The Best Weapon for Peace

The Best Weapon for Peace

Maria Montessori,
Education, and
Children's Rights

E R I C A   M O R E T T I

THE UNIVERSITY OF WISCONSIN PRESS

The University of Wisconsin Press
728 State Street, Suite 443
Madison, Wisconsin 53706
uwpress.wisc.edu

Gray's Inn House, 127 Clerkenwell Road
London ECIR 5DB, United Kingdom
eurospanbookstore.com

Printed in the United States of America
This book may be available in a digital edition.

Library of Congress Cataloging-in-Publication Data
Names: Moretti, Erica, author.
Title: The best weapon for peace : Maria Montessori, education,
and children's rights / Erica Moretti.
Other titles: George L. Mosse series in the history of European culture,
sexuality, and ideas.
Description: Madison, Wisconsin : The University of Wisconsin Press, [2021] |
Series: George L. Mosse series in the history of European culture, sexuality,
and ideas | Includes bibliographical references and index.
Identifiers: LCCN 2020051821 | ISBN 9780299333102 (cloth)
Subjects: LCSH: Montessori, Maria, 1870–1952. | Pacifism. |
Children and peace. | Children's rights.
Classification: LCC LB775.M8 M595 2021 | DDC 370.92 [B]—dc23
LC record available at https://lccn.loc.gov/2020051821

ISBN 978-0-299-33314-0 (pbk.: alk. paper)

to Ivan and Viola

Contents

Illustrations

Acknowledgments

Having grown up as one of four sisters, my knowledge of children as instruments of peace is arguably mostly academic. Though I study the ways children can bring peace to the family and the world, I probably made my own family life even more complicated. And yet I owe the completion of this book to that chaotic family. My mom Mirella's love and deep knowledge of history encouraged me to enter this profession. My father Enzo's sense of justice and love of the environment made me passionate about the themes at the core of this work. To my sisters Silvia, Laura, and Lucia, I owe the stubbornness to want to finish this project in the face of new and ever-shifting obstacles. Long summers of research in Italy were only possible thanks to their cooperation, support, and love. My husband, Ivan, knows every twist and turn of my work. This book would not exist without him. Our daughter, Viola, constantly surprises and confounds my expectations about early childhood education. Fiercely independent, gutsy, and charming, she has been an endless source of awe. I am grateful to all my family members, Italian and American, young and old, by blood, by marriage, and by zip code, who have supported me in the process of thinking and writing.

Beyond that, I am grateful to my broader academic and professional family. The main ideas of this book were conceived during my years as a graduate student at Brown University—a place that challenged and stimulated me deeply. In particular, I would like to thank my advisor, Suzanne Stewart-Steinberg, and my readers Caroline Castiglione, Massimo Riva, and David Kertzer for their generous mentorship. Cristina Abbona has been a friend and a supporter in both work and life. I have her to thank for endless discussions of the ethics of our profession. All the other mentors I have found along my academic journey, from Università degli Studi di Firenze to Smith College, have deeply shaped my way of thinking and feeling about history. Thank you, Lorenzo Benadusi, Anna Botta, Jim Hicks, Alessandra Lorini, and Sharon Wood.

Colleagues and students at Mount Holyoke College and the Fashion Institute of Technology have provided invaluable support for my academic work. My colleagues in the Department of Modern Languages and Cultures at FIT-SUNY have been unfailingly supportive. Within the college at large, Patrick Knisley, Amy Lemmon, Daniel Levinson Wilk, Evelyn Rynkiewicz, and Amy Werbel have sustained me with their humor, kindness, and endless advice. The seminars in Italian Studies at Johns Hopkins and Brown University, the NYU History of Education Writing Group, and the Five Colleges Seminar in Italian Studies, as well as the Seminar in Modern Italian Studies at Columbia University, have all provided solid criticism of my early drafts, improving my work in innumerable ways. Financial support from numerous institutions was also crucial to the completion of this project. Fellowships from the Barbieri Endowment in Modern Italian History, the Center for Italian Modern Art, the Laura Bassi Foundation, and the Literary Encyclopedia Grant have been crucial in supporting my lengthy research periods abroad. The Leonard Hastings Schoff and Suzanne Levick Schoff Memorial Fund at the University Seminars at Columbia University provided invaluable support in finishing my work. The Remarque Institute and the Center for European and Mediterranean Studies at NYU were vibrant intellectual communities in New York City.

Molly Tambor, Matteo Pretelli, Eden Mclean, Vanessa Roghi, Roberta Pergher, and Joseph Viscumi provided attentive and productive close readings of the manuscript at various stages. In addition to their own work, their collective insight into thinking about modern European history has been indispensable. Fellow Montessorians Christinia Cheung, Renato Foschi, Alice Graziadei, Emily Green, Paola Trabalzini, and Joke Verkeul have shared the burden of doing scholarship on someone larger than life. The team of the *Gender, Sexuality, Italy* journal has shared help, friendship, and knowledge on many occasions. I have also benefited from the support, encouragement, and camaraderie of my colleagues and friends Anna Aresi, Anna Argirò, Franco Baldasso, Patrizio Ceccagnoli, Laura Di Bianco, Rebecca Falkoff, Nicola Lucchi, Anita Pinzi, Stefania Porcelli, Michela Ronzani, and Victor Zarour Zarzar, all of whom have nourished my intellectual and emotional growth in incalculable ways. My gratitude for their friendship and intellectual sustenance is boundless. My friends, scattered throughout the world, have furnished many opportunities to take much-needed breaks from writing, and for that I am forever indebted to them. Anita, Laura, and Valentina, Allison and Khristina, Cici, Courtney, and Sara, thank you for reminding me that there is life outside academia.

The Best Weapon for Peace

Introduction

Ten-year-old Madeleine Mahière was a Belgian refugee who had fled to Paris in 1914 seeking shelter from German soldiers. She had witnessed both the so-called Rape of Belgium and the invasion of northern France by German troops in the opening months of World War I. Forced out of her home and traumatized by the horrors of the conflict, Madeleine recounted, "I heard my grandmother scream. . . . I looked behind and [she] was lying on the ground with her hand on her knee, and my aunt's face was all covered with blood, and she was on the ground too, only she did not scream."[1] At the time, traditional medical, scholastic, and custodial spaces for children could not adequately treat Madeline's experience. The frequency, intensity, and characteristics of the new mental traumas inflicted on children by ongoing tension, exposure to death, physical toil, and disrupted emotional life were causing specialists to rethink old diagnostic and therapeutic paradigms. Professionals, such as specialized nurses or teachers, capable of addressing the plight of young civilians affected by armed conflict were rare.

But young Madeline began to receive care and instruction in an institution that sought to address the new physical and psychological problems created by a war that had encompassed all aspects of life—a place in which the discoveries of modern psychiatry, the findings of progressive education, and the philanthropic spirit of the Italian feminist movement could coalesce. She had become part of a group of students housed at an experimental school in the French capital, established to rehabilitate war-affected children. The school adopted the approach pioneered by the Italian educator Maria Montessori, who conducted psychiatric and pedagogical research on the children there. Montessori found that the pupils had experienced "a special form of mental disturbance, which constituted a real mental wound."[2] Ahead of her time, she designed activities to rehabilitate and educate them to become fundamentally peaceful human beings.

These efforts were part of a critical yet understudied aspect of Montessori's work. Though historians have acknowledged the significance of Montessori's pedagogical theory, they have so far failed to recognize the importance of her views on pacifism as the foundation of her pedagogy.[3] *The Best Weapon for Peace: Maria Montessori, Education, and Children's Rights* recovers Montessori's pacifist work in relation to both her educational activism and the greater international conversation. Her goal was peace; teaching was the method—the weapon, as Montessori herself put it—by which it would be achieved, originating within children in an ordinary classroom.[4] Those brought up in the Montessori method—free to move, play, and explore—would be liberated from the disciplinary constrictions of other contemporary educational theories. This pedagogy had the goal of educating children to become members of a new world, wherein empathy, social responsibility, and solidarity among people would be the most essential values. Achieving peace was a twofold process: first, the child would be called to develop an internal peace, a harmony with the environment, and a moral sense to guide her acts. Competition, injustice, and abuse of power found no place in a Montessori classroom. Thanks to an innovative pedagogy, the child would grow in response to her own bodily and intellectual needs, fulfilling her own potential. Second, having developed into a satisfied adult, she would be gratified by her own work and would be able to find a place within the larger ecology of the world. The resulting adult would have a natural propensity toward peace; she would find joy in her work and in her relationships with people. Montessori's progressive approach would produce self-determining adults naturally opposed to war. To further her aims, Montessori also worked for societal reform through humanitarian and legislative intervention (both at the national and international levels) to promote the rights of children, and, in a rippling effect, propel a global, peaceful revolution.[5]

Though Montessori was a well-known pacifist in her day, historians have generally considered her writings on peace to be secondary to her pedagogical efforts, which have been regarded as the intellectual side project of a woman more concerned with the practical goal of educating youth. The unilateral and top-down view historians have of conflict resolution, peace building, and humanitarianism has undermined the coherent and sophisticated "big picture" of Montessori's thought, favoring instead the practicality, intuition, and nurturing aspects of her work on childhood. This book redefines the terms of Montessori pedagogy, which was never about an individual child—or even about the children of a single nation—but instead about the mission for global peace.

Indeed, Montessori's approach to peace does not strictly align with contemporary attempts to foster it through cultural internationalism, such as the creation of student exchange programs, international lecture circuits, and other activities that have come to be identified as foundational to the field of pacifist education.[6] Content-oriented efforts at peace were not sufficient to build a harmonious world, Montessori argued. While she put forward proposals to promote the rights of children and to create political bodies to support their growth, she did not engage directly in debates on international arbitration, arms reduction, or diplomatic dialogue among nations. Whereas conflict resolution was considered the work of politics and politicians, a reformed educational system was in Montessori's view the cornerstone of a peaceful society.

The end of the nineteenth century signaled a profound redefinition of children's roles within the family and the nation, and my analysis of Montessori's project is situated within this shift.[7] At the time the educator was first joining pacifist groups and feminist organizations, two historical trends were developing throughout the Western world: an increasing recognition of the social value of childhood and the growth of tutelary regimes—in other words, a surge in public and private action meant to protect children in danger.[8] During this historical period, politicians and public intellectuals began to recognize the need for social intervention on behalf of children. Reproduction and child-rearing became the object of new sciences, technologies, and government praxes. This interest eventually led to the formation of new social practices for the study and regulation of pedagogical approaches capable of molding the child. One of the central issues in what was slowly becoming a puerocentric society was how children (especially the disadvantaged) should be raised—and by whom. My work analyzes the ways in which Montessori attempted, amid these efforts, to provide appropriate and viable teaching strategies for educating young citizens.

This Western awakening to children's issues and needs included Italy as well. It was a country in the process of remaking itself, one whose politicians looked to public education as a powerful tool to accelerate national progress. Through an analysis of the "Age of Pinocchio" (1861–1914), a time in which child-related concerns were at the center of the political agenda of Liberal Italy, this book investigates the birth of Montessori's pedagogical experiments to demonstrate the relevance of the vast and diverse constituencies engaged in reshaping attitudes toward child-rearing and education.[9] Seen closely, the beginning of Montessori's work in the district of San Lorenzo demonstrates a local attempt from the Roman municipal government to restructure a series of buildings in what at the time constituted the periphery of the capital; a single educator and a group philanthropists, feminist activists, local artists, and politicians assembled to rethink the future of a small group of lower-class children. But what the first Casa dei Bambini truly reveals is the rationale behind the reformist zeal to expand education to the realms of morality, art, and movement, as inspired by pacifism, social welfare, and state democratization. Furthermore, it sheds light on the myriad lay and religious organizations devoted to saving marginalized children. It speaks to the changing structure of philanthropic organizations reconceived according to scientific principles, and to the slow but steady formation of public welfare agencies. The significance of Montessori's educational experiments for culture and politics—specifically having to do with state interventions into educational practice in Italy and beyond—has yet to be laid out.

Montessori's theorization of an adult capable of cultivating peace stems from a larger debate about population size, natality, fertility, and migration. Within the last decades of the nineteenth century, many Western European countries grew concerned with depopulation and degeneration, as nation-states competed for military and imperial dominance. These concerns led politicians to legislate in favor of women and infants, with special attention paid to reducing child mortality and promoting children's health. Pedagogues, doctors, psychiatrists, and anthropologists worked to reconceive ways to sustain a healthy national citizenry. This effort often focused on avoiding supposed racial degeneration, a category that furnished a spurious biological explanation for phenomena such as crime, vagrancy, prostitution, and alcoholism. At the center of this debate, the Italian school of anthropological criminology worked to classify and typify so-called degenerates, attributing to pathologies solely organicist origins and connecting disabilities to moral and psychological weaknesses.[10] A strong supporter of the redemptive role of medicine, Montessori argued against a purely deterministic approach to children's pathologies, claiming that a regeneration of the disadvantaged was indeed possible. It was the duty of education, specifically of a *pedagogia riparatrice* (restorative pedagogy), to amend whatever environmental, hereditary, economic, and social factors had harmed the child. A scientific education would produce an adult who would resort to peace naturally.

Montessori's efforts to shape a child's upbringing and education can be read through Michel Foucault's concept of governmentality, in order to address questions about governance and the politics of the social, an examination of the range of mechanisms through which political groups and forms of knowledge in the West regulated, controlled, and policed the lives of citizens.[11] The Foucauldian study of political power expands the notion of state intervention to include a complex set of alliances between political and nonpolitical forces; in order to control its subjects, the state used a wide variety of nonpolitical professionals—such as doctors, social workers, and criminologists—to establish an "artificial normalcy" to which its citizens had to conform. The construction of an industry devoted to the psyche, what social theorist Nikolas Rose has called the "psy complex," conferred power on the state but simultaneously rendered this power invisible by entrusting the enforcement of normative behavior to private professionals.[12] Such professionals, of which Montessori was a prominent one, were, in turn, central to the process of drafting new legislation on child-rearing. As a result, they played a crucial role in the state's work to establish the boundaries of a new class of citizens: healthy subjects capable of regenerating the social body. The act of monitoring the lives of disadvantaged children, in Montessori's case, must be contextualized not as an act of policing, but in light of her own struggle as a woman, particularly as a woman in the male-dominated fields of medicine and psychiatry.

Amid this puerocentric culture, Montessori's approach to the study of children's needs proved to be unconventional. While states and organizations were focusing on a paternalistic approach to protecting defenseless children and molding future citizens, Montessori was arguing that the child was the "father of mankind," the true agent of change within society. Children were what Montessori called *forgotten citizens*, in that their potential as active political subjects was largely ignored. Montessori's work therefore changed the conversation on child-rearing and education by bringing children's rights to the forefront of the international political debate and by arguing that, if a healthy upbringing and education were guaranteed to them, children would be able to reform humanity.

Owing to the breadth of Montessori's pedagogical and political project, in this book the term *childhood* does not refer to a specific age. The reason for this is twofold. First, most of Montessori's writings mention *il bambino* (the child, in the masculine neutral form) and refer only to developmental stages, rather than to exact years, because the structure of Montessori education entailed mixed-age classrooms and often utilized the same principles across grades and ages. The second reason is that I read Montessori's thought on peace through a historically defined notion of childhood, one that is shaped by the emergence of mass politics, and which often corresponds to an artificial and symbolic construct. Therefore, childhood cannot be interpreted as a biological category, or a sociological one, but instead as a political classification.[13] All in all, the period analyzed is not just the "century of the child," as the famous book defined it.[14] It is also the century of boys, girls, adolescents, babies, foundlings, pupils, and all these young people who became the objects of new policies; who attended compulsory schooling;

who became consumers; who were conscripted into the military; who became the beneficiaries or at least targets of humanitarian efforts—and, most of all, who came to occupy a new space in society.[15] What I intend to capture here is the intrinsically liminal nature of this category of analysis, which makes the child a subject in transit.[16] No specific age group is at the center of my work, nor even is a specific gender (which Montessori did not differentiate), but rather the process of development itself, a child's transition from infancy to adulthood. And if Montessori reimagined this development, she was competing with many forces that were trying to shape the child into a citizen, a soldier, a member of a specific party, and so on. What I suggest is therefore a reading that takes into account these competing forces.

Montessori's vision of reform was unconstrained by geographical or socioeconomic boundaries. As a result, it aspired to spread globally and to make her name a synonym for children's well-being and development everywhere. In her eyes, her success would be unbridled, the recognition of her work universal. Yet this universalism should not prevent historians from digging deep into its roots, probing what is behind an approach conceived to be applicable to any child in any country. Indeed, Montessori's educational projects cannot be studied without taking into account the political, economic, religious, aesthetic, and social contexts that generated them. Whether Montessori was a Catholic or a Theosophist, to point out only one dimension of her theoretical underpinning, is not at the center of this work. Her reflections on religious syncretism, spiritualism, Roman Catholic doctrine, and Catholic antiwar activism, however, deeply informed her broad conception of the child and of human rights, and are therefore essential to my analysis. It is precisely Montessori's political intuition, her subtlety in interpreting matters of foreign affairs, her interest in questions of faith and spiritual development, and her ability to gauge diplomatic opportunities that allowed her to generate an all-encompassing vision of childhood. If we look at Montessori only for her vision of the child, the woman dissolves into her mission. We miss the complexity and the seemingly irreconcilable sets of beliefs that shaped her thought; we see the successes, not the struggles and compromises that so much conditioned and enriched her life.

Montessori's revolutionary conception of children and their rights did not develop in a vacuum. It resulted from her myriad collaborations, discussions, and confrontations. Her work was deeply embedded in the emerging transnational sphere of international organizations, congresses, and networks devoted to children's welfare, and, more specifically, to children's newly recognized right to education. Transnational reform networks—or, using Peter Haas's term, epistemic communities—worked to reform educational systems according to the principles of progressive education.[17] Parallel to the growth of nation-states and to increasingly regimented national educational systems, these networks of educators, social workers, and intellectuals gathered to discuss how to improve child-rearing and upbringing.[18] New educational demands caused by the extension of compulsory education, changes in the parameters used to evaluate pupils, and the necessity of forging national elites brought these people together in lively debates, ultimately creating a global grammar of schooling affected by mutual and continuous adjustment.[19] By collaborating with organizations such as the Genevan International Bureau of Education, publishing in journals such as *Pour l'ère nouvelle*, and attending conferences organized by the New Education Fellowship and others, Montessori was enriched, and in turn altered, by a vast conversation on the need for education reform.

The turn of the twentieth century also signaled the formation of several new organizations aimed at fostering world peace. Promoting a variety of approaches, many of these associations were able to circulate their ideas on a global scale for the first time. Montessori benefited especially from participating in the discourse on humanitarian practices and humanitarian law, and more specifically children's welfare. This discussion originated with the Geneva and Hague Conventions (1864, and 1899 and 1907 respectively), which constituted the foundation of international law agreements for the treatment of civilians and noncivilians during wartime; it grew in size and scope from there. In particular, the first postwar period saw the rise of the practice of humanitarian intervention. The protection of all victims of war became the work of numerous activists, who often chose to focus on child protection. Whether that occurred under the aegis of the Child Welfare Committee of the League of Nations or via the work of nascent organizations such as the Save the Children Fund, the plight of hundreds of thousands of child refugees or displaced children became a nonpartisan issue, the focus of international organizations in a continent otherwise ruined by the conflict. Directly and indirectly, the Italian educator's work to create organizations and agencies to protect children was informed by this surge. While elaborating her own pacifist agenda, Montessori became a key interlocutor in global discourses on humanitarianism, disaster relief efforts, and pacifist actions, often anticipating techniques and strategies that would be implemented only in the aftermath of World War II. Her writings on these topics dealt with pedagogical activities to help children cope with severe trauma and called for the organization of governmental agencies to represent the rights of children, such as the Ministry of the Child and the

Social Party of the Child, new political organs that would guarantee children's direct participation in the body politic.

This work maps out a varied set of debates and practices aimed at rehabilitating disadvantaged youth, providing an alternative historiographical framework to the fields of humanitarianism and human rights.[20] Countering a top-down perspective that highlights the actions of government and military officials and international agencies, this analysis of Montessori's work sheds light on how nonstate actors and transnational networks attempted to bring about institutional and normative changes.[21] By looking at the educator's theorization of children at the margins, I bring attention to a vast and diverse array of professionals that contributed to the transition to scientific philanthropy, in a multilayered reading of how human rights were defined by humanitarian practices.[22] The history of human rights and humanitarianism and the history of education have frequently been unaware of each other. Often, the former takes a transnational approach, centering on how international networks and organizations produced shared knowledge.[23] The latter is instead based on national and comparative studies.[24] By bringing these two historiographical traditions together and, more specifically, by using the tools of cultural history and history of education to reflect on the history of humanitarianism and human rights, we can expand our understanding of the debates on children rights and nongovernmental interventions to benefit disadvantaged youth.

Within the discourses on child-related concerns and humanitarianism, Montessori often focused her attention on children suffering from poor health, lackluster education, and diminished economic circumstances. With her work, she went on to include a broad variety of marginalized children, such as those from the impoverished areas in and around Rome, the orphans of the 1908 Messina-Reggio earthquake, the refugees of the Great War, and ultimately the deprived children in India during the Second World War, whom she intended to help.

The examples provided here are in stark contrast with the current reality of Montessori schools in the United States. Symbols of progressive education, freedom, and creativity, they are often private and cater to affluent families.[25] There are many reasons for this, chief among which is that the Montessori method has often been considered an outlier in traditional educational circles. Its marginal position has resulted in a limited availability of training courses and scarce access to its didactic apparatus. Many Montessori principles are indeed part of national education systems that, at least nominally, have over time adopted a student-centeredness, multisensorial materials, and a policy of following the child's predispositions. But the number of public

Montessori schools is still small. Since the opening of her first schools, Montessori worked with children of all socioeconomic backgrounds. Children from wealthy families, such as those from the via Famagosta's Casa dei Bambini, which opened in 1908, would also thrive through a pedagogy designed to create self-determination and autonomy in children.[26] While her findings were (and still are) applicable to any child, her writings concerning peace often sprung from her work with disadvantaged youth specifically.

Intellectually and emotionally impeded by a lack of resources, these children misbehaved, disrupted classroom activities, and provoked conflicts with classmates and family members. She claimed that these children were most affected by a lack of educational stimuli and were therefore more likely to grow up as unbalanced individuals who would resort to conflict. Influenced by the growing fields of behavioral science and psychiatry, Montessori designed activities to stimulate the children's conduct, intellectual growth, and muscular development, therefore instilling in them a sense of inner peace and outward kindness. The story of little "Otello the Terrible," a pupil of the via Giusti Montessori school in Rome, is an excellent case in point. Otello "met love with hate, kindness with malevolence, sociability with taciturn aloofness," and "wrought confusion in the beauty." At home his mischief was met with "the brute force of the adult." Instead, in the Montessori classroom, there was "no word of blame, no command, *you must not.*" Montessori argued that Otello's behavior was caused by a lack of freedom. According to her, "the child who is choked at home by an artificial environment and chained by the commands of his parents will develop into a crooked, blasted man." The constraints of parents and previous teachers had caused little Otello to misbehave, commanding him not to touch certain objects, not to litter the adult's space, not to say certain things. But when adults "act as jailers," the child will inevitably rebel, Montessori contended. Instead, she argued, education had to free the child and his innate "unlimited capacity for good."[27] Montessori maintained that a school based on a fundamental misunderstanding of the child's needs—in other words, based on the cult of his abnegation, committed to predetermined objectives, obsessed with self-interest and competition—instead of seeking the free unfolding of the child's potential would always result in an "Otello the Terrible." Paving the way for thinkers, educators, and radical pedagogues such as Don Lorenzo Milani, Montessori worked to change the very way education was conceived. Children did not learn for a prize or to avoid a punishment; they learned because they were engaged in an activity that was calibrated to their developmental needs. They learned when they were free to move around the classroom and to choose what was most appropriate to them. Montessori envisioned a school that welcomed each child, without distinctions of class, gender, ability, or upbringing, a school that would flourish anywhere—including juvenile detention centers and conflict zones—one that would favor the achievement of individual capacities and desires, promoting free will and social mobility. Montessori's vision was not only a radical educational reform but also a firm denunciation of the existing contemporary school system.

The Best Weapon for Peace analyzes the development of Montessori's thought on pacifism. I argue that the educator repeatedly reconceived her theory of peace, with each revision expanding it to include a larger set of relationships and agents. Her vision evolved in concentric circles of influence, first as a form of harmony between the child's own body and immediate environment, then with the family, and then further outward with the nation-state and the world. While working with the disadvantaged children of San Lorenzo in Rome in 1907, Montessori focused on how the child, through education, could become a peaceful individual in harmony with himself and his surroundings. This new capacity to "move gracefully" (*grazia dei movimenti*) within the classroom and at home would eventually inspire peers and relatives to seek the very same harmony, thereby spreading change on a local level and turning the child into an agent of reform. When Montessori worked with the refugees of the Great War, this pacifistic progression in turn grew to include the nation at large. Montessori believed that children affected by the conflict could be physically and mentally rehabilitated by her approach. As an outgrowth of her work with the children harmed by World War I, Montessori started elaborating a methodology that would foster peace and prevent the occurrence of war altogether; at the same time, she advocated for the role of governments and international organizations in supporting the rights of infants and children, anticipating a trend that would persist throughout the Western world. In fact, her work on how children could become agents of peace did not stop there. She went on to conceive a new relationship between the child and the environment, one in which the ecology of the entire planet would be respected and all human beings would be able to live peacefully. As a result of her successive reevaluations of the child's role in society, Montessori had a plan for creating a model citizenry.

To trace the history of Montessori's pacifism is to map a global history of ideas. As historian Patricia Clavin reminds us, "Transnationalism is first and foremost about people: the social space that they inhabit, the networks they form and the ideas they exchange."[28] Montessori's life trajectory is mapped out across transnational distances to constitute a global life.[29] Building upon Linda Mahood's work on humanitarian Eglantyne Jebb, I use the techniques of microhistory and what Liz Stanley terms "feminist biography."[30] I therefore proceed from the notion that a "micro- and biographical scale" offers a privileged viewpoint to understand "the entanglement of cultural traditions produced by the growing contacts and clashes between different societies."[31] Microhistorians, as historian Jill Lepore puts it, "even when they study a single person's life . . . are keen to evoke a period, a *mentalitè*, a problem."[32] Montessori's life trajectory is therefore used here to reveal the broader contours of social, cultural, and political issues, and her life becomes "an allegory for broader issues affecting the culture as a whole."[33]

Within feminist biography, I draw from three main points. First, my work recognizes the impossibility of creating a biography of a "coherent, essentially unchanging and unitary self," or of presenting a complete view on a person's life.[34] Instead, it can only strive to offer a picture that captures the simultaneous, often opposing, forces peculiar to the individual, the result of which often differs from the "great lives" or more canonical biographies usually concerned with the lives of upper-middle-class white men. Second, I contextualize my subject deeply within her historical background, in order to build not a narrative of exceptionality but one that locates her in an overlapping net of social groups and collaborations.[35] Third, I rely on this feminist form of writing because it sheds light on how "power and powerlessness are complex matters, and most certainly not two poles of a dichotomy," insofar as Montessori, a prominent pedagogue and someone with access to the help of renowned intellectuals and politicians, also experienced obstacles and profound criticism in her attempts to bring forward her theory of pacifism.[36]

My goal is not merely to rehabilitate our understanding of the life of an exceptional woman but to use her life as a lens to see how the discourse on peace, humanitarianism, and war prevention took different turns and was adapted to different contexts. To see this, one has to dig deep into Montessori's own narrative of the self and her disciples' view of her. The traces and clues left behind by the educator about her battles and compromises are scarce. But Montessori's intimate thoughts surface at times through the texts, and they transpire behind the curtain of her students' biographies—a curtain she must have created over years to affirm herself. This work attempts to go beyond the image of Montessori as a selfless, devoted teacher and to limn a figure fiercely complex and volatile, who surrounded herself with disciples and asked for a cult-like devotion. Montessori was an educator who staunchly advocated for the freedom of the child and left little liberty to the people around her. She was a materialist, a Catholic, and a Theosophist, a dreamer of a radical transformation of the rights of children, and a savvy

promoter of her own patented material who often cut off disciples and followers who did not adhere to her directions. To understand the core of
Montessori's thought, one has to take into account all of her contradictions.
In the end, one must listen to Montessori herself, who, according to a biographer, refused to study and emulate the lives of great women (as assigned
by her teacher) and had no interest in becoming a "great woman" herself—
arguing that she "cared too much for the children of the future to add
another biography to the list."[37]

In telling this story, I draw on material from private correspondence, leaf-
lets, lecture notes, ministerial publications, governmental reports, and
photos. These materials have been accessed from a variety of archives,
libraries, museums, schools, and private collections. Additional evidence
comes from my own direct observations at Montessori schools in the United
States and at the Kalakshetra Foundation in India. The Opera Nazionale
Montessori and the Association Montessori Internationale retain some private documents and many otherwise hard-to-find writings by the Italian
educator, such as her early lectures and articles. But Montessori's writings
on peace are scattered throughout numerous minor collections, obscure
magazines, and Montessori's own smaller publications. The Archivio Centrale dello Stato and the Archivio Fondazione Giovanni Gentile per gli Studi
Filosofici have provided me with the papers on Montessori and Fascism.
The documents regarding her attempt to constitute the humanitarian organization the White Cross (for war-affected children) have mainly been retrieved
at the Archivio Apostolico Vaticano. Montessori's collaboration with the
Theosophical Society has also been reconstructed through materials found
at the Archivio Apostolico Vaticano, at the headquarters of the Theosophical Society's Surendra Narayan Archives, and at the Private Archive of
Francesco Randone. Smaller archives such as the Archivio Storico Società
Umanitaria, Archivi delle Arti Applicate Italiane del XX Secolo, the Associazione Nazionale per gli Interessi del Mezzogiorno d'Italia Archives, the
Archivio Fondazione Gramsci, and the Kalakshetra Foundation yielded
documents that led me to reconstruct Montessori's diverse and original
theory of peace.

The Best Weapon for Peace adopts a chronological narrative approach. It
would be impossible to understand the full trajectory of Montessori's internationalist philosophy and commitment to social responsibility without
analyzing her studies, her civic engagement, and her social activism. Chapter 1 traces the roots of Montessori's pacifism back to the earliest conception of her pedagogical methodology, in the first decade of the twentieth
century. I examine how her work occurred at a time of radical revisions to

the role of childhood in Italian society, whereby politicians, intellectuals, artists, and educators all worked to reassess the child's needs, reconsider public intervention in the education of youth, and develop new ways of helping marginalized infants. Within these efforts, Montessori envisaged child-centered education as a tool to promote responsible citizenship and political enfranchisement. The classroom was a gateway to reshaping society. Through a close reading of her 1909 text *Il Metodo*, I argue that Montessori's work with the children of San Lorenzo began as an attempt to educate the child to be at peace with his own body, mind, and surrounding environment. Through her work on sensorial education, Montessori aimed at shaping a child who, through the unfolding of his inner capacities, could grow according to his natural predispositions and would therefore behave with respect for his peers and environment.

Chapter 2 provides an exhaustive overview of Montessori's efforts to rescue war-stricken children, through an analysis of the conversations she initiated over the course of the Great War—conversations with educators, psychologists, and social workers; the Italian state; prominent members of the Roman Catholic Church and eventually Pope Benedict XV; and the Milanese socialist organization Società Umanitaria. In 1916, Montessori studied nurseries in the occupied territories of Belgium and northern France, arguing that her methodology was "a veritable cure for all those ills" caused by war. A year later, the educator started planning a new humanitarian organization that would assist children distressed by war, an entity she called the White Cross. Although this organization did not materialize, the process of trying to create it had an important influence on Montessori's evolving pedagogy of peace.

Chapter 3 offers a close reading of four unpublished peace lectures that Montessori delivered in San Diego in 1917. My analysis reveals that Montessori's conception of children as vehicles for constructing a peaceful society began nearly twenty years earlier than previously thought. The educator's lectures about viable solutions for peace were inspired by her desire to find support for those who were experiencing the catastrophic effects of the Great War. After working toward the creation of the White Cross, Montessori found that educating the child survivors was not enough; she therefore shifted to using education to prevent such catastrophes altogether. The educator's reflection on pacifism developed both as an outgrowth of her political militancy and as a long-term project to transform society through educating the next generation.

Chapter 4 examines a time when Montessori paused her direct commitment to pacifism, during the 1920s, while receiving financial support from the Fascist regime. The chapter begins by contextualizing that support. I maintain that this period corresponded to a gestational phase for Montessori, in which she privately reworked some of her theories on pacifism. Current historiography tends to downplay or erase Montessori's attempts to return to Italy in the first decade of the dictatorship. This chapter provides an exhaustive overview of the educator's relations with prominent members of the Fascist Party and contextualizes her own projects of reform amid the changes occurring in the public education system, which was seen as the primary tool to indoctrinate Italians in the principles of the dictatorship.

Chapter 5 looks at the peace lectures Montessori delivered between 1932 and 1939 in order to share her work on peace publicly and forcefully at educational conferences and peace congresses throughout Europe. I argue that this is the period during which Montessori worked for the first time to theorize viable strategies for fostering peace at the political and social level, as opposed to merely in the classroom. While lecturing throughout Europe, the educator worked to emphasize the neglect of children and to call for an institution that could secure children's rights within an educational system that otherwise suffocated their potential. She then urged every nation to establish the Social Party of the Child, a political party in which children would be called to be active members and represent their rights. As to the question of who would take care of a child lacking proper parental authority, Montessori found another solution: the Ministry of the Child, a nonpartisan institution that would guarantee the rights of this new citizen. For the first time, the educator called for the creation of specific public institutions that had the ultimate goal of producing peace.

Chapter 6 looks at how Montessori's work on pacifism, specifically the notion of cosmic education, was affected by her stay in India (1939–1949). Invited by George Sidney Arundale, president of the Theosophical Society, and his wife, Rukmini Devi, dancer and choreographer of the Indian classical dance form Bharatanatyam, Montessori and her son, Mario, spent almost a decade in that country. This chapter first analyzes how Indian nationalists such Rabindranath Tagore and Mohandas K. Gandhi helped Montessori situate herself within the discourse on education and the environment. While looking at the dialogue among the three intellectuals, I also analyze Montessori's work against the larger framework of the anticolonialist debate, specifically the opposition to Western educational thought. An investigation of the lasting influence of Theosophical principles in the Italian educator's oeuvre follows, specifically of the notions of One Life and Universal Brotherhood, which provided the foundation for Montessori's cosmic vision of peace. According to Montessori, a global approach to early childhood education was necessary so that the development of knowledge would proceed in a holistic way, by integrating all aspects of the individual in relation to every other living being on the planet.

One hundred and fifty years after Montessori's birth, her pedagogical approach continues to be successful. There are almost three thousand accredited Montessori programs in the United States alone, and many more throughout the world that are influenced by her in a less official capacity. The Montessori approach retains its appeal across geographical, class, and religious boundaries. The reason for this widespread appeal is the complexity of Montessori's thought, informed by the vast networks of artists, educators, social workers, feminists, politicians, Theosophists, modernists, and Catholic thinkers who shaped her expansive conception of education. This complexity builds on the notion of *histoire croisée*—that is to say, a history of experimental psychology, psychiatry, and pedagogy that takes into account research outside of conventional sources, found through unorthodox ways of approaching scientific problems, lost threads, and unexpected inspiration, all of which constitute the foundation of Montessori's thought on pacifism.[38]

CHAPTER 1

Peace from Within

How the Montessori Method Came About

> And there, right at the gates of Rome, among these shepherds and primitive nomads formed a certain flock that the cosmopolitan civilization of the capital seems to ignore: a flock, or better, a herd of men driven to labor like beasts of burden, guided by watchmen armed with a prod or whip, with which they "invite" the malnourished and malarial laborer to work . . . just as they do with the herds of famous Roman buffalos.[1]
> —Maria Montessori, *Caratteri fisici delle giovani donne del Lazio*

Neglected and barren farmland encircled the newly built residential quarters of Umbertian Rome, near the grand ruins of the Roman Empire.[2] Despite living "at the gates" of the city, countryside residents at the turn of the twentieth century did not benefit from the bustling renovations intended for new administrators, small-scale industrialists, and service-sector workers.[3] Instead, this rural area known as the *agro romano* housed a "wild and savage population" who migrated throughout the malaria-infested plains seeking seasonal agricultural work.[4] They were "so close to the metropolis, yet so far from Civilization."[5] Maria Montessori was intimately familiar with these peasants, the *guitti*; she had already conducted an anthropological study on the physical characteristics of women from the Lazio region.[6]

A few years later, she returned to improve the peasants' living conditions, this time with a diverse group of activists: feminist writer and journalist Sibilla Aleramo; poet and editor in chief of *Nuova antologia* Giovanni Cena; artist and educator Alessandro Marcucci (brother-in-law of the renowned painter Giacomo Balla); artist Duilio Cambellotti; nurse and president of the Unione Femminile Nazionale's Roman chapter Anna Celli (née Fraentzel) and her husband, epidemiologist and parliamentary deputy Antonio Celli. This initiative exemplifies the spirit and eclectic nature of Montessori's

Peasant woman in a *tukul* (cone-shaped hut) in the *agro romano*. Photograph taken for the 1911 Turin International World Fair. Duilio Cambellotti Collection. Courtesy of Archivi delle Arti Applicate Italiane del XX secolo, Rome.

early collaborations, which shaped her conception of education and, consequently, of pacifism. Indicative of Montessori's early activism and civic engagement, this collection of artists, intellectuals, and educators, fueled by a Tolstoyesque desire to fight for the oppressed, together conceived new ways to understand infancy, to rethink public intervention in the upbringing of youth, and to uplift the disenfranchised.

The disconcerting conditions of the peasants in the *agro romano* marshes had risen to national prominence, thanks to the work of statesman and

Duilio Cambellotti, *La capanna dell'Agro*, 1911. Ink on paper. Duilio Cambellotti
Collection. Courtesy of Archivi delle Arti Applicate Italiane del XX secolo, Rome.

economist Stefano Jacini, whose 1880s research revealed the incomplete
and inaccurate view, typically held by foreign travelers, of the countryside as
a bucolic paradise.[7] Only a few years later, sociologist Werner Sombart painted
an even more vivid picture, sharply condemning the wealthy landowners (*lati-
fondisti*) whose exploitation of the peasants led them to live "in the degradation
of this destitute and horrific misery," often in "natural caves" and "grottos"; the
peasant who did not find refuge therein would often be "satisfied with nest-
ling under temple ruins or under the rubble of the collapsed buildings of old
villas and monuments . . . worn out and broken by the demands of modern
civilization."[8] This marginalized populace, especially its youth, suffered gruel-
ing working hours, unsanitary living conditions, and an unhealthy diet, which
stunted their growth. In the words of Aleramo, they "live[d] in huts with no
floors; they, too, seem[ed] made of mud. Children and elderly people look[ed]
on, astonished . . . [in] groups of veritable tukuls [cone-shaped huts], abandoned without medical assistance and without schooling, and they looked at
me as if I'd wound up in Africa."[9] The Republican deputy and public-health
advocate Celli maintained that the conservative approach taken by the government, the unchallenged power of the landowners, and the widespread effects

of malaria prevented any progress.[10] Redemption for the peasants was unlikely. All they knew was submission, and education was unavailable to them.

Described by historian and politician Gaetano Salvemini as "the most miserable and oppressed peasants in Italy," they suffered from malaria, which decimated the population seasonally.[11] In fighting the disease, the group of activists received help from the Italian Red Cross.[12] Though the agency normally only gave care during wars, it intervened because the crisis was deemed similar in scale and urgency to a war. Funds were provided by several benefactors. Montessori was close to the organization, as she had been appointed lieutenant for local infirmaries in 1897.[13] The Red Cross opened seven stations throughout the *agro romano*, equipped with forty doctors, nurses, ambulance drivers, and stretcher bearers.[14]

Though quinine was the direct antidote to the disease, prominent members of the activist group, Anna and Angelo Celli, argued that education was the primary weapon in the long-term struggle against malaria.[15] Preventative care could only become a reality among farmers if they had a greater hygienic consciousness: not only basic hygiene awareness, but knowledge of the rights granted to them under the new quinine legislation, and an understanding of preventative measures. A physical redemption would only come from a redemption of the mind.[16] The teacher, Celli argued, had to be an equal partner (alongside the doctor and agronomist) in the farmers' spiritual and sanitary rehabilitation: "the master of the alphabet" was to transform the "sluggish and coarse human machines" into "colleagues and partners of the new agricultural life."[17] A concern for the sanitary and social welfare of the disadvantaged characterized the whole endeavor and was one aspect of the contemporary debate on "social medicine"—or the shift from a classic interpretation of the medical discipline as curative of diseases in favor of a preventive approach to eradicating illness entirely. In accordance with this new thinking, society would be treated with a system of economic, social, and educational reforms constituting a "social prophylaxis."[18] Medicine had the task of saving humanity, just as Montessori had recently assigned education with the salvific task of redeeming disadvantaged youth. Access to education was imperative to guaranteeing this physical and social transformation.

On a governmental level, the farmer had been the target of an extensive series of policies throughout Western Europe aimed at integrating everyone into the modern (which often meant urban) culture of the new nation. The prevailing belief that the rural masses were uncivilized, and that they had yet to be assimilated into a supposed national discourse, prompted intellectuals and politicians to pass legislation with the goal of consolidating

Children and huts in the *agro romano*. Duilio Cambellotti Collection. Courtesy of Archivi delle Arti Applicate Italiane del XX secolo, Rome.

the populace into a polity, creating collectively shared values by fiat. As historian Eugen Weber describes it in the French context, the process of forming a national community was contingent on the implementation of "agencies of change"—that is to say, developing infrastructure, implementing military service for citizens, and creating a schooling system, among other initiatives that would eventually transform peasants into citizens.[19] Schools certainly existed in the most remote parts of Italy prior to the diffusion of mass schooling, but they served the local community and catered to local interests. In the late nineteenth century, the Italian national school system came instead to serve national objectives and to respond to new and modern paradigms designed to fit national needs. The propagation of these agencies of change (e.g., the school and the infirmary) in the *agro romano* stemmed from such focus, though it also worked to preserve local cultures from completely assimilating into the dominant national civilization.[20]

These activists' efforts led to the first school in the Roman countryside in Lunghezza, along via Collatina in 1904.[21] It was one of a series of schools established by Anna Celli and supported financially by the Roman branch of the Unione Femminile Nazionale (Women's National Organization). Open during evenings and holidays for accessibility, the schools belonged to a broader philanthropic tradition led by feminist organizations focused on public medical services for children, on infirmaries, and on sanatoria for women affected by consumption.[22] Though these were mostly public-health initiatives, they also popularized women's role in science. Like other philanthropic and humanitarian groups, Unione Femminile focused on the fight against illiteracy in rural areas.[23]

Headed by Alessandro Marcucci, the Comitato per le Scuole dei Contadini (Committee for Farmers' Schools) worked quickly to increase the number of schools in the Roman countryside to provide instruction to child agricultural workers. Pushed by the novel notion that schools belonged to students, "groups of teachers scatter[ed] regardless of the weather, on bicycle, in carts, on foot . . . , as the sun set in the desolate darkness of the *agro*, to go to school in the *guitterie* and the huts."[24] According to Marcucci, schools not only provided material benefits derived from educational attainment but also allowed children to affirm their rights as citizens, and simultaneously to denounce an economic system that oppressed them. Therefore, education in these unserved areas had to be accessible through mobile school stations, traveling libraries, flexible schedules, and didactic material that was appealing and relevant to the target population. These were no ordinary schools, and they sprang up in every viable place: huts made of reed and mud, disused train cars, and churches. In the words of Marcucci, which were later echoed in Montessori's *Il Metodo*, the school "must adapt and adjust . . . to the civil life of rural populations; it must, by degrees, expand, beautify, and perfect itself, according to the progressive improvement of local conditions, beginning with the essential minimum of hygiene, decorum, grace, and comfort that is legitimate to ask for and obtain anywhere."[25] Schools were to serve the needs of the child and to provide the necessary tools for citizenship.

The Comitato per le Scuole dei Contadini also opened several nurseries employing the Montessori method (Case dei Bambini). In 1906, the Comitato deemed these schools models for future initiatives, to such a degree that the participants of the 1908 Congresso Nazionale delle Donne (National Women's Congress, which Montessori herself attended) went on a guided tour to witness their impressive results.[26] Marcucci, who headed the *agro romano* program's logistics and adapted school curricula around the exigencies of the lives of farmers' children, believed in Montessori's work—in the scientific foundation of her methodology, and in her focus on the child's personality—and shared with her a profound respect for the child's individual freedom. According to Marcucci, "the didactic and educational impact of the [Montessori] sessions was superior to that of the others." He observed

A school hut in Concordia, with the teacher, Bruno Flamini, among his students.
Alessandro Marcucci, *La casa della scuola: Relazione sulle scuole per i contadini dell'agro romano e delle paludi pontine* (Rome: Le scuole per i contadini dell'agro romano, 1925).
Courtesy of Archivi delle Arti Applicate Italiane del XX secolo, Rome.

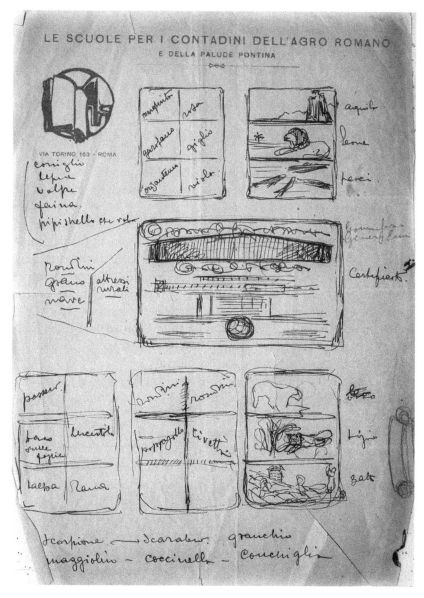

Sketches and notes by Duilio Cambellotti for the *agro romano* schools. Duilio Cambellotti Collection. Courtesy of Archivi delle Arti Applicate Italiane del XX secolo, Rome.

that all those who saw children brought up in this approach "remained in admiration of the children's spontaneous grace, their carefree activities, and the orderliness, precision, and cleanliness of their habits." They were "all children of very poor country people," and their rough upbringing often left them alone in the huts or looked after by an older sibling, yet "without physical punishment or humiliating practices, they were as diligent and calm as their tender age can and should allow."[27] As a result, the method spread across the *agro romano* and later *agro pontino*, a marshland extending along the southeast coast of the municipality of Rome, sprouting up from San Cesareo to many more villages such as Colle di Fuori, Palidoro, and Mezzaselva.[28]

The opening of Montessori schools generated much popular interest. Even the great actress Eleonora Duse visited them, with "a spirit torn between pity before so much misery and happiness at [such a] project of redemption."[29] But neither the local nor the national government funded public nursery schools. The Unione Femminile sponsored the first schools through private donations and through funds from the Commissione per l'Istruzione Primaria nel Mezzogiorno (Committee for Primary Education in Southern Italy). The City of Rome donated school supplies. In 1908, the Ministry of Public Instruction and the Ministry of Agriculture started giving small subventions.[30] At that time, however, children younger than age six were not provided with a caregiving space during the workday.[31]

Though infant care and education were still not the object of any broader governmental policy and were mostly private, small improvements began to occur in the last decades of the nineteenth century.[32] Inspired by the *asilo* (nursery school) movement pioneered by Ferrante Aporti, the founder of the first Italian charitable *asilo* in Cremona in 1830, many small private and public initiatives had mushroomed throughout the peninsula. These preschools were often established by priests, who provided religious education and practical skills for children ages two to six. The offerings were uneven, however, concentrated in cities in northern and central Italy; moreover, they were mostly run by Catholic organizations or a single municipality, in which the bourgeois liberal elite would co-opt funds and take responsibility for the well-being and education of youth.[33] Nurseries, classified by the state as charitable projects, fell under the purview of the Ministry of the Interior and were subjected to Francesco Crispi's 1890 *Opere pie* reform that sought to transform the old charitable order of benevolent institutions into a new system of public assistance, based on citizenship rights.[34] Within this slow and often inefficient shift toward a new approach to welfare, philanthropists, social workers, and intellectuals expanded the outreach of charitable institutions to lower-class families, working women, and unattended children of farmers (or workers). *Pro infanzia* conferences (in favor of infant children), women's organizations, and an overall greater concern for the public good transformed these interventions on behalf of children. The success of Friedrich Froebel's kindergarten, the development of the Agazzi sisters' approach, and the birth of the Montessori method all contributed to this conversation and, in turn, prompted changes by local and state governments. In 1904, the Unione Nazionale Educatrici per l'Infanzia (National Union for Early Childhood Teachers) was formed and held its first national congress.[35] Marcucci noted these innovations and argued that "public opinion and the public authorities . . . seem to have understood that schooling is fundamental for the real and lasting regeneration of men and things."[36]

The 1904 Orlando Law mandated compulsory primary instruction until age twelve, which necessitated "preparatory courses" for younger children.[37] Nevertheless, as the investigation led by the director for primary instruction Camillo Corradini reported for the scholastic year 1906–1907, the existence and distribution of nurseries throughout the country were scarce and uneven. More than three thousand municipalities lacked them entirely.[38] Mayor Ernesto Nathan's liberal-democratic administration (1907–1913) favored the diffusion of nurseries in Rome and its surroundings, especially those schools associated with Montessori, with whom the mayor had a personal and long-standing friendship.[39] Prominent people such as Enrichetta Chiaraviglio Giolitti, daughter of the minister Giovanni Giolitti, spoke in favor of disadvantaged infants' education.[40] In a 1908 report on schooling in rural areas, the inspector of the Ministry of Public Instruction, Pacifico Passerini, wrote that it was of paramount importance to improve scholastic services. He recommended opening nursery schools to protect and educate the farmers' children, often left unattended while their parents worked. Public institutions had to care for these children, guaranteeing "the right to health, without which life is a punishment."[41] A council member responsible for public instruction of the municipality of Rome argued that "as a form of spiritual adoption, the municipality takes the child from the mother's arms to restore to life a complete citizen." The children of the lower classes and those of the countryside—"poor people that are ignor[ed] except by the revenue authorities and the Ministry of War"—deserved a better education, and this handful of intellectuals spearheaded the change.[42]

By the time Montessori established her first Casa dei Bambini in 1907, she had participated in several humanitarian initiatives that had shaped her vision of the child and of education's transformative and redemptive role for humanity. As the *agro romano* shows, Montessori's first endeavors occurred during a time of profound redefinition of the role of childhood in Italy. Her work would have extensive ramifications for governmental interventions in impoverished areas, the role of international relief organizations (established to serve victims of war) during peacetime, and the decline of private charity in favor of governmental welfare agencies. Montessori positioned herself at the crossroad of the movements to advance women's rights, labor rights and protections, and universal literacy. She lived and breathed an atmosphere of change fomented by numerous wide-ranging artistic and political groups, all involved in improving the lives of those at the margins of society. Inspired by these intersectional forces, she elaborated an education system geared toward helping a child grow into a balanced individual, capable of peacefully interacting with her peers and inhabiting her environment.[43]

This chapter examines that transition: how the various intellectual and social developments of early twentieth-century Italy inspired Montessori's conception of a child at peace with his surroundings. It is divided into two parts. First, an analysis of Montessori's education and social activism sheds light on her philosophical foundations, providing background for the first step toward her theory of pacifism in the classroom. Her eclectic collaborations influenced her formulation of a pedagogical approach that accounted for the diverse facets of a child's development: intellectual, emotional, artistic, physical, and moral. All these initiatives involved marginalized subjects: the mentally challenged and the disadvantaged, especially women and children. Montessori's collaborations furnished her with many insights into how education could create a more just, equitable society, where all people could thrive. According to Montessori, the first step toward a fairer society began in the classroom, where a physically and mentally healthy child could be shaped through restorative education. Educated through the Montessori method and perfected by this multifaceted approach, the child would gradually establish peaceful and meaningful relationships. The second part of this chapter explores the steps that would transform a child to be at peace with her physical environment and the people around her—Montessori's first inkling of a lifelong approach to creating a peaceful society.

Montessori's Own Progression

Montessori's upbringing, education, and early activism formed the foundation of her pedagogical approach, a far-reaching project of reform that would eventually identify the child as the key agent for pacifism. The first years are characterized by the personal and professional identity formation of the young Montessori. Her overlooked early writings present not the classic image of a middle-aged woman with a seraphic smile, contemplating the child from a distance, but rather Montessori's impatience with injustice and her vigorous, almost unbridled passion for her causes. The reader feels the urgency of the universal mission that would undergird her later work.

This section investigates the educator's life before the opening of the first Montessori nursery, the San Lorenzo Casa dei Bambini. In particular, it examines three societal trends from her time—social medicine, interventions on behalf of disadvantaged youth, and feminism—to show the crucial role they played in shaping Montessori's *pedagogia riparatrice* (restorative pedagogy).[44] Owing to these influences, Montessori's view was that education must be understood as a tool to prevent, or at least to halt, the gradual deterioration of a child's physical and mental wellness. Her pedagogy provided for the restoration of physical, intellectual, and moral strengths damaged by "unhealthy living conditions, diseases, or intrinsic physiological issues."[45] This restorative pedagogy was meant not only to rehabilitate children with developmental or physical delays but also to provide the foundation for a plan to produce a physically and psychologically sound citizenry. All children, now self-assured and passionately absorbed in their own work, would naturally resort to peace, averting disruptive movements and violent behaviors.

In the preface to the 1912 English translation of *Il Metodo*, professor of education Henry W. Holmes argued that the Montessori method was the product of "a single woman's creative genius," contributing to a broader belief in Montessori's achievements and discoveries as personal epiphanies or "mystical revelation[s]."[46] For example, Montessori's disciple Anna Maria Maccheroni recounts that Montessori witnessed children who would "throw themselves on the floor to pick up the crumbs with their mouth" after meals at the psychiatric clinic at the Santa Maria della Pietà Asylum; she cited this event as the inspiration for Montessori's emphasis on providing children with appropriate stimuli.[47]

In reality, however, Montessori's work was the product of varied and convergent forces. Her approach to scientific inquiry can be seen, to borrow historian Renato Foschi's definition, as a "multiple science," shaped by a vast array of currents.[48] One must, therefore, unpack the densely layered history of her life to account for the complexity of Montessori's early thought on the role of education in fostering peace.

Montessori's was a life of unconventional choices.[49] At the turn of the twentieth century, she was a young woman with a degree in medicine and a thesis on psychiatry.[50] Though she was not the first woman in Italy to graduate with a medical degree, her journey toward this achievement was an arduous one.[51] Hagiographical accounts narrate that Pope Leo XIII interceded to help her enroll in medical school; once enrolled, she had to overcome several

obstacles, such as a deep revulsion for the anatomy room—which she conquered by hiring a man to smoke cigarettes to cover up the overpowering
odor of corpses.[52] The fact that she chose such a difficult course, even with
the help she might have received, speaks to the resilience, creativity, and
resourcefulness that would serve her throughout her professional life.

The study of medicine and psychiatry provided a strong and interdisciplinary background for Montessori's subsequent interest in pedagogy. Her
university had a specific approach to teaching these subjects. Prior to Montessori's enrollment in 1890, La Sapienza university in Rome had under-
gone expansion owing to the enrollment of the growing bourgeoisie.[53] As
historians Valeria P. Babini and Luisa Lama emphasize, there had been a
gradual shift among the faculty toward an experimental approach to medicine. This shift coincided with an influx of new scholars, the majority of
whom took democratic and socialist positions.[54] As positivists who perpetuated "il mito della scienza" (the belief that science produced objective truth),
several of Montessori's professors, such as physiologist Jacob Moleschott,
hygienist Angelo Celli, and psychiatrist Clodomiro Bonfigli, looked at the
social, economic, and political causes of pathologies. Consequently, these
faculty members conceived their field of inquiry through the lens of social
medicine, a preventative approach to the physical and psychological conditions of the lower classes. This approach expanded the scope of medicine
beyond hospital recoveries to encompass, as Babini and Lama put it, a "physical, moral, and social regeneration of the young nation."[55] Montessori
endorsed her mentors' strong belief in the scientific method and adopted
their approach to social medicine. She argued that science was first and
foremost a means to improve the conditions of the marginalized. Montessori also maintained that the dissemination of scientific information would
prevent the development of aggravating circumstances for those who lived
at society's margins.

At the time, scientific inquiry into the social body was not confined to the
field of medicine. The second half of the nineteenth century and the early
part of the twentieth witnessed a shift in the conversation on pathology and
degeneration, one that gave rise to a pervasive medical model of human
behavior in political debates and social movements across the political
spectrum.[56] This medicopsychiatric view of national decline invoked the
notion of physical degeneration, wherein individuals could be distinguished
from the healthy by various physiognomic traits. Doctors, teachers, anthropologists, and others began to widely apply the binary terms "normal" and
"pathological" in justifying their interventions in political and social matters.[57]
This dichotomy was ductile and was extended to other dualities that served

to describe the social body: corrupt/moral, morbid/wholesome, sane/insane, criminal/honest. As Robert A. Nye puts it, medicine and its ancillary sciences granted themselves a social authority "to pronounce on the nature of the norm," to mediate between deviance and compliance.[58] This discursive shift encompassed diverse schools of thought, many of which influenced Montessori.

Within this medicalization of the public discourse, deviance was often analyzed in deterministic terms. This line of inquiry classified regional human typologies and pinpointed, through medical and anthropological studies, so-called degenerates (criminals, people with disabilities, poor people, etc.). The Italian school of thought within anthropological criminology focused on racial degeneration and interpretations of pathologies as having purely organicist origins; it also equated biological malformation with moral and psychological weakness.[59] Theorists of degeneration argued that race and gender were marks of evolutionary difference, and thus they devised a taxonomy of human development.

However, as historian Rossella Raimondo argues, even within Italian positivist anthropological criminology, there was some belief in the possible redemption of the child.[60] Cesare Lombroso hinted at the possibility of rescuing children, through education, from a future of marginalization and criminality.[61] Enrico Ferri described the impact of environmental factors on the behavior of delinquents, who therefore could be raised and educated not to commit crimes even if they were predisposed to do so, as Ferri believed, by hereditary biological traits. With appropriate changes to the social and economic environment, even individuals termed "born criminals" by Lombroso could be educated to become functional members of society.[62]

Also embedded in this crusade on behalf of the lower classes, young Montessori carved her own path on this issue. What shaped her deeply humane conception of the disadvantaged was her work at the Lega Nazionale per la Protezione dei Fanciulli Deficienti (the National League for the Care and Education of Mentally Deficient Children), founded in Rome in 1898 by the director of the Asylum of Rome and of the Psychiatric Institute Bonfigli, with the help of the minister of public instruction Guido Baccelli. There, she started to lobby for the creation of special classes for the so-called feebleminded and elaborated her own response to the problem of degeneration, one that would come through the "previously unsuspected" "union between medicine and pedagogy."[63] In an understudied writing titled "La teoria lombrosiana e l'educazione morale," the young pedagogue distanced herself from a deterministic approach to pathology, maintaining that the redemption of the disadvantaged was "the duty of the teacher of the future."[64]

Educators must not only consider the environmental causes of the pupils' pathologies but also study "each single individual, to distinguish each person's constitution and adapt for every single person the educational approach that is most congenial."[65] Wherever science entered the classroom, rehabilitation would ensue. Until then, as she would declare in 1915, the school had "to become a source of grandiosity and redemption."[66]

Montessori's conception of degeneration, as Foschi argues, stood in between that of anthropologists Léonce-Pierre Manouvrier and Giuseppe Sergi—the latter had become her mentor in 1902 while she was pursuing a degree in philosophy at La Sapienza.[67] Following Manouvrier, Montessori considered criminal tendencies, and more generally all pathologies, to be degenerative and hereditary, but she also saw education as having a rehabilitative role and worked to devise tools (such as the *cartella per lo studio individuale del bambino*, a chart for studying each individual child) to catalog and monitor all anthropological and physical information on the child, as Sergi had done. Supporting the environmental theories of crime, she distanced herself from the Lombrosian school of criminal anthropology and argued that the identification (and punishment) of criminal anomalies in adults did not lead to the betterment of society because it did not prevent anyone from committing crimes. Instead, it was by educating the so-called degenerate child that crimes might actually be prevented.

Schools had to be reformed, Montessori contended, and educators had to rethink how they assessed students. According to Montessori, academic outcomes were determined not only by physiological differences but also by anthropological circumstances that highly affected student performance.[68] Through a combination of bodily measurements (mainly of the cranium and thorax) and anthropometric data on the biological and social status of the household (diet, family members, parents' professions, and housing), Montessori worked to demonstrate that intellectual development resulted from a vast array of environmental, social, economic, and biological factors, all variables that could be adjusted through public intervention in the life of the disadvantaged. Therefore, teachers needed to acquire a new "sense of justice," one that took into account previously unused parameters. It was important to examine biological and anthropological aspects of the students' upbringing and to reconsider the role of reward and punishment.[69] A new pedagogy based on scientific principles and rigorous observation of the child would act as a preventative measure against possible degeneration.

Positivist science formed Montessori's entire background. It manifested in her work through direct observation, scientific rigor, and an analytic method. But during these formative years, she had already distanced herself from determinism and mechanism, opening herself up to science in a dynamic way. She exalted the qualities of the scientist—patience, respect, and perseverance—and found these same attributes in the teacher, described by Montessori as "a religious woman with regards to nature," whose objective is to "gather information from nature, awaiting its revelations."[70] Notably, these first attempts to combine a scientific pedagogy with her interest in religious syncretism were already present at this moment in her work, and they would remain in tension throughout her life. Her approach to science was marked from the very beginning by a spirituality that she articulated in reflections on morality, esthetics, and religion. Though a mere inkling at first, this element would become far more pronounced in subsequent years.[71]

Montessori's multifaceted approach to children's education and welfare also reflects the diverse public and private agencies that had just begun to take an interest in youth and infants. Alongside the aforementioned innovations in child psychiatry and psychology, and late positivism's broader anxiety about population degeneration, an interest in the child began spreading throughout the Western world.[72] The dawn of the famously so-called century of the child signaled the surge and diffusion of a transnational debate on child-related concerns.[73] Networks of educators, social workers, and politicians recognized the necessity for public intervention into children's needs. According to historian Carl Ipsen, Italian politicians' desire to follow the lead of other countries, as well as "the combination of social peace, economic growth, and reformist zeal," drove a broad spectrum of political figures to discuss the condition of children.[74] As a result, the Giolitti government (1901–14) passed a series of laws aimed at protecting Italian children from labor and neglect.[75] This academic, political, and popular interest in youth and infancy provided a fertile ground for the development of the first welfare policies in favor of children in need. Despite this growth, Liberal Italy's social insurance system had fewer actual initiatives when compared to other nations' emergent welfare provisions. Nonetheless, Prime Minister Giolitti paid significant attention to the system of *beneficenza pubblica* (public welfare) and attempted to improve it by increasing government control over denominational charities, in order to hold them accountable.[76] Montessori's theorization and social activism originated in this vibrant conversation.

Montessori's interest in the restorative power of education was strengthened by a grassroots militancy that brought her to volunteer on the streets of Rome in institutions such as the Asdrubali maternity ward in the Esquilino district and to canvass in favor of reforming juvenile detention centers.[77]

She conceived a new form of assistance for those living at the margins, which entailed creating a public system of support and passing social legislation in favor of the lower classes, women, and children.[78] When speaking about the "feebleminded," for example, Montessori argued in 1898 that "[their] education [did] not concern only the sentiment of the single individual, instead it concern[ed] the right to social protection of each person; it [was] not an issue of *opere pie*, but of political economy and penal law."[79] This statement represented a bold stance in redefining charity as a state duty, not a duty solely of Catholic institutions.

The fight for women's rights was also central to Montessori's activism. It became a defining feature of her early campaign to bring about social and political change, which would end up informing her expansive redefinition of children's welfare. The social and political enfranchisement of women was central to the early formulation of Montessori's theory of restorative education. As historian Paola Trabalzini argues, Montessori at the beginning of her career considered women and children, particularly mother and child, an indissoluble duo; emancipated women would become the means to promote the wellness and welfare of children.[80] Montessori argued that during pregnancy and breastfeeding, hereditary and environmental factors affected the mother as well as the baby. Adequate food, a suitable environment, and a workplace where women did not experience discrimination all contributed to the health of the fetus. According to the educator, protecting and promoting the mother also meant taking preemptive action against any diseases that would affect the baby. With this in mind, Montessori spoke against female exploitation at work, promoted the education of young women (specifically, encouraging them to study science), and fostered women's participation in the political arena: "as soon as she [the woman] becomes a free human being with her own social rights, she *will begin to work for peace*: she will know how to ignite the divine light among the minds that lose it in selfishness, and instill in the hearts the holy love of humanity—which is widespread maternal love in the world."[81]

For Montessori, women must change to become capable of leading this reform movement. In these years of her scientific and political growth, the educator used diverse platforms to espouse female emancipation. In March 1896, she became vice secretary of the Roman branch of the organization Associazione Femminile Italiana (Italian Women's Association), which aimed at promoting sisterhood among women. A representative of Italy at both the 1896 International Women's Congress in Berlin and the 1899 International Council of Women in London, Montessori delivered lectures on the rights of working women, including equal pay for equal work, and decried the working conditions to which minors were subjected. Montessori's feminist speeches and articles are characterized by the strength of her convictions and her poise in tackling complex issues. She presented herself as a "new woman," one who would promulgate a "scientific feminism," capable of reforming society.[82] She argued that several benefits would ensue: women would not only reform scientific fields, enriching them with female viewpoints, but also claim their own "intellectual identity" and economic independence and act as catalysts for scientific knowledge, popularizing it among lay audiences.[83]

Bringing about this female-led scientific rehabilitation of the child was not going to be an easy task, given the general opposition to women entering male-dominated fields. Through lectures and opinion pieces in magazines and newspapers, Montessori also spoke out against what had probably been years of academic marginalization and firsthand experience with prejudice against women from her mentors and colleagues.[84] Several criminologists, among whom were the aforementioned Lombroso and Sergi, argued that women were inferior to men. Based on their preconceptions about women's nature, they claimed that their lower status was hereditary and evident in their physical bodies. As paraphrased by Montessori, Lombroso argued, "the woman is biologically, that is to say, entirely, inferior, . . . the volume of her brain is destined by its nature to inferiority. There is nothing to be done about it."[85] Sergi, as Montessori put it, "[did] not bother to discuss feminism because he consider[ed] it a 'bore,' a topic suitable for a congress on humor." Nonetheless, Montessori was not to be discouraged. For her, the time when women were told "to be passive, to annihilate [their] will in favor of that of their husband" was finally over. Through her public engagements, she encouraged women to be out in the world and to take charge of change. Montessori promoted the era as one in which the woman would rise; this new woman would go on "to achieve justice and world peace!"[86]

Thus it is no surprise that Montessori collaborated during these years with those women who entered the public sphere confidently with the goal of change: women such as Ersilia Majno, who, while part of a governmental committee on juvenile delinquency, argued that degeneration among young people is rooted "in the disregard for the rights of the child . . . —the right to love, to education, and to joy—the right to always know who gave them the unsolicited, and often fatal, gift of life. A new civilization will rise up healthy and purified if these rights are recognized."[87] These were the "new women" of the Italian feminist movement who would leave an indelible mark on Montessori's pedagogical approach.

At the turn of the twentieth century, Italy experienced a new kind of feminism, grounded, unlike its precursor, in social charity.[88] Italian women's
associations did not fight for political rights directly but instead engaged in
social activism to reshape the female presence in the public sphere. Historian Annarita Buttafuoco calls this strategy "practical feminism" or "philanthropy as politics" and pinpoints these women's associations as attempts to
create structures for assistance and education. Italian feminists were primarily concerned with reforming and assisting working-class women and
their children, with the general goal of "giving them theoretical/practical
tools . . . useful to face battles for reclaiming civil and political rights, and,
above all, to experience the emancipation once the [political battles] would
have been won."[89] The movement's goal was to provide a cultural formation for the female political individual and then to use this model to fight
for political rights. The movement attempted to obtain social and legal parity
between the sexes by arguing for the *equivalence* between men and women.
Its tenets were rooted in the cultivation of a "new female ethics," as feminist thinkers called it, which emphasized the difference between genders
that did not hail one as superior or subordinate to the other. Motherhood, for
instance, became a way for women to participate in the political discourse of
the time. Using Montessori's words, feminists believed "wom[e]n's social victory will be a maternal one."[90]

Until the rise of Fascism, Italian feminism was characterized by its "mater-
nalism," also referred to as the "culture of the maternal." Women were
encouraged to fight for their rights without relinquishing the putatively
defining traits of their gender, especially their reproductive functions.[91] The
movement's purview extended far beyond the maternal realm, however, to
accommodate broader political projects: reforming civic and penal codes,
granting civil rights for single mothers, and protecting women against rape
and incest. Despite these tangible and far-reaching plans, feminist associations were rarely endorsed by political parties, even by those with whom
they shared an ideology. Socialists, for example, supported the struggle for
female emancipation, but they failed to advocate for female suffrage. And
yet feminist organizations manage to accomplish significant goals. These
groups added their own initiatives to the nascent welfare state, and in the
case of Rome and Milan, they were backed by progressive city administra-
tions to create funds for pregnant women in need, first aid stations, and
courses on child medicine, among other programs. In fact, when the law
approving the Cassa Nazionale di Maternità (National Maternity Fund)
passed in July 1910, these movements "had thirty years of practical and

theoretical engagement in the issue of the relationship between mother-hood, the state and women's citizenship."[92]

It was in this climate that Montessori began to formulate her thoughts on the role of the mother in the child's upbringing. Her theoretical contribu-tion to feminism drew on her studies in medicine, philosophy, and anthro-pology (which she was eventually qualified to teach at the university level in 1902). Montessori argued that feminism's ultimate goal was for women to reclaim their "own biological work," which is to say "the creation of their own children."[93] This did not mean relegating them to the private sphere but instead giving them the most important task of all: preserving humanity.[94] Montessori's feminism appears to be founded on biological determinism; her vision of womanhood is based on a supposed biological interpretation, encapsulating women in a sort of biologism (the equation of women's iden-tity with certain biological and specifically maternal functions). From a current perspective, as philosopher Caterina Botti puts it, biologism discounts a history of personal, social, and political efforts that aim at affirming women's diversity by conceiving of womanhood vis-à-vis hegemonic institutions.[95] Though Montessori's feminism was characterized by Catarsi and Genovesi as moderate, her positions must properly be evaluated in light of the sociohis-torical context that produced them: the notion of maternity as a choice was mostly ignored in the political sphere in Montessori's era and was scarcely taken into consideration even by the newly founded feminist movement.[96] Her feminism is tethered to a specific and narrow conception of woman-hood, but several other points of her agenda (e.g., women's place in the work-force, equal salary, women's right to vote) could be considered innovative.

According to Montessori, women were to lead a scientific revolution. Women, "pure, sweet, strong, with holy ideals of love and *universal peace*, with [their] eyes fixed on that civic progress shining toward the future," were to end the perils of degeneration which, if left untreated, were transmittable and could eventually be fatal.[97] Women must become acquainted with and adopt scientific principles to use them in their most intimate decisions: those pertaining to their families and their lives. They were to enjoy conscious and free choices in selecting their partners, using principles of science to make better sexual decisions. According to Montessori, women had to

> use reason to appeal for peace; and make the argument that a long period of decadence follows any war, and that this is a real fact; since women who are pregnant in times of war produce degenerate offspring because of the extreme emotions they are subject to. Say that you don't want war not only

because it weakens us numerically and financially, but because it also makes us produce weak children.[98]

Bearing the weight of a conscious maternity, and consequently the responsibility of maintaining a healthy "species," "new women" would have a renewed place in their relationships, families, and society.[99] Men would have to accept the women's renewed role to reach "well-being, *universal peace*, that is to say, the absolute progress, which can be achieved only when the whole of humanity is aware of its true rights and duties, will work together for the universal good."[100] This "new woman" must make a practice of informed sexual choices, for children's well-being and the health of the species. Education, the bastion, the "sovereign leader . . . of the biological becoming of the species," must guide women's choices. As Montessori declared, "The time has come for a new morality and a new education."[101] She spent the next years of her life devising a new education that would foment a new morality.

Achieving Grace through Motor and Intellectual Education

In the midst of the evils affecting society, the poverty of the present, the uncertainties of the future, everyone understands that the most efficient remedy cannot but come from education, understood not narrow-mindedly as it has been by many until today, but in the nobler and broader sense: education of the mind and of the heart, capable of broadening our host of ideas, of eradicating evil tendencies, of teaching truly to think, love, and work, of cultivating in the child and in the youth the future man, ready to take on the struggles and disillusionments of life with serenity and strength.[102]

Montessori's eclectic upbringing, her education, her interests in social medicine, her feminism, and her commitment to the betterment of humanity through activism all converged in a pedagogical approach focused on children living harmoniously. This conception of "a child at peace" was rooted in Montessori's earlier and numerous collaborations, studies, and initiatives, which contributed to her understanding of how to mold an individual to "think, work, and love" and who would, in turn, become a citizen "ready to take on the struggles and disillusionments of life with serenity and strength."[103] By the time she attended the 1898 Primo Congresso Pedagogico (First Pedagogical Congress) to speak about developmentally challenged children, Montessori had already identified education as the principal tool for changing society by generating the true agent of that reform—the child.

To this end, Montessori's approach reshaped the child's relationship to his immediate environment, as well as to his peers and family, by rethinking ways of teaching not only intellectual and motor skills but also moral values and principles. Being at peace—or acting in harmony—with the environment was a twofold notion for the Montessori child: his actions and gestures would be restful and composed, and he would act morally and respectfully, seeking good for his community. This layered approach included moving gracefully, acting in accordance with physical surroundings, and also behaving altruistically, learning to feel empathy for peers and family. Moving erratically, or behaving carelessly or recklessly, was rare in the Montessori classroom.

Crucial to building this child-environment interaction was children's motor and intellectual skill development. The Montessori child possessed the so-called *grazia dei movimenti*: she moved with grace and discernment not because she was disciplined to do so but because she could identify—thanks to a proper education—the reasons and ways to move through her environment with deliberation and agility. Montessori stressed progressive motor skills refinement and its direct connection to intellectual development. The child's growth depended on having unguided interactions with the environment. This was a noticeable departure from the misconception guiding educators until then, rooted in René Descartes's philosophical tradition of separating the intellect from the body. In contrast, Montessori insisted that the education of the mind could not come at the expense of the physical body. The two worked together, and any movement was strictly interwoven with the development of the child's intellectual faculty. As Montessori observed in her later work, if movement was obstructed, the child would fail to develop intellect and personality; overall well-being would be at risk, potentially creating an adult incapable of seeking peaceful and harmonious interactions.

Therefore, "unity between the nervous system and the muscle" must be favored through specific activities, so that the child's first manifestations of growth, most often related to movement, could begin.[104] Building on this understanding, Montessori created a baseline assumption of her method: the developmental process was ignited by the brain's sensory and motor activities that would, in turn, lead to the growth and development of higher-order functions, such as language and complex thought. Neurobiologist Alberto Oliverio describes this process as an "interactive synchronism" between psyche and body that manifests itself even in newborns who react to voice and language via micromovements.[105] Ignoring this connection between psyche and body, Montessori argued, leaves children incapable of controlling the way they interact with their circumstances: "Beyond lack of interest, there is, in common children, a muscular anarchy, whereby every muscle does as it pleases and refuses to obey the mind. Adults prevent children from having experiences at the age in which muscles have to be dominated by the will, and so the muscles are left without master, without control, and when the individual wants to use them, they are nowhere to be found." Motility and thought must be trained simultaneously, so the child could unify them himself—and therefore build his own personality, "which otherwise would remain confused, and almost fractured."[106]

When speaking about this union of body and mind, Montessori referred to the importance of sensorial education to prod cognitive development, but also to the rehabilitative practice of *psychomotricité*, or psychomotility, based on the notion that mind and body were inseparable and continuously influencing each other. Psychomotility had been conceived by French neuropsychiatrist Philippe Tissié, who developed physical education activities as a remedy for the *degenerescence* of French youth and as a treatment for illnesses of the nervous system at the end of the nineteenth century. It was later embraced by French psychiatrist Ernest Dupré, who first elaborated on the connections among congenital anomalies, motor debilities, and cognitive impairments.[107] This field had a significant impact on Montessori's approach. One central claim was that a child's movements were influenced by social, emotional, and affective personality components; these sensory-motor activities would then drive the child's affective-emotional, cognitive, and social faculties, creating a feedback loop. Following this school of thought, Montessori argued that the education of physical movements should precede intellectual processes so that it could influence psychological traits.

This conversation was also taking place within Italian education circles. Since 1878, when minister of public instruction Francesco De Sanctis introduced *ginnastica educativa* (educational gymnastics) for boys and girls at all grade levels, physical education was deemed essential for the Italian school system.[108] According to De Sanctis, gymnastics was indispensable to the child's upbringing because "it create[d] moral energy, which is the foundation of initiative, perseverance, and seriousness in pursuing a goal, and character." Informed by thinkers based at the Turin Società Ginnastica, the first gymnastic programs were the result of a collaboration between the Ministry of Public Instruction and the Ministry of War and therefore had a militaristic character evident in the goal of developing a "sentiment of order and bravery."[109] Gymnastics was a means to "make young men's aptitude for military service simpler, more active, and more widespread."[110] Following the decree, educators were forced to rethink their curricula in light of this new pedagogy.

Though De Sanctis believed that a child's mind and body must be shaped in order to become an adult, applying the 1878 law proved difficult because of school districts' financial difficulties and limited resources.[111] Further-more, Italian intellectuals rarely addressed the overall psychophysical development of the child—and when they did, they hardly considered this development an organic process. For example, Emilio Baumann, a school-teacher and proponent of regimented training, promoted the development of the child's physique through collective and militaristic exercise.[112] Rethink-ing the role of movement in education had more to do with disciplining the body and correcting the character to shape, as political commentator Pasquale Turiello argued, a reformed Italian through a school system mod-eled on the military where "virile discipline" reigned.[113] As historian Silvana Patriarca notes, gymnastics were central to the militarization of the educa-tional system to subject bodies to regimented preparation for participation in a model citizenry.[114]

This shift to an alternative epistemic principle, based on knowledge through the body before that of the mind, a form of sentience in kinesis that art historian Zeynep Çelik Alexander terms *kinaesthetic knowing*, gained momentum at the turn of the twentieth century.[115] Several European educa-tors were concerned with the connection between motor and intellectual skills, the study of which contributed to the understanding of psychomotil-ity. Swiss composer and music educator Émile Jaques-Dalcroze served as an inspiration to Montessori's work. His colleague, neurologist and child psychologist Édouard Claparède, wrote in 1906 that Dalcroze had arrived "at the same conception of the psychological importance of movement as a support for the intellectual and affective phenomena."[116] Indeed, as a music teacher, Dalcroze maintained no one could learn music if they used only their ears and hands; instead, he designed activities for students to respond to music, thereby integrating their emotions, intentions, nerves, and senses. Educators needed to rethink music instruction to incorporate what he termed *gymnastique rythmique*, or eurythmics—a systematic approach to rhythmic and bodily training. According to Dalcroze, "To be a well-rounded musi-cian, a child must possess a set of physical and spiritual factors and quali-ties that are, on the one hand, the ear, the voice, and the consciousness of sound, and on the other, the whole body (resonant frame, muscles, nerves) and the consciousness of body rhythm."[117] The composer established a sys-tem of bodily coordination with the goal of provoking "a current of con-sciousness," which would lead to more unified perceptual faculties, integrating sensory details between the eyes, ears, body, and mind.[118] In referencing Dal-croze, Montessori argued that "those who follow with rigor, with precision, this classical rhythmic gymnastics, feel in them a moral transformation, a greater clarity of intelligence, and a new life."[119] Music was, therefore, a means to an end, and, according to Dalcroze, a way "of forging links," to create synergy among parts of the body.[120]

Dalcroze's *gymnastique rythmique* converged with Montessori's idea of precision in the child's movement, a feature that often surprised observers of her students: their successful completion of complex activities was unparalleled in children of similar grade levels. As emphasized in a later essay by Montessori, coordinating the education of body and mind merged one's entire personality toward a specific goal, which resulted in more deliberate movements. In this quest for precision, a previously unseen spatial equilibrium would emerge: a new relationship of ease with the environment and congruity among movements would ultimately sharpen the child's attention and intelligence.[121] As Patrick Frierson puts it, the Montessori child would strive to build character, an individual process that occurred through concentration, precision, and effortful work.[122]

Two elements were essential in reaching this objective: gradation (or gradual progression through activities) and repetition.[123] Montessori materials guided children through the curriculum, as they increased in complexity. The teacher presented the materials in sequence to the child, from easiest to hardest, following children's developmental needs and interests. In a series of articles on reform instead of punishment for young criminals, Montessori reported on the San Michele reformatory, where skilled Roman artists trained young boys to become cabinetmakers, tailors, and plasterers. She described how the maestro Michele Vinci had articulated the process of making a shoe, so students could visualize distinct stages, understand the complexity of working with particular materials, and so forth. After accomplishing activities such as shaping the wood for the shoe's heel, students would design complex tridimensional shapes. Montessori argued: "Gradation leads from the simple line engraved on clay or carved on cardboard to the fundamental geometrical figures, to their combinations in drawings, as well as to their applications in the composition or analysis of useful or artistic objects." Progressive engagement with the material alone was not enough. Children must become involved in each activity, Montessori explained, "to eviscerate it in all its depth." The mastery of each action required "a laborious conquest, a cultivation." The child's personality, her inner being, and individuality "builds and extends only at the price of patience, of stopping, of repeating." This is a necessary step, Montessori emphasized, that the teacher must "repeat without boring, that is, without tiring."[124] By reiterating the same action or movement many times, the child would conquer disorderly behavior.

Education of movement (and therefore of the intellect) brought balance to the individual and constituted the first step in the achievement of a peaceful attitude—the first metaphorical step toward Montessori's pacifist development. The refinement of movement not only shapes the child's self-awareness but also develops her will and promotes her independence by mastering her actions. Grace was achieved by motor skill refinement and through developing sensorial activities, which would, in turn, develop "the highest part of man's psyche, because mankind must use it as a clear guidance to his own conscience."[125] Peace, therefore, was at the child's fingertips.

But how could a child master her actions and thereby achieve peace? The key point, for Montessori, was the notion of *work*, interpreted both as an unabridged engagement of the child's attention and as stimuli to his intellectual and physical capacities. As contemporary pedagogues understood, activities that kept children anchored to their desks inhibited their movement while they directed their attention toward curricular goals. At the other end of the spectrum, gymnastics was imposed as a collective muscular discipline in which a teacher would "imperialistically" determine assignments for those who were inactive.[126] What Montessori sought instead is best illustrated by one of Giovanni Pascoli's poems, which was published a few years before the opening of the first Casa dei Bambini and happens to reflect her ethos particularly well:

> It was sunset: two boys were intent
> on boisterous amusements
> in the golden quiet of the shaded avenue.
> At play, *as seriously as at work* . . . [127]

Just like Pascoli's two boys (*i due fanciulli*), Montessori's children were fully absorbed in what they were doing because of the scientifically designed didactic apparatus that stimulated them in response to their physical and mental needs. Concentration and absorption would follow. A concrete example of these activities was the *attività di vita pratica* (daily-life activities), made possible by Montessori's development of child-sized furniture and utensils.

Ordinary daily activities fit the developmental needs of children ages three to six, prompting them to become "conquerors of themselves": to direct their latent mental and physical energies toward a specific goal, which eventually leads them to gain motor (and therefore intellectual) skills. Folding rugs, polishing shoes, and washing floors were all activities that used a full range of movement and, at the same time, refined children's motor skills without tiring them. Furthermore, children carried out these tasks repetitively to keep their environment clean and orderly, which also provided a sense of satisfaction upon completion. This new form of gymnastic movement, Montessori argued, would perfect itself over time. It was only natural

Young children at a Montessori school engage in practical life activities, including washing dishes and rolling out fresh pasta. Maria Montessori, *Il Metodo della pedagogia scientifica applicato all'educazione infantile nelle Case dei Bambini* (Rome: Loescher, 1913). Courtesy of Opera Nazionale Montessori, Rome.

that children would not master these activities immediately. At first, they would have "a roughness, a coarseness that spoils the harmony of the person," but eventually the children would learn to avoid superfluous movements. Through tasks such as rolling fresh pasta for a meal, setting the table, or washing glasses and dishes (as shown in the photograph that follows), children would come to discern which motions were necessary, arriving at a true "economy of movement."[128]

Only through repetition and avoidance of unnecessary moves could an action be learned to the point that it was precise and therefore perfect. Then, and only then, stressed Montessori, "the aesthetic movement, the artistic attitude, comes out as a consequence." Through this process of perfection, the child escaped adult control as he recognized his awareness of the environment and others. Therefore, he would free himself and thus elude his "biggest danger": that of having his personality restrained by adult judgment.[129] Montessori warned that ordinary chores must have an observable outcome and not be geared toward imaginary tasks. Children who prepared a meal had to share the fruits of their labor with their classmates; those who cleaned should not see the teacher clean the same area more effectively right after them. Tasks had to have a tangible goal, one that made sense within children's own worlds.

Two young children at a Montessori school demonstrating practical life activities such as cleaning and working on a dressing frame. Maria Montessori, *Il Metodo della pedagogia scientifica applicato all'educazione infantile nelle Case dei Bambini* (Rome: Loescher, 1913). Courtesy of Opera Nazionale Montessori, Rome.

Immersed in these activities that responded to the child's inner developmental needs, the child would grow physically and mentally. According to Montessori, what propelled this development was the child's aspiration for self-actualization, for developing his character based on sets of impulses and stimuli or the attempt to fulfill the physical and mental unfolding of his personality. As Montessori educator Paula Polk Lillard put it, the child's "emotional and physical health will literally depend upon this constant attempt to become himself."[130] This, however, was not to be interpreted as a selfish plan to self-actualize and self-perfect *at the expense* of others or of the environment. Self-construction was a process that allowed each child to find his place of service to humanity while seeking personal happiness.[131] Over time, this approach would be clarified to include a specific vocation or purpose; in the context of her first pedagogical experiments, though, Montessori interpreted it as a necessity for the child "to construct his own body to be an instrument that will enable him to have his own special behavior in the environment."[132] The child's full personality would blossom in a well-designed scholastic environment.

In this quest to self-actualize, the child also developed a sense for community life, a "*sentimento sociale*."[133] This sense of community was achieved through a key element of Montessori's approach: developing responsibility toward one's environment, accomplished by encouraging the children to consider the classroom as their own. All material was geared toward children's needs (intellectual, emotional, and physical); they also took care of the classroom, returning the didactic material to cabinets, cleaning up tables, watering plants, and so on. According to Montessori, once children appreciated their environment and the didactic apparatus, they naturally developed a sense of pride in the order and beauty of their space, and sought to preserve it.

Moreover, children would develop a sense of responsibility for one another. This notion sounded counterintuitive to many early observers of Montessori's classrooms, who criticized the educator for not urging a sense of cooperation among peers.[134] "And how will the social sentiment be developed," they asked, "if each child works independently?"[135] Montessori responded that giving children freedom in how to socialize, and showing them that they had to limit their actions only when they hampered the rights of others, indeed nurtured a spontaneous empathy. This process also benefited from grouping together children of different ages, often with older peers helping younger ones.

One example of this phenomenon is the story of young Bruno and Piccola, who attended Montessori's via Giusti Casa dei Bambini.[136] Little Bruno was an orphan of the 1908 Messina-Reggio earthquake. The Associazione Nazionale per gli Interessi del Mezzogiorno d'Italia (National Association for the Interests of Southern Italy) had selected the Montessori method for the schools in Sicily and Calabria.[137] The association helped recovery efforts in the two regions, counting among its members intellectuals and politicians such as senator Leopoldo Franchetti, who, at that time, was also an advocate for Montessori's work in Italy and abroad.[138]

Traumatized by the horrors Bruno had witnessed, "such as the death-cry of his girl mother" and "the evil things done to him during his babyhood in the tenement," he seldom participated in classroom activities, "his timid fingers fumbled by the big pink and blue letters . . . ; they tried to button, to lace, to match color, but not very effectually."[139] As recalled by the North American journalist Carolyn Sherwin Bailey, the only thing that helped him overcome his state of dullness and apathy was his empathy toward a younger girl who had been bullied:

> A new little one had come and, full of disorderly impulses, had snatched at the vari-colored carpet of carefully arranged color-spools Piccola had spread on her table, scattering them to the floor. Red, green, orange, yellow, Piccola's painstaking work of an hour lay in a great colored, mixed-up

heap. . . . She dropped her curly head in her arms and sobbed, big, gulping sobs that wouldn't stop, that strangled her. Bruno, watching her, *found his muscles*. He ran to her, putting one kind little arm around her waist and with the other drew her head down to the shoulder of his little ragged blue apron and smoothed her hair, talking sweet, liquid nonsense all the time that made Piccola's sobs grow less and less, and comforted her. When she smiled and drew away to watch the group of children who had hurried to pick up her colors for her, Bruno slipped back to his corner and the old, dull look settled back in his face.

"The little man has the conscience-sense. He shall have a chance to use it," thought the Montessori directress who had been watching the scene.[140]

Injustice had awoken little Bruno's conscience (manifested first through the awakening of his muscles)—being able to reassure and take care of somebody had touched him so deeply that he was stirred from his torpor. As his muscles twitched, his conscience awoke. If this spontaneous display of empathy demonstrated the presence, within each child, of an innate tendency toward kindness, Montessori aimed at systematically "turning these manifestations of inner sensibility into morality," to harness these isolated episodes to generate an individual capable of choosing the common good and that of others.[141] To do so, she struggled over her career with ways to integrate morality into a plan for education. This next section looks at her early reflections on this topic.

Education to Morality or How to Shape a Gentle Soul

The development of moral traits—the ability to distinguish between good and bad actions and to recognize and anticipate the consequences of one's behavior—was also a fundamental aim of Montessori's approach. This subject of her early career, however, has remained an understudied part of her work. The child's capacity to act altruistically, to empathize, and to behave in concert with peers and family came from Montessori's efforts to develop a feeling of "*simpatia*," as understood according to its Greek etymology *sympátheia*, derived from *pathos*, or feeling for something suffering for someone, and the prefix *syn*—with, or together.[142] According to Montessori, the development of an emotional or spiritual life was possible because certain senses already existed within the child for responding to his emotional and spiritual environment, and, therefore, for expressing compassion for others. The idea that it was the duty of education to foster this sense of morality serves as the second step in my reading of Montessori's approach to peace.

To understand this aspect of Montessori's approach, one must examine her little-known essay, "Norme per una classificazione dei deficienti in rapporto ai metodi speciali di educazione," written while she was working with "feebleminded" children at the Scuola Magistrale Ortofrenica in 1901.[143] The essay drew on her earlier work with children with developmental delays, and it later formed the backbone of her approach. The prevalence of confinement, neglect, and dereliction among this special subset of children, as well as their isolation and the lack of governmental and social efforts to rehabilitate them, inspired Montessori to take up their cause. She elaborated pedagogical strategies to foster in these children a sense of morality, which would, in turn, help them to become active and productive community members.

This essay signaled Montessori's temporary "scientific divorce" from the physician and educationist Édouard Séguin; she had abandoned his purely sensorial and intellectual educational approach as the key to educating children with developmental delays.[144] Instead, "inspired by a deep feeling of justice for the weak, the inept, the mentally challenged, [Montessori] pointed humanity to the way forward, for the redemption of those vanquished," and maintained that a moral education would allow for the rehabilitation of all children.[145] Building on her experience at Scuola Ortofrenica, the educator argued that education's end goal was to develop a preventive social and educational care system, so children with developmental delays would not become part of "that low social stratum where vice, idleness, and crime represent the joys of life and its means of subsistence."[146] A solid moral education could rescue these children and lead them toward a productive life.

Montessori's objective was to ensure these children would morally and physically "adapt to the social circumstances in which they will have to live."[147] Montessori had gained public influence as a contributor to the conversation on the recovery and integration of youth affected by mental impairments. Her engagement drew public attention when she attended the Primo Congresso Pedagogico. Meanwhile, an Italian anarchist assassinated Elizabeth of Bavaria, empress of Austria and queen of Hungary. Montessori was able to use this occurrence as an example to speak in favor of reforming the educational system to include criminals, who were considered to have developmental delays.[148] As she addressed the crowd at the Congress, she cried to the audience:

> You will reform the methods for the *moral education* of the school in vain
> if you do not think that there are individuals, precisely those capable of

committing such heinous crimes, who go through school without being touched in any way by education. . . . The reform to be imposed is that of school and pedagogy, so it may lead us to protect all children in their development, including those that prove to be resistant to social life.[149]

Montessori explained a new approach to education, a "pedagogia riparatrice" that would ameliorate the lives of the disadvantaged.[150] Schools had to become strongholds for preparing individuals, even marginalized ones, to enter society and become full citizens. In opposition to the positivist Lombroso, who argued that there were such things as born criminals, Montessori asked people "not to condemn the wicked but to redeem them through education and that solidarity that comes from a shared blame."[151] It followed, she argued, that for "each school that opens up, a prison shuts down," insofar as schools assumed a central role in the reeducation of those who followed disruptive tendencies.[152] Teaching morality assumed a central place in this project.

To prevent and address delinquency and intellectual idleness among these children, she returned to Édouard Séguin's psychomuscular education approach, which proposed that psychosensorial growth led to intellectual and eventual moral development. Although Séguin served as Montessori's point of departure, she argued that he had neglected to explain how one could receive moral instruction through intellectual education. This was a problematic lacuna, one that urgently needed to be addressed. Montessori wrote:

> The one leads individuals to be productive and procure for themselves a series of elements of material and intellectual well-being, the other leads them to adapt to the social climate in which they will have to live, namely, among a certain number of analytical rules of conduct that have a utilitarian significance—and among the other rules of moral synthesis that have a philosophical or religious significance.[153]

Séguin maintained that children developed intellectually and, consequently, progressed automatically into a development of their morality through a sensorial education. According to Montessori, however, Séguin contradicted himself. Drawing upon the Enlightenment tradition of the French philosopher Étienne Bonnot de Condillac, he asserted the centrality of sensorial education in the development of the mentally challenged child, failing to recognize the Schopenhauerian notion that man can only reach an education in morality through an education of the will.

Montessori referred to German philosopher Arthur Schopenhauer's argument that the essence of our being and of reality corresponds to *Wille zum Leben*, or will to live.[154] According to Schopenhauer, man can only possess knowledge on a phenomenalist level. Man can, however, possess the knowledge of his own essence—and the essence of the universe—through his physical body, which allows him to acquire an awareness of the *Wille zum Leben*, to be interpreted as a blind striving, an unfulfilled desire, without consciousness and impossible to satisfy. Reality cannot be known through the intellect but only through corporeality and through will, or desire. Man does not reach a moral behavior through rationality but through experiencing life *cum patior*, with compassion or empathy, the feeling of someone else's suffering as one's own. Montessori borrowed this notion from Schopenhauer and investigated the way education could promote empathy and henceforth generate a sense of morality in children.

While speaking of children with developmental delays—who, Montessori thought, were at risk of having a decreased inclination toward empathy— she drew again from the German philosopher and argued:

> What commonly manifests in the perverted, who are of an infinite variety, is a special deficiency of the so-called "moral sense," namely, "sympathy," "altruistic inclinations," "a sense of justice," which are diminished, suppressed or perverted; the representation of other people's good and evil suppressed or perverted leaves insensitive: egoism triumphs, with its consequences.[155]

Educators must therefore devise new ways to address deficiencies of altruism, generosity, and similar qualities. While exercises in inhibitory control could be designed from practical activities, Séguin had not suggested anything specific to foster these attributes, which he believed would be generated in the child via activities that stimulate the intellect. Conversely, Montessori argued the necessity of both corporeality (an education of the body) and specific activities that would generate a sense of morality.

Montessori thus turned to Schopenhauer. Overall, she drew extensively from the European pedagogical romantic tradition—particularly Jean-Jacques Rousseau of France, Johann Heinrich Pestalozzi of Switzerland, and Friedrich Froebel of Germany—without idealizing the child, yet recognizing the value of childhood as a stage of life and scrutinizing it with a scientific eye.[156] Schopenhauer's "will to live" allowed Montessori to bridge a scientific approach to early childhood education and a nondeterministic way of understanding the education of the child, overcoming, as Montessori's collaborator at the Scuola Magistrale Ortofrenica Giuseppe Montesano termed it, Séguin's "fatalism" about the innate potential of the child.[157]

By taking this stance, Montessori entered into dialogue with a school of thought introduced by her professor Clodomiro Bonfigli. In his opening speech delivered for the inauguration of the 1894–1895 academic year at La Sapienza medical school (at which Montessori was present), Bonfigli argued for the crucial role of education in the development of morality in so-called feebleminded children.[158] Most psychiatrists at the time considered curing and educating children to be completely separate activities; in particular, the debate revolved around whether morality was the crucial distinction between curable and incurable mental disease—and thus morality was a determining factor for whether a "feebleminded" child should be interned in an asylum or educated.[159]

According to Bonfigli, morality resulted from a nondisordered use of the cerebral inhibitors' functions and therefore would work better or worse depending on whether the child's inhibitors were compromised. Both education and the environment, however, had a profound impact on the child's moral development. Drawing on his research at the asylum in Ferrara, Bonfigli examined those affected by mental disabilities, in order to argue that psychiatry must consider individuals in their environment. He distanced himself from a positivist view that approached the child from a biological standpoint, without accounting in any way for upbringing, education, personal habits, and family habits. Education and the environment, both understood broadly, were therefore singled out by Bonfigli as key factors in the development of morality.

Though Montessori recognized the centrality of moral education in producing a sound adult psyche, she did not elaborate on it until she systematically organized her own pedagogical approach in *Il Metodo*; she then continued to expand on the subject throughout her life. According to the educator, a teacher had to impress a sense of morality that "must have the purpose of instilling the principle: 'do not do to others what you would want done to yourself.'"[160] Children needed to be imparted with a respect for their peers and surroundings.

To elicit such respect, she outlined two solutions. First, the child should be exposed to "religious functions, with their sweet music, artificial lights [candlelight or electric lights], [and] the smell of incense, [all of which] can be beneficial to that appealing purpose."[161] Here a young Montessori referred to the power of suggestion, or the ritual conditioning associated with religious functions that could, for young and impressionable minds, leave a positive, morally instructive mark.[162] Still far from the Catholic fervor of later years, Montessori was captivated by the humanitarian impulse of both

Theosophy and "mystic and philanthropic modernism" that enthralled so many female educators at the time.[163] Second, she added that if religious education was insufficient in providing children with a sense of morality, art education would. A merely intellectual education (such as the one provided by Séguin) could help a child predict the outcomes of her actions, but only a moral education (through drama, religion, music, and the arts in general) could stimulate socially appropriate actions and inhibit the will to misbehave. According to Montessori, Séguin had "forg[otten] the moralizing action that, even from such fully formed ideas, could originate from nature, art, or religion."[164] Education in morality cannot consist only of practical activities and projects geared toward exercising morality. According to Montessori, the arts broadly understood (and later an education in religion) would become the vehicle for the child's evolution beyond his biological conditions and for his integration within the scholastic and familial environment in peace and harmony.

Montessori's attempts to integrate the arts (and consequently morality) into her methodology for children up to age six did not begin until 1907 in San Lorenzo.[165] She adopted the approach of artist and educator Francesco Randone, ceramist of *arte vasaja* (the art of making vases or working clay) and founder of the Scuola di Arte Educatrice, an institution for children of working-class parents who could not afford to send them to school or to keep them busy after school hours.[166] Built inside the ancient Aurelian walls of Rome, on tower XXXIX, the school operated from the first Sunday following the spring solstice to New Year's Eve, when children would gather at midnight to make ceramics, a ritual believed to bring good luck for the new year. At the school, "an all-Tolstoyan conception of freedom" reigned: attendance was optional, and children followed their own pace, free to express their own artistic interests.[167] Ten years after her essays on moral education, Montessori incorporated Randone's suggestions to create an inspiring atmosphere in the classroom. As she wrote enthusiastically, "Randone turned the Mura Aureliane into a fantastic nursery school. With brilliant, scientific insight, he put together rooms with intensely violet and yellow lights intercepting sun rays with special glasses. Whoever comes in feels a sense of calm, as well as the sense of being in a sacred space, but above all a great joy at being so close to an artist." Students attending Randone's courses would come to appreciate art and, most important, would develop "an artistic sentiment, aimed at making people kind and intelligent."[168] Art would make the child's soul kind (*ingentilire*).

Randone and Montessori probably met at La Sapienza's medical school, where he produced scientific sketches for anatomy classes. They had friends in common, including Angelo Celli and the *agro romano* group, and both were members of the Theosophical Society as well.[169] Just like the *agro romano* endeavor, Randone's school represented the attempt to provide free education for the lower classes, an eclectic artistic debate, and the notion that beauty could uplift the disadvantaged. This latter element was central to Montessori's theory on thoughtfulness and harmony in the classroom.

Montessori maintained that Randone's goal was to "educate youth to be kind to the environment—namely, to respect objects, buildings, and monuments: a truly important part of civic education." His society, Giovinezza Gentile, embodied the very goal stated in its name—kind youth. Montessori observed that it "could not insensitively be founded on theoretical preaching about the principles of civility—or on obligations taken on by the youth out of a sense of morality; but that it had to proceed from an artistic education."[170] Art was, therefore, not an end but a means to have children appreciate and respect the environment and people around them. With regard to his own pedagogical approach to art, Randone later wrote, "Contrary to other schools, we teach art not as an end, but as a very efficient means to lead the child's thought toward a spiritual life full of identity; toward an appreciation of the beautiful and the good; toward love and the respect of monuments, animals, plants; toward gratitude, toward the homeland; toward Latinness [*latinità*]."[171] Through art, specifically pottery and ceramics, and by working toward the creation of useful objects, the Montessori student would be taught kindness and respect for others. The child's conscience would be "refined."[172] Children created useful objects, but they also had the chance to decorate them, expressing their own taste and capacities, free from a teacher's interference.

According to Randone, "all teachings should guide us toward goodness."[173] In his school, a student's goodness was measured by his ability to "reflect in his work the beauties hidden in his soul. . . . and develop in his breast the duty of moral and material charity toward his neighbors," while "a special educational discipline rises in the spirit of the community and the individual."[174] To this extent, several initiatives were implemented to "guide the soul of the child on the path to a spiritual and visionary life."[175] One of them was a week devoted to celebrating kindness, when children would prove their warmth and altruism and would be educated through "a new form of . . . noble welfare, or brotherhood, or compassion."[176] For Randone, art implied spiritual elevation; this is what Montessori sought to borrow for her Casa dei Bambini. Through art and beauty, children could accomplish moral growth necessary for societal reform.

In sum, training children's muscles through ordinary activities was meant to provide them with the grace necessary to harmonically interact with their scholastic environment. Morality, interpreted as the practice of respectfully engaging with others, was internalized through the creation of an artistic product. Such an object always had a specific purpose, one that taught the child an appreciation of the good and the beautiful, and prepared him to replicate this feeling when interacting with peers. These approaches converged in practice at the first Casa dei Bambini. There, motor and moral education occurred within and by way of a reformed environment. The child's gradual changes would eventually create a ripple effect, transforming his family and his immediate surroundings. Modern design and an appreciation for a beautiful environment contributed to igniting and propagating peace.

Educating by Design: The First Casa dei Bambini in San Lorenzo

The opening of the first Casa dei Bambini in 1907 conjured another redemption story for Montessori, one about children confined to the "edge of a city."[177] At this first Casa, physical harmony and peaceful interactions converged in what came to be known as the Montessori method. Montessori also experimented with how these qualities could be exported beyond the classroom, first radiating from the child to the family and then to the child's and family's surroundings. Via the Montessori didactic material and an aesthetically pleasing environment, the child would become an agent of peace.

While Montessori worked to conceptualize her method, a new spatial segregation had emerged in Rome in the 1880s. Poverty was sectioned and confined to specific neighborhoods, and children were left unattended while their parents worked in low-wage jobs.[178] Past the Aurelian walls of Rome, the district of San Lorenzo became the target of a series of urban and architectural renovations by the Istituto Romano dei Beni Stabili (IRBS; Roman Association of Good Buildings) in 1905. Its manager, Edoardo Talamo, put Montessori, a well-known activist at the time, in charge of an empty room and a group of undisciplined children. This was the first time that Montessori worked with children without developmental delays, all belonging to lower-class families. Montessori experimented with her approach to teaching children to be at peace with their peers, their immediate surroundings, and in a classroom designed entirely by her.

IRBS had been in charge of remodeling several buildings in run-down districts throughout San Lorenzo that had decayed since the construction industry's financial crisis of 1887. Over time, San Lorenzo had become a case for social reformers as it was riddled with crime, populated by sex workers, and infested with disease. Migrant tenants from the countryside, who provided cheap labor for the capital, were crammed into dwellings. Unattended children roamed the streets, often begging or engaging in petty theft. In the early 1900s, the district numbered 18,000 inhabitants, a total of "2,500 destitute families crammed in poor homes, where physical and moral filth lived next to the most dismal misery."[179] Of these inhabitants, "2,000 had a criminal record, 80 had been admonished, and just as many were kept under surveillance."[180] The district furnished newspapers with "the raw material that is called, in journalism, crime news."[181]

Politicians from across the political spectrum focused on issues caused by the concentration of the lower class in unhealthy districts near the city center. First and foremost, they were concerned by the loss of morality, assumed to be caused by migrants' living conditions. Their homes *caused* immorality, this narrative ran; migrant homes were often described as a potential epidemic, one that could spread and contaminate the whole city, especially its so-called respectable citizens.[182] According to this rhetoric, prostitution, alcoholism, idleness, and intemperance were rampant: the inhabitants were subject to *urban demoralization*.[183] Street clearance schemes, the construction of model dwellings, and sanitary laws were the most common reaction to the perceived epidemic, measures undertaken within the first decade of the twentieth century.

The slow but steady building of city slums as spatially secluded areas, a process common to many industrial metropolises throughout the Western world, entailed the segregation of poverty, now ghettoized at the city's outskirts.[184] Montessori condemned this segregation, arguing that previously aristocrats and commoners lived side by side, while now the city "has cleansed itself from all bad things," isolating indigents and leaving them to themselves, exacerbating their poor conditions so much so that anyone who had a "social conscience" would be concerned.[185] In a similar observation, Sibilla Aleramo, who was also engaged in programs for disadvantaged women and children, wished to "drag" to San Lorenzo "all those who enjoy the light, fresh air, beautiful things, simple or refined, necessary or superfluous; all those who stroll through buildings and fountains, and crowd together around shows" to open their eyes to these conditions.[186] Social workers, philanthropists, and activists from clerical-conservative groups and lay-Masonic-progressive organizations dedicated themselves to ameliorating these conditions, often focusing on children and women.

IRBS led one of these projects. The *risanamento*, or slum clearance program, brought several changes, which blossomed "like a beautiful, fresh flowering plant in the midst of a pigsty."[187] Before the clearance, each dwelling was designed to cram a maximum number of tenants to obtain higher rents, a common pattern in working-class housing projects throughout Western Europe in the late nineteenth and early twentieth centuries. After the clearance, IRBS transformed the buildings according to "modern criteria, with regard to construction as well as hygiene and morality." Each new unit was fashioned according to its intended buyers: Talamo divided the apartments among lower-, middle-, and upper-class dwellings, each with distinct amenities and characteristics. For lower-class accommodations, the main goal was to guarantee brightness and cleanliness, since in the old slum "no social or hygienic motive had guided the constructions."[188] The *risanamento* entailed renewing the architectural structure of the building (e.g., removal of external toilets, courtyard expansion, street paving) and upgrading the services it offered (i.e., Casa dei Bambini); this would lead to hygienic conditions and lifestyle improvement (i.e., smaller housing without extra tenants), as well as to an appreciation for beauty and hygiene. All of this would ultimately converge for the inhabitant in stimulating a desire for physical harmony and moral tranquility.

IRBS's project in San Lorenzo was part of a larger conversation about ameliorating the living conditions of working-class families. Several intellectuals in Montessori's circle debated similar issues. Duilio Cambellotti and Alessandro Marcucci, who had been involved with Montessori in the *agro romano* project, were among a group of artists inspired by the Arts and Crafts movement who had, concurrently with the IRBS project, proposed "a radical reform of domestic habits and home management."[189] In particular, Cambellotti had attempted to rethink lower-class housing (*case operaie*), similarly to Talamo's projects. Relying on his experience with the *guitti*, his style of applied arts and furniture design "convey[ed] motifs and impressions of a local flavor, of [his] sensation, and of the Roman countryside in particular, of which [he] kn[e]w every secret and which [he] love[d] deeply," which was the place of his radical commitment and activism as well as the source of his aesthetic.[190] Cambellotti was one of the founders of the bimonthly magazine *La Casa*, a publication on the aesthetic, décor, and administration of the modern home. The magazine hosted contributions from several friends of Montessori, including Olga Ossani Lodi, who had first recommended the name Casa dei Bambini to Montessori.[191] *La Casa* devoted much attention to the Primo Congresso Femminile and reported on the energetic discourse between philanthropist Giuseppina Le Maire and Montessori about subventions for public housing. Le Maire, who "dealt with communities in the poorest neighborhoods," wrote of the necessity to reform these spaces to avoid the promiscuity that affected the lower classes, while the "lively and brilliant doctor Montessori described to what extent work is being done in certain Roman neighborhoods to improve the moral and physical state of the population, and to make their houses spacious, airy, and comfortable, and therefore healthy."[192] The magazine captured the discussion around urban peripheries, slum improvement, and state intervention in the lives of the poor.

Cambellotti's contributions to the magazine tackled issues related to the modern home, which needed to become a "wholesome, comfortable, and beautiful" place where people from all classes could find "moral and material solace," a place where a communion of the useful and the beautiful "in rational harmony" took place.[193] In his article "Progetto di casa per famiglie di lavoratori" for *La Casa*, Cambellotti recommended the principles of simplicity and durability when building small homes (*case minime*) for the working class.[194] But architecture had to be considered as a means to elevate the masses to the appreciation of beauty, and Cambellotti, who mixed the influences of the new liberty style and Henry Van De Velde's early rationalism, recommended that each room be "plain, decent, and respectable."[195] Abiding by the humanitarian principles guiding his *agro romano* endeavor, Cambellotti designed this model for popular housing for the Istituto per le Case Popolari (Institute for Popular Housing), founded in 1903 by the Giolittian politician Luigi Luzzato. As part of his ethical mission, the home—"an instrument of social redemption"—inspired by medieval quarters in the popular districts of the city of Rome, was made with local materials and incorporated vernacular artistic traditions.[196] According to Cambellotti, beautiful homes would provide well-deserved solace to working people.

Parallel to Cambellotti's work on popular housing, *La Casa* also hosted pacifist intellectual Teresita Bonfatti Pasini's writings, which presented Talamo's project as the solution to the contemporaneous housing crisis. These dictates included a fair-priced, well-kept apartment, respected and cleaned by its tenants, who were not to sublet. The owner, in fact, would not speculate on the tenants' rent, considering the money and time saved on upkeep and on looking for new tenants. According to Bonfatti Pasini (who wrote under the pseudonym Alma), the owner need not be a philanthropist, for what worked for the tenant also favored the owner's interests.[197] To

Housing project for working families drawn by Duilio Cambellotti. Duilio Cambellotti, "Progetto di casa per famiglie di lavoratori: L'arredamento," *La Casa* 1, no. 13 (December 1, 1908).

support this virtuous cycle, the owner should also invest in services for the tenement, especially a school: Montessori's Casa dei Bambini.

According to the article, school and home environments had to be harmonious: inspired by the same principles and aspiring to the same goals. Construction and educational overhauls proceeded together to improve the situation of those who lived in the building. Cultivating the morality of its inhabitants was a key attribute of both the school and the home. The idea that morality would emerge through the home's beauty and decency was at the foundation of Talamo's project, who said that the house, "beyond being healthy, clean, and comfortable . . . must also reflect the affective

Housing project, exterior. Alma [Teresita Bonfatti Pasini], "Un buon affare e un'opera buona: La 'casa moderna,'" *La Casa* 1, no. 11 (November 16, 1908).

Montessori classroom in a housing project. Alma [Teresita Bonfatti Pasini], "Un buon affare e un'opera buona: La 'casa moderna,'" *La Casa* 1, no. 11 (November 16, 1908).

and moralizing aspects of the family, as to make it a desired and loved refuge, integral to a civil education."[198] Montessori's project in the IRBS building synthesized her social reform aspirations: via modern design, and
through public intervention, the school environment could become transformative for those who inhabited it. As Montessori later recalled, the first
Casa dei Bambini "emerged not as a pedagogical institution, but exclusively
as a *social* one; it didn't arise as a work of charity, but as an endeavor of
social life . . . being in the housing block, this home was always open to
the mother and the father . . . in this way school and family were fused
together."[199] The reform of the school and house were therefore coupled to
the reform of those affected by poverty and neglect. To restore "the core of
a social community" that was lost as a result of poor living conditions, Montessori and Talamo maintained that the tenements necessitated a modernization of the living situation as well as the help of social workers and
activists to repair the fabric of the community.[200]

Montessori also argued for keeping this new scholastic environment visible to the observing eyes of the state and of social activists during the opening of the first Casa dei Bambini on January 6, 1907. Supervisors were
available to guide the behavior of those living in the building: teachers, nurses,
and doctors would help them maintain the decorum and cleanliness both
Talamo and Montessori had in mind. If the home were to be monitored and
brought up to higher hygienic and moral standards, the Casa dei Bambini
itself worked to impose these norms on the child, in turn expanding the
best practices he acquired at school to the families and their homes. A child
educated via the Montessori method would so internalize hygienic, behavioral, and moral norms that the effect would eventually spread to his family.
The teacher also functioned as a point of reference for the families, insofar
as she embodied a high social function and had to be "a true missionary, a
moral queen among the people."[201] A weekly conversation with her informed
mothers of their children's progress and granted her indirectly the possibility of checking on the family itself.

The strong presence of specialized personnel such as nurses, chefs, or
housekeepers in the tenements would provide support for the family, insofar as "the transformation of the house [should have] compensated for the
lost presence of the woman [who had] become a paid worker outside the
home" (*un lavoratore sociale*). The socialization of homemaking activities,
all of which were mostly covered by women and mothers, would allow for a
scientifically trained teacher to teach age-appropriate material to the children.
It would also address, Montessori pointed out, "the problems of feminism

that seemed unsolvable to many. What will become of the house, then—it was said—if the woman leaves it? The house will be transformed and will assume the former functions of the woman. I believe that in the social future, other forms of socialization will come, i.e. the nurse."[202] As a result, the school played a crucial role in reshaping the dynamics between the scholastic (and therefore social) life of the child and the child's private family relationships. Talamo argued that parents understood the Casa dei Bambini as a common good, insofar as it "also allowed housewives to leave their homes without worries in order to look for daily work."[203] Moreover, through the monitoring structure of the tenement, its residents would "almost unconsciously improve themselves through the example of order and education set at home, every evening, by their young ones; eventually, [they would] leave the *osteria* to create around their children—every day kinder—the familial intimacy from which their previously dark, filthy, and unhealthy homes distanced them."[204]

Montessori summed up the goal of her approach through her commentary on the first Casa dei Bambini in *Antropologia pedagogica* in 1910: encouraging children's consciences through a tranquil and beautiful environment would produce what she vaguely termed a "sentiment of peace":

> The adopted pedagogical methods are such as to create a gradual series
> of psychic stimuli that are perfectly adapted to children's needs: the
> *environment* encourages every individual in his own psychic development,
> according to subjective potentials: children are free in their expressions, and
> they are approached with friendly displays of affection. I believe it's the first
> time we've created such an interesting pedagogical experience: namely, that
> of planting in the children's consciences, in a tranquil environment, a
> feeling of affection and peace.[205]

And though this sentiment was only a germinal idea of what she would elaborate in the coming years, the seed of her future inquiry on pacifism had started to sprout.

The school environment is the last element to analyze in reconstructing Montessori's first theorizations of peace. If art was to *ingentilire* the child, or make her kind, beauty would also inspire the use of the didactic apparatus. The notion that beauty would uplift the child's spirit began to circulate in Europe at the beginning of the twentieth century.[206] The famous pedagogue Ellen Key, who fought against the homogenization of school programs and the so-called school barracks, recommended an environment for individuals to flourish, where "the feeling of beauty will be directly encouraged."[207]

Education in beauty appreciation as a tool to transform society was also at the core of school reform plans put forth by utopian socialists Robert Owen, John Ruskin, and particularly William Morris involving reflection on peace in the classroom, instilling an appreciation for the arts, and a valorization of human dignity.[208] As historian Tiziana Pironi emphasizes, Montessori was surely aware of Key's *The Century of the Child*—she probably knew the educator personally through their mutual friend Sibilla Aleramo—and was also influenced by the artistic conversation revolving around the pedagogical works of the aforementioned intellectuals.[209]

It is precisely from this debate that Montessori worked through the last educational component that would allow children to achieve peace: a beautiful and inspiring school environment. In the Montessori classroom, nothing was left to chance. She recommended "lightweight furniture . . . plain and economical . . . if washable, better, especially because children will learn to wash it, and by doing so will engage in a very educational and pleasant activity."[210] "Above all," she continued, it is of tantamount importance that furniture "be beautiful, artistic." Beauty was not to be understood as an elitist concept insofar as "it ha[d] nothing to do in this case with the superfluous and luxurious, but rather with the grace and harmony of lines and colors, united in the simplicity demanded by the lightness of the furniture."[211] Objects in the classroom had to be "attractive."[212] "Colour, brightness, harmony of form, are all sought after in everything that surrounds the child," not only in the didactic apparatus but also in the environment itself that will ultimately draw the child to it "as, in nature, brilliant petals attract insects to drink the nectar which they conceal."[213] Referring to the production of Montessori material in Palidano in collaboration with her friend Maria Maraini Guerrieri Gonzaga, who sponsored the effort, Montessori argued the specific artistic style did not matter, since "every corner in Italy hides a local artistic treasure. . . . Objects comfortable and pretty, created with a view to practicality by an artistic instinct," must be utilized in the classrooms; her designs were inspired by "the old, local, rustic art," bringing back to life, just as in Cambellotti and Marcucci's endeavor in the *agro romano*, "country art."[214]

A few years later, Alessandro Marcucci, a fervent Montessorian throughout his life, would argue that he believed in "the need for an intimate spiritual communion between the teacher and the artist," and thus he saw "the esthetic function tightly linked to the educative function of the school."[215] In the words of the *agro romano* coordinator, Montessori's statement on the beauty of the classroom, which he termed "aesthetic environment," needed to be achieved in each classroom.[216]

Interior of the Casa dei Bambini in Palidano di Gonzaga. Courtesy of GonzagArredi Montessori Archive.

Alessandro Marcucci, desks with seats, 1920s. Duilio Cambellotti Collection. Courtesy of Archivi delle Arti Applicate Italiane del XX secolo, Rome.

Alessandro Marcucci, desks with seats, 1920s. Duilio Cambellotti Collection.
Courtesy of Archivi delle Arti Applicate Italiane del XX secolo, Rome.

Casa dei Bambini with didactic material and library, 1920s. Duilio Cambellotti Collection.
Courtesy of Archivi delle Arti Applicate Italiane del XX secolo, Rome.

A Montessori classroom in the Roman countryside, 1931. Duilio Cambellotti Collection. Courtesy of Archivi delle Arti Applicate Italiane del XX secolo, Rome.

Children at work with Montessori material, 1920s. Duilio Cambellotti Collection. Courtesy of Archivi delle Arti Applicate Italiane del XX secolo, Rome.

Classroom of the Casa dei Bambini in Scauri, 1920s. Ugo Ortona, "La casa della scuola," *La casa bella*, July 1928. Courtesy of Archivi delle Arti Applicate Italiane del XX secolo, Rome.

Classroom of the Casa dei Bambini in Scauri, 1920s. Ugo Ortona, "La casa della scuola," *La casa bella*, July 1928. Courtesy of Archivi delle Arti Applicate Italiane del XX secolo, Rome.

Marcucci noted that this milieu "[was] conducive to the formation of an internal discipline . . . ; it [was] born out of happiness, becomes conscience, and results in will." In the *agro romano*, each child was educated in a beautifully decorated Montessori classroom, "felt the charm of that harmony between colors and forms, and adapted to it by developing inside him— more or less rapidly, but always in a spontaneous fashion—a refinement of feeling and taste, in relation to himself, to others, and to things." In such a school, the child would act, added Marcucci emphatically, in an orderly manner, "aesthetically."[217]

Via an aesthetically pleasing didactic apparatus and school, the child would learn grace and precision in his actions. He would learn to appreciate beauty. He would emanate all of these qualities to his surroundings. Change would radiate from the Montessori child to the family, the neighborhood, and finally, the community.

Conclusion

To restore the physical and mental well-being of the child, Montessori created an approach to foster harmony of movement and peaceful interactions. Her refinement of this pedagogy began with her work with children affected by developmental challenges, then moved to research on instruction in juvenile detention centers, and was completed while working with children without cognitive impairments but who were impacted by severe economic challenges in the neighborhood of San Lorenzo. There, her approach was systematized to reflect the broad and kaleidoscopic set of influences that had radically shaped her young life.

At the San Lorenzo Casa dei Bambini, Montessori's educational approach aligned the child with the environment, helping him find coordination of movement, balance, and confidence in accomplishing tasks, promoting his growth in the context of his surrounding community's needs. A scientifically trained teacher children would expose children to sequentially organized didactic material. They had to repeat the activities until they perfected fine and gross motor skills. Moving gracefully in this carefully designed environment, however, was not enough. The Montessori child was also respectful of others, a goal achieved through an *ingentilimento*, the process of making somebody kind. Montessori would pursue this goal by experimenting with various teaching strategies, first and foremost through the teaching of arts, specifically the art of making vases as elaborated by potter Francesco Randone. An appreciation for beauty would complement the child's education to reach a "feeling of affection and peace."[218] Last, Montessori came to think of the child as an advocate of peace; through a restorative pedagogy, the child would extend the balance achieved at school beyond the walls of the classroom, to improve the lives of those living around him.

The years following the 1909 publication of *Il Metodo* marked a profound change in Maria Montessori's life. Her involvement with feminist associations ceased to be a major active influence on her, though it would continue to resonate in her work for years to come.[219] Her participation in the Primo Congresso delle Donne Italiane (First Congress of Italian Women) in 1908 was her last public appearance in this circle.[220] Instead Montessori began to focus on the elaboration of a pedagogical methodology. As Montessori's disciple Edwin Mortimer Standing writes, "her mission in life had crystallized. . . . She felt the duty of going forth as an apostle on behalf of all the children in the world, born as yet unborn, to preach for their rights and their liberation."[221] The development of an organic approach became the purpose of Montessori's work; she took time away from her lectureship at La Sapienza and discontinued her practice as a physician. According to Kramer, this bold move corresponded with her desire to focus entirely on the diffusion of her method, transforming the "[Montessori] movement into a business, a kind of franchise operation in which [she] had a vital stake in such matters as copyright of the materials and official certification of teachers."[222] She decided to focus on the creation of an organic system and its propagation.

As her book circulated throughout Western Europe and North America, the Montessori method attracted a following. By 1913, when the second edition of *Il Metodo della pedagogia scientifica* was published, the fame of its author had already reached an international scale.[223] In the same year, Montessori traveled to the United States, where she gave a series of lectures on the method, which met with great success. The pedagogue also published the English version of the text under the auspices of the Department of Education at Harvard University and wrote a series of articles on her methodology that found favor with the general public.[224] A Montessori fever spread throughout North America and, more generally, the Western world.

Up until the First World War, Montessori's research expanded to the early elementary years and new sets of stimuli for the child, such as music and religion. Her quest to educate the child toward physical and mental health did not end, however, but it was subsumed under the everyday necessities of building transnational networks of educators, philanthropists, businesspeople, and parents interested in her method. These competing influences on her attention and time were aggravated by Montessori's tendency to control every aspect of what was becoming a global pedagogical enterprise. Nevertheless, her plan for pacifism through education became a priority with the outbreak of World War I. She returned to the child as an advocate for peace, stunted this time not by developmental challenges or by economic disadvantage but by the traumas of war: "the only way out for individuals is that all humanity is saved."[225]

CHAPTER 2

The White Cross

*Rehabilitating War-Stricken Children
to Prevent War*

While working with war-stricken children over the course of the Great War, Maria Montessori came to the conclusion that her methodology was "a veritable cure for all those ills" caused by the conflict.[1] In 1916, the educator studied the effect of her pedagogy on children in nursery schools in the occupied territories of Belgium and northern France. Whereas before World War I she had envisioned educating children to peace through a prepared environment and scientifically trained teachers, she now observed the traumatizing effects of war and realized that her approach—and even education per se—was not enough. The war had such a profound and long-lasting impact on the child's psyche that new practices were needed in order to restore his mental and physical capacity and bring him back to being a collaborative individual, able to live harmoniously within society.

Traumatized by the horrors of the conflict, children suffered from what she termed "mental wounds."[2] Anticipating the conversation on what would later be classified as posttraumatic stress disorder, Montessori pointed out the effects on children of witnessing and experiencing a catastrophic stressor, such as the Great War, that was outside the typical human experience. Unable to sleep, eat, and interact with others, they needed an educational approach able to address the dysfunction caused by the horrific events and restore emotional well-being. If left untreated, Montessori suggested, the children's symptoms would progress and over time lead to the degeneration of their mental capacities. Instead, once they found a physical and psychological balance, they would be able to establish positive connections, first with their peers and surroundings, and later with society as a whole, with the ultimate goal of promoting peace and harmony.

This conviction pushed Montessori to envision and seek support for the creation of a supranational humanitarian association that she planned to call the White Cross. *White* was chosen to stand for the nervous system, as distinct from the red of the Red Cross, which represented the blood of wounded soldiers. According to Montessori, this organization would develop the use of her pedagogy in war zones, in order to restore the mental and physical health of traumatized children. Its trained personnel would work in tandem with the Red Cross to cure the mental and physical wounds of civilians, especially children and their mothers. Montessori-trained teachers would be assisted by nurses and psychiatrists trained to administer first aid. Such an organization would have a complementary role to that of the recently established Red Cross and would promote the care of civilians, children in particular, making the organization the first of its kind. Montessori believed that, after the war, the children who were educated by the White Cross would not only be healthier individuals but also be better able to promote a peaceful world.

Owing to the lack of sponsorship, the White Cross never became a reality. But as Montessori sought financial and ideological support for her project, she engaged in a series of fruitful conversations with intellectuals and organizations both in Italy and abroad; planning how to rehabilitate those affected by the conflict consumed most of her time. This chapter provides a comprehensive overview of Montessori's practical efforts to rescue war-stricken children through an analysis of the conversations she initiated over the course of the Great War—conversations with contemporary educators, psychologists, and social workers; the Italian state; prominent members of the Roman Catholic Church and eventually Pope Benedict XV; and the socialist Milanese organization Società Umanitaria (SU).

First, this chapter contextualizes how Montessori chose to focus on rehabilitation, and it outlines her contemporaries' thought on the subject of physical and moral support for a civilian population during war. It then assesses the efforts on the part of the Italian government to imbue children with militaristic discipline, shaping over time a scholastic system that differed drastically from Montessori's vision, thus pushing her to seek support elsewhere. Next, it investigates her efforts to collaborate with the papacy, one of the major entities that provided relief efforts for civilians, especially children, and her attempts to foster international conversation to end the conflict. Last, this chapter looks at the correspondence between the educator and members of the SU, with which Montessori had collaborated since 1908 and which was at the forefront of providing services for displaced people and refugees in Lombardy. In addition to the SU's direct help for those affected by the conflict, many members of the organization belonged to the internationalist and pacifist wing of the Socialist Party that remained committed to protesting the "bourgeois war," furthering the argument for a truce among the participating nations.

Even though the White Cross never came into existence, Montessori's efforts to attract these collaborators significantly refined and extended her original approach and her understanding of the child as an agent of peace. In other words, the White Cross's failure to materialize served as a continuous motivation for the development of Montessori's methodology. Furthermore, her activism shed light on her participation in the international development of a discourse on the battles that civilians, especially children, waged on the home front. By looking at these four conversations, this chapter shows how Montessori contributed to the conversation on measures to protect populations against certain consequences of war, as well as the necessity to set apart the most vulnerable segments of the population: the wounded and sick, as well as the infirm, expectant mothers, and children. She strove to launch assistance programs for children traumatized by war and to protect them against pillage and harsh treatment—with the goal of rehabilitating their bodies and minds.

Rehabilitating War-Affected Children: The Historical and Intellectual Roots of the Debate

It was a well-to-do New Yorker, Mary Rebecca Cromwell, who first applied the Montessori approach to the children affected by the Great War, children "whose fathers [were] so nobly and conscientiously united in the great task of defending life itself." A philanthropist with an interest in social work, she had moved to France in 1902 and later became so interested in Montessori's work that she joined the many Americans who travelled to Italy to observe its implementation. Impressed by its results with the children of the impoverished neighborhood of San Lorenzo in Rome, Cromwell applied it to war-stricken children. In response to the number of unsupervised children in Paris during the conflict, she inaugurated five schools in Saint-Sulpice and Fontenay-aux-Roses in 1915. According to Cromwell, these schools hosted "little bewildered Flemish and French children, many of whom had come from the Front on foot or being dragged in big rambling carts—sometimes upset on the way—[who] still suffered from the shock of that frightful exodus."[3]

In the early months of the war, Paris became home to numerous refugee children who had fled to escape the German troops' advance into Belgium and northern and eastern France.[4] The violation of Belgium's neutrality (described by allied propaganda as the "rape of Belgium"), its invasion, and the creation of the western front by the end of 1914 caused many

Classroom for French and Belgian refugees in Fontenay-aux-Roses, France, July 1916. Courtesy of Musée du Domaine Départemental de Sceaux.

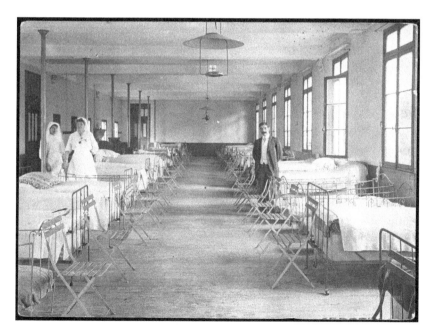

Cromwell Dormitory, Fontenay-aux-Roses, France, July 1916. Courtesy of Musée du Domaine Départemental de Sceaux.

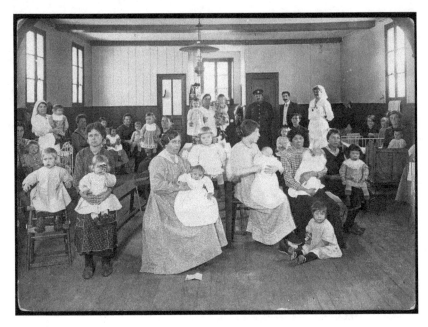

Nursery, Fontenay-aux-Roses, France, July 1916. Courtesy of Musée du Domaine Départemental de Sceaux.

people to seek refuge in Paris. Among them, there were at least 150,000 refugees, mostly children and women, who lacked any livelihood.[5] Echoes of the atrocities perpetuated during the German occupation, especially those involving women and children, resonated throughout the continent and generated a strong movement of compassion and solidarity. Montessori and Cromwell, deeply struck by the situation, found themselves in conversation.

Although the French government and the Parisian municipality had halted in providing help for civilians, the two educators' initiative did not occur in a total vacuum. Cromwell was in fact part of a large contingent of North Americans who volunteered to assist soldiers and civilians in Paris over the course of the global conflict.[6] Many North American organizations intervened in the invaded territories of the Entente powers. American Red Cross workers assisted soldiers on both sides of the conflict under the guidelines for neutrality set by the 1906 Geneva Convention and the principles of the Red Cross.[7] In particular, the American Red Cross contributed its own Children's Bureau to establish much-needed public services for

French children. Influenced by the outpouring of help from some of her own relatives, including sisters Dorothea and Gladys, Cromwell shared Montessori's belief that her greatest contribution to the war effort would be to support war-affected children.[8] Consequently, in 1916, Cromwell gathered a number of children, mainly French and Belgian refugees, and used Montessori material to educate them at her own expense. She recruited and trained Belgian and French widows to aid her in the endeavor. Because of the soothing effects of some of the activities, and the stimulating class material that awakened senses numbed by the horror of the war, Cromwell quickly found that the Montessori method could help children overcome trauma. She also requested that the municipal authorities utilize the Red Cross fund to expand her efforts.[9]

A few months after the inauguration of Cromwell's schools, Montessori went to France to visit them and gauge the validity of her method as applied to those children. As she later explained, they were affected by "a special form of mental disturbance, which constituted a real mental wound—a lesion that is as serious as, if not more serious than, wounds in the physical body."[10] Montessori described the children's affliction as a "disease of degeneration; a weakening of the entire nervous system involving loss of energy and intelligence and so affecting the whole life of the individual that these degenerative tendencies [were] passed on to the succeeding generations."[11] Cromwell had also observed that the children were "haunted by a desire to reconstruct, . . . at once individual and cooperative"; notably, they were particularly stimulated by building blocks, a crucial part of some Montessori activities, which seemed to symbolize the slow but steady capacity to restore harmonious human interaction, a hallmark of the educator's approach.[12]

Because of the extraordinary trauma the children had experienced, Montessori believed they represented a unique category of subject for study. She argued that just as one must more generally distinguish civilians from combatants, so too was it necessary to consider those children who, "under the threat of the invasion, were taken away or were lost in a mob scared by the explosion of bombs disseminating death."[13] These children needed to be treated according to a special protocol that took into account the disturbances they had endured. After her visit to Cromwell's classes, Montessori asserted that these children "arrived at the school in a stupor, incapable of understanding anything, frightened by everyone, constantly afraid." They were often affected by "convulsive states . . . very insufficient development."[14]

Focusing overwhelmingly on their mental, rather than the physical, injuries, she argued that the children were psychologically mutilated. If not treated adequately, these wounds in the mental system would become chronic and expand to cause a "disease of the generation or era."[15] In speaking of this "disease of deterioration," Montessori was drawing from French psychiatrist Augustin Bénédict Morel, who saw mental deficiency as the end of a process of progressive mental degeneration.[16] According to Morel, who elaborated the so-called theory of degeneration, pathologies were the consequence of physical and/or moral injury, manifested in the nervous system. Crucially, damage to the nervous system was transmitted across generations, not in the form of specific conditions but as a predisposition to suffering certain neuroses. Heredity was therefore a biological determinant of madness and would eventually cause the death of those affected. The psychiatrist also called for an etiological study of mental diseases that differed from mere symptomatologies. Montessori, who had worked with children with developmental challenges early in her career and continued to pay particular attention to this debate, had adopted Morel's perspective and would continue to do so.

According to the educator, children affected by mental disturbances would degenerate into unbalanced human beings, incapable of fostering peaceful dialogue and understanding with their peers. A cure to these "mental wounds" was at the center of Montessori's conception of the White Cross.[17] She suggested that White Cross personnel could cure these "mysterious psychological wounds" by means of education and hygiene of the nervous system. As a result, White Cross workers would ideally be trained both as teachers and as nurses who specialized in nervous (and mental) diseases. The nurse-teacher's education centered on "first aid, knowledge of nervous diseases, dietetics for infants and children, isolation, special psychology, domestic science, agriculture, language and a theoretical and practical course in the Montessori method as specially applied to those children."[18] The Montessori teacher would restore the child's diminished mental capacities and return him to being an individual capable of fostering peace.

Cromwell had assured the Italian educator that the method had enabled her to "restore the minds" of those who were affected by the conflict.[19] Upon their arrival, Cromwell observed, these children benefited from exercises of "natural gymnastic as understood by Madame Montessori; . . . the care of birds and plants and the charge of the classroom [also at the foundation of the approach] became an absorbing occupation for the little ones." The American educator continued, reporting that "modelling and drawing were of unending interest, and children five years old begged to touch (their eyes blindfolded) the sandpaper letters and the movable pink and blue alphabet," all activities that were characteristic of the method.[20] The "method has a wonderfully calming influence on nervous children"; it "allows for a moderate, continuous, and pleasant activity that keeps the children engaged without tiring them—so to reorganize their perturbed mental faculties."[21] Children were soon capable of returning to calm by being engaged with activities that deeply interested them. It could therefore be used for this peaceful crusade, necessary at a time of such gruesome violence.

Montessori was aware of the difficulties of training in her method and purchasing her patented didactic material, especially during wartime. She therefore recommended simple measures that could be used regardless of a school's resources. One such example was starting class by having the children wear colorful pinafores. Though this might have seemed like an insignificant thing to the intellectual community engaged in rescue operations for these children, she assured them that "the refugee children she had seen in Paris were greatly helped by the fact that once a week each had a clean, brightly colored pinafore of a different color . . . a bright ribbon, something fresh and new [that] may penetrate the mist surrounding these little souls."[22] According to the educator, small measures such as stimulating children through color would awaken and initiate their psychological recovery.

Over the course of the Great War, Montessori was not alone in her focus on mental health; other intellectuals and psychiatrists were also concerned with it, but their attention was on combatants. Thanks to psychiatrists such as Enrico Morselli and Augusto Tamburini, the debate on mental diseases expanded considerably during and after the conflict.[23] The "total" nature of the conflict created a staggering number of new mental disorders, forcing doctors to review their therapeutic and medical approaches to psychiatry and pushing for new research in the field. Certain types of injuries, such as physical paralysis, mental impairments, and the blank, unfocused gaze of battle-weary soldiers, were so unprecedented that treating them called for organizing a neuropsychiatric service in war zones. Cases born of the war were hardly classifiable in the traditional psychiatric paradigms.

Historian Bruna Bianchi has argued that battlefield doctors usually attributed new symptoms to the soldiers' anthropological inferiority and would frequently send them back into combat without proper treatment, despite serious health issues.[24] Combat trauma—usually the result of concussive injury to a combatant's brain, otherwise known as "shell-shock"— was treated only superficially in hospital camps with the goal of sending the soldier back to the battlefield as soon as possible. In the case of mental distress imposed on noncombatants (i.e., support personnel or civilians directly affected by the war, such as the women and children Montessori intended to treat), these symptoms were usually disregarded or seen as a form of weakness linked to being a woman or a child.[25] As a result, when these symptoms were diagnosed in noncombatants, they were not treated at all; these traumas are therefore not represented in official statistics.

Although the medical community had begun to address combatants' well-being, there was still limited interest in curing noncombatants. Few social reformers and humanitarians acknowledged the unprecedented number of traumatized children coming out of the war. One exception from Montessori's time was the North American author Maude Radford Warren, who traveled through France during the conflict and collected memories of children distressed by war, some of whom had been educated with the Montessori approach. Echoing Montessori's words in her postwar work *The White Flame of France*, Warren described "thousands of such children whom France is rearing for the new nation, hundreds of them weakened by exposure and shock, all of them precious, each of them a convincing argument against any future war." One Montessori child recounted to Warren the horrors she was exposed to during the German occupation of her Belgian village: "So when we got to the little trenches our soldiers had made we walked in them. I carried my doll and held my little brother's hand. We had nothing to eat. . . . We were tired and we all cried. So then we got into a train and the baby died. And oh, *madame*, on the train I broke my doll, and mamma made me throw it away." Warren argued that these children "can be diverted easily" because they did not fully comprehend all they had lost. Commenting on the memories she recorded, she maintained that "when older children write of their experiences their sense of proportion seems less grotesque. But whoever reads sympathetically between the lines will see the deep traces of ineradicable fear, of human losses for which no tenderest fostering can ever quite atone."[26]

Montessori concluded that her pedagogy, if applied extensively to children like the Belgian girl who spoke to Warren, could cure their wounds and restore their damaged nervous systems. The routine of the Montessori activities would first bring children peace and tranquility while providing a stable and stimulating learning environment; it would then allow them to work on their damaged senses through sensorial education. Its implementation would rehabilitate the mental conditions of those affected by the disease of degeneration. She believed the only way to save war-distressed children from becoming unbalanced human beings capable only of perpetuating their suffering and spreading it to others was through the rigorous implementation of her pedagogy. She would task the White Cross with carrying out this campaign within the expanding war zones. And even though the White Cross was never created, Montessori was part of the initial stages of an invaluable conversation that took place in the following decades about the necessity for psychological therapy for civilian populations, which is now part of the modern approach to disaster relief. As analyzed in the following chapters, Montessori's view of child protection in times of distress would be at the center of the 1924 Declaration of the Rights of the Child endorsed by the League of Nations, and in the formation of international agencies such as the United Nations International Children's Emergency Fund (UNICEF).

Italy's Search for a National Pedagogy: The Child as Peacemaker or Soldier?

In the years leading up to the war, the Italian state—informed by imperialistic, nationalistic, and militaristic values—searched for an educational method that could turn the Italian child into a docile citizen, yet one who would take up arms against other countries when needed.[27] In contrast, Maria Montessori sought to develop a pedagogy that would guide children to become balanced human beings who could ultimately end war. Though the pedagogical goals of Montessori's approach and the methodology sponsored by the Italian government diverged, both sprang from an interest among Italian intellectuals and pedagogues in early childhood education. Montessori's interest in children affected by war was in fact rooted in an international debate on childcare and the role of the state in raising a population's children. In Italy, this discursive trend was inaugurated in the 1870s. Italy's questions about appropriate parental care and the state's duty to look after children arose alongside its desire to emulate other European countries and in response to the slow but steady increase of women who joined the industrial workforce.[28]

Since the nation's unification in 1861, the school had functioned as a channel for national values and identity, one that would mold the populace according to the principles that were guiding the Italian nation-state. Despite the lack of a concrete agenda with which the education system would shape a specific national character, instilling respect for the new state and, more generally, engendering a sense of belonging to the newly unified nation permeated the earliest national education programs and guided pedagogues in shaping the first national curricula.

In the first decade of the twentieth century, the Italian intellectual discourse still emphasized nationalism and imperialism. Among other events,

the propaganda for the colonial enterprise in Libya; Enrico Corradini's founding of the nationalist alliance (the Associazione Nazionalista Italiana); and
the proliferation of movements promoting the idea of an Italian *Über-
mensch* (superman) and the importance of improving the Italian race
highly influenced the prewar political discourse and, in turn, the debate
around the education of the Italian child. These developments in Italian
society tested the delicate sociocultural equilibrium of the state, which
worked at what historian Gaetano Bonetta describes as the "modernization of socialization, and of scholastic socialization in particular."[29] Nursery and elementary schools became the primary tools for assimilating the
masses to the values of the nation, such as allegiance to the state, at the
same time that these masses began to claim a political voice. In the years
immediately preceding World War I, the increased attention that the state
paid to schooling and the national use of belligerent rhetoric pushed educational theorists to create new methodologies that would respond to the
need for a system that was "in its turn capable of creating . . . a little soldier
of the nation."[30]

   This interest in early education climaxed with a state initiative aimed at
finding a national pedagogy for Italian preschools. In 1914, minister of
public instruction Luigi Credaro convened a royal commission charged
with examining and evaluating pedagogic methods in Italy.[31] Over the course
of this investigation, the educational theories of Maria Montessori and Carolina and Rosa Agazzi came under intense public scrutiny.[32] Broadly,
whereas the Agazzi sisters' approach supported the ludic quality of the Italian nurseries and kindergartens, finding it unnecessary to expose children
to reading and writing, the Montessori child was trained to develop these
skills in an environment that fostered the free unfolding of his capacities.
Thus, the Agazzi approach considered learning as an activity separate from
playing, whereas Montessori saw play as a tool for learning. Ultimately,
however, the text that resulted from the commission's inquiry, *Istruzioni,
programmi e orari per gli Asili infantili e Giardini d'Infanzia* (Instructions,
Programs, and Schedules for Preschools and Nurseries), called for a didactic orientation essentially in line with the pedagogy of the Agazzi sisters.[33]

   In choosing the Agazzi method, the Italian government envisioned shaping the Italian child to be a docile citizen, one who conforms to "traditional"
(e.g., not upwardly mobile) social roles and obeys authority, especially when
called upon to serve the country in military service. In the words of anthropologist Giuseppe Sergi, this approach suppressed "every mental and physical initiative," it fostered "passivity in the child through unceasing suggestion

[and] automatism for every sensory faculty and action."[34] He described the Froebelian approach as a "formalism that sterilizes teachers and children," among whom the latter would become like puppets in the hands of their masters.[35] Sergi also argued that children educated by methods such as the Agazzis' would not develop any mental freedom and would suppress voluntary actions; "cerebral functions, . . . now guided step by step, would not develop their promptness and speed." Also, this method would not allow for the "development of the child's personality, of his own character, what distinguishes men among them, and provides them with that sentiment of responsibility that is so necessary in our daily conduct for our individual and social life."[36]

In the Agazzi method, the scholastic environment was modeled after the home, and it aimed at stimulating the child's development in continuous dialogue with the adult, as within the family. Moreover, the Agazzis maintained that the mother was "the first natural guide of the spontaneous development of the child," and that in the classroom, the teacher had to perform this role "to create in class that domestic climate that assures the nursery school's success."[37] The sisters appropriated certain elements of Froebelism, particularly the "the spontaneous concept of education" that emphasized "the importance attributed to play" over activities that would advance the cognitive, physical, and emotional growth of the child.[38] By contrast, the Montessori approach fostered these latter capacities, educating a child who "is cognitive, industrious [and] conquers the instruments of knowledge."[39]

Another fundamental characteristic of the Agazzis' pedagogy that differed from the Montessori method was the rural setting in which it developed. Many of the educators who visited the Agazzis' school in Mompiano commented favorably on the fact that the environment furnished an ethical education "intent on making the young country children acquire that mentality that is more appropriate to their social class and to the life that they must conduct in the future."[40] These comments echo Dina Bertoni Jovine's reflections on the liberal ruling class's approach to popular instruction at the time: on the one hand, there was a desire to bring education to the lower classes, and on the other, there was great concern about the threats such an education might bring to Italy's historically immobile social structure, which had always assured some stability in the nation.[41] Supporters embraced the Agazzis' emphasis on the rural "Italian" environment, one of whom remarked: "The merit [of the Agazzi sisters is that of] having given back the character of sincere, unsophisticated *italianità* to our playgrounds, with a completely new general direction, with practical and common tools, directly useful, derived from the same environment of the small rural world."[42]

In contrast, Montessori encouraged an educational environment designed to stimulate peaceful encounters among the children. As Sergi put it, Montessori sought to incentivize "liberty, and continuous communication among all [the children], so to develop that social sentiment that leads to fondness and reciprocal love. I did not see any sign of aversion among the children, no sign of teasing or contrast, but a perfect harmony, because there is not competition in games, in the places children can use, in moving or acting in a certain direction: [the Montessori school] looks like a small and well balanced society."[43] Furthermore, Montessori's methodology responded "to the social needs of urban infancy and of the working class." Organized in a climate of engagement and freedom, the Montessori environment urged the child to develop at his own pace, nurturing each pupil's aspirations without class distinctions. Bonetta has argued that "the Montessorian child . . . seems to represent the most progressive child of Italy [and] aims at surpassing the traditional agricultural society. . . . [The method is] oriented toward industrial society, conceived upon a different use of human resources to be prepared with an education [and is] realized in a climate of commitment and liberty," based on developing individual discipline.[44] At a time when the Italian state sought to shape docile citizens, therefore, its educational administrators rejected the Montessori approach, which stood in fundamental opposition to such a goal.

The interest in imbuing children with militaristic discipline became even stronger when Italy joined the Great War on the side of the Entente in May 1915. The belligerent Italian state adopted a national rhetoric and imagery that employed the themes of youth and childhood to promote the war. Historian Antonio Gibelli has argued that the Great War became an experiment in a political pedagogy oriented toward the masses, one that centered on the image of the child: Italians became *il popolo bambino* (child population).[45] Italian children were at the center of a nationalist campaign that used childhood to speak about national mobilization as "a pledge, a warranty for the future, a concentration of patriotic feelings, a metaphor for what one fights and dies."[46] This political propaganda used the concept of childhood in two ways: on the one hand, through the *infantilization* of the population *tout court*, and, on the other hand, through the *militarization of infancy*, or the spreading of new images of childhood that were modeled after the classic iconography of war. For example, postcards available to soldiers at the front would often picture children playing with planes or with games that mimicked war. Furthermore, the entire population was infantilized in war propaganda (e.g., the wounded soldier, the Red Cross nurse), making the idea of war less frightening for the Italian audience.

National mobilization also called for a reorganization of the family and educational structures.[47] According to Gibelli, the "war drastically diminish[ed] the educative function of the parents"; while fathers were usually absent because of conscription, mothers were called to fill the economic void left by their male breadwinners.[48] On a societal level, the state took on the roles of both mother and father, first and foremost for the children of the nation's fallen soldiers but eventually for all of Italy's children. This growth of a tutelary state corresponded to the reduction of paternal power within the family. This process reached its climax at least on a rhetorical level in the Great War: during this time of dislocation, who would parent and educate the children of the nation?[49]

At the infrastructural level, the answer to this question was weak. The national school system was seldom capable of supplying an education for children in the absence of parents. Many private organizations were run by "patriotic volunteers," most of whom were schoolteachers, and they invested in promoting scholastic and paraeducational spaces that were custodial in nature and designed to give the children a patriotic education, often devoid of an academic curriculum.[50] Organized under no specific school program, these institutions guaranteed the supervision of the children, allowing mothers to join the workforce. At the same time, children were exposed to what historian Andrea Fava has defined as a "war education," through reading "daily military bulletins, followed by the 'geography of the front,' and [listening] to anecdotal and edifying versions of Italian history."[51] The war ended up accentuating some of the characteristics of the Agazzi sisters' method in both private and public institutions, where its only requirements were a teacher with a maternal instinct and a focus on simply guarding and entertaining the children, rather than imparting academic content.

Ultimately, then, by 1916, the goals and methods of the Italian educational system differed drastically from Montessori's. It was unlikely, therefore, that Montessori would find support from the Italian state for an international organization in favor of war-stricken children that was based on her methodology. However, Montessori was determined to rescue these children from "a disease of degeneration," and this desire led her to contact members of the Roman Catholic Church—an institution aligned with her commitment to pacifism—to see whether they would endorse her educational project.

"Children Are Often the Greatest Missionaries of Peace in the World":
Montessori's Attempts to Collaborate with the Papacy

In 1916, when Montessori began looking for support in creating her organization to care for war-distressed children, rescue efforts for civilians were
not yet part of most humanitarian organizations' agendas.[52] Previous large-
scale campaigns in Europe had only provided minimal care for noncombatants. The historiography on the Great War has tended to reflect the meager
contemporary conversation about the effects of the war on noncombatants,
as it has primarily focused on combatants as the victims of violence, leaving
the subject of violence against (invaded, occupied, deported, displaced)
civilian populations partially understudied.[53]

The second half of the nineteenth century saw a rising global awareness
of the need to care for the war wounded throughout the Western world. The
International Committee of the Red Cross (ICRC), founded in 1863, and
the conventions that followed were pivotal in establishing the standards of
international law for the humanitarian treatment of wounded combatants.
However, the protection of civilians, even those near war zones, played a
limited role in this conversation. Still, the civilians' suffering did not go
completely unnoticed when they experienced shortages, famine, and displacement on an unprecedented scale during World War I; some organizations began debating how to provide care and support for the affected
populations.[54] Humanitarian groups, such as the ICRC and the Fight the
Famine Council, as well as lay and religious societies, made contributions
to the relief effort for civilians.

World War I was not confined to the trenches. It affected the entire territories of the participating nations, and it involved an unprecedented number of civilians. Contemporary observers were struck by its "tremendously
new" capacity to destroy, a total war that affected all the populations and
territories involved.[55] The new and all-encompassing nature of the conflict
ignited nonetheless only a limited debate on this topic, among only a few
intellectuals—including Montessori and prominent members of the Roman
Catholic Church.

Alongside the ICRC, the papacy in Rome, as represented by Pope Benedict XV and his nuncios, was the other major entity trying to relieve the
suffering on both sides of the war. Benedict XV and Cardinal Secretary of
State Pietro Gasparri engaged in diplomatic actions between the Allies and
the Central powers in an attempt to save civilians as well as soldiers.[56] By
mid-1915, the papacy geared itself toward taking a peacemaking role among
the nations involved, remaining the only institution actively advocating

for conflict resolution.[57] This ambition culminated in the *Peace Note* of August 1917, a seven-point peace plan addressed to all the warring nations.[58]

Ignored by most countries, the *Peace Note* identified the main points for reaching peace as the simultaneous and reciprocal reduction of armaments, the establishment of international arbitration, and the evacuation and restoration of all occupied territories, with special mention of Belgium and northern France. The suffering children in these territories had been one of Benedict XV's main concerns. In 1916, he appealed to the clergy and laity of the United States for money to help the children of Belgium.[59] It was probably because of the pope's interest in the welfare of children distressed by the war, and his insistent call for peace, that Montessori, right after the *Peace Note*, asked for the pope's help in the establishment of the White Cross.

Meanwhile, Montessori also pursued experiments in religious education and expressed interest in enriching her pedagogy with activities that fostered children's moral growth through the knowledge of a higher plane of life—or, more specifically, God's love. Through this work, Montessori contended that children's spiritual development would better prepare them to contribute to society and work peacefully, both as individuals and in cooperation with others. In 1915, she moved to Barcelona, where her disciple Anna Maria Maccheroni had preceded her and opened a small school, the Escola Modelo.[60] While there, Montessori tested the use of activities based on religious education to strengthen the spiritual growth of the child. In a 1922 book based on her experiment at the Escola Modelo, Montessori maintained that her approach "seemed Catholic in its very essence[:] the humility and the patience of the teacher, the fact that facts are more valuable than words, the sensorial environment as the beginning of psychological life, the children's silence and concentration, the fact that the child's soul is free to perfect itself, . . . the respect for the interior life of the child."[61] According to the educator, the new focus on religious education in the classroom would allow the teacher "to penetrate deeper into the soul of the child" and to therefore inspire love, respect, and harmony among the children.[62]

When her correspondence with the papacy about the White Cross began, Montessori was heavily involved in these experiments. In particular, she was working to create a small-scale altar to allow children to participate in the Mass and to gain a deeper understanding of the rituals associated with it.[63] According to the educator, liturgy could be defined as the pedagogical method of the Roman Catholic Church, insofar as it embodied the main concepts of Catholic doctrine and allowed believers to experience them.

Therefore charity, and a profound respect for the interior life of the individual, could be understood through these practices by children.[64]

Despite her involvement in the study of religious education, her letters to the papacy did not delve into the details of how her experiments could be useful to reeducate the child affected by war, beyond general statements in which she reiterated religion's usefulness in expanding the child's moral growth. All the letters she exchanged with prelates and nuncios echoed the points she made in general informational material about the White Cross, emphasizing the rescue of children from the trauma of war.[65] There are, however, two noticeable differences between the material she produced for the general public and the materials she presented to papal nuncios and the pope himself. First, when writing to the papacy, Montessori accentuated her personal commitment to Catholicism and, more broadly, the role of religion in both the constitution of the White Cross and the formation of the child. She also expanded on the training of the personnel, describing in depth the kind of woman who was to be selected to take part in the White Cross: a Catholic (ideally chaste and pure) woman trained in the Montessori method, knowledgeable in subjects that spanned first aid to special psychology.[66]

Contacting the papacy was not an easy endeavor, not even for a renowned educator like Montessori. Her persistence, however, eventually paid off. She first tried to contact Basilio Pompilj, cardinal and secretary of the Sacred Congregation of the Council at the Vatican.[67] In a draft of her first letter in 1917, Montessori introduced the first leitmotif of the correspondence: the need to create a Catholic organization in favor of war-distressed children—namely, the White Cross. The letter repeated the core themes of previous pamphlets and articles on the topic, first and foremost that through her method children are engaged in a moderate, continuous, and pleasurable activity.[68] The correspondence did, however, try to appeal to the members of the Catholic Church through a *captatio benevolentiae* by pledging allegiance to Catholicism. Montessori wrote:

> My aim is to declare to you that whatever error may have been found in it
> I am ready to correct, because I believe that all the truth is in the Catholic
> Church, and whatever is contrary to it is certainly an error, the repercussion
> of which would fall back on the destiny of humanity.
>
> Nevertheless I believe that not only in my sentiments is there nothing
> against the truth of the Church, but if there has appeared in any of my
> writings anything which seems against it is an error of expression, an
> involuntary error which I would immediately withdraw. Furthermore I am

convinced that this is precisely my religious faith which had inspired me
in my method, which I have indeed taken from the Church.

I believe that this method of education is an instrument placed by God in
my hands; and that God has showed me the instrument and placed it in my
hand for His own ends.[69]

In the missive, Montessori was willing to forgo her earlier disagreements
with the church if it meant she could get funding for the establishment of
her organization. She further asserted that, in the education of a child, "a
prominent role must be given to religion."[70] This first letter continued with
a brief sketch of the White Cross, an association that, according to the educator, would further the papacy's commitment to pacifism.

In making her case to the papacy, Montessori also detailed the irreversible
mental and physical wounds inflicted on the French and Belgian children
conceived as a result of rape. She called for special attention to these "pure
children menaced by the terrible and fatal upset of their nervous system;
the mother's state during the conception and the gestation period influence
the health of the fetus and must not be ignored."[71] According to the educator,
these children were traumatized first by occupying soldiers and then dismissed by their own government; they would constitute a primary focus of
White Cross initiatives. Conceived in the midst of a violent act, the "children
of the enemy" were "developmentally arrested" even further by the state of
shock in which the mother found herself during the pregnancy.[72]

The plight of these children was at the center of a heated debate among
Italian psychologists, physiologists, educators, and politicians who saw rape
as a "national threat to individual dignity, social tranquility, and race and
hygiene."[73] When discussing these children's fates, nationalists feared the
nation's degeneration: these children of rape were born with mental challenges, and they were perverting the physical and psychological sanity of
the nation's race. Their atavistic tendencies, it was believed, would eventually cause criminality and subversion at unprecedented levels.[74] In the words
of criminologist Scipio Sighele, "all over the world, youth is morally sick as
it has never been," and as a result, governments needed to take precautions
against the contamination of the race by reeducating these children, or by
preventing their birth altogether through abortion.[75] As argued by gyne-
cologist and politician Luigi Maria Bossi, "the children born out of these
brutally forced sexual intercourses can only be feebleminded degenerates
dangerous for the family, for society, and, above all, for the nation."[76] Distancing herself from these positions, Montessori recognized the challenges
of children born out of the violent acts but did not participate in the public

debate directly and instead worked toward possible solutions to educate these children while requesting help from Catholic nuncios.

Montessori's letters follow this structure with minimal variation. Despite her efforts to reach the papacy, none of her missives ever reached Cardinal Pompilj. All of them were intercepted by Monsignor Umberto Benigni, founder of the Sodalitium Pianum, a secret organization that enforced the condemnation of modernism by the previous pope, Pius X.[77] Her last attempt to gain the papacy's support was contained in a letter sent directly to Pope Benedict XV on August 15, 1918, a year after the letter to Pompilj.[78] In it, Montessori called for a papal benediction of the White Cross, which she described as a "humanitarian, neutral, and universal" organization.[79] The association would be based in Barcelona: the king of Spain, Alfonso, and Monsignor Reig y Casanova had already endorsed it. The letter did not contain the profession of faith present in Montessori's earlier communications; instead, it emphasized a common interest in the oppressed children, shared by Montessori and Benedict XV. She also devoted a significant portion of the letter to the description of the nurse-teacher who would educate the children, a role requiring both a nurse's knowledge of medicine and a teacher's training in the Montessori method.[80] In previous pamphlets, Montessori had seemed to envision that the education of the war-distressed children would be performed by a figure similar to the one she described for the children of the San Lorenzo's Casa dei Bambini: a scientifically trained teacher with a deep knowledge of medicine and psychiatry. In the letter to the pope, however, Montessori mentioned the necessity of the nurse-teacher being Catholic because of the faith of the children. Montessori added:

> The nurses must be kind women who possess the benevolence that is the sense of spiritual motherhood. In order to become true "nurses of the spirit," they must be well prepared for a predominately educational mission—they must be soaked in charity to soothe the misfortunes of those children who must first be cured and then educated. Who more than the profoundly religious woman, who loves Jesus Christ, could humbly undertake such a noble endeavor? Who better than she could understand the physical needs of these children who have suffered as the victims of human hatred and greed? Who better than she can cure them and instill in their healthy little bodies a sense of fear and love for God? All this will be possible for women, in particular those who are virgin, humble, and devout docile daughters of the church, when they join the White Cross. With the blessing of the church in their mind and chastity in their hearts may they move ahead to seek out innocent children, while the adults, having lost sight

of the charity of Christ, continue to tear one another to pieces, implacable sowers of massacres and anger.[81]

Beyond the highly specific scientific training the personnel had to complete, Montessori indicated to the pope that the nurse-teacher must have a sense of "spiritual maternity." These "nurses of the soul" must first heal and then educate the children by "planting the fertile seeds of love for Christ."[82] These spiritual mothers must be religious, and they must impart a love for Jesus Christ to the children.

Despite Montessori's efforts to receive support from the papacy, her letter bears a handwritten note, from Benedict XV himself, indicating that Montessori had been told (in person) that the papacy did not give its blessing to her project. The note reads, "Said aloud [to Montessori] that the Holy See does not give its blessing to the projects but waits to applaud and bless the new institutes once they have been established."[83] The note added in parentheses that Montessori and her entourage did not welcome the dismissal with enthusiasm. Only three months later, however, Benedict XV gave a papal benediction to Montessori's *Il Metodo*, and he ordered that her works be included in the Vatican Library.

The pontiff's refusal probably resulted from Montessori's initial ambivalence toward Catholicism and her connections to various individuals and associations directly opposed to the Vatican (such as the Freemasons and members of the Theosophical Society). She did not consider either her Catholic faith or her more general interest in Catholicism to be incompatible with other intellectual pursuits. Although experiments in religious education occupied Montessori during the war years and beyond, they did not preclude her engagement with Theosophist organizations, nor did they prevent her from maintaining some of her materialist beliefs. And that was probably all too visible to Catholic nuncios. All along, Montessori and the Catholic Church had a fundamental divergence of views that precluded her receiving full sponsorship from Catholic authorities. The educator's attempts to mediate her positions over the years were, in fact, doomed to fail.

Montessori's correspondence with the papacy shows her attempts to work in collaboration with an organization that was promoting a similar and parallel campaign to help those who suffered from the injuries of war. It also highlights the importance of her experiments with religious education to rescue children affected by war. Montessori cited the integration of practices related to the Catholic doctrine (i.e., training personnel, and the curriculum itself) to convince the papacy to collaborate. Although it was not effective, this correspondence suggests Montessori's burgeoning interest in religious education, crucial in her quest to develop an educational organization, and later method, to form a peaceful society.

"Save the Children": The Società Umanitaria and Montessori's Plight to Rescue Children from the Damages of War

While seeking support from the papacy, Montessori also contacted Augusto Osimo and Giulio Cesare Ferrari, members of the Milanese association Società Umanitaria, which had ties to the Italian Socialist Party.[84] Montessori had started collaborating with the SU on the specific issue of rescue efforts for children affected by war during a training course for Montessori teachers in 1917. The following year, she asked the secretary general and a member of the association to sponsor the White Cross.

Montessori had reason to believe the SU would support her work, as it was a progressive experimental community for the disadvantaged, built on the idea that access to innovative education and culture would improve their circumstances. Between 1908 and 1923, this institution was crucial in the elaboration and diffusion of the Montessori method and central to the educator's thought on pacifism. The association had hosted one of the first Case dei Bambini and several Montessori training courses. The training courses allowed the educator to continue experimenting with pacifism and to spread her credo. Among those who gave lectures were Ferrari, psychiatrist and director of the mental hospital of Imola, who led a class on child psychology; hematologist Pio Foà, who taught hygiene; and physician Gino De Din, who taught anthropology and physiology. Though these intellectuals did not deal directly with pacifism, the content of their courses would later become central to Montessori's plan to eradicate the scourge of war and to reeducate children toward harmony and peace. The lessons taught by Ferrari, Foà, and De Din were in fact expected to constitute the backbone of the training for White Cross personnel.

As recorded in the annual report by Lola Condulmari, director of the 1917–1918 training course, the majority of the children under the care of the trainees in Milan had been devastated by the conflict:

> Some of the children had nervous systems affected by the frequent arguments in the family (how many fathers coming back from trenches found, or brought, fights and quarrels); [they were] distressed by anomalous and harmful environmental conditions, and found the necessary psychological equilibrium in our *Casa*, with our method so effective with happy children, but even more for that youth that has been affected by the pains of life.[85]

The emphasis on restoring the minds of those affected by traumas in the SU training courses was also demonstrated by the many Montessori teachers who, after graduation, played a significant role in the rescue efforts of catastrophe-stricken children. Several Montessori teachers who had been trained at the SU became active in the areas affected by the 1915 Marsica earthquake, in the region of Abruzzi. Many of those who did their traineeship at the San Barnaba school of the SU went on to work in SU-sponsored institutions throughout Lombardy that hosted children affected by the First World War, such as the School for the Children of Conscripts (Scuola per i Figli dei Richiamati di Guerra) where Montessori alumna Elettra degli Uberti was the director, the Institute for the Derelicts (Istituto per i Derelitti) in Milan, and the Preschool for War Refugees (Asilo Profughi) in Monza.[86]

Montessori's work with the SU also informed her research on pacifism on a practical level. In 1910, she had started collaborating with the socialist reformer Alessandrina Ravizza to create a workshop to have Montessori didactic materials built by hand in the Casa del Lavoro, an SU institution for the unemployed. The Casa del Lavoro soon became the principal producer of patented Montessori material, so much so that the educator requested that Ravizza increase the production to export the sets of materials to the United States and Northern Europe, where the method was in use.[87] By working with the SU, Montessori aimed to expand her project of societal renewal to the underprivileged Milanese workers of the area. In her view, societal renewal had started at the Casa dei Bambini, where children learned to live in cooperation with one another, to respect each other, and to value hygiene. Her belief was that these children would consequently export these values to their family and then to their neighborhoods and communities at large. Montessori created a similar initiative when she visited the schools for Belgian and French refugees. As the war progressed, it became harder to export the material to France, and Cromwell, in concert with Montessori, opened a workshop for manufacturing the didactic material for *mutilés* (soldiers mutilated on the battlefield).

A hub for political reform, the Società Umanitaria was active in facing the emergencies caused by the outbreak of World War I. Following Italy's entrance into the conflict, the city administration of Milan had to confront a growing number of displaced people, including young children. Alongside many public and private, lay and confessional organizations, the SU tried to support a city that had become "a crossroad of desperation, a place for refugees and repatriates."[88] The society opened a second Montessori school in 1916 for the children of soldiers, gathered funds for opening a shelter for refugee children in the Casa degli Emigrati (Home for Emigrants),

Montessori class with French and Belgian refugee children, Paris, ca. 1916. "Work in the Garden." Atelier de Fabrication du Matériel Montessori par les mutilés de la guerre. Courtesy of Association Montessori Internationale Archive, Amsterdam.

Montessori class with French and Belgian refugee children, Paris, ca. 1916. "Rest in the Garden." Atelier de Fabrication du Matériel Montessori par les mutilés de la guerre. Courtesy of Association Montessori Internationale Archive, Amsterdam.

"The children initiate the mutilés [wounded soldiers] in the application of the Montessori material" and "Study of Grammar," ca. 1916. Atelier de Fabrication du Matériel Montessori par les mutilés de la guerre. Courtesy of Association Montessori Internationale Archive, Amsterdam.

"The mutilés [wounded soldiers] initiate the children in the fabrication of the Montessori material," ca. 1916. Atelier de Fabrication du Matériel Montessori par les mutilés de la guerre. Courtesy of Association Montessori Internationale Archive, Amsterdam.

"Atelier [workshop] of painting and varnishing" and "First exercises of the senses," ca. 1916. Atelier de Fabrication du Matériel Montessori par les mutilés de la guerre. Courtesy of Association Montessori Internationale Archive, Amsterdam.

Outdoor activities at La Gioiosa summer camp. Courtesy of Archivio Storico Società Umanitaria, Milan.

Refugees and displaced children in the kitchen at Cocquio Sant'Andrea summer camp, 1922. Courtesy of Archivio Storico Società Umanitaria, Milan.

Refugees and displaced children with their teachers in front of the summer house Cocquio Sant'Andrea, August 1918. Courtesy of Archivio Storico Società Umanitaria, Milan.

Refugees and displaced children in the summer house Cocquio Sant'Andrea Cafeteria,
1922. Courtesy of Archivio Storico Società Umanitaria, Milan.

established nurseries and schools for displaced refugee children, and later
opened Montessori schools in the liberated territories of Venice, Treviso,
Belluno, and Udine.[89] The Cocquio Sant'Andrea and La Gioiosa summer
camps sponsored by the SU also hosted refugees and displaced children.

Osimo's description of the children hosted in these institutions sponsored by the SU echoed the ones Montessori and Cromwell used to describe
the French and Belgian refugees:

> The little refugees arrived [at the schools] in the most miserable conditions:
> not covered, dirty, hungry, oppressed by the fatigue of a long and disastrous
> voyage, desperate from not receiving a maternal caress . . . sickened by the
> emotions and by all the discomforts; and the older anguished also by the
> sudden tragedy of which they understood all the terribleness, with still in
> their senses and their soul the tremendous and thunderous in war scenes.[90]

It is no surprise that after Osimo received a letter from Montessori describing the plight of children affected by war, he responded with enthusiasm
and published it with an insightful introduction in the magazine *La Coltura
Popolare*.[91] In his introduction, Osimo lamented the state of public school-

ing in Italy, arguing that "a preschool is, in many cases, a gray, melancholic place, merely custodial . . . where children are only kept briefly." He describes how the few children who had the privilege to attend school did not find psychological support in the teacher or in the educational approach and remained "in the gloomy sadness that weighs on the anguished family." He ended his plea by touching on the theme of racial degeneration that was discussed in most of Montessori's pamphlets for the constitution of the White Cross, and he recalled the "deep scars left by this violent tear in the brains and hearts of these poor exiles." Osimo's piece concludes with an excerpt of a letter sent by the Belgian minister of education, who had just received from the SU sets of Montessori materials for the children of invaded territories. In exchange, the Belgian minister asked Osimo to welcome two Belgian teachers to the Montessori training courses in Milan. Osimo finished by asking his readers, "What will become of these children of ours—men of tomorrow—who lived among tears, abandoned, and among the scary memories of this terrible war?"[92]

Montessori's letters to Osimo and Ferrari follow the leitmotif of her previous material on the White Cross, though she highlights that psychological assistance to children should be given by intellectuals who have experience in psychology and social services for the disadvantaged. The "psychological cure," Montessori insisted, is of crucial importance, as shown by the "high number of those who present signs of psychological deterioration."[93] The White Cross "aims at revealing nervous disorders in children due to the psychological traumas caused by war."[94] One of the White Cross's tasks was to collect psychological evaluations of war-stricken children. Ferrari would be one of the doctors to train personnel for these evaluations. Montessori urged him to contact Osimo, who would help him organize for the tasks ahead.

According to Montessori, the fate of the human race was at stake. Those born during the war, whose nervous systems had been severely impaired from that tragedy, would not be able to reconstruct a peaceful world. The educator argued that the promotion of peace required enormous effort that only a generation of superb intelligence could accomplish—only those with a balanced nervous system could achieve "the colossal task of reaching a future peace." This new generation was to be molded through education, implemented via modern associations, such as the SU, which could coordinate initiatives aimed at "gather[ing] these innocents, seeds of life, from these fields of slaughter, to save them, and so to prepare the bringers of peace."[95] Osimo published Montessori's letter and promoted the initiative, but it was never realized. Despite the intellectual alignment between the SU and Montessori, they never created the White Cross.

Conclusion

Although Maria Montessori's visionary plan of creating an association of educators who could heal children affected by war—the White Cross—was never achieved, the conversations that Montessori initiated during the Great War helped her define the type of intervention she wanted to implement in favor of war-stricken children. Among Montessori's interlocutors, it was intellectuals and politicians interested in first aid initiatives who provided the theoretical background for her endeavor. From this limited yet fruitful dialogue on rescue efforts for civilians, Montessori envisioned a large-scale initiative for war-affected children. The attention devoted to early childhood education from the Italian state helped the pedagogue situate her own approach relative to that of contemporary Italian educators, and to continue asserting the importance of a method that fostered the free unfolding of the child's spirit.

It was, however, Montessori's conversations with the papacy and the Società Umanitaria that proved to be particularly productive and had a measurable impact on the educator's thought. The letters she sent to the papal nuncios and to the pope prompted Montessori to analyze the positive effects of religious education on children's development, particularly on their emotional and psychological development. Montessori's ongoing collaboration with the Società Umanitaria also inspired the educator's project by showing her the practical application of her methodology to war-stricken children through the small-scale initiatives sponsored by the institution in Lombardy and adjacent regions.

The apparently jarring swings in Montessori's search for someone to support the White Cross can be explained by her endless quest for allies in the expansion and diffusion of her pedagogical work. This quest led her to drop out of groups that were anything less than wholeheartedly supportive. As a result, she was constantly seeking a new coalition of advocates and believers. In addition to her undeniable pragmatism, Montessori's deep-seated complexity can shed some light on these sways. Recent historiography has produced two irreconcilable images of Montessori, two dialectic readings that depict someone who is either irredeemably secular or profoundly devout.[96] All in all, this period in her life was characterized by a strong interest in Catholicism, so much so that Montessori attempted to create "a kind of rule of life, a project that seems to concern a secular congregation of Montessori teachers."[97] Within this pious union, what she called a Catholic partnership, Montessori envisioned a movement of reform grounded on the salvific power of education, as well as the implementation of a scientific pedagogy applied to the neediest, wherein religious devotion would be geared toward the welfare of the child. This did not diminish her commitment to the scientific method, as her ongoing attention toward the psychiatric and psychological needs of the child attest. While fundamentally irreconcilable, the papacy and the Società Umanitaria (and more specifically Pope Benedict XV and Augusto Osimo) probably each seemed perfect to Montessori's single need: the desire to create an organization whose work was scientifically rooted and inspired cultlike devotion from a group of women invested in ameliorating children's lives. To her, the church and the socialist Milanese organization were probably two sides of the same coin. In her mind, the core of her mission would have not been compromised by refashioning parts of her message and image. In doing so, she responded to an all too personal conception of science and spirituality, wherein "the firmament of the saints and blessed Itard, Séguin, Fabre, Madame Curie and Thomas Edison, and almost certainly Lamarck and the founder of experimental medicine Claude Bernard would shine [and] of course Maria Montessori too."[98] The changes she did make to her appeals were superficial to her, while the substance of her requests did not waver.

Though the White Cross did not become a reality, Montessori's attempts marked a new phase of her conception of pacifism, one in which her practical work to rescue children pushed her to elaborate on how to train Montessori personnel in rehabilitation. Indeed, her practical attempts to create an organization were accompanied by a series of lectures in which the educator started elaborating on her pacifist philosophy. During the course of those lectures, delivered in California in 1917, Montessori would come to highlight the major deterrents to war and to rethink the role of education not only as a tool to regenerate those negatively affected by conflicts but also as an instrument to prevent war altogether. Children educated by the principles of her approach would become peaceful human beings, humans who would ultimately be able to prevent the occurrence of war. A thorough analysis of those lectures is the focus of the next chapter.

CHAPTER 3

Ending Conflict
with Education

The 1917 Peace Lectures

In the spring of 1917, Maria Montessori delivered four lectures on pacifism
to the Women's Board of the city of San Diego, California, as part of a training course for elementary-level Montessori education.[1] Probably inspired by
the raging conflict in Europe, members of the audience asked her to opine
on the state of contemporary affairs, and she took the chance to discuss
topics on which she "had only just started to reflect."[2] She saw the series of
talks as an opportunity to develop issues that were personally compelling:
the education of children and pacifism. At the beginning of each lecture,
she cautiously reminded her audience that they "[should] not give absolute
importance to the things [she was saying], in fact [she was speaking] of
them for the first time now, and [she was] glad to do so amongst friends, in
a small group, intimately." Though she was still formulating her ideas,
Montessori explained the relevance of her talks by noting that they were
germane to the current "horrible scourge of the European war."[3] Through
them, her audience glimpsed how much the global crisis—particularly its
effects on children—influenced her pacifist philosophy.

As Montessori's first attempt at a complete theorization of how to achieve
world peace through education, these lectures established the foundation
of her thoughts on global pacifism.[4] The educator first provided an overview of contemporary society and its difficulty with preventing war. Assess-
ing the pacifist movements and tactics of her time, she demonstrated their
inefficacy and argued for drastic social reform. To prevent war and achieve
perpetual peace, humankind needed to be altogether reshaped to save
humanity from itself. But to reach such a goal, society needed to embrace
new models of education. Over the course of her third and fourth speeches,
she advocated for the rediscovery of the "laws of life" and their pedagogical

application, ultimately arguing that her approach could form a person capable of respecting others while protecting the unfettered development of his own spirit. By establishing meaningful and respectful relations with the people around him, the child would transform humanity and bring peace.

These reflections on pacifism developed as both an outgrowth of her political zeal and a long-term project to transform society. Montessori's desire to help the disadvantaged and the marginalized brought her in touch with many feminist and pacifist organizations, through which she was exposed to the main currents of national and international pacifism. Her grassroots activism—particularly her efforts to realize the White Cross— and her work to bring about peace through political and civic engagement exposed the educator to contemporary debates on war prevention, conflict resolution, and peace-building strategies. Still, Montessori responded to such conversations by calling for the end of war in a unique way, from the ground up, by reforming the educational system. In other words, the educator argued for a radical transformation of society—and a complete cessation of war—through the education of society's youngest members. Indeed, a close reading of the San Diego speeches demonstrates that most pedagogues, social reformers, and politicians considered Montessori's agenda to be radical. Unlike other pacifists of the time, she did not consider propaganda, rallies, or demonstrations viable tools to spread a pacifist message among people, nor did she support half measures in school curricula aimed at integrating activities promoting peace. Peace was to come from the child. She advocated for spreading an educational system that would allow children to develop as individuals who seek peace and foster understanding. If children were educated according to the "laws of life," in harmony with their own spirit and their immediate environment, they would grow up to become mentally and physically healthy human beings, leading the way to perpetual peace in adulthood.

Pacifism through Political Activism and Theoretical Engagement

From the 1890s, when she attended La Sapienza, to her 1909 publication of *Il Metodo*, Montessori engaged in numerous social-renewal projects and collaborations with feminist organizations. This early activism, always closely tied to her pedagogical work, put her in touch with several schools of thought on pacifism, conflict prevention, and resolution. Her exposure to these diverse perspectives proved to be foundational to her own understanding of pacifism in these years, and later in the formulation of her pacifist agenda.[5] Her political connections, her social activism, her work-related travel to countries including England and France, and especially her participation in international feminist associations deeply influenced her pedagogical, political, and pacifist thought. Her engagement in improving society was rooted in these connections and projects.

While Montessori was a student and activist in Rome, the discourse on pacifism was spreading throughout both Italy and the rest of Europe. With the 1891 constitution of the International Peace Bureau, many pacifist organizations, antimilitarist groups, antiviolence leagues, and associations for civil disobedience joined forces and began circulating their messages across the continent. By the first decade of the twentieth century, myriad organizations aimed at establishing peaceful dialogue among nation-states flourished throughout the Western world.[6] Promoting various approaches to peace, many of these associations were able to circulate their ideas on a global scale for the first time. Reflections on how to construct a peaceful society were no longer the work of a few isolated intellectuals but instead took on the scope of political organizations that could sway general public opinion.

Scholarship on pacifism has highlighted two strains of thought above all others.[7] In Great Britain and the United States, pacifist movements mostly relied on a positivist and evolutionist approach to pacifism, originating with the progressive free traders. This school of thought, championed by intellectuals including philosopher and propagandist Herbert Spencer and liberal economist Richard Cobden, rested on the notion that the Industrial Revolution transformed traditionally militaristic societies so that they would eventually evolve toward discarding war as a method of conflict resolution.[8] This passive and deterministic view, also termed *positive pacifism* by historians, did not find a considerable following in continental Europe. There, antiwar philosophy rested on completely different premises. Most of the European peace activists were informed by the idea that war was a means to achieve perpetual peace, hence the definition of *negative peace.*[9] Pacifist movements following the latter approach saw peace almost as a utopian objective to be realized through violent means, a target toward which to aim but never to be reached, a "definition that is violence oriented, peace being its negation."[10] Achieving peace was often cited as the basis for belligerent actions. The ultimate dream of peace—obtained through fighting—was a leitmotif as the lines between pacifist and belligerent viewpoints were blurred.

Modern Italian pacifist thought was first elaborated in the aftermath of Italy's 1861 unification, and it mostly belonged to the negative peace category. The first generation of Italian activists who created peace committees in the 1860s and 1870s had participated in the national liberation movements of the preceding decades. For example, young Ernesto Teodoro Moneta, winner of the 1907 Nobel Peace Prize and leader of the Italian pacifist movement, took part in the riots against the Austrians during the "Five Glorious Days of Milan" in 1848.[11] Within the Italian discourse on peace, the liberation of the oppressed peoples of Europe was a condition for obtaining international peace. War was seen as a necessary step toward a peaceful society.[12] Giuseppe Garibaldi, the leader of the Italian independence movement, was invited to preside over the 1867 inauguration of the Ligue Internationale de la Paix (International League of Peace) in Geneva, and he remained the honorary president of the league for several years afterward. As Victor Hugo put it in a description that evokes the spirit of Italian pacifism, Garibaldi was "one of the heroes of peace who traversed war; the just sword."[13] Military heroism, a belligerent quest for freedom, and peace became conflated under the flag of Italian pacifism.

By the beginning of the twentieth century, however, these positions had lost their influence, and the idea that national liberation and nation building depended on sacred warfare began to fade—that is, until the government declared war on Turkey over Libya-Cyrenaica in 1911. Intellectuals, including Montessori, started engaging in debates to find alternatives to the concept that conflict could act as a means to achieve peace. The new antiwar movement became known as *continental pacifism*. At the center of this movement were the debates over whether arbitration and arms reduction could resolve international conflict. Many peace activists throughout the continent returned to arguing that Europe was a single culture, despite national differences and animosities, and that it needed strong international relations and arbitration to prevent conflicts. Furthermore, they argued, internationalism was a logical outgrowth of nation-states, not a subversion of them. In this view, a unified Europe could finally solve long-standing issues—such as the tumult in Alsace-Lorraine—while maintaining its national and ethnic diversity as championed by Giuseppe Mazzini in his writings on "Young Europe."[14] According to these currents, dialogue on positive approaches to peace was to be preferred over armed conflict resolution.

Many of the Italian thinkers influenced by continental pacifism also belonged to feminist groups, who advocated ending all war through propaganda and lobbying.[15] Historian Franca Pieroni Bortolotti argues that many early feminist cells in Europe originated as pacifist organizations aiming to promote peace as well as to politically and culturally unify the continent.[16] As with pacifist movements, feminist groups often advocated for conflict resolution through arbitration committees and the abolition of permanent standing armies.

Among the many issues addressed in their platforms, such as women's suffrage and equal juridical status for women, some Italian groups and associations focused their efforts on ending the colonial oppression of African peoples. Building their criticism of contemporary European gender roles on an analysis of rhetoric regarding female colonial subjects, Italian emancipationist groups often expressed strong criticism of their government's colonial enterprises.[17]

Montessori's political contribution to pacifism had its roots in the democratic feminist emancipation movement of the late nineteenth century. Her interest began as a generic desire for universal peace and social justice connected to her political and medical work in favor of the disenfranchised, and it was often expressed in speeches on equal rights and women's emancipation, and in protests in favor of the education of women.[18] Moreover, her quest to promote the rights of marginalized subjects expanded beyond national borders to include a struggle against colonialism. In 1896, Montessori began collaborating with the Roman feminist association Per la Donna (For the Woman), a group aimed at "infusing in women a spirit of solidarity and sisterhood."[19] The organization was linked to the Unione Internazionale Femminile per la Pace (International Women's Union for Peace), an association that called for women across all classes to work together toward universal disarmament. Per la Donna expressed its official support for the International Union of Peace Societies with the goal of expanding the debate on peace across national borders.[20] As her first act as the organization's vice secretary, Montessori launched a petition against the colonial occupations in East Africa. Following the 1896 battle of Adwa in which Ethiopian forces defeated the Italian army, Montessori, together with other women from the newly established Associazione Femminile di Roma (Women's Association of Rome), demanded the end of the "menacing African war."[21] Counting Virginia Nathan and Giacinta Martini Marescotti among its members, the group divulgated an anticolonial manifesto titled *Alle donne italiane* wherein war was described as "inhumane" and "opposed to our nation's traditions." The manifesto maintained that "the honor and the majesty of the Fatherland—now that its civility has opened up vaster horizons—are no longer based upon conquests or the sword, but on work, and on the judgment of our citizens."[22] Embracing the organization's far-reaching political program, Montessori placed herself among the radical feminists who disapproved of Prime Minister Francesco Crispi's occupation of colonial territories and manifested their dissent throughout the country.[23] With the occupation of Libya a few years later, however, enthusiasm for colonialism would unravel the Italian pacifist movement.

At the International Women's Congress in Berlin in 1896, Montessori began her lecture on the rights of working women and addressed Italian women's collective disapproval of colonialism.[24] Her plea did not conform to any specific political agenda, yet it did resonate with a growing anti-imperialist spirit in an expanding number of feminist organizations founded on a deep respect for all human beings. She argued that women must fight for "the great humanity, [which] has only one, imposing and majestic [political] party, advocating for wellness, universal peace, and absolute progress."[25] The debate on peace policies was also at the center of the International Council of Women, held in London in 1899, also attended by Montessori. The committee in charge of discussing strategies to achieve peace among nations focused on youth education, the implementation of arbitration and mediation for conflict resolution, and ways to increase media coverage for those ideas. The words of Austrian pacifist Bertha von Suttner, who would soon receive the Nobel Price for Peace, reminded all the participants of the consequences of modern warfare.[26]

These early political efforts were intertwined with the educator's pedagogical work and prompted her to start thinking of an approach to education that could transform children into proponents of peace, a thought process that led her to a more complete pacifist agenda in 1917. She wasn't entirely alone in her thinking. At the turn of the century, a small movement called Education to Fraternity promoted spreading peace through school curricula.[27] According to this school of thought, children were to be educated with the ideal of democratic citizenship, preparing them to become members of a democratic society. While Italian educators debated how best to promote the children's allegiance to the newly constituted Italian state through school programs, this approach fostered understanding and global citizenship, advancing what was termed *educazione al mondo* (education in the world). This methodology asked educators to promote the notion that students are members of humanity, as opposed to members of a specific nation. The movement's core principles required children to form relationships beyond their immediate surroundings.[28] Among the pacifists who embraced this approach, essayist Romain Rolland and feminist Ellen Key highlighted education system reform as a tool to build a new conscience among young children. They pleaded for the importance of the child's individual freedom as advanced by contemporary pedagogical methods; they also suggested art as a way of transmitting universal values.[29] Both saw scholastic institutions as the propeller for a pacifist revolution, the formation of a European conscience, the valorization of coexistence and diversity, and the overcoming of national stereotypes. Key argued for mothers to lead the antimilitarist campaign and for children to promote a cosmopolitan pacifism.[30] According to the Swedish thinker, children should learn the consequences of fraud and deception and develop inhibitions to stop that kind of behavior, honing their ability to control instincts, desires, drives, and so on, "and from this state of mind of the individuals of a nation will an international self-control be developed."[31]

Montessori encountered this school of thought in its early stages, and it was later employed by philosopher Henri Bergson, activist Mohandas Gandhi, and educator Aldo Capitini; today it is at the core of intercultural curricula and a tool for educating youth in cross-cultural understanding.[32]

Montessori's approach to pacifism, as understood through the 1917 lectures, had a similar universalistic mission, one that the next generation was to carry out. The child was at the very center of this project, taking him away from the conventional and oppressive pedagogy of the day and out of a society that aimed at his normalization, not at his growth. In *Il segreto dell'infanzia*, Montessori compared the child to Christ, incarnated in a world where his people did not recognize him in his full potential and redemptive power.[33] Through her lectures, Montessori further unveiled the true nature of the child, the only one who can save humanity from an apocalyptic future.

Despite the private audience for Montessori's 1917 lectures in San Diego, it is likely that her ideas had started to circulate through kindred pacifist circles. One indication is an unpublished letter Montessori received from Frances M. Witherspoon, one of the founders of the War Resisters League and of the Woman's Peace Party, an American association that counted among its members the famous philanthropist Jane Addams.[34] By the time Montessori received the missive, she had distanced herself from Italian feminist organizations, probably as a result of her desire to concentrate on promoting her methodology.[35] Nonetheless, her prior participation caught the attention of North American organizations. In 1917, Witherspoon wrote to Montessori requesting a contribution for the Woman's Peace Party's monthly bulletin on the issue that was dividing women's political associations: Should women stand in support of the war, or concentrate their efforts on finding possible solutions to end the conflict? Which sentiment should prevail: patriotic duty and belonging to a national community, or the spirit of international collaboration developed in the years preceding the conflict? According to the letter, the Woman's Peace Party considered Montessori an esteemed member of an international community of women pacifists and wanted her to contribute an article. In particular, Montessori was asked to write a "much neglected note [on] broad internationalism in these days of universal warfare and national strife." In inviting Montessori to write about the destructive effects of war on the Italian school system, Witherspoon noted that the association felt "very much in the dark about what the women of Italy are doing and what sentiment there is for peace and internationalism."[36] The article would have eventually contributed to the debate started in 1915 by Mary Sheepshanks, director of the International Woman Suffrage Alliance (IWSA), who had published an editorial entitled "Patriotism and Internationalism" in the magazine *Jus Suffragii* in which she asked, "what is left of the internationalism which met in congresses, socialist, feminist, pacifist, and boasted of a coming of an era of peace and amity?"[37]

There is no evidence that Montessori responded to this letter, nor is there any record of her contributions to the bulletin. The 1917 lectures may, however, be read in part as a response to Witherspoon's exhortation, for two main reasons. First, her initial lecture was delivered only a month after she received Witherspoon's letter, and it picked up many of themes touched on in the bulletin, such as grassroots strategies to expand the debate on conflict resolution among citizens of all ages, and the inefficacy of current political tools used to foster anti-interventionist propaganda. Second, Montessori's words seemed to echo Witherspoon's references to internationalism, specifically in advocating greater political and economic cooperation among nations and people with the help of her proposed supranational organization, the White Cross.

It is worth noting, however, that despite Witherspoon's communication with Montessori, there were fundamental differences between the Italian educator and the North American Woman's Peace Party. The most significant was in the way each sought to create a peaceful society. Montessori maintained that her pedagogical methodology was necessary for educating children to live in harmony, whereas the Woman's Peace Party promoted an agenda that offered practical solutions to contingent classroom issues. The Montessori child achieved peace through an internal process of development; the Woman's Peace Party argued instead for an external method involving politics and pragmatic changes within school curricula. Between 1914 and 1917, a period during which US President Woodrow Wilson's administration gradually abandoned attempts at mediation with other countries in favor of outright American military intervention, the efforts of the Woman's Peace Party became even more urgent. On a pedagogical level, the members considered a variety of ways to establish a peaceful classroom, such as fostering discussions on peace among the teachers and eliminating any texts that depicted human history as a succession of wars. Tellingly, no party members discussed the necessity of an altogether new pedagogy; it was just not crucial to them.

Such efforts were not uncommon. Prior to the Great War, Italian intellectuals had also considered the possibility of simply modifying units of the schools' curricula to educate children in what they defined as civil and pacifist behavior.[38] In a 1905 article in the journal *La vita internazionale*, Moneta had recommended teaching a common morality to the Italian people: "If you don't want sad days to repeat in the future, days more disastrous than those we had in the past, I only see one way, which is to have only one morality ruling on public life. The first notions of this morality are the only ones worth teaching in schools. This morality should not be antireligious, nor antichristian, but only fruitfully civil."[39] Although these isolated initiatives probably influenced Montessori, she would eventually aim to implement a broader project that was organic and systematic.

Debates on pacifism came to a halt when the Great War broke out. Very few European intellectuals continued to support scholastic initiatives aimed at promoting peace. Generally considered unpatriotic, such proposals received harsh criticism. In 1914, Belgian, French, and Italian pacifists accepted the catastrophe of war as necessary in support of sovereignty, freedom, and the holiness of the motherland.[40] European governments justified it as defensive, and all the arguments that had been put forward over the previous decades by pacifist associations and antiviolence leagues were swept away. Notably, when the neutrality of Belgium was violated and European governments intervened, they were supported by pacifist associations. The majority of Italian pacifists were in favor of intervention before the Italian government decided to participate in the conflict on the side of the Triple Entente (France, Great Britain, and Russia). The organizations and political parties that continued campaigning against intervention were labeled traitorous and quickly silenced. Echoing the message of the unification-supporting Risorgimento pacifists, the politician Gaetano Salvemini argued for Italy's intervention in World War I as the war that would bring peace: "It is necessary for *this* war to kill all wars, [it is illicit] to abandon the war for peace."[41] Montessori's conviction that peace would come from a radical transformation of humankind and not from war was thus exceptional during the war years. To realize her philosophy, she slowly became involved in new training courses and projects in Spain and the United States, neutral nations during the early part of the conflict.[42] These activities helped her focus on education, which she would argue was the only tool to transform people into agents of peace.

San Diego, 1917

The 1917 teacher training workshop in San Diego was not Maria Montessori's first trip to the United States; she had traveled there repeatedly between 1913 and 1917.[43] Her first trip, in 1913, was a promotional tour organized by the publisher Samuel McClure; many well-known American philanthropists and educators who were interested in her methodology supported her trip financially and logistically.[44] Welcomed as "the Italian apostle of a new libertarian education," Montessori enjoyed a great deal of popularity and decided to come back in 1915 to participate in the Panama-California Exposition in San Diego and the Panama-Pacific International Exposition in San Francisco as well as to lead a demonstration class at the San Francisco World's Fair early that year.[45]

On October 9, 1916, Maria Montessori returned again to the United States to give training courses, this time with Adelia Pyle, her American protégé. Pyle had spent the preceding years traveling with Montessori throughout Europe and the United States, transcribing and translating Montessori's lectures. Blanche Weill, a young woman who had previously assisted the psychotherapist Alfred Adler in his lectures, also accompanied the educator.

Only Montessori's disciples and student-teachers attended her lectures. Though she was still formulating her ideas, Montessori explained the relevance of her talks by noting that they were germane to the current debate in the so-called New Education movement, which saw children as having inalienable human rights—as competent, active agents—and sought social change through education in Europe and North America.[46] Broadly, the international

"Little Pupils of the Montessori Children's House, New York: Demonstrating the System of Rhythmic Exercise, under the General Direction of Dr. Montessori, Who Is in the Country as a Guest of the State Board of Education of California." *New York Times*, May 30, 1915. Courtesy of Library of Congress, Washington, DC.

Maria and Mario Montessori, group photo for a training course, United States, 1915. Courtesy of Association Montessori Internationale Archive, Amsterdam.

Maria and Mario Montessori in Los Angeles, 1915. Courtesy of Association Montessori Internationale Archive, Amsterdam.

movement on New Education campaigned against a traditional methodology that saw teachers as sources of information and authority, students as passive receivers of information, and schools as detached from the community and the family. According to this school of thought, the personality of the child had to be a central concern, and education must serve human betterment, eventually leading to a new era.[47] Montessori herself was an advocate of this movement.

In addition to situating the lectures within this debate, the educator pointed out that they were pertinent to her new research on pacifism, as well as to the conflict that was then devastating Europe; education was in fact key to reforming humanity and constructing a peaceful society. Indeed, wars would stop occurring altogether after the educational systems of the world were redesigned, she contended.[48] The first two lectures offered an overview of the political and social changes that have brought humanity to become a single organism whose main cultural and economic processes—including war—have become interconnected. For example, she posited, if one nation were to experience an epidemic, the entire world, through an intricate system of alliances and organizations, would act swiftly to contain it and to protect those who were infected. The global conflict made it plain: only a global approach could eliminate war. Having highlighted the issues at stake, Montessori then proceeded to delineate the only solution—education— progressing from a general analysis to a series of specific suggestions.

Overall, the four talks were somewhat repetitive and, as Montessori acknowledged, were more spontaneous reflections than developed arguments. Some of the topics she touched on had been part of her *Antropologia pedagogica* or would soon surface in other writings.[49] The way the talks were recorded underscores that they were open-ended dialogues; Montessori adopted this practice more fully in the 1920s, when much of what was published under her name consisted of ideas transcribed from her speeches, which had often been delivered during her training courses.[50] Montessori, who rarely used notes, delivered the San Diego talks in Italian; Pyle was beside her, translating her remarks into English as she spoke. This English transcription is the only record that remains, and it may contain some degree of inaccuracy and interpretation.[51]

Montessori's lecturing style was described by biographer Rita Kramer as relying on a "romantic and mystical . . . sometimes embarrassingly florid prose."[52] The speeches, in fact, followed the same stylistic approach as Montessori's early writings, in which she drew from various semantic fields such as philosophy, literature, and the scriptures, with abundant use of metaphors; she tapped into her knowledge of child nutrition, classroom management, social medicine, and international relations. The result, however "florid" it may have been, was captivating prose that shed light on her multifaceted scientific influences.

The First Lecture: Three Scourges—Famine, Pestilence, and War

In the first lecture, delivered on February 18, 1917, Montessori gave the audience an assessment of contemporary global relationships among nations, in which she laid the foundation for the idea of humanity as a single organism. Because all humans are interconnected, intellectuals, educators, and politicians must study the repercussions of this relationship attentively and work to find solutions to the numerous potential problems.

The speech began with a comparison of the "three scourges of life" (famine, pestilence, and war) and an analysis of how humankind had changed its approach to those three threats. During the last forty years, she said, people had found efficient ways to deal with famine and pestilence, though they had not been able to find viable solutions to the third problem, war. Though war had remained "occult and hidden," famine and pestilence had been at the center of a vast movement of reform that led humanity to unite. As a result, humankind was able to intervene wherever people lacked "the material necessary for the life of the body" and provide supplies.[53] To determine which responses had been successful, Montessori investigated the social response to famine and plague, which involved international cooperation. But, as Montessori argued, this very strategy was not effective for war. In the case of World War I, national alliances had caused a domino effect, in which nations were dragged into the conflict one by one, and therefore their initial cooperation in fact escalated the scope of the conflict.

In explaining how humankind overcame the scourge of famine, Montessori drew upon two metaphors: the world as a human organism and the earth as a family in which brothers prepare food for each other. The forces that fought famine were similar to those combating plague. A "brotherhood of men" fought against the spread of disease, a global threat that had almost disappeared thanks to a new consciousness regarding hygiene. During emergencies, Montessori claimed, humanity functioned as a single organism, sustaining itself just as the human body supports a single organ during disease, through its immune system.

Anticipating post–World War I trends—for instance, the creation of international agencies such as the League of Nations—Montessori argued that cooperation among nations was necessary to improve living conditions everywhere. Montessori devoted a large section of her first speech to describing how humankind was able to improve its living conditions through social renewal. One crucial agent of such renewal would be a still vaguely defined new organization that would help provide food supplies and promote hygiene on a global scale, giving humanity a self-sustaining system to over-come hardships: "As in the case of famine, so in the case of pestilence, there has been made a new social organ whose work compares with that of the circulation of the blood. Just as there is something in the circulating blood of the individual that counteracts the germs and the microbes, so is there something in the social circulation that defends us from pestilence." She went on to describe the ties that connected individuals around the globe in the shared goal of protecting humanity against the hardships of plague and famine as "unions" or, more broadly, the "brotherhood of mankind." Accord-ing to the educator, people, institutions, and nations all collaborated toward the eradication of these two scourges. This common goal was entrenched in society to the point that helping one another became a process "so purely mechanical" that soldiers dying in the battlefield were helped by organ-izations such as the Red Cross—regardless of what side of the conflict they belonged to.[54] Even in conditions as extreme as the war, where nations fought one another, humankind had been able to act as a single organism and provide care for the wounded, regardless of national affiliation.

Montessori declined to address the nature of a "new social organ" that would gather all of man's unions around one goal. In fact, her use of this expression was metaphorical, referring to a collective commitment rather than any specific institution. Yet her efforts during this time to create an organization that would serve children in distress, named the White Cross, offer valuable insights on the structure of this commitment. One could infer from the lecture that Montessori wished for the creation of the "new social organ" in the form of a supranational organization. This group would overcome national barriers and act impartially in the extirpation of famine and plague. By advocating for it, Montessori anticipated the debate on human rights that would come in the aftermath of World War II and would lead to the formation of international agencies that regulate food security, such as the Food and Agriculture Organization (FAO), and global health, such as the World Health Organization (WHO), both coordinated by the United Nations. Though Montessori's contributions to the founding of political organs in defense of children's rights are well known, her participation in a larger debate on the creation of intergovernmental organizations to pro-mote international cooperation remains largely unexplored.

Yet Montessori also believed this new form of international collaboration had potential drawbacks. Though a supranational organ had the power to counter pestilence and famine, it did not have the capacity to prevent or stop war. In fact, the "unions" that were so important to stopping the spread of famine and plagues also allowed for the globalization of war. According to Montessori, "The fact that [the current] war has spread in such a way is due to this other fact of the union of mankind." Montessori explained that the formation of a global network of alliances meant "all nations are thrown into war" whenever two countries were in disagreement.[55] She therefore opposed the formation of a supranational social organ aimed specifically at stopping war because the array of tight-knit alliances of such a united world would make global conflict more likely. She used World War I as an example of how global diplomacy and alliances had failed. More generally, she claimed, international laws and treaties were ineffective; not only did they fail to prevent wars, but they also had often transformed local conflicts into multinational affairs.

Montessori also addressed other solutions contemporary politicians were suggesting as possible remedies for war, such as granting nations the right to self-determination. According to Montessori, granting nations their "natural territory" would not prevent war; in fact, such a position was a delusion, "for those who have the largest territory are those who make war."[56] This assertion was probably influenced by her view of Italian irredentism, a movement that aimed at the unification of Italian-speaking peoples and territories deemed to be Italian lands, and which was the foundation for Italian interventionists pushing to enter World War I.[57] During the Giolitti era, this campaign assumed militaristic and nationalistic tones, with the goal of establishing Italian hegemony on the Adriatic Sea. Such a stance, with its warmongering rhetoric, was in stark contrast to Montessori's plea.

Of course, the Italian discourse on irredentism was not Montessori's only influence; one must read Montessori's remark on the principle of self-determination within the context of the American debate on pacifism in early 1917, which understandably revolved around the larger public discourse on US participation in World War I. On January 22, 1917, only a few weeks before Montessori's first lecture, President Woodrow Wilson had delivered an address to the US Senate entitled "A World League for Peace," discussing the possibility of an armistice without victory, a peace that would "make it virtually impossible that any such catastrophe should ever overwhelm [humanity] again."[58] The speech was part of a series of addresses to the Senate on principles such as open diplomacy and free trade that were to foster the creation of a peaceful society. Wilson's speeches on this issue would be further developed in his famous Fourteen Points, delivered in January 1918, and again in the formation of the intergovernmental organization the League of Nations.

By January 1917, however, Wilson had already highlighted the necessity for all the nations engaged in the conflict to adhere to a league for peace. A strong proponent of international arbitration operated by supranational agencies, organizations, and lawyers, Wilson maintained that "mere agreements may not make peace secure . . . it will be absolutely necessary that a force be created as a guarantor of the permanency of the settlement so much greater than the force of any nations now engaged or any alliance hitherto formed or projected that no nation, no probable combination of nations could face or withstand it."[59] Owing to the resonance of the president's speech in the months preceding the United States' entry into the war, it is likely that Montessori was responding to the president's call for a league of peace when she denied the validity of any such solution. As the United States debated whether to join the Allies, and peace demonstrations took place across the country, Montessori's comment emphasized her opposition to the president's strategy for peace.

Disillusioned by how little she accomplished during her militant years in feminist organizations, Montessori was skeptical of the common practices carried out by other pacifist and nonviolent associations, and she ended her first lecture with a warning: "Processions of women calling for peace" would not suffice to end war. "Everyone must work for this from morning till night. . . . And we can imagine a society where all [people] work, at all times, against a war that never comes . . . just as now we fight continually against the epidemic that never comes."[60] According to the educator, only a radical reformation of society would avert the perils of new conflict. Montessori, however, had yet to elaborate on the tools needed to enact this transformation.

The Second Lecture: Education for a Peaceful Society

On March 11, 1917, Montessori gave her second speech on peace.[61] Over the course of this lecture, the educator outlined exactly how humankind could achieve peace for the first time: her vision called for every citizen to live a physically, morally, and psychologically healthy life. The second lecture's structure was not as coherent as the first; often Montessori compared and contrasted historical periods without giving the audience necessary context, or she would lose her train of thought in a long digression. She did, however, connect this talk to the previous one in her initial review of international law, reiterating that it is insufficient to prevent the occurrence of war.

Her second talk centered on the notion of "law," defined as what guided both a man's actions and the relations among nations. According to Montessori, a scientist interested in fostering peace should not focus on the legal and economic agreements that bind nations together but instead should concentrate on the "conditions of life," or the biological, cognitive, and moral laws that guide an individual's development.[62] As highlighted in the first lecture, jurisprudence and agreements were not sufficient to prevent war; instead a change within humankind was necessary, one that could only be achieved by following these interior laws. Montessori did not delineate those laws in this lecture, but she referred to her concept of "deep laws" that had played prominently in her early pedagogical writings. Defined in her seminal text *Il Metodo*, these "deep laws" could be seen in the rules children spontaneously follow in the course of their development.[63] "Deep laws" corresponded to inner aids the child would use to explore an aspect of the environment. For example, during a specific phase in the child's development, that Montessori later named the "sensitive period," the child would be absorbed in a specific activity (or set of activities), which he repeated over and again. New skills were learned through repetition, ultimately fulfilling developmental needs. For example, from birth through the first eighteen months of life, the child would be extremely concerned with actions related to movement; he would seek out activities that require motion and exercise. According to Montessori, the Montessori-trained educator, like a scientist, must observe and suggest activities to the child that facilitate the unfolding of the child's spirit. The existence of these general principles made any educator more of an interpreter of preexisting laws rather than a creator of new approaches. Montessori's methodology itself could be defined as the pedagogue's identification of the universal laws of human development playing out before her.

Although it would not become explicit until her third lecture, Montessori suggested in the second that only the rediscovery of the laws of life—and their pedagogical application—would allow for the creation of a peaceful society. Yet to discover them, men could not rely on their own capacities. Instead, they must look to what she conceived as the foundation of religion. Once again, the educator relied on her syncretic view of religion to approach an entirely scientific matter. In fact, she proceeded with her argument by using a religious metaphor: a "divine light," which could be interpreted as either God or knowledge, must guide the search.[64] Men should not fight over territory or riches; they should fight those who oppose the unfolding of a child's natural self and wage a war for reaching a higher plane of moral and intellectual life. The educator drew a distinction between contemporary soldiers who fought hoping not to die and "Christian soldiers" who fought on the strength of their faith during the Roman Empire and were unafraid of death. At the core of Montessori's analysis stood the distinction between fighting for something unjust and fighting for a greater good. Whereas the soldiers of her day were fighting to kill and were thus uninterested in implementing the "virtues of life," the earlier Christian soldiers made a sacrifice "in order to give life" to allow other believers to freely express their faith, an act that made them martyrs, according to Montessori. If these first "priests of Christ" were to come back and judge contemporary society, they would say that the "virtues of life" had not changed; in other words, the moral principles or "deep laws" that must govern a man's life were still the same.[65] Those virtues, however, did not serve God as they had in the past; they served the devil, "not life but Death." In the Great War, men were fighting only for war's own sake; a pointless war was raging across the globe, a war that would not generate a society guided by higher principles.

Montessori concluded the lecture by criticizing once more the strategies of contemporary peace movements that only protested war without searching for a superior law that could guide humanity away from conflict:

> He who was to work against war and work for peace, should put himself into a different combat, into a great work that cannot be that of simply abstaining from war, of protesting with words and making law against war, but he must do great works. . . . Christ cannot be put back into the world simply with words, for the form of Christianity is the form of the human spirit and should enter into the spirit as a help to life. But this help to life must come through some actions—that is, we must discover and follow [the] laws of life that also has its laws to be followed.[66]

In addition to rediscovering the laws of life, then, humankind must abide by Christian values, not simply through words but by accomplishing great actions. In doing so, Montessori argued, man might yet reach salvation.

The second lecture ended with an analysis of childhood as a stage of life in which people were closer to God and therefore had greater knowledge of the aforementioned laws. In drawing this comparison, Montessori referenced William Wordsworth's *Intimations of Immortality*, an author and poem she had previously mentioned in *Il Metodo*.[67] By citing the British poet, Montessori highlighted the fact that children possessed what she called a luminous spirit, or what Wordsworth called a "memory of heaven." They both conceived of infancy as a life stage in which sensorial experiences were more immediate, lively, and able to transmit the secret laws of life to the child. According to Montessori, children experienced a connection to heaven that made them see nature's glory more clearly. The luminosity within the child was directly connected to the "divine light" that Montessori had previously indicated was necessary to guide men in their search for peace. As the child grew, this connection gradually weakened.[68] When developing new curricula, an educator should be guided by the knowledge that the child must be encouraged to cultivate certain skills and values before a particular age. Therefore, to create a methodology that fostered peace and implemented the organic development of the child's spirit, the educator must closely observe the child. Both here and in *Il Metodo*, Montessori referenced Wordsworth to discuss the child's capacity to remain faithful to his true nature, his *vita naturale*.[69] She was inspired by his pantheistic and Neo-platonic conception of the universe, wherein God is immanent and visible, and nature has moral value.

Any attempt to discern Montessori's position on the role of religion in the education of the child, and in her own life, is a complex task and often reveals inconsistencies. First and foremost is her deep commitment to Catholicism, followed by her numerous connections to Theosophical organizations. At the time of the lectures, the educator had just conducted experiments on religious education in Barcelona with her disciple Anna Maria Maccheroni. This work was so important to her that it would soon inspire her to write three books on the subject. But Montessori had not severed her ties with democratic-Masonic forces in Italy and abroad. She had just attended the Panama-Pacific International Exposition in San Francisco, accompanied by a longtime supporter of her work, the anticlerical grand master of the Masonic Grand Orient of Italy, Ernesto Nathan. Furthermore, she was collaborating during this time with the Società Umanitaria (which had links of its own to Freemasonry) and with the Theosophical Fraternity in Education.[70] Her work continued to mirror this intricate web of relationships, with all the contradictions therein.

Her devotion to fostering the child's moral growth would continue to be deeply entangled with her adherence to scientific principles. This time of religious fervor did not change the nature of her work. The reference in her lecture to the importance of reinstating Christian principles, which she makes explicit for her private audience, had more to do with a broader call to prompt children to love one another, humankind, and the universe, and to do unto others as one would have them do unto oneself. This reliance on, and promotion of, religious tropes and language did not undercut the universalism of Montessori's public message. According to Montessori, scientific observation of the child went hand in hand with teaching basic principles of what she identified as Christianity, which included nondenominational notions of respect, kindness, and love for all. They were indispensable tools to achieve the harmonic physical and intellectual growth of the child, and ultimately the redemption of humankind.

The Third Lecture: An Approach for Body and Mind

Montessori began her third speech, delivered on March 18, 1917, by advocating for a thorough study of the human body and hygiene.[71] For healthy development, including being at peace with the world and with others, children should be taught healthy mental and physical habits. A child who took care of his own body and hygiene, Montessori argued, would be able to, in turn, take care of the environment around him, learn to cooperate with others, and so on. After having spent her lecture the previous week highlighting the general principles that should guide educators in the rediscovery of the laws of life, she moved on to suggest practices to foster the child's healthy growth. Through the scientific observation of the human organism, she argued, a teacher would be able to detect the laws of life and create an environment that favors them. As explained throughout Montessori's oeuvre, the adult must not set specific rules for the child's development because children are born with vital tendencies (also described as interior laws or inner forces), and because they strongly seek independence. When children are exposed to an environment without obstacles, she explained, "it is as though an arrow had been sent flying from the bow and it goes straight, sure and strong. So does the child proceed along the path of independence. A vital force is active in the individual and leads it toward the child's own evolution."[72] Specific laws or tendencies govern when certain sensitive periods in development occur. As Montessori observes, "life makes itself manifest—life creates, life gives—and is in its turn held within certain limits and bound by certain laws which are insuperable."[73] An educator must not interfere with these laws—she must respect them, so that a child may develop free of constrictions, into a healthy individual who respects others.

Montessori went on to explain that her pedagogical approach "favors life" through an environment that was designed and organized around these laws, a notion that formed the foundation of her approach.[74] Montessori asserted that to develop a renewed society, the child must be educated according to the laws of life. She proceeded to argue that these rules must be traced by observing and studying the child, an operation that Montessori herself carried out while elaborating her educational methodology. Following these laws would guarantee the physical and psychological health of the child, both of which were necessary to form a balanced human being capable of creating a peaceful world.

To determine the "rules of practical life," Montessori proposed, one began by scientifically examining a child's biology and then the environment in relation to the body. According to Montessori, at the core of the human body was the circulation of blood, her basis for a scientific and complete study of the human being. This circulatory system connected the entire organism. Through the circulation of blood, the digestive, respiratory, and excretory systems could be studied for information on the condition of the body and its functions. According to Montessori, scientific observation revealed the importance of these systems and demonstrated the necessity of promoting the health of the body through hygiene, in the form of appropriate nourishment, life in the open air, physical exercise, and bathing. All these principles, as demonstrated in the first chapter of this book, were the foundation of the educator's philosophy.

The study of the child's biology, Montessori further claimed, needed to be complemented by a study of the relationship between the child and his surroundings. Montessori-trained educators had to rigorously examine the physical development of the child. It is through such observations that Montessori had surmised that the laws that govern children's lives were different from those of adults; as she elaborated, "linguistic exercises, a systematic sense-training, and exercises which directly fit the child for the duties of practical life" served to stimulate the child toward healthy development, and they ultimately formed the foundation of Montessori's pedagogy.[75]

A Montessori educator then had to prepare the environment and offer the child age-appropriate material. Montessori argued that children would succeed, slowly and with perseverance, in accomplishing many complicated actions if the end results were agreeable to them, such as getting dressed and undressed, washing themselves, eating, setting and cleaning the table, and so on. While completing such actions, they remained patient, "overcoming all the difficulties presented by an organism still in process of formation."[76] Through these activities, set up with the didactic material in the Montessori classroom, the child established meaningful relationships with the surrounding environment. The "sensorial world [acted] as a stimulus" to the "inner part" of the organism, the nervous system, fostering an education through the senses that allowed for a healthy intellectual and physical development of the entire organism.[77]

Montessori continued her speech by arguing that a new science that fosters the hygiene of this "superior part," the nervous system, must arise to provide consistent incentives to further the growth of the nervous system. She contended that humankind must stop considering motion as something separate from life and abandon the prejudice that those who use their muscles are not using their intellect. "Motor expression must not be limited to gymnastic movements," Montessori wrote, as it was central to the development of this "superior part" and forms obedience, which is "the purpose of our lives." If the child were left free in his expression, his educator could see the child's "way of responding to [that which showed] the functioning of his center—a slow working."[78] By observing how the child regulated his muscular expressions, in both the practical activities of daily life and his thoughts, the educator could see how the child's "inner part" worked, and the learning environment could be structured accordingly.

Toward the end of her third lecture, Montessori made a connection between the hygienic lifestyle promoted by her pedagogy and the cultivation of a superior, more peaceable human being. Montessori argued that people who followed a lifestyle that accounts for the health of the entire organism were frequently the ones who performed menial tasks, commonly considered the "work of servants." Generally, children in Montessori schools performed work—that is to say, they were fully engaged in the activities they themselves chose and that they considered meaningful to their development. Without interacting with the teacher, inner impulses linked to the aforementioned sensitive periods guided the child toward a specific part of the didactic apparatus. The child's own nature brought him, at a certain time and in a certain way, to perform a specific activity, and guided him to accomplish a particular goal, developing his "psychological organs" in the process. A child who performed his work, even tasks such as lacing his own shoes or serving food to his classmates, would learn more than those who are served by so-called servants. Therefore, Montessori concluded, a man educated through his own senses and allowed to freely choose his own work according to his natural inclinations would be a superior human being. Echoing the words in her foundational *Il Metodo*, she explained that his "superiority will lead [him] to new action, concentration, peace, slowness in action, repose, a repose active in form in which one hears the voices of other souls and hears the voices of nature."[79] Such a person, Montessori believed, would oppose belligerent actions.

The Fourth Lecture: The Child and Society

Montessori delivered her fourth and final lecture of this series on March 25, 1917. The speech did not appear to work toward a clear conclusion; rather than wrapping up the topics introduced in the previous lectures, the talk delved further into the connections between the child and society, a relationship that Montessori argued had to be revitalized to rejuvenate humanity.[80] The lecture focused on the development of morality during childhood.

According to Montessori, children's moral development was connected to the implementation of social skills and to the sense of human unity, or a "brotherhood of mankind." Once the child had acquired a sense of belonging to human society and came to respect that sense, he would also become a transformative agent for a new and harmonious society. In this lecture, Montessori sketched strategies for educating children toward this goal, a plan she would later elaborate through her conception of the Four Planes of Development.[81] This first draft of her theory proposed that the child could internalize this ethical code by loving his closest surroundings—the family and the educational environment of the Casa dei Bambini.

Though the intellectual development of the child had been the object of much scientific research, Montessori stated that no study had yet been conducted that focused on the development of morality in children. She pointed out that morality had so far been linked to intelligence: an individual was thought to choose moral acts because he had acquired knowledge of the law and because he could measure the benefits of his actions in relation to his community. According to Montessori, however, morality and intelligence had nothing to do with each other. Morality had so far been considered the submission of the child to the will of the adult. Educating a child in ethical behavior was considered to be a form of adult sovereignty over the actions of the child. Therefore, the foundations of ethical behavior remained "rather obscure."[82] Only religion—not to be construed as a specific system of faith and worship—had highlighted the basis of moral education: love. To study morality—and ultimately the possibility of perpetual peace—Montessori argued in this final lecture, one should study the emotional life and affections of the child.

It was through loving one another and the environment that children themselves became the means for society's moral progress. To succeed at improving society, children must freely love the people around them to develop what Montessori named "a social sense," or an attachment and caring for one another. With this sense of connection, she explained, the child would become "more and more conscious of the other human beings around him, and little by little [would become] interested in an affectionate way in all that happens to his companions." This love was the first step toward a higher kind of affection, one that opened "the world of the soul, and the . . . heart to humanity, . . . a revelation to the world of love."[83] Montessori provided another example: the Virgin Mary, through loving her son, had a revelation of God's love for humanity and of the capacity of any person to feel this love. By comparison, contemporary society, especially its school system, promoted competitiveness and individualism. According to the logic of that system, love weakened the child. Yet Montessori offered examples of people who had not repressed love but had become stronger by conquering higher levels of love. For example, the writer she referred to as Carmen Sylvia lost a child, but nonetheless she wrote in praise of God for having had the chance to know love in a way she never would have otherwise.[84] Montessori recounted the way in which Sylvia was transformed by experiencing maternal love and was able to transfer that love to humanity: "It is a high interpretation of maternal love, so strong it opens the world of the Soul, and the mother's heart can love all humanity. As in the symbol of Mary, the mother of Christ, love of her son became love for humanity, and it is this son who gives the revelation of the world love." To further substantiate her argument for the need to experience a higher level of love, Montessori reflected on the life of a French aristocrat, Jeanne de Chantal. When her husband died, "instead of feeling the void, she noticed that she loved much more widely, that she was conscious of the human beings she had never been aware of before; she noticed she love[d] the poor, but with a great and perfect love like the love for her husband and children." Chantal started receiving beggars in her home, hand-washing their clothing, and making them food. She had "heard the voice of humanity," a call that urged her to leave her home. "So she became the celebrated Jeanne de Chantal whose divine mission was to do as did Saint Vincent de Paul, to found hospitals. This woman, noted as a mother, abandoned her children, and this makes one remember the words of the teacher of Love, who said: 'Unless you leave parents and brother, husband and wife, and all to follow me, you are not worthy.'"[85] Referring here to the Gospel according to Matthew, Montessori described the passage between different levels of love.[86] According to the educator, a series of steps must be taken to achieve this higher and spiritual love for those in need. One must pass from an earthly love for one's neighbors to a more perfect, more universal, love. Building on the cautionary tale of Jeanne de Chantal, about the need to feel and express love for one's neighbors, Montessori concluded her fourth lecture by arguing that one must first feel "inferior love" in order to feel the "superior love," a love for God, a necessary condition for acting in the care of disadvantaged people, and, more broadly, of everyone.[87] Here Montessori referred to a transversal notion of love, not in a religious or even a Catholic sense but one that is foundational to numerous religious and humanitarian perspectives. Loving one's own family and relatives was the first step toward that higher level. From this followed a love for all humanity, one that allowed people to act in favor of the disadvantaged. According to Montessori, a renewed humankind would build a peaceful world.

Conclusion

Montessori's 1917 lectures highlighted the importance of studying the causes of war, the only one of the three scourges that had not been defeated. Whereas remedies for famine and plague had already been found, the contemporary tools being used to prevent war (such as political alliances and pacifist rallies) were shown to be ineffective. To prevent conflict, Montessori proposed, humankind must be educated following the deep laws that universally regulate the child's body and mind. If the child were thus educated, he would grow up with a sound psyche and develop into a harmonious human being, capable of loving his peers, and, later, society. Such a person would be able to establish meaningful relations with his surroundings and to repudiate conflict. A society made up of such people would always reject war.

The four lectures set the theoretical foundation of Montessori's thought on international pacifism. Her early political and social activism, as well as her pedagogical research, motivated her to formulate an approach that could turn children into agents of peace, forming a new humanity that would resist the urges of conflict and would eventually prevent the occurrence of war altogether. As demonstrated through a comparison with her contemporary pacifist and grassroots initiatives, the educator benefited from a broad array of perspectives and influences to frame a relatively radical solution to the problem of war. Throughout her numerous travels in Europe and the United States, Montessori observed the inefficacy of the established practices—such as demonstrations, rallies, and small-scale class-curriculum initiatives—which, she claimed, would not stop the conflagration of a new war. A different kind of education was necessary to save humanity.

Montessori's interest in peace did not end with these speeches; it continued through the educator's entire life, occupying a growing importance in her work. Her second and more famous phase of writing on this topic, which led to the publication of the collection *Education and Peace*, built upon many of the issues discussed in these early lectures. The themes of the three scourges of life, the consequences of individualism, and the necessity of a new physical, mental, and moral hygiene reappeared in a more articulate series of lectures delivered throughout the 1930s. The references to World War I would be replaced by comments on contemporary dictatorships and their tendency toward warfare; likewise, the role of the child in society was described through metaphors that would become central to the educator's subsequent writings, especially with regard to the child as savior of humanity, "as a messiah, as a savior capable of regenerating the human race and society," and as a forgotten citizen.[88]

CHAPTER 4

Montessori in Fascist Italy

In a 1927 letter to Prime Minister Benito Mussolini, Maria Montessori complained about having to go to London to teach a training course for Montessori teachers. In her view, her approach to education and the sites in Italy where she had developed it were inextricably linked. Montessori was therefore "doubly sad to have to go down there—that is, to leave [her] homeland to teach this method which [was] known to be notoriously born in Rome and to give, through [her] presence, a disillusion to those who have come from so far away, to meet only the person, and not its environment, to study in schools so far from the wonderful country where [her method] originated." She wished she could run her courses in Rome, where it all began. Rome was, to her, the "place toward which all the people in the world aspired, especially in this great moment of renaissance and great hope."[1] At the time of the letter's composition, Montessori, a true nomad, had traveled for the past ten years, living in Barcelona, spending long stretches of time in the United States, and doggedly promoting her methodology across Europe. But in some of her writings to Italian politicians and intellectuals throughout the 1920s, she expressed a desire to return to her country and to permanently establish her schools and training courses there. She seemed weary, almost helpless, calling herself a *povera signora* (pitiable lady).[2] Despite her desire to return to Italy, she did not actually diminish her travel, nor did she change her intellectual stance toward nationalism. The core principles of her work remained intact. She did not, however, write about peace.[3]

Montessori's letter to Mussolini reveals a tension that characterized her life in the 1920s, during which she paused her direct engagement with international pacifism to focus instead on her own methodology. It is important to note that she did not fully divorce herself from international pacifist and humanitarian movements. She continued to follow their development and made personal contacts with notable individuals within them. That said, during the 1920s Montessori principally pursued recognition for her work in her country of origin, to "bequeath her spiritual legacy to Italy."[4] This desire to reside in her homeland and to obtain financial support from the Italian government occurred in the context of the establishment of the Fascist regime.

From 1922 to 1934, Montessori worked under the patronage of the Fascist government. Though the collaboration lasted for more than a decade, her biographers often attempt to soft-pedal it. She herself apparently did not examine her relationship with the regime critically until the beginning of the 1930s. It is hard to reconcile the common view of Montessori, a pedagogue globally renowned for educating children through an emphasis on individual freedom, with that of someone who collaborated with a dictatorship. This tension, however, must not go unexplored, as it sheds light on "the collective responsibility of a people, but in the first place on the role of cultural elites, to whom the privileges of culture and of social rank deny the margins of innocence granted to the masses."[5] Understanding Montessori's choices within the realities of Italian Fascism opens a critical window to her political views and the complexity of this historical moment.

Montessori undeniably accepted the patronage of the Fascist regime while she carved out an independent place for herself within the Italian educational panorama. Simultaneously, she laid the foundation for her future work on pacifism by connecting with a vast array of organizations advancing peace through education. In 1932, when the regime seemed to threaten her capacity to work freely, she refused its financial support.

Scholarship on this subject tends to depict Montessori's association in light of her professed apolitical nature and to argue that she only cared for the development of children rather than any specific political agenda. According to this view, Montessori had a presumed "excessive ingenuity" when it came to politics—a lifelong lack of interest in state affairs, amounting to an artlessness that allowed her to conceive of the Fascist government as a suitable patron for her pedagogical vision.[6] Notwithstanding Montessori's progressive bona fides—such as fighting for women's right to vote and vehemently opposing the "terrible scourge" of the Great War—her collaboration with Benito Mussolini and his regime is typically viewed as a decadelong misunderstanding on her part.[7] According to this interpretation, when she sought Mussolini's support in 1922, she did so without realizing, at least at first, the ambitions and extent of his political project.

In reality, though, Montessori was a keen political observer. As the previous chapters have shown, she confidently navigated diverse partisan forces and negotiated with an array of powerful figures when seeking support for her work. Indeed, her political savvy extended beyond the realm of children's rights.[8]

Montessori was willing to use money from the Fascist regime to pursue the good of children in Italy and across the globe. She appealed to and cooperated with Mussolini for pragmatic purposes. Her ambitious projects needed ongoing financial backing, and Montessori thought, as did many other Italian and international intellectuals, that she could carve her own niche in this new political landscape.[9] The prospect of being able to directly help the children of her native country, the appeal of returning to Italy and being recognized at last for her work, and the promise of gaining funding to continue her research pushed the educator and her son to solicit Il Duce for support, at least for a time. When Mussolini's impositions became unmanageable, she left the country.

At the same time, it would be willfully naive and dismissive of Montessori's intelligence to assert that she did not understand the nature of the dictatorship. Recent historiography has provided a new wealth of primary sources that complicate Montessori's attempts to obtain support from the regime.[10] Examining Montessori's relationship with Fascism restores her agency, effectively returning her to the center of her story. Over the course of her partnership with the regime, Montessori did not publicly advocate for peace—a remarkable and notable change. While her writing maintained the foundational tenets of her pedagogy—the child's quest for inner peace and harmony with the environment and the family—it did not directly engage with projects dealing with political peace, as had the lectures she presented in San Diego in 1917 or her attempts to create the White Cross under the auspices of the papacy or the Milanese socialist organization Società Umanitaria. Instead, in the years between 1922 and 1932, she focused on implementing new pedagogical activities, influenced by her interest in Roman Catholicism and the moral education of children. These themes are clearly visible in the considerable changes made to the 1926 edition of *Il Metodo*.[11] During this period Montessori benefited not only from the regime's financial backing but also from the public endorsement of its most prominent intellectual, Giovanni Gentile.

In the 1930s, Montessori shared her theories of pacifism publicly and forcefully, through a series of conferences around Europe. It is difficult not to conclude that her interest in international pacifist and humanitarian movements did not vanish but that she simply felt constrained from participating in them because of her relationship with the regime. The 1920s were a gestational phase in her engagement with pacifism, a period in which the educator privately reworked some of her theories before sharing them with the world.

This gestational phase coincided with a drastic turning point in the world of humanitarianism, as both humanitarian action and humanitarian discourse: international humanitarian associations came to occupy a seminal role throughout Europe, as they addressed the deep economic and societal shocks caused by World War I.[12] Many of these humanitarian organizations (especially their child welfare programs) borrowed heavily from a broad intellectual and moral climate that saw children as the creators of peace. In this school of thought, Montessori's writings, her initiatives, and her pedagogy more generally loomed large, despite the conspicuous absence of her voice.

At a time when Montessori withdrew from public canvassing on behalf of children affected by war or from advocating for them as agents of pacifist reform, numerous child-focused organizations rose to prominence in the field of humanitarianism and engaged in the debate on child welfare that led to the development, refinement, and definition of transnational children's rights. Innovative child welfare initiatives radically changed the conversation on aid to children and children's rights. It is thanks to the work of some of these organizations that the League of Nations ratified the Declaration of the Rights of the Child in 1924.

At the same time, several organizations that were engaged in fostering international understanding and peace through progressive education began organizing congresses and symposia to avert the perils of another war. Scholars, school administrators, social workers, or just hopeful internationalists all took part in these initiatives, ultimately aimed at fostering cooperation among countries, student-exchange programs, and lecture circuits. They also monitored new outlets and agencies to prevent hostile or inflammatory coverage of foreign nations and to promote accurate depictions of issues in international affairs.[13] The period between World Wars I and II also saw the emergence of new organizations rethinking education as the cornerstone of a peaceful world. Moral disarmament, peace through education, and more generally an opposition to dictatorial control on the part of schoolteachers became part of a heated debate on global stability, enflamed by the inefficacy of traditional tools such as arbitration and economic cooperation in solving international disputes.[14] Organizations such as the New Education Fellowship and the International Bureau of Education (IBE) funneled the work of the aforementioned pacifist intellectuals. Montessori, though she did not participate in these activities herself, paid close attention by having her collaborators attend.

The discussion following the Declaration of the Rights of the Child in turn inspired Montessori's theorization on this subject, as did the necessity of educating children to peace. In the early 1930s, she returned to issues of public health and pacifism and rejoined European lay forums as she herself was spurred by the connections she had nurtured throughout the 1920s. By then, the conversation on these topics had advanced, and new initiatives throughout Europe and the United States had flourished. She thus rejoined the debate and began to speak publicly about topics that were at the core of her project to reform humanity, making her plea to transform society through education a public conversation for the first time.

Montessori's Attempts at Dialogue with Intellectuals in Power

During the 1920s, Montessori attempted to move the bulk of her pedagogical activities back to Italy. In 1922, she held a series of conferences in Naples at the invitation of the minister of public instruction, Antonino Anile, under the auspices of the last Liberal prime minister, Luigi Facta. In July of the following year, Anile's successor, philosopher and pedagogue Giovanni Gentile, expressed his own interest in Montessori's method and his intention to collaborate with her to spread her work throughout the country.[15] Gentile, long a proponent of children's self-education, looked favorably on the Montessori method.[16] As the head of the Ministry of Public Instruction under the new Fascist government, Gentile was leading a series of reforms that was changing the Italian educational landscape. Montessori, whose success had become global, would be a valuable collaborator in this endeavor.

Montessori and the Fascist regime both recognized that her global reputation offered the new Italian government a source of legitimacy. Aware of her fame and her connections abroad, the educator understood that the Fascist project would benefit from counting her among its supporters.[17] Both sides attempted to leverage this fact for their own ends. In the winter of 1923, Mario Montessori wrote to Mussolini asking that his mother's method, now spread throughout the world, be given due consideration in her country of origin.[18] Mussolini did not write back, but he did request that the minister of foreign affairs investigate the Montessori schools abroad—and, because Maria Montessori was in Rome at the time, Mussolini asked to meet her.

Biographer Rita Kramer has investigated Mussolini's intentions for this meeting and has plausibly surmised that Il Duce was less concerned with building a nation of freethinkers than in harnessing the method's striking academic reputation.[19] There was some overlap in their interests, to be sure. Mussolini had to deal with the high levels of illiteracy throughout Italy and was committed to addressing this issue with the help of Italian pedagogues. Montessori wanted to bring about an "explosion of writing" in Italian children, to initiate a process by which children, without ever being taught, would seemingly erupt into speaking, reading, and writing.[20] Mussolini came to see her method as a means to his main end: modernizing the Italian state with a pedagogical method that delivered remarkable results. To do this, her approach needed to be incorporated into the scholastic system, which had recently been reorganized as a result of the Gentile reform of 1923.

For her part, Montessori sought the government's support throughout the 1920s to promote her pedagogy, with the ultimate goal of returning to Italy—particularly to Rome, the "center of everybody's aspirations in the world, especially in this moment of great rebirth and hope," as she wrote in a letter to Mussolini.[21] Toward this end, she made superficial changes to her work, bringing it into dialogue with the leading cultural and political forces in Italy. Specifically, in her 1926 revisions to *Il Metodo*, the educator toned down the positivist emphasis of her early texts to "affiliate herself with the most influential trends in the field of educational policies"—namely, idealism and Catholicism.[22] Hoping to return to Italy permanently, she focused on strengthening diplomatic and personal relationships with Italian intellectuals, principally Gentile.

The Fascist attention to education, and more generally to youth, began early and was present in the government's propaganda at the outset. In large part, Fascist educational philosophy was founded on *actual idealism*, a branch of Hegelian philosophy, which, within the field of education, emphasized the formation and development of the child's spirit. Gentile, considered the philosopher of Fascism, was the main force behind its initial restructuring of the educational system while he was minister of public instruction. His 1923 scholastic reform, later known simply as the Gentile Reform, delineated the philosophy of Fascist education that Montessori had to confront on her return to Italy. Styled as *riforma fascistissima*, or, in Mussolini's words, *la più fascista delle riforme* (the most Fascist of reforms), the Gentile Reform was the first comprehensive education act in twentieth-century Italy.[23]

For the most part, the reform was not a drastic departure from previous legislations put forward by Liberal governments, nor did it constitute a dramatic change from the contemporary pedagogical debate. As argued by historian Tina Tomasi, Gentile himself had perorated it profusely in the previous years, highlighting its "faithfulness to the liberal, bourgeois conception of the school system, one that was foreign and beyond political and social fights."[24] Despite often being described as one of the most prominent intellectuals in the regime, Gentile was accused of moderatism from the radical fringes of the Fascist Party and counted numerous outspoken opponents within the political establishment.[25] Consequently, Montessori's return to the conversation in Italian pedagogy was not a dramatic departure from her experience prior to 1922. At the same time, the political framework in which the Gentile Reform was implemented gradually altered the practical program to the point that it was hardly recognizable as the result of an international conversation.[26]

The Gentile reform, the first significant piece of legislation of the Fascist government, was intended to play a central role in the education of the youngest citizens of the regime. Based on the notion that education was the "most powerful instrument of civilization" in shaping the spirit and mind of the people, the reform's ultimate goal was to create an educational system capable of remolding the Italian mind and spirit into the image of the new Italian—a new adult brought up according to Fascist principles.[27] The legislation was the first act of a gradual centralization of the scholastic and extracurricular systems that completely delineated the lives of children and young adults, nurturing them into becoming active supporters of the totalitarian regime. Children were to be inserted into a collective project wherein the individual sacrificed his needs in favor of the nation. They had to be "courted, organized, trained, entertained, and indoctrinated."[28] Gentile's idealism served as the theoretical backdrop for this endeavor.

Gentile's philosophy interpreted reality as a manifestation of the ideal principle of pure action, or reflexive awareness (*pensiero in atto* or *soggetto transcendentale*). The empirical subject—that is to say, a single individual—was considered an object of the transcendental ego, or the self that comes to consciousness. Each such individual was sublimated into a single collective entity, the Ethical State. This state, the political manifestation of a community—the nation—embodied the will of the collective; simultaneously, the collective was meant to embody the will of the state. As a result, the state's main obligation was to train its citizens, ideologically subsuming them into the collective.[29] The individual, meanwhile, was an active part of the whole, and contributed to the realization of the community of which she was part.

The new educational reform focused primarily on secondary, postsecondary, and professional education, while Montessori's approach was mostly implemented for children in the age groups from birth to age three, three to six, and six to nine. Perhaps most notably, the mandatory school age was extended by two years, requiring all children to attend school until the age of fourteen. But a greater standardization of curricula was also enforced in public and private schools, and a system of state examinations was imposed to determine whether students would graduate from one grade to the next.

Furthermore, the law consolidated certain subjects (for example, combining physics and mathematics) and reorganized the system of checks and inspections to monitor teachers and administrators. Both at the curricular and at the administrative level, the reform promoted the centralization and consolidation of a rigid system of control—for example, in the strengthening of the role of school principals, who had the duty to act as a "vigilant sentinel who has absolute, militaristic, and unconditional devotion to the duty given to them, regarding it as a sacred thing."[30]

There were, however, also significant changes in the primary-education system. Primary education was key to the Fascist project to mold a new Italian, since three out of four Italians concluded their education at the elementary level.[31] In particular, religion was introduced to elementary grades as a compulsory subject—a significant departure from policies adopted by Liberal governments since the 1870s, which, with various degrees of uncertainty, left religious instruction at the discretion of those who requested it.[32] Structurally, the elementary school cycle increased from three to five years, dividing it into a *grado inferiore*, grades one through three, and a *grado superiore*, grades four and five.

The changes introduced by the Gentile Reform were not wholly new, and many of them grew out of long-standing discussions and debates from the Liberal period. The approach of pedagogue Giuseppe Lombardo Radice, in charge of the reform for primary grades, "oscillated between liberalism and statism."[33] His reorganization of the elementary curriculum incorporated the principles of progressive education, but somehow he concocted "a mix of contrasting elements, of advanced innovation, and reactionary measures."[34] At a practical level, he reinforced the ties between curricula and the students' environments, building on the principles of the preschool reform enacted by the Royal Decree of 1914. At a philosophical level, teachers were asked to play a more central and leading role within the classroom. These two changes built upon and strengthened characteristics present within the Italian educational system.

Indeed, Montessori, who centered her methodology on the development of the child's distinctive potential through an individualized approach, would seem an unlikely supporter of this educational vision, to which individualism could not be more distant, and this discrepancy was evident even to idealist intellectuals. In the words of Gentile himself, Montessori children "are always at the center of their own thoughts," lacking social skills and a connection to real life and their own surroundings, which he believed would eventually lead to the development of "introverted children rather than extroverted ones."[35] Excessive individualism, the absence of lecture-based instruction, the marginal role of the teacher, and a "pedagogical anarchism à la Tolstoy," as Lombardo Radice put it, constituted a radical departure from the principles at the foundation of idealism.[36]

By contrast, Montessori's method envisaged teachers as mere observers, whose didactic material was standardized. Despite these evident differences, Montessori made changes to the 1926 edition of her main text, Il Metodo, in an attempt to enter a dialogue, at least superficially, with idealist approaches.[37] Montessori minimized the references to the positivist sciences and to scientific naturalism that provided so much background to previous editions. In particular, as Paola Trabalzini puts it, Montessori's comments on experimental psychology became more critical, and references to names of positivists such as Cesare Lombroso, Achille De Giovanni, and Giuseppe Sergi—previously defined as "those who prepared the masses' conscience to embrace scientific development"—disappeared.[38] As historian Tina Tomasi has observed, Gentile had "demolished positivist pedagogy" because of presumed "ideological inconsistency, moral weariness, and educational pessimism."[39] Striving to frame her work in ways more palatable to the educators who were in power, Montessori appears more deliberate at this time, almost "cautious" as to appease her contemporary respondents.[40]

In trying to engage with the major pedagogical forces at play in Italian society, Montessori had to contend not only with philosophical idealists but also with Catholic intellectuals, whose influence was deeply embedded in the Fascist educational program. Fortunately, she had already been in the process of rethinking certain aspects of her approach to comply with the main principles of Roman Catholic pedagogy. The years preceding Montessori's return to Italy had marked a period of religious fervor for the educator, who progressively became more and more invested in her own spiritual and religious growth and consequently in the development of religious education.

As recent scholarship has emphasized, Montessori intensively solicited Catholic intellectuals, for multiple reasons and through diverse channels.[41] While she attempted, unsuccessfully, to gain the support of Pope Benedict XV for the creation of the White Cross, she was also in touch with Jesuit Pietro Tacchi Venturi, whom Montessori asked for advice on creating a sort of religious order; she also collaborated with the Capuchin Joaquín de Llevaneras and the Vincentian Antonio Casulleras to devise activities for the moral and spiritual growth of the child.[42] Catholic Barcelona had provided a favorable backdrop for her religious interests, and so, it seemed, did 1920s Italy, where a gradual realignment of the papacy with the civil government was taking place.

The most important potential allies for Montessori's goal of returning to Italy were the educational idealists and Catholics. These two groups combined their efforts when Gentile mandated religious instruction as "the foundation and coronation of elementary instruction," a collaboration that would culminate in 1929 with the signing of the Lateran Pacts (*Patti Lateranensi*) by the Kingdom of Italy and the Holy See.[43] Broadly, the Fascist regime's incremental alignment with the papacy manifested itself pedagogically as a new consideration on the teaching of religious education. The Gentile reform served as the cornerstone of this collaboration, upon which the cooperation with the Vatican was constructed.[44] The reorganization of the educational system welcomed many elements of the traditional Catholic program: teaching religion in elementary schools, the crucifix on the wall, state exams, and freedom of school programs. With the signing of the Lateran Pacts, religious education was extended to all grades.

Before returning to Italy in 1922, Montessori had received timid signs of approval from Catholic thinkers. The first arrived with the 1918 papal benediction of *Il Metodo* and the text's addition to the Vatican library, marking the first public recognition of Montessori's work since her collaboration with the Franciscan nuns of the via Giusti convent in 1910.[45] A "comprehensive critical overview of the Montessori method" in *Civiltà cattolica* by the Jesuit Mario Barbera offered the first positive, if not uncritical, commentary on the approach. Though Barbera did not appreciate "the emphatic tone" used by the educator and criticized the "materialist exaggerations of scientific pedagogy" in the text, he maintained that Montessori had "clearly applied with genius, in her *Children's Houses*, in such a beautiful and sophisticated way, the Christian principles that great educators put into effect for the successive ages of childhood and adolescence."[46] After the positive articles by Barbera, Montessori published *I bambini viventi nella chiesa* in 1922, a manual for teaching Catholic doctrine to children; she also lectured on original sin and the child in 1921, and then wrote *La vita in Cristo* (published in 1931) and *Mass Explained to Children* (1932).[47] This brief period of encouragement spurred Montessori to engage openly with religious education, an interest of hers that had previously remained secondary to her pedagogical inquiries.

Throughout her time in Italy, Montessori revised elements of her work that had been criticized by members of the Catholic intelligentsia, seeking an endorsement from the clergy, which represented an influential interest group in the field of education. According to Hélène Leenders, Montessori made alterations and adaptations to the 1926 edition of *Il Metodo della pedagogia scientifica* in response to Barbera's commentary.[48] The changes addressed Barbera's criticism very closely. The guidelines for these changes were likely approved or even dictated by Pope Benedict XV himself, who, after having denied support for the White Cross, likely indicated which adjustments Montessori could make to better fit Catholic doctrine.[49] The end of Benedict XV's pontificate in 1922 and the rise of Pius XI to the papal throne, however, ended this opening. The new pope's condemnation of naturalism in pedagogy in the encyclical *Divini illius magistri* signaled the end of the church's positive attitude toward the educator.[50] The disappointment that must have followed probably led Montessori to end her direct engagement with religious education.

The Fascist Government's Response

Montessori's attempts to cultivate Catholic approval of her work and to engage in dialogue with idealist philosophy were well received by the Fascist government. With its new emphasis on educational reform and, later, on pronatalist policies, the regime provided institutional and economic resources for the Montessori approach to spread nationally.[51] In April 1924, the Società Amici del Metodo (Society of Friends of the Method) became the Opera Nazionale Montessori, with Gentile named its president.[52] A robust campaign promoting the Montessori method began: by summer of that year, the number of Montessori schools had already increased notably throughout the peninsula. Maria Montessori was nominated as honorary president of the association, followed, in 1926, by the nomination of Mussolini as its actual president, with Gentile serving as director of the organization in Rome.

Mussolini had become aware of the Montessori method's growing international success; its resonance throughout the world impressed Il Duce and his government and offered a way to burnish Fascism's international reputation. Pietro Fedele, the minister of instruction from 1925 to 1928, called the opening of Montessori schools in Rome a "matter of national decorum."[53] Alessandro Marcucci, who was the chief inspector for the Milan school district, argued that she could in fact bring "new credibility" to the Italian education system, demonstrating to other countries the Italian government's desire to implement the Montessori approach in vast cities like Milan as well as the smallest rural schools.[54] That, according to Marcucci, was a "precise mandate [. . .] of the Head of State, of Il Duce of the Italian renaissance," who could see how in Montessori "Italy's name has credit and admiration from all the civilized world."[55] Having given her its full support, Fascist Italy could boast of having such an influential native intellectual.

Along with the benefits that Montessori could bring to the Italian education system, Mussolini wished to use the pedagogue's fame to expand his own influence internationally.[56] He believed that Montessori could become a symbol of the rebirth of the country. In the words of Fedele, the Montessori method had "a very Italian structure" and fostered in children a "real pride, and hence a passion, in being Italian."[57] The same woman who, only a few years before, had been indirectly accused by a government act, the *Istruzioni*, of having created a method that had little to do with the basic characteristics of the Italian child now became a symbol of Italian character— *italianità*—throughout the world.

Montessori's global reputation was useful to the regime in both domestic and international contexts. As the newspaper *La Stampa* reported, "the great expert and Italian educator [. . .] has generated such great interest in her work that the most developed foreign cities, such as Paris, London, and New York, competed to invite her to speak to both families and educators about her methodology."[58] Since Montessori continued to travel extensively and to receive awards, including an honorary doctorate from Durham University, she was suitable for representing the regime within a variety of contexts. Now, in the words of Montessori to Il Duce, "an exquisitely Italian approach could honor the name of the Fatherland throughout the world."[59]

To place her activities in context, Montessori was by no means the only Italian celebrated abroad who was used by the regime to enhance its reputation. According to historian Adrian Lyttelton, Mussolini had appointed Gentile himself precisely for his international standing and thus his capacity to encourage support for Fascism abroad.[60] Similarly, the inventor and engineer Guglielmo Marconi was favored by the regime as one of the most influential intellectuals and was called on by the Italian government to play a key role in the Italian scientific landscape and thereby raise Italy's international prestige.[61]

The Fascist government put in place an "active cultural policy" aimed at supporting intellectuals who would ideologically bolster Fascism.[62] The regime inaugurated an unprecedented series of reforms aimed at providing funds and new social status to intellectuals. Subsidizing artists, scholars, and intellectuals with either a stable monthly income or small subventions over time became a "totalitarian practice."[63] With the creation of unions such as the Confederazione Italiana del Lavoro Intellettuale (Italian Confederation of Intellectual Work) and the Confederazione Nazionale dei Professionisti e Artisti (National Confederation of Professionals and Artists)—whose president, Emilio Bodrero, was also the president of the organization Opera Nazionale Montessori—intellectuals and artists enjoyed generous benefits.[64] The amount of support varied, but at least some scholars and intellectuals

obtained a new "economic tranquility," which allowed them to "give a measure of one's own intelligence," as poet Vincenzo Cardarelli put it.[65]

This is the context in which Montessori attempted to obtain support
from the Fascist government. She had always been a pragmatist when it
came to financing and advancing her work, and the endorsement of the
Italian government must have been personally and deeply appealing. She
had tried for decades to gain recognition in her native country, with fairly
limited success. In 1926, only 4.5 percent of Italian preschools used the
Montessori method.[66] Moreover, Montessori had a dire need for financial
aid. Economic stability and the Italian recognition of her contributions
must have been powerfully, if not irresistibly, enticing.

Years later, her son, Mario Montessori, would recount the money struggles that seemed to have plagued the family for decades: everybody seemed
to want to benefit from the educator's discoveries by sponsoring her initiatives, only to manipulate her and take credit for them. Several "powerful
organizations" and personalities had over the years attempted to collaborate with Maria Montessori, only to abandon her when she insisted that she
could not compromise her work and integrity, leaving her in what she
described as "the most dejected situations," Mario recounted. The choice to
collaborate with the Fascist project was a difficult one, not only in aligning
her work with Fascism, but also for the potential consequences a refusal
might entail. Mario Montessori later explained the collaboration as follows:

> When the organization was of such power—as, let us say for example, the
> Catholic Church, or a Mussolini, a Hitler, a Stalin, at the peak of their
> might—if you, an individual without finances or an organization of your
> own, are offered their mighty help toward power, riches, glory, and you do
> not go with them; then it is the usual story: "If you are not my friend, you
> are my enemy." [. . .]
>
> "WHY, WHY not accept the riches, the world power and glory," as my
> lawyer [. . .] told me in London when I informed him that we had gone away
> from Italy because of our idealism and refused to collaborate with Mussolini."[67]

Montessori's work during the 1920s can, according to her son, be understood
as one attempt in a long quest to find financial stability, a quest that led her
to unlikely partners and sponsors, including Mussolini.

With the benefit of hindsight, Mario described a lifetime of financial
struggles, notwithstanding numerous offers, coming from multiple organizations and governments, throughout the years. Mario's post hoc rational-
ization, however, understates the extent of Montessori's cooperation with

Italian Fascism, at least in the early days. Luisa Lama suggests that Montessori believed the regime's attention to educating infants and youth was genuine, and Lama points to the possibility that Montessori could have seen, in Fascism, the potential for realizing the "century of the child."[68] Indeed, the year that Montessori was named an honorary member of the Fascist Party— her only formal political affiliation—was also the year the regime founded the Opera Nazionale Balilla, the youth organization tasked with spreading Fascist political and military education.[69] The importance of education reform within the Fascist narrative, and its emphasis on physical education, might well have appealed to a woman who had tried to push the Italian political agenda in this direction for decades.

This interpretation, however, does not take into account the fact that Montessori was intelligent and experienced enough to evaluate the content of the Fascist educational programs. It is unlikely that she would have failed to recognize that the regime's goal was to indoctrinate children rather than to educate them to freedom. Even if one accepts the dubious contention that Montessori did not see a fundamental conflict between her method and the goals of Fascist educational policy, it is difficult to imagine that the regime's mounting violence, and the 1924 murder of socialist politician Giacomo Matteotti, would not have alarmed her. After this event, other pedagogues such as Lombardo Radice argued that serving in the current administration "would have meant . . . living a lie," compelling them to sever connections with the Fascist Party.[70] But it did not for Montessori. At least not at that point.

What convinced her of the incompatibility between her work and Fascism was probably a change in the educational landscape. As scholarship on the education system under Fascism has demonstrated, over the course of the 1920s a gradual Fascistization (the process of conforming to Fascist ideology) took place. In particular, the adoption of a state-mandated national textbook (*testo unico di stato*) for elementary grades in 1929, deep changes to the curricula for the purpose of producing a "Fascist regeneration" in 1930, and the transformation of the Ministry of Public Instruction into the Ministry of National Education all entailed increasing governmental control over the educational content and approach given to the students.[71] To any keen political observer, these changes would not have gone unnoticed—and, in fact, the beginning of Montessori's split from Mussolini was not far off.

Montessori's cooperation with Mussolini worked for a time and gave her some hope that her method would spread in her native country. However, when the secretary of the Fascist Party changed with the nomination of Achille Starace in 1931, the Fascistization of the schools quickened, making it necessary for the regime to control Montessori institutions. With these shifts began a new paradigm that sought to educate the child according to the principles of Fascist doctrine. Shortly thereafter, the favoritism that Montessori had enjoyed began to wane.

The change in the government's stance toward Montessori can be seen in two instances in which the educator dealt with the regime directly, and which follow the ongoing Fascistization of the scholastic system. On April 4, 1927, Montessori sent the letter to Mussolini that was quoted at the beginning of this chapter; she lamented the fact that to train teachers in the method she had developed in Italy, she was forced to go to London, thus "distancing [herself] from [her] homeland to teach what is well known to have been born in Rome."[72] To continue her work in her native country, she explained, she needed more financial and institutional support. She concluded her letter by requesting funds from Mussolini for a study center in Rome—a request that the head of government immediately satisfied by opening a Montessori school for teacher training and by financing the magazine *L'idea Montessori*, an official part of the Opera Nazionale Montessori. At the end of the same year, Mussolini presented a decree for the establishment of another center for training teachers in the Monte Mario neighborhood, to be opened in January 1929. During the inauguration ceremony of this second center, Montessori professed her own noninvolvement in politics. Her interest was restricted to the child, she said, asserting that "we are here not for the work of a person, nor author of a specific text" and that her audience had convened "only in the hope of doing even better for the children, believing that one can succeed by following the best ways to ameliorate the lives of children."[73] She claimed publicly that she was working without any real political ties, and that she only cared for the child. The self-proclaimed *povera signora*, insisting she "had reached an age in which people normally rest," responded with an almost timid "respect my silence" to the numerous compliments that her method received at the ceremony.[74]

In this speech, we see the beginning of Montessori's retreat from her acceptance (however tacit) of the regime's backing. The imposition of religious education and fascist culture, and the progressive changes in the scholastic system, had over time tested her willingness to receive help. What began here as a timid declaration of sole commitment to the child, and an intention to stay above the politics of Fascism after the 1920s, slowly became a firm stance toward understanding childhood as the crucial period in which an attitude toward peace could be developed, and ultimately a disavowal of the deepest principle of Fascism: an insistence on grooming youth to fight for the regime.

Giovanni Gentile's inaugural speech, XVI Montessori Training Course, Rome, 1931.
Seated from left: Maria Montessori, Balbino Giuliano (minister of national education),
and Boncompagni Ludovisi (governor of Rome). Speaker standing at table is Senator
Gentile. Courtesy of Opera Nazionale Montessori, Rome.

As one might expect, Montessori's relationship with the regime started
fracturing after this point. Increasingly, over the next few years, the Fascist
police investigated her activities, and there were many anonymous accusations of antifascism reported to the police against Montessorian teachers.
Among these anonymous letters and notes, one suggested a "Montessori-
anism without Montessori." The writer contended that because the presence of Montessori "would not guarantee the [Fascist] faith of the school, it
is necessary to find the courage to transform the Montessori school into a
Montessori type of school, eliminating the *dottoressa*," and that a version of
the approach without Montessori's "greed, instability, vindictive fits and
ambiguous faith" would eventually be easier to bend to the requirements of
the regime.[75]
     Over the course of the 1930s, the pedagogue slowly abandoned her
declared political neutrality, which had marked the previous years. Montessori confirmed her decision to return to the broader mission of international
peace when she expressed her own pacifist views to the League of Nations
in the first months of 1932.[76] Mussolini clearly could not accept the independence of a strong personality that was so little disposed to collaborate.

During the 1920s, Montessori had already discreetly maintained a communication network with pacifists and liberal organizations by sending her closest collaborators to attend international gatherings. She witnessed the radical transformation of the debate on children's rights from afar, probably thinking about her next steps, which she would so forcefully undertake in the 1930s. This maze of connections and acquaintances, conferences, private correspondences, and mission statements allowed Montessori to continue her international work for the welfare of the child and to believe in the promotion of peace and understanding through education. These principles contradicted those of the Fascist regime and eventually brought the collaboration to an end.

A Missed Chance for Montessori

In the aftermath of World War I, children came to be seen as primary instruments in the promotion of peace. Organizations and intellectuals from diverse fields of study argued that a peaceful future was intertwined with the future of children. Postwar reconstruction was to begin in the crib. This notion had extensive ramifications in the interconnected fields of humanitarianism, children's rights, and pedagogy. Montessori had contributed extensively to all of them. And yet throughout the 1920s, the Italian educator did not take the lead, nor participate directly, in this shift. While Montessori focused her efforts on developing her pedagogy under the support of an increasingly nationalistic and authoritarian government—leading her to retreat from public engagement on children affected by war—new actors and organizations brought about seminal changes within the field of children's rights, and within education as a tool to foster peace. Occupied as she was with spreading her pedagogy within Italy and constrained in her ability to speak on some of these issues, Montessori did not actively participate in most of these developments. That is not to say that she was not engaged with these discussions and new movements. She actively monitored new developments and was deeply interested in them. But only when her relationship with the Fascist regime broke down did she reemerge as a central figure in international pacifism.

The dire conditions facing children throughout Europe called for new types of interventions. Devastation and famine had not ended with the signing of the armistice in November 1918. At the heart of Europe, children were still suffering. The years of conflict had deeply scarred the continent and created a profound humanitarian crisis, leaving millions starved, homeless, and orphaned. Diseases spiked: malaria and typhus surged to alarming levels. The two-year influenza pandemic that had emerged at the beginning of 1918 caused millions of deaths worldwide. Within this climate, social workers, pacifist volunteers, and educators pleaded for international cooperation, especially in protecting children and their rights. Their pleas were strengthened by the hundreds of thousands of child refugees, orphans, and displaced minors created by the war, which warranted international intervention in the eyes of the public.[77] Children's welfare could be presented as a nonpartisan issue, one that was unlikely to disrupt the fragile postwar equilibrium, which was otherwise fueled by xenophobia and public distrust of internationalism. As historian Dominique Marshall argues, "sympathy" toward children helped steer movements that had been created to address wartime issues toward international cooperation in peacetime.[78]

The issue of protecting the child in need therefore became an apolitical priority for organizations that intended to expand humanitarian action beyond national boundaries. Governments and voluntary agencies focused their work on ending children's suffering in the hope of inspiring a sense of duty and therefore triggering broader humanitarian action. The war-affected child represented neutral ground, a new point of departure for the devastated European continent—a starting point for renewed cooperation, a way to heal some of the deep fractures. As a result, many international organizations in favor of children's rights thrived in the postwar era. This surge of interest came to constitute "a brave new world of international organizations," aimed at promoting the health and welfare of society's most vulnerable members.[79]

In this new environment, confederations, associations, and committees mostly worked under the intergovernmental organization the League of Nations—specifically, within the Social Section of the league, which became a hub for transnational institutions.[80] The league, founded in 1919 by the Versailles peace conference in order to foster worldwide security, took over many of the prewar initiatives serving children's welfare.[81] The hub of organizations that rotated around the league had transformed and reorganized the transnational sphere, making it more dynamic and creating an intricate web of welfare initiatives.[82]

Amid the rising tide of internationalism, organizations such as the Save the Children Fund were able to set aside the divisions of the Great War to engage in "constructive philanthropy and reparative nation-building."[83] The emphasis on these issues led to great victories, chief among which was the 1922 landmark Declaration of the Rights of the Child, adopted by the League of Nations in 1924 as an affirmation of its commitment to protect children's economic, social, and psychological needs throughout its member nations.

As a result, the Child Welfare Committee was created to establish norms, draw up reports, organize conferences, and promote the implementation of new organizations to foster child welfare.[84]

The surge of interest in child protection during the interwar period did not occur in a vacuum. These organizations integrated an established, ongoing tradition of activism, dating back to turn-of-the-century philanthropy, that had transformed the relationship among children, family life, and public institutions. In the preceding decades, a transnational discussion about the rights of children had influenced domestic reforms, but these efforts remained national in scope. During the so-called *sortie de guerre*, domestic reforms took on Wilsonian principles of promoting peace and security among countries through reparative interventions.[85] Every single nation needed to achieve political and social stability for continental peace to prosper. In this climate, humanitarians sought "to shift the responsibility for child welfare into the international arena," thereby "expand[ing the] ethic of collective responsibility" beyond national boundaries.[86]

The Declaration of the Rights of the Child was drafted within this climate of collaboration, during a moment in which the entire international community took an interest in protecting youth, adolescence, and childhood. Drafting the charter involved many highly trained educators, social workers, and humanitarians from child welfare organizations, all of whom were connected to a committee led by Save the Children International Union (SCIU) volunteer Victoria de Bunsen. The declaration was the product of a vital conversation among diverse actors and associations, including the International Council of Women (IWC).[87] For instance, the IWC's president, Lady Ishbel, Marchioness of Aberdeen and Temair—an old acquaintance of Montessori from the IWC conference in 1899—had the goal of rebuilding the organization in the postwar years by depoliticizing it and focusing on drafting a children's charter, which eventually came to be part of the final version of the declaration.[88] The document was ultimately drafted by SCIU founder Eglantyne Jebb.

The declaration contained many elements that were to become influential to later children's rights activists such as Montessori herself. First and foremost, it incorporated a call to foster children's spiritual development, highlighting their need for moral and emotional support in time of distress. It established the principle of "children first" for receiving relief in emergencies, paving the way for an axiom that is now universally accepted and breaking with a tradition of considering noncombatants and the weakest members of the population as a government's least valuable and most expendable citizens.[89] It also brought up the principle of universality, according to which all children—regardless of nationality, faith, race, or any other characteristic—were entitled to protection. At a time when antipatriotism could result in imprisonment, this document took a courageous stand. Article 4 "evoked a right to protection," distinguishing the child as being vulnerable to exploitation and therefore in need of being protected.[90] The last article of the declaration stated that "the child must be brought to a consciousness that his talents must be devoted to the services of his fellow man"; its utopian tone was typical of the early days of the League of Nations, though it did not actually describe a particular right possessed by children.[91]

From a political standpoint, the declaration failed to inspire effective action, yet it marked the first international agreement on fundamental rights for children. Adopted by the League of Nations in 1924 in what Susan Pedersen defines "the most striking example of such humanitarian entre- preneurialism," the document commonly known as the Geneva Declara- tion of the Rights of the Child was not binding for member states, which were only invited to follow its principles.[92] No obligations were attached to its acceptance; it outlined the rights of each child to a normal development but did not require particular steps to ensure them. Though revolutionary, the document "was [also] principally concerned with the provision of children's economic, social, and psychological needs."[93] Like the organ- ization that promoted it, the League of Nations, "it was a radical departure from the past, [and] in other ways it fitted squarely into an earlier Victorian tradition of Great Power paternalism."[94] It followed a pattern throughout Europe in the first decades of the twentieth century, in that it was devoted to the traditional areas of prevention, protection, and provision for children. Yet while it did not include the term "human rights" or "children's rights," the declaration showed an implicit concern with respect for the inherent dignity and worth of each single human being.[95]

The declaration echoed Montessori's emphasis on the child's individual capacities and the necessity of connecting with the world in exercising one's own freedom. It was divided into two parts: what society owed the child and, in the final statements, what the child would give back as an adult. It therefore contained both mutual aid and social responsibility for the child, central principles in Montessori's conception of child welfare. It also recalled many of the main points put forward in Montessori's earlier writ- ings. For example, the first point of the resolution, titled "Prenatal Care," demanded "instruction in sexual hygiene for boys and girls by specially trained teachers," to prevent the spread of venereal diseases.[96] Nurses and midwives were to instruct pregnant women, who would be forbidden by law to work six weeks before and after delivery. Medical care had to be free and available during the breastfeeding period, and couples about to marry had to show their responsibility to the next generation by attending courses on childbearing and child-rearing—a goal that recalls Montessori's *La morale sessuale nell'educazione*, a speech she had delivered in 1908 at the Congresso Nazionale delle Donne Italiane (Italian Women's National Congress).[97] Broadly, the document synthesized various schools of thought, from fields as diverse as psychiatry, early childhood education, and welfare rights advocacy, speaking to a wide audience of specialists and making social action toward all children the responsibility of all nations.

Several organizations that advocated for children's rights argued for a direct connection between a child's development and growth, and the spreading of peace. Close to the spirit of the League of Nations, nongovernmental agencies such as the Brussels-based Union of International Associations, the Geneva Jean-Jacques Rousseau Institute, the IBE (founded in 1925 by the governing board of the Rousseau Institute), and the League of Nations' International Committee on Intellectual Cooperation gave considerable momentum to the spread of peace education. In particular, the IBE, where "the Montessori pedagogy circulated concurrently with explicit pacifist proposals," became a hub for the conversation on this issue.[98] The institution's purpose was sanctioned in 1927 by an international conference, titled Peace by the School.[99] There, IBE convened delegates from various international education societies, peace organizations, and League of Nations agencies. They met in Prague, under the auspices of the Czechoslovakian government, to discuss the theme of education for peace, to bolster "the set of psychological conditions that favor the emergence of pacifist and internationalist behaviors, as well as the eradication of the prejudices that oppose them."[100] From 1925 to 1929, the organization was directed by Pierre Bovet, who had written the preface to the Swiss edition of *Il Metodo*; among its founding members were pedagogue Adolphe Ferrière and peace activist and educational progressive Elisabeth Rotten.

While Montessori was not a vocal participant in these processes, she was careful to stay abreast of developments. Within the nebula of organizations that constituted the conversation on peace and education in the 1920s, both the IBE and the New Education Fellowship (NEF), a movement with Theosophical roots that connected educational reformists and major scholars in the disciplines of pedagogy and psychology, were the main links between Montessori and the international world of education. These connections—namely, to Bovet, Ferrière, Rotten, and the NEF's Beatrice Ensor—allowed the educator to monitor the debates of the time and to gestate her future work.

Deeply embedded in the intricate web of experts, these two organizations shared many scholars, debated similar issues, and ultimately worked to create a "transnational sphere" of exchange.[101] The NEF—based on the notion that education had to be reformed to spur change—had ramifications throughout continental Europe and the United States. The goal of the organization, established in 1915 by Ensor as the Theosophical Fraternity to Education, was to prepare humankind for the new demands of a changing world; it emphasized internationalism and cooperation among nations. Since its inception, the NEF had maintained strong ties to Montessori. It was born through a collaboration with the organizers of the New Ideals in Education conferences, chief among whom was Edmond Holmes, head of the English Montessori Society.[102] Toning down its Theosophical roots in the 1920s, the organization changed its name to NEF to expand its reach and brought together seminal thinkers in the field through seven international conferences.[103]

Though the three executive committee members of the NEF—Ensor, Rotten, and Ferrière—came from very different backgrounds, they shared the conviction that an education that encouraged children to think independently and fostered their development as whole human beings would be an instrument for peace and international harmony.[104] Prominent supporters of the New Education movement, they continued to collaborate with the Italian educator in the interwar years, seeing education as the most important tool to bolster a rebirth of the wounded continent. Indeed, they assigned children the mission of fostering peace and emphasized the role that educators had in creating a pedagogy that would make this possible. Broadly, the organization's principles and aims coincided with Montessori's central tenets, especially when it came to the role of education in shaping self-reliant, self-disciplined children who would also be free to express themselves and to develop a scientific spirit of inquiry.[105] It drew attention to the necessity of creating "world citizens [which was] as important for the safety of modern civilization as the creation of national citizens."[106] To this end, the NEF attempted to intervene in government-run educational programs that were deemed to violate certain basic tenets of morality.[107] As argued in an editorial in one of NEF's official journals, *Pour l'ère nouvelle*, "When it comes to peace, we do not mean only the negation of armed conflict among nations, but the cessation of hatred among races, and of the injustices within the nations themselves, where children are unleashed against one another."[108] This educational paradigm ushered new models of freedom for the child—namely, the principle of self-education, and pacifism itself.

Through the 1920s and early 1930s, NEF conferences served as the occasion for most of Montessori's international lectures and training courses. As a recurrent platform for her work outside Italy in the interwar period, the organization and its three journals—the French *Pour l'ère nouvelle*, directed by Férriere; the German *Das Werdende Zeitalter*, directed by Rotten; the English *The New Era*, directed by Ensor—became a privileged site for debating Montessori's work, making it visible to educators, psychologists, and social workers invested in promoting peace through education.

The founding event of the organization, the Calais conference of 1921, sheds light on Montessori's place within the hub of educators, intellectuals, and progressive thinkers. Steeped in the climate of the postwar reconstruction through education, the summer school convened such experts from the New Education movement as Ovide Decroly, who had also been engaged in the rehabilitation of war orphans at Le Foyer des Orphelins.[109] As reported by Ensor in *Pour l'ère nouvelle*, among those who were supposed to attend were Montessori-trained teacher Mary Rebecca Cromwell, who had worked with Montessori on the education of children affected by war; Anna Maria Maccheroni, who was replaced in the conference by Claude Claremont, director of the Montessori training courses in London and Cranleigh; and a Mademoiselle Stiernon, a Montessori teacher.[110] But, as a report on the congress by the *Revue Pédagogique* stated, "nowadays, we are all more or less faithful Montessorians," even though Montessori herself was not present.[111] In addition to the two presentations by Montessorians, the attendees visited a small Montessori school, which was still housed in a barracks among the ruins of the village of Bailleul, an area devastated by the war.[112] Montessori's presence also pervaded the issue of *Pour l'ère nouvelle* that followed the conference. Among the signatories of the nascent organizations listed in the periodical were Montessori's collaborators Giulio Cesare Ferrari and Augusto Osimo, who had worked with the educator through the Società Umanitaria. Furthermore, her method was extensively featured in its articles, one by Ferrari, and one by progressive educator Roger Cousinet, who stated that his organization *La nouvelle éducation*'s mission was "a continuation of Mrs. Montessori's work, simply because one of the main merits of her pedagogy has been the creation, via the Montessorian material, of the most appropriate milieu for the mental development of the little children."[113] Broadly, the journal was a platform for a "network of women trained in Montessori in international courses" who extensively published in the journal itself, spread Montessori's work, and ran some articles by Montessori herself.[114] The wide international recognition given by the hub of educators maintained Montessori's name at the forefront of the debate on peace and education, and because her own disciples were in attendance, she was kept abreast of the conversation at hand.

Yet Montessori seemed disengaged from this array of educators and humanitarians, who credited her as foundational to their own work in the New Education movement. The unusual reservation that surfaces in her letters to Mussolini is confirmed by long-term colleague Adolphe Ferrière, who, after a visit to Montessori schools in Milan in 1926, stated in his personal journal on April 29 that "the impression [Montessori] made on me has changed. She seems less womanly, and more lady-like than I believed; an elegance of a simple queen, an almost detached but enigmatic smile; with a self-possession that puts a veil on passions."[115] In a report in *Pour l'ère nouvelle*, Ferrière conveyed this impression to his readership, explaining the new reserved attitude: Ferrière recognized that few people were as famous as Montessori, but also that "few people have been able to get in touch with her," since she refrained from attending conferences. Ferrière gives a possible justification by saying that "she loves to listen [. . .] not to speak. She loathes conversation."[116] And listen she did. This demure attitude would soon be replaced by a series of public engagements in which she spoke about peace education.

Evidence of this slow shift back to a lively international public presence can be seen in her development of a Montessori Training Course with the NEF conference in Elsinore, Denmark, in 1929. Among the many educators present were Jean Piaget, who spoke about moral judgment in children, and Helen Parkhurst, who gave a lecture on the Dalton Plan. Montessori's talk was more of a summary of her child-centered approach, but she spurred the audience to seek "a quest [. . .] to change [. . .] society so as to make it more open, more responsive to the needs of [citizens with] balanced personalities."[117] The jargon of her future lectures on peace was starting to come together in front of a receptive audience.

Conclusion

The Fascist government officially recognized and celebrated Montessori's international fame and worked to establish her schools throughout the country. For her part, Montessori continued to profess a distance from politics and failed to acknowledge the mounting violence that was sweeping the country. Her decade-long quest to engage with the major pedagogical forces at play in Italian society, namely philosophical idealists and Catholic intellectuals, did not yield the support the educator had hoped to receive. Eventually, the government's interference in the organization of her training course and selection of personnel became unmanageable, straining their relationship to the breaking point. The creeping Fascistization of the Italian school system and the attempts to alter Montessori's process brought the collaboration to an end.

The center of gravity for her work could not be Rome. Between the end of the 1920s and the beginning of the 1930s, Montessori started accepting more and more engagements outside of Italy, moving the bulk of her operations abroad. During this period, the Montessori family travelled extensively to hold training courses in Vienna, Dublin, and London, to name a few cities. She eventually relocated to Barcelona, until the outbreak of the Spanish Civil War pushed the Montessori family to leave again. Meanwhile, the Association Montessori Internationale had been promoting her method internationally. Its headquarters were first in Berlin, but by the time it moved to Amsterdam in 1935, Montessori decided to make the city her home, in large part because her methodology was growing rapidly throughout the Netherlands.

Montessori's work outside of Italy during the 1920s helped her maintain a steady relationship with intellectuals, educators, humanitarians, and social organizers throughout Europe, all involved in promoting international cooperation, peace, and understanding through education. Despite not participating directly in these conversations in the aftermath of the Great War, Montessori weaved a close-knit web of relationships with organizations in favor of promoting peace through education. This "humanitarian moment," during which collective hopes for human rights legislation became reality, provided Montessori with a springboard for her subsequent work on children's rights. In fact, strengthened by her decade of silence and propelled by the extensive debate on children's rights, her first public speeches on peace, between 1932 and 1939, ushered in a new paradigm of children's welfare, whereby the child would be understood to possess rights and not simply be regarded as a defenseless human being in need of protection.

CHAPTER 5

Montessori's First Public Lectures on Peace, 1932–1939

During the 1930s, Maria Montessori's reflections on peace were formulated in a series of international public forums that she participated in while dividing her time between Rome and Barcelona.[1] In her public speeches, the educator's message was stronger and tighter than in her earlier unpublished lectures, and the connection between the moral and political growth of the individual had become more apparent. Montessori was dismayed by the impact of totalitarian regimes on international organizations: the disempowerment of networks of child welfare experts, the disenfranchisement of transnational advocacy groups, and the boycotting of leagues' meetings. Despite the obstacles posed by the political climate, Montessori was able to find a new voice and, over time, to elaborate direct criticisms of totalitarian regimes.

Through the first half of the decade, Montessori struggled to keep alive the very institutions that she had developed in Italy with the help of the Fascist government, while also directly collaborating with transnational organizations dedicated to peaceful dialogue among nations. It is clear that she felt silenced under the regime, and in fact she would leave Italy in 1934, abandoning all the activities and institutions that bear her name. Her participation in pacifist and humanitarian conferences and her collaborations with pacifist organizations, as well as the pressure from Fascist hierarchies to control her work, caused her to terminate her relationship with the regime. Her public speeches openly declared an interest in pacifism and in radically reforming humanity through education. This message thrived in nondogmatic contexts where she could finally be applauded for both her pedagogical work and her social endeavors.

All in all, the educator's speeches in the 1930s called for a regeneration of the educational system, with the aim of supporting the emotional, spiritual, and physical growth of the child into a healthy adult. The tools to achieve this drastic change had, however, become more specific, in Montessori's view. Humankind was in a state of "moral paralysis"; people were guided by an "insidious madness."[2] Education would solve the current situation and improve the "social status of children," for "never had law so forgotten the rights of man as when that man was a child."[3] The lectures Montessori delivered on pacifism in the 1930s were the foundations of an organic vision of the child. Connected to society through his own labor, this child would, in turn, transform society and, in spreading outward, humankind as a whole.

These series of works can be read as building blocks with which Montessori learned to own her voice and contributed to the public conversation on pacifism and humanitarian action. Up to 1936, the year of the last significant report on her by the Fascist Political Police, Montessori offered only veiled commentary on the political situation. Her tone was subdued, her references to current events were vague, and the rise of nationalism was never mentioned directly. Despite continuous interference from the Fascist regime, she continued to speak about peace, and during this period she developed many of her ideas. Though it was only after 1936, while on pilgrimage throughout Europe preaching for peace, that her voice on these issues became stronger and her advocacy free from constriction, the groundwork had already been laid.

Montessori's 1932 Speeches and Articles

When Montessori returned to discussing peace, she did so by leaning on organizations and intellectuals with whom she was already familiar. Her first public speech was delivered in Nice in 1932, at the invitation of the International Bureau of Education (IBE), which was connected to a vast array of organizations including the New Education Fellowship (NEF), the International Peace Bureau, and, at the intergovernmental level, the League of Nations.[4] Relying on the "vitality of networks during the interwar years," the pedagogue took advantage of the groundwork these associations had laid over the course of the previous decade, as she capitalized on networks constructed by colleagues and friends such as Pierre Bovet, Édouard Claparède, Adolphe Ferrière, and Elisabeth Rotten.[5] As a result, she reentered the conversation on pacifism as if she had never left it.

At the time of the speech, the IBE had become a beacon for scholars interested in achieving peace through education. Its chair, developmental psychologist Jean Piaget, part of the "new generation" of IBE scholars, had spoken in favor of peace at the NEF's sixth world conference in 1932 and would continue to do so throughout the 1930s.[6] When it came to education as a tool to achieve peace, Piaget shared much with Montessori. An opponent of neo-Darwinism, Piaget believed that love and altruism—and not their negation, war—were inherent to humanity. A child's innate tendency toward goodness was corrupted by other human beings, who exposed him to the concept of war. Therefore, according to Piaget, "to struggle against war is to act according to the logic of life against the logic of things, and that is the whole of morality."[7] The "diplomat of education" also maintained that teaching international cooperation and writing more just and balanced history textbooks—the two major initiatives undertaken by the League of Nations' International Committee on Intellectual Co-Operation and by the IBE—were not enough, for they did not foster the intellectual and moral growth necessary to propel genuine and altruistic collaboration.[8] So far, argued Piaget, "the aim was much more to fill the minds of students with the same variety of international mystique and to provide them with ready-made options regarding the League of Nations than to bring out in depth the intellectual and moral tendencies conducive to true collaboration." Education was to be reformed at a national level and, thus, lead a global readjustment.[9]

Broadly, Montessori's 1932 speech was in line with the goals of the IBE, which hosted many like-minded scholars. She called for a new organization that would prepare individuals to be responsible citizens and active members of a civically conscious society; there must be a moral organization of the masses in which people would be brought up to regard themselves as part of a greater community. Montessori proposed a transformation of the way people understood and engaged with the public sphere. Human beings needed to connect with one another, and it was the duty of adults to collectively promote peace. Human strengths had to be reorganized and channeled toward the creation of a new kind of person.

An "epoch of miracles" was about to begin, if humankind's potential could be reformed.[10] With that phrase, Montessori the scientist, the doctor, and the anthropologist was probably referring to the numerous discoveries that characterized the first decades of the twentieth century, such as Albert Einstein's theories of relativity and Guglielmo Marconi's wireless telegraphy.[11] As a woman of science herself, she claimed that science had to spur change and that education was the tool to do so. With a new kind of education, one geared toward enhancing children's potential, a new generation would emerge. Montessori warned, however, "If man remains earthbound and unconscious of the new realities, if he uses the energies of space for the purpose of destroying himself, he will soon attain that goal, for the energies now at his disposal are immeasurable and accessible to everyone, at all times and in every corner of the earth." In her view, humanity was at a crossroads.

Technology had become so powerful that humankind faced a stark choice between self-renewal or continuing down the road of violence, greed, and consumption. The latter was tantamount to self-destruction and, therefore, it would be necessary for humans to develop in a healthier way to survive this new era and fully develop their potential. The solution would be the child, exposed to a new educational system that promoted harmony. This new type of child would be regarded "as a messiah, as a savior capable of regenerating the human race and society."[12]

According to Montessori, there was an ongoing war between the adult and the child, given that the adult used his power to mold the child. This happened both within the family and within the school. Therefore, the child could not accomplish what Montessori called her "spiritual gestation," or her moral growth. Her great capabilities would be instead suppressed, forcing her to conform to the expectations of adulthood. And when, in this delicate moment of the child's life, this form of "enslavement" is committed, "the seeds of life will become sterile, and it will no longer be possible for men to carry out the great works that life has summoned them to perform."[13] Current school pedagogies that demanded obedience from the student and punished mistakes with public humiliation were exactly the wrong approach, she argued:

> These many [. . .] kinds of conditioning [. . .] lead to a sense of inferiority, opening the spirit to unthinking respect, and indeed most mindless idolatry, in the minds of paralyzed adults toward public leaders, who come to represent the surrogate teachers and fathers, figures upon whom the child was forced to look as perfect and infallible. And discipline thus becomes almost synonymous with slavery.[14]

For Montessori, overweening authority and misdirected classroom discipline had clear parallels with totalitarianism. This stance signaled the beginning of the educator's critique. Montessori believed that misplaced admiration of and deference toward authority—whether it had to do with classroom discipline, the relationship between the child and the adult, or the lack of confidence that often affected young adults—was a critical problem. This feeling resulted from the "obedience forced upon a child."[15] Children, and later adults, did not have the means to rebel against imposing figures (e.g., the father, the teacher).

Montessori's criticism could be read as an indictment of Mussolini, the metaphorical father/teacher of the nation who imposed his will on the students/children (or citizens), suppressing their instincts. In the same speech, she also commented extensively on the lack of collegiality among students, a behavior that was encouraged by a system in which "if [the child] spied on or denounced others, he [is] met with tolerance."[16] A clear denunciation of Mussolini's culture of fear, the statement described a society in a constant state of surveillance, where people were stripped of their basic freedoms and encouraged to report those who did not conform to the regime's dictates. In her view, the classroom had become a microcosm of Italian society.

Montessori was not alone in critiquing authoritarianism as reflected within the classroom and the family. As argued by historian Celia Jenkins, post–World War I democratic reconstruction centered its rhetoric on a strong critique of authoritarianism, holding governmental educational systems responsible for the children's failure to reject war.[17] This became a recurrent theme in editorials throughout the 1920s. Journals such as the NEF's *New Era* extensively debated this topic, denouncing an aggressive and nationalistic mentality that permeated the public sphere so much so that it reached the school environment. Also problematic was the punitive father who used physical violence and commanded through fear—an archetype analogous to any authoritarian, from Il Duce to a despotic teacher. Calling for a pedagogy of emancipation, authors such as NEF chair Beatrice Ensor questioned the inculcation of blind obedience in children and dismissed the use by past governments of "arbitrary authority, which implied both arbitrary discipline and arbitrary suppression," inspiring Montessori's inquiries into peace.[18]

Notably, the lecture's hopeful proclamations of technological accomplishments are accompanied by an overall tone of dismay and stern warnings about the current state of European affairs. Although Montessori did not explicitly condemn Mussolini or Italian Fascism, limiting her lecture to the problems of overly hierarchical classroom or familial relations, her linkage of "discipline" and "obedience" with slavery was sharply critical of excessive authority. The commentary, however, remained on a social rather than political level, as Montessori was attempting to remain somewhat circumspect. She was, after all, still struggling to receive governmental support in her native country.

Indeed, the Fascist regime reacted to this speech very critically. Montessori sent a copy of her lecture to Mussolini via her collaborator Giuliana Sorge, prior to the conference.[19] Though Il Duce did not comment directly, he commissioned the president of the Opera Nazionale Montessori (ONM), Emilio Bodrero, to attend the lecture in Geneva and write a report.[20] Bodrero disparaged Montessori by depicting her as an unscrupulous social climber in search of new supporters for her projects. In his account, the application of the Montessori method to peace was an oversimplification of her curriculum, which itself was "grotesque and puerile," and he further intimated that her method was only made to appear peace-related so that she might join the conference and gain additional support.[21] He argued that, in fact, the Montessori method hardly fostered peace within the classroom and that the educator's interest in peace was only momentary. He went on to assert that a proper education should instill the "principle of war"; as evidence, he noted that he could not think of any game for children that did not symbolize or imitate war. Further, Bodrero declared that all members of humankind structured interpersonal relations on emulation of one another, and since every action contained the principle of war, it followed that every human relation was based on war. Bodrero also reported that the assembly greeted Montessori by cheering, "Hurray for Montessori, down with Fascism!"[22]

Bodrero was not the only one appointed by the regime to report on the Italian educator. The Organization for Vigilance and Repression of Anti-Fascism (OVRA) sent one of Montessori's inveterate opponents to spy on her: Monsignor Umberto Benigni, known as Spy Number 42.[23] Benigni was the very same prelate who had prevented Montessori's letters about the White Cross from reaching Pope Benedict XV.[24] According to Benigni, the method was "nothing but spiritually antifascist," and the government had to "shut Montessori's enterprise down." In his view, Montessori, a *"malafemmina"* (woman of ill repute), was not to be trusted.[25]

For the regime, several parts of the speech were problematic. According to Montessori, the regenerated human being would call for an equal redistribution of all wealth among nations and their citizens, "rather than the patrimony of one country," to create an environment "that [. . .] will set no limits on man's boundless aspirations."[26] Greed drove the morally crippled human being to engage in war; hence, redistributing wealth among the nations was necessary to prevent conflict. Furthermore, Montessori stated that if earthly resources could be parceled out equally, humanity would have no need for borders, and nations would have no basis to claim territorial rights. People had to resort to resources such as solar energy that were theoretically available to everyone.

At the same time that Mussolini was calling for the abnegation of the individual in favor of the state, Montessori's evolving pacifist ideology was anticipating the withering away of national borders.[27] Clearly, the educator's plan was opposed to both the Fascist project generally and the strategy of colonial expansion specifically, both within the territories acquired by Liberal governments in the Adriatic Sea as well as through the robust repression of Libyan and Somali revolts. In addition to occupying a central place in the political discourse, the virulent rhetoric surrounding the colonial enterprises had permeated textbooks and school programs. It was becoming apparent that the Fascist regime and Montessori had irreconcilable differences.

Around the time of her speech, Montessori published an article in the NEF's *New Era* titled "Disarmament in Education," lamenting "a state of warfare" in child development in which the "teacher is often the persecutor of the child," and "fathers and mothers are dictators, judges from whom there is no possible appeal."[28] The article gave the educator a venue that reached an international audience of educators and political activists.

The topic capitalized on a heated debate that was taking place among numerous international organizations and that culminated in a conference on arms reduction at the League of Nations in 1932. Galvanized by the 1928 ratification of the Kellogg-Briand Pact, which barred war as an instrument of foreign policy, nationally based disarmament campaigns achieved a transnational dimension thanks to "the establishment of *super*-international and non-governmental organizations [. . .], the staging of a massive unofficial World Disarmament Conference in Paris, and the circulation of arguably the largest petition in history."[29] The debate on disarmament preceding the conference stirred a conversation that involved exploratory committees and preliminary conferences to debate possible proposals. The suggestions came from the most disparate associations, from student organizations such as the World Alliance of YMCAs and World YWCA, to religious groups such as the Universal Christian Council on Life and Work. Among the participants, the Women's International League for Peace and Freedom compiled a manifesto on disarmament that, citing "scientists and technicians" from all over the world, requested the "peoples of the world [to] unite and testify [their] desire for peace by demanding universal disarmament" and recommended the renunciation of war as a tool for international politics while adopting peaceful means to settle international disputes.[30]

The League of Nations hosted the World Disarmament Conference, which met intermittently from February 1932 to June 1934, when it was readjourned sine die. This long-awaited event involved representatives of sixty countries, among which were Russia and the United States; for many, this conference presented the last chance to prevent another war on a global scale. From the start, the event was overshadowed by the depressed global economy and the growing ultranationalist movements in Italy and Germany. Disarmament was of crucial importance for all the intellectuals and politicians who believed in the league's mission. This issue had dominated the organization's debates and resources since its inception. The arms race preceding the First World War was considered a critical factor in the escalation of violence during that war. Reducing national armaments was therefore included as one of the articles of the league's covenant and continued to be a central point for the organization.

At the conference, the notion of disarmament was approached at large. Albert Einstein, for example, who intervened on May 23, 1932, to restart the sessions that seemed to be on the verge of stalling, criticized national governments for their inability to implement both material and moral disarmament. He argued that the promotion of both forms of disarmament had to occur concurrently and ultimately could not be spearheaded by national governments. As nation-states had failed to relinquish their sovereignty, a condition to a reduction of their armies, and had heretofore resisted an intellectual renunciation to war, they were clearly incapable of leading an effort toward global disarmament. Consequently, Einstein argued that "intellectually and morally independent people" had the duty to demand "a complete disarmament within five years" and to renounce "all methods of warfare under any circumstances."[31]

Disarmament through education, or moral disarmament, was also a core issue.[32] This notion had been debated throughout the 1920s across the Continent along two main viewpoints. The pacifist one emphasized "the transformation of the aggressive, vindictive and revengeful mentality into a conciliatory one."[33] It was believed that this would lead to a drastic change in society's value system. A notable champion of this viewpoint was Caroline Playne, a council member of the International Peace Bureau. Philosopher Théodore Ruyssen, secretary-general of the International Federation of the League of Nations' Societies, promoted as an alternative an internationalist approach, wherein moral disarmament was the prerequisite to military disarmament, established through an international security system implemented by a supranational authority.[34] Through this system of supervision and by deploying a comprehensive education program that included revised textbooks, the elimination of warlike images from media, and the imposition of an international and impartial press agency, moral disarmament would be achieved. By the end of the decade, the notion of disarmament had gained momentum, especially in educational circles.[35]

Thanks to the creation of the Moral Disarmament Committee with the 1932 Disarmament Conference, the issue of moral disarmament reached international prominence. The committee recognized the links among arms control, international security, and international understanding, conferring legitimacy on this very approach. To increase mutual understanding among nations, the committee issued a draft convention emphasizing goodwill measures. These included, for instance, broadcasting "films intended to foster a peace spirit" and organizing trips for primary and secondary school-children to foreign countries—in effect, scholarships abroad that would turn students into "soldiers of peace and friends of international intellectual cooperation."[36]

Yet the committee's actual accomplishments were limited to distributing informational pamphlets and making recommendations. Disparate national policies in the field of education and, more broadly, the diverse political systems throughout Europe prevented the committee from taking any concrete steps. Countries governed by authoritarian regimes with centralized school systems did not relinquish control over their educational policies and mass media. Liberal governments, often characterized by decentralized school systems, opted for voluntary programs to promote peace. The committee's ambitious recommendations mostly fell on deaf ears, especially when it came to Italy.

The Italian government, through the minister of foreign affairs, Dino Grandi, made a pretense of peaceful intentions and orthodox diplomacy by showing a cooperative attitude toward disarmament negotiations.[37] But this was simply a smokescreen for international consumption, as Mussolini's domestic rhetoric continued to belittle the League of Nations and glorify war. In "Discorso di Firenze," a speech he gave in Florence, he argued, "Words are a truly beautiful thing, but rifles, machine guns, ships, aircraft and cannons are even more beautiful; since, oh Black Shirts, the Law, if it is not accompanied by strength, is an empty word, your great Niccolò Machiavelli warned that all disarmed prophets had perished."[38] All in all, the participating nations did not come to an understanding because none of the national committees would endorse any significant limitation to national armaments. Furthermore, Nazi Germany withdrew from both the conference and the League of Nations in October 1933, invalidating the basis of the negotiations.[39]

While still in Italy, Montessori published an abbreviated version of the Geneva speech in the journal *Rivista pedagogica*.[40] She also argued for de-escalating tension in the realm of education. Though she was not a formal member of the committee on moral disarmament, she did voice her opinion while the issue dominated the debate. Borrowing from the fields of international relations and humanitarianism and tapping into both schools of thought within moral disarmament, she argued, once again, for ending the oppression of the child. This time Montessori used terminology employed in the public arena to debate arms limitation and control and took a clear stance in support of the league's efforts to reduce nations' armaments, and she established a parallel conversation to the league's political and civic attempts via reforming education. She argued, "To avoid war in international affairs we say we must enable the people to know one another. Hatred endangers precisely the capacity to understand. War in the human soul begins at birth, and this struggle is reflected in the relations between child and the grown-up. This struggle is a prime begetter of error and evil." One way to "de-escalate" the continuous war on the child is to alleviate the oppression he experiences from birth onward, she asserted. Since "all [political and civic] reforms aim at alleviation," Montessori argued for applying that principle to education by, for example, removing examinations and tests, increasing the number of hours students are outside in nature, and similar measures. Alleviating the spirit of the child would become "the true work of disarmament." To this extent, Montessori continued, the child should leave school altogether when she reaches puberty and "have a holiday for three years." The educator, posing the foundation of her plans to educate adolescents, expressed the desire to "see children leave their narrow homes and go into the hills or to the sea, or into the country, where they will be in touch with nature and learn some practical trade. Here they can meditate and their innate sense of justice and life will blossom tranquilly under ordered labor and this natural existence." Children would resume schooling at the age of sixteen, with a "feeling that they understand something of life and have achieved a sense of direction."[41] Through contact with nature and being lifted from the oppression of discipline and meaningless authority, the adolescent would flourish into an altruistic adult, Montessori concluded.

Montessori's participation in the international conference and her article on disarmament were only two of many growing sources of tension between the educator and the regime. When their differences became evident, neither Mussolini nor Montessori made any attempt to reconcile. The straw that broke the camel's back was control over the content of the training course and the choice of personnel within Montessori schools. Montessori's need to manage every aspect of her own methodology was reported by almost all of those who collaborated with her throughout her life. Often, she would distance herself abruptly from previous friends and promoters over disagreements. When the Fascist government insisted on selecting the personnel for the Scuola Regia di Metodo Montessori, Montessori could not tolerate such interference—or she used it as an excuse to distance herself altogether. Additionally, there were disagreements with Bodrero on the management on the ONM. The educator accused him of getting in touch with unauthorized Montessori societies abroad in an attempt to escape her scrutiny and further the regime's presence using her methodology.[42] As a result, she resigned from the ONM and from the Scuola Regia, asking that her name be removed from it.

Montessori's desire to be part of an international community promoting peace and collaboration continued in the following years, while her family moved to Spain, where they gained the support of the Spanish Republic's government. Once she had permanently moved out of Italy, the educator took up her campaign to promote peace with renewed strength. With Fascism in Italy and National Socialism in Germany growing stronger, Montessori continued agitating for a radical mobilization against war. This task occupied her intensively, and afflicted by the unceasing threats of further war, she worked restlessly.

Montessori's 1936 Speeches and Writings

After her departure from Italy, Montessori increasingly aligned herself with the international Left. For instance, when the Spanish Civil War broke out, she sketched a plan for an organization to support all civilians harmed by it. Building on her previous project to establish an organization to rehabilitate children affected by conflict, Montessori conceived of an association for all those "disabled or ill because of the war." The project, conceived by Montessori herself, was less detailed than her plan for the White Cross, and it appears among the OVRA papers with a handwritten note that says it was "found in possession of Nayno Yosher," who is otherwise unidentified. This time, the organization would take care of all disadvantaged people, even adult civilians who had "until the revolution lived off public charity, wandering peddles, or similar trades."[43]

The civil war had an effect on children, but they were also affected by the lack of innovative pedagogy in Spain, so much so that all the children who returned after the war would be at a considerable advantage, having benefited from advanced pedagogical methods such as those used in countries such as France and Russia. Here the educator was referring to the evacuation of children from conflict areas that occurred over the course of the war, organized by republican authorities. The roundup started in 1936, with the orphans of the first republican casualties, those who lost their families because of the bombardments, and refugees from other areas of conflict. They were joined by a massive number of children who had fled orphanages and juvenile delinquents who had escaped reformatories. The government responded by first creating experimental colonies removed from the front line, an "ideal tool for educating citizens and also for testing radical educational reforms," and later by evacuating thousands of young children to the United Kingdom, France, Belgium, Mexico, and the Soviet Union.[44]

The Levant had become the emblem of suffering children, and Montessori responded to their plight. According to the educator, all children younger than age eighteen should be differentiated based on the degree of the war's impact on them (e.g., their physical wounds, neuroses, psychoses) and gathered in schools for rehabilitation. Montessori's intended audience for this is unknown, but it remains an ambitious yet isolated attempt to conceive an organization to protect civilians of all ages from the ravages of war—a war that would prefigure the ideological divide between liberal and nationalist governments seen in World War II. Furthermore, her initiatives were consistently aligned with the republican government. It is certain that in these years the Italian educator started discussing her project with the European Left.

In fact, in September 1936, Montessori attended the Rassemblement Universel pour la Paix (RUP) convention for universal peace, convened by the RUP's copresident and founder Lord Robert Cecil, in Brussels, where she gave a presentation on the idea of erasing national boundaries.[45] The association was founded according to League of Nations principles, with the objective to safeguard those international organizations that guaranteed the respect of international law and cooperation. With the slogan "Save the League of Nations to Save Peace," the RUP comprised a vast array of organizations: trade unions, veterans' leagues, religious groups, and feminist associations, all deemed by the Comintern as compatible with its popular front policy and all engaged in educating public opinion on international diplomacy and collective security.[46] The conference was organized in response to Italy's invasion of Ethiopia.[47]

The Ethiopian crisis and the overtly aggressive turn in Italy's foreign policies had caused the League of Nations to impose sanctions on the country. In the fall of 1935, the Italian delegation at the league started boycotting meetings and discussions. Italy's official withdrawal from the league came on December 11, 1937.[48] The Abyssinian debacle signaled the deterioration of post–World War I internationalism and the unstoppable decline of the League of Nations. The outcry generated by the invasion of Ethiopia, a member nation, inflamed Europe's public opinion. As a result, the RUP had more than five thousand attendees belonging to forty international organizations, and 750 national associations representing thirty-seven countries, among which were the Soviet Union, the United States, France, and Great Britain, all in favor of radical pacifism and united in an organization that had clear antifascist aims.[49]

The convention's goals included reasserting the importance of the League of Nations and guaranteeing collective security and arms reduction. This much was clear from the initiatives that came from the congress: the RUP called into question the impact of negative propaganda on foreign countries; it sponsored speakers who would travel across Europe to counter heavily slanted and belligerent reporting; it prompted the establishment of a film exchange program throughout continental Europe to foster international cooperation, and created a day for a European peace plebiscite, all of which was made more urgent by the declining impact of the league.[50]

Moral education was also an important issue during the conference. In her address Montessori described the purpose of education as the creation of a peaceful society, which remained more or less unaltered from her earlier speeches. She focused her lecture on the need to eliminate divisions between countries; if men continued grouping themselves by nationality and fighting over interests, they would only destroy themselves, she said. As World War I had demonstrated, "a conquered nation is an illness [from which] all mankind suffer[ed]," an illness that afflicted even victorious nations. Montessori emphasized:

> We are all a single organism, one single nation. By becoming a single nation we have finally realized the unconscious spiritual and religious aspiration of the human soul. "Humanity as an organism has to be born"; the superconstruction that has absorbed all man's efforts from the beginning of his history has now been completed. In a word, contemporary man has citizenship in the great nation of humanity. He is the new citizen of the world—a citizen of humanity.[51]

Throughout the text, the necessity to dismantle state structures figures preeminently. Drawing from the larger debate on limiting absolute sovereignty of the European states, a condition that hindered the functioning of organizations such as the League of Nations, Montessori extended this notion. According to Montessori, single states were no longer necessary, since humanity had conquered what she called "the third dimension"—space itself, with all its resources. People could now connect with one another from every place on earth. As a result, national borders needed to be overcome in the name of a "single organism."[52] Material resources should belong to humanity as a whole, not self-interested groups constantly trying to claim them at the expense of others.

Delivered only a few months after Mussolini's declaration of the Italian Empire, the speech did not find favor with the Fascist police that monitored the congress. A report noted that the event itself was a maneuver organized by the Third International in conjunction with members of Freemasonry. According to the document, the meeting in Brussels had the goal of "creating a mystique of the popular front against authoritarian regimes" and was meant to encourage a bigger divide between democratic and Fascist Europe, in order to ignite a war that would have favored the establishment of Communism throughout the continent.[53] The political polarization in Europe at the time, exacerbated by the 1936 victory of a Popular Front government supported by the Communists in France, was being played out in the Spanish Civil War (1936–1939), in which the larger international struggle between authoritarian and democratic forces was being symbolically enacted. According to the Fascist police, the Montessori family took a side: Mario Montessori joined the Popular Front militia in Huesca, Spain, under the leadership of antifascist Carlo Rosselli (who was at the head of an Italian antifascist volunteer group) against the nationalists led by General Francisco Franco. The OVRA spy in charge of following the Montessori family in Spain, Santorre Vezzari, who signed as "torre," argued that the Montessoris were "rigorously protected by anarchist groups." Vezzari reported that Mario had joined the resistance, encouraged by Ventura Cassol, founder of the Escola Nova Unificada, an organization aimed at promoting free lay schooling in Catalan.[54] And while Mario's active militancy in the Popular Front militia is not confirmed by sources related to the Montessori family, their support of Catalan republicans is evident by their collaboration with Francesc Macià i Llussà, acting president of the Generalitat of Catalonia, and it is corroborated further by the opening of schools in the main office of the Generalitat, for the children of workers and the indigent children of the Iberian Anarchist Federation.[55]

The RUP congress was, indeed, organized principally by French militant socialists of the Comité Mondial Contre la Guerre et le Fascisme (Global Committee Against War and Fascism) and attended by communists and, more generally, members of European movements from the Left. It gathered activists from all around the Continent who were interested in de-escalating conflict and rearmament and fighting against the rise of totalitarianism.[56]

A few months before the conference, the Fascist police had begun filing regular reports on Montessori. Fascist surveillance in Barcelona, where Montessori had returned in 1934, became more frequent after the outbreak of the Spanish Civil War. The family was accused of having antifascist sympathies and connections to the "utmost buffoon Lord Robert Cecil."[57] One letter dated only a few days before the Brussels conference reveals the Fascist police's discomfort with Montessori's political views and her participation in the European peace meeting. As this unsigned letter demonstrates, the fascist regime was wary of her collaboration with idealist intellectuals, and her ties to the dictatorship were questioned: "Dr. Montessori, who lives in Barcelona with Prof. Montesano, is politically very untrustworthy; she is definitely hostile to fascism and has communist tendencies. She has hidden her sentiments under a thin veil of love for fascism for personal gain, which she has achieved."[58] Comments like this had become common after Montessori left Italy. A brief handwritten note at the bottom of the page is particularly blunt: "This miserable woman was spared years ago because of the intercession of the Minister of National Education."[59] A stamp on the page reads "seen by the Head of Government," suggesting that the handwritten note was written by Mussolini himself: the handwriting also resembles his. According to the letter, Il Duce had stopped trusting (or perhaps had never trusted) Montessori's dedication to the regime and had supported her educational projects only because of the minister of national education's interest in her method.

Though the pedagogical approach was still of interest to the regime, the goal was to have a Montessori approach in Italian schools without Montessori to lead it.[60] Her lifelong effort to avoid aligning herself with any political party was probably seen unfavorably by Mussolini, who regretted giving her his support.[61] His handwritten note could also have been written after she openly dedicated herself to pacifism, which led her to a more thorough and engaged analysis of contemporary society, instead of what had appeared to be a circumscribed interest in early childhood education.

Montessori now pushed her analysis outside the walls of the classroom and into the realm of contemporary politics. Together with the anarchopacifist and antimilitarist Bart de Ligt and British philosopher and representative of the Peace Pledge Union Aldous Huxley, whom she met at the RUP conference, she began plans to establish a Peace Academy, the task of which was to develop a science of peace, an objective Montessori had tried to achieve since her 1917 lectures.[62] In supporting the creation of the academy, de Ligt argued:

> The science of peace should elaborate a whole system of nonviolent fighting and prepare a new system of education for individuals and the masses. In a word, whereas the science of war, having reached its culminating point, can only aim at [total] war, the science of peace can only aim at [total] peace. This means that all the moral and intellectual forces of [people], in all professions and all branches of science and art, must be mobilized in the service of peace and its natural complement: social justice.[63]

Active in international networks of antimilitarists, de Ligt played a seminal role in the promotion of peace through education. His knowledge of the Montessori method came from a rather uncommon source that dates back to 1927 and to Montessori's connections to the NEF: his wife, Ina de Ligt-Van Rosem, had entered a contest promoted by an "orthodox [. . .] Dutch organization" in which teachers throughout the country were asked to sketch out an informational pamphlet on the method's principles. De Ligt-Van Rossem won the contest, and her work was published in *Pour l'ère nouvelle*.[64] She argued that contemporaneous educational methods super-imposed militaristic and regimented mental structures on the child's psyche, from which a mental detoxification was necessary. With his wife, de Ligt investigated numerous educational approaches and selected those that spoke to their anarchist and pacifist beliefs: those inciting the child's self-emancipation and those in which discipline would be replaced by a principle of self-organization. According to de Ligt, governments have mistakenly construed violence as the only means of subordinating their citizens. Instead, referencing educator Maria Patricia Willcocks and Montessori, de Ligt argued there is "another force, more secretly and fatally neglected," which is confidence.[65] De Ligt maintained that teaching children to cooperate with their peers would lead to the disappearance of any external authority and naturally evolve into a self-regulated society. Children would therefore acquire a *bonté impérieuse*, a capacity to avoid violence, which would free them from the "yoke of the State, even of the best organized State." To create this "new army," a "new code of honor" was necessary, one generated by progressive education and modern psychology, which were contrary to any form of compulsion or cruelty. This would generate "real pacific mentality."[66] These strategies would form persons willing to adopt nonviolent means of struggle. Similarly, the quest for a total peace is what motivated Montessori's work.

During her subsequent speeches on this topic, she came to include a subtle analysis of the political situation in Europe; her writings became increasingly political. She began to synchronize her pedagogical mission with a reformation of society as a whole, to alter its very political structures. She maintained that "science without politics is like thought without action," meaning that scientific progress that yields only a novel theory does not result in any real, much less radical, change in the lives of children. To make that sort of difference, the crusade for the child "must arm itself with the legal defenses that society has established, and these defenses have now taken the form of the people's representation in the government."[67] Montessori highlighted a new path of political action for all those interested in reforming society. This signaled a new chapter in her life, one apart from Italy and Fascism.

Loud and Uncensored: Montessori's Pacifist Discourse, 1937–1939

Since the beginning of the 1930s, the educator had been delivering public lectures on pacifism internationally. Her ties to the Fascist regime had nevertheless diminished the strength of her message and forced her to be more reserved, at least while she was still in Italy. Now, completely untangled from Fascism, the educator had no one to appease.

In the summer of 1937, Montessori advanced her reflection on pacifism at the Sixth International Montessori Congress held in Copenhagen. Despite the belligerent rhetoric raging across Europe, the conference, titled Educate for Peace, was well attended. It was organized under the auspices of the Danish government and held in the presence of numerous luminaries, such as the minister of education, as well as foreign delegates. Many representatives from the League of Nations attended, despite the absence of delegates from Italy, Germany, and Russia.[68] During the event, Montessori delivered a series of lectures on peace, wherein she argued for the defense of the child, the "forgotten citizen." According to the educator, the contemporary moral sickness affecting civilization was causing hospitals to overflow with people affected by mental disabilities. Governments had to act quickly to prevent a society of "stunted homuncul[i]." Education, which had to be approached as a "social question," was the solution.[69]

In the Copenhagen lectures, Montessori argued that humankind had two moral imperatives: achieving the welfare of all humans and creating a governmental structure that engaged citizens positively from childhood.[70] The earlier speeches treated the subject of child development in the neonatal phase, making an important contribution to the conversation on the physical and psychological needs of newborns. During this first part of the congress, she expanded on the notion of a "spiritual embryo," or a child who undergoes what she termed a "spiritual gestation," the emotional and physiological growth during the first months of life.[71] In line with the theme of the congress, Montessori only analyzed this concept in relation to the social and political repercussions of neglecting children's postnatal development, though this notion would become central in her later pedagogical writings. She then engaged in a subtle political commentary on contemporary society. In particular, she pointed out the importance of a worldwide social mission that would rescue humanity from the incumbent tragedy of war.

At the time, psychological development for newborns was the subject of an international debate among scientists, educators, and psychoanalysts. One of them, Jean Piaget, pioneered the field of early childhood education and shared with Montessori the idea that children develop in a well-defined sequence.[72] Studying this sequence and adapting the environment according to the child's progressive needs was tantamount to fostering organic mental growth.

The discovery of this period of the child's life was at the core of Montessori's notion of reforming education and, hence, uplifting humankind. Reeducating humanity had to start with the identification of a crucial phenomenon in the child's life: the incarnation, "that mysterious force which animates the helpless body of a newborn child." "When a spirit enclosed in flesh comes to live in the world," his intellectual development starts, she asserted.[73] The educator argued that we must pay attention to this period, during which a great deal of the child's psychic and physiological growth occurs. Every newborn is a "spiritual embryo" that possesses a psychic life at birth. He therefore needs a special environment that protects him from the trauma of leaving the womb while stimulating his senses. Neglecting the child in this special phase of her life meant stunting her growth, resulting in an adult with limited capacities.

At birth, according to Montessori, the child is forced to come to terms with his surroundings and the efforts entailed in the development of his personality. This gradual activity requires a continuous effort on the part of the adult to identify the periods in which the child is sensitive to particular stimuli. For example, within the first year, children start developing a specific desire for order, inherently different from that of the adult insofar as it corresponds to an inner necessity. Building on Piaget's research, Montessori argued that children "derive their principles of orientation from the environment which they must later master, [. . . and] that order produces a natural pleasure." When an object is seen somewhere other than its normal place, the child experiences discomfort. Parents usually mistake this behavior for a tantrum, though it is just a manifestation that certain psychological needs are not being met. Adults must therefore learn to read the child's needs and be guided by them. But in reality, the adult is instead "a dictator, whose wishes the child must blindly obey." If, Montessori continued, contemporary society had considered dictatorship as "one of [the adults'] problems," it should now see it as a "social problem of children," insofar as the adult imposes his will on the child. Thus, education was the only tool to eradicate dictatorships.[74]

Building on this emphasis, Montessori's subsequent lectures dealt with more political issues, demonstrating her capacity to evaluate the political climate of a continent on the verge of a new global war. In particular, her assessment of human beings' place in society under various types of governments shed light on her political stance and her analysis of contemporary

Europe. While speaking at the International Montessori Congress in Copenhagen with her son, Mario, she elaborated an astute study of diverse forms
of government. In particular, she contrasted the efficacy of the tools utilized
by authoritarian regimes to indoctrinate youth and the relative failure of
democratic governments to educate their citizens and inspire young people
to love and support their country.[75] Looking at state initiatives for children,
she criticized democratic governments for declining to allocate resources to
educational reforms, scholastic programs, and extracurricular organizations.
She argued that education did not occupy a prominent enough role: "The
place education holds in the great interests of humanity is secondary—it is
considered a luxury rather than a necessity. In times of stress, if any cuts
are to be made, it is the budget for education which usually suffers. This is
because, especially in democratic countries, education plays the minimal
role of imparting, in an abstract way, certain ideas contained in a standard
syllabus."[76] Democracies also did not offer enough opportunities for their
citizens to participate in the public life of the nation. As a result, citizens of
democratic nations were raised in a state of moral ignorance and, in turn,
did not feel a strong allegiance to their governments or to ideals linked to
the fatherland.

On the other hand, within "unitary forms of government" (i.e., totalitarianism), individuals felt that they were an integral part of society by playing
an active role in national ceremonies, by attending school programs that
fostered national allegiance, and by participating in parascholastic activities.[77] Through state-organized initiatives, citizens felt as though they took
part in the achievement of national goals. According to Montessori, these
initiatives enhanced a person's dignity and inner value, making him a more
participatory member in the national discourse. Within these forms of government, intellectuals and educators understood the need to ascribe value to
the personal formation of the individual. Montessori recognized that although
this "valorization is built around the ideals of the respective regime, it is
nevertheless a valorization and it starts from a very early age [which pro-
vides] an immense impulse to the formation of the character."[78] The Fascist
Political Police shadowing her praised her convention speech—for speaking highly of those nations "that glorify war" and for grasping the importance of educating children from infancy—although she likely would have
been chagrined to know that they approved.[79]

Montessori was far from naive in her analysis of state initiatives in
nondemocratic regimes. In the lecture, she pointed out that authoritarian
regimes restricted their citizens' rights and liberties, and that whereas the
tools these governments employed to integrate youth within the national

discourse were positive, the message of totalitarian governments was far from praiseworthy. Indeed, during her own ten years in Italy, she had the chance to observe the enthusiasm that young people demonstrated for propaganda-backed state initiatives. Young people who felt called to be part of a national mission were often willing participants:

> Even at four years of age, when [a child is] passing in front of a general, the [general] renders [the child] the same military salute with the same dignity as he renders to the adult soldier. Is it to be marveled at that, in individuals so valorized that constructive enthusiasm forms part of the psychic constitution, sacrifice appears as a pleasant means to achieve an aim, and discipline and obedience are sought with joy?[80]

Montessori thus argued that the same investment in educational resources must be made in democratic societies and directed toward stimulating the child through an education of freedom. She also questioned how much so-called democratic governments truly valued the concept of freedom. The failure of elective governments to encourage children's personalities to thrive with innovative educational approaches put the lie to many of the foundational claims of liberal nation-states, in Montessori's opinion. By denying young citizens the capacity to exercise their full potential, these states only practiced a very limited version of freedom. The educator pointed out a misconception: those who deplored any "attempt to restrict personal liberty" judged the democratic state the most suitable form of government and considered it "the careful protector and cultivator of the independent human personality."[81] But even though these governments protected the adult's individual freedom, they did not protect the child's.

According to Montessori, when it came to children, "democracies ha[d] a dictatorial regime, worse than any witnessed in the past or in the present." Adults governed the child's life tyrannically, weakening her will and raising her into an "apathetic, depressed, unconsciously humiliated, dissatisfied" adult citizen, one "unable to act without continual guidance." The problems of this weakened individual did not manifest fully until maturity, when the time came for him to become politically and civically active: now "he [threw] himself into the group which seem[ed] to embody ideas that express his inner dissatisfaction."[82] Here Montessori was probably referring to authoritative figures such as Mussolini, whose post–World War I rhetoric captured the attention of those dissatisfied with liberal governments and with the outcome of the Versailles peace treaty. It was no wonder that these people became passive and accepted violence with resignation, the educator claimed.

According to Montessori, what liberal governments did to foster an understanding of peace had so far been futile. Here, she was referring to the
small-scale efforts from pacifist and international advocates, such as textbook reform (in particular history books), to resolve conflicts or promote
reconciliation among previously hostile nations.[83] But, she argued, asking
children to memorize the founding principles of the League of Nations, or
to remember a series of dates for battles and wars, would not help humanity find common ground. Even learning a literal common language to
"reach a common understanding and solve conflict by discussion instead of
violence," for example, proved to be useless—in Spain, where Montessori
resided, civil war was tearing apart the nation in spite of a common language. Hence, education in democratic states had to be radically transformed to allow individuals to satisfy "their innate tendency"—that is, to
achieve "an increasingly refined form of independence growing from basic
functional independence to mental abstraction and social acquisitions."[84]
In light of the failures of international organizations such as the RUP and
others, a more radical approach to pacifism would be necessary.

Traditional educational approaches that did not favor the growth of the
individual meant that respect and harmony in the classroom could only be
reached through discipline. In this environment, as soon as a teacher would
leave the classroom, chaos would ensue. Similarly, when "the government
and the commanders of the army los[t] control," then "arson and murder
[were] committed, convents [were] burned, priests and innocent citizens
[were] tortured by people who, until some days before, had led peaceful and
respectful lives."[85] Instead, through the valorization of each individual's
personality, governments would enable real freedom, not meaningless for-
mality, for their citizens.

To attain this goal, the educator urged that "new sciences must begin,
new disciplines that shed light on the new ideals and disseminate them the
way conflicting ideologies have broadcast their propaganda." The new tools
employed by conflicting ideologies (Fascism and Communism) to indoctrinate their populations shed light on the necessity for governmental engagement of citizens. The content of the regimes' propaganda had so far been
flawed. According to Montessori, nationalism had prevented people from
leaving their countries, restricted the circulation of money through protec-
tionism, and "promote[d] an artificial attachment to their fatherlands by
training them from birth to go along with what are essentially narrow national
interests." In a similar fashion, "political internationalism" had attempted
to indoctrinate people. However, this trend was not able to promote positive
values around which humanity could unite because it was "based on the

elimination of the rights of the remainder of humanity and the destruction of their particular moral features."[86] Montessori began to elaborate a sharp and sweeping criticism of not just totalitarianism but also the conventional political wisdom of the day.

Montessori, dissatisfied by the inefficacy of the proposals put forward by democratic governments and international organizations, and alarmed by the continual threats to and progressive erosion of freedom by nationalism, exaggerated her criticism of democratic forms of government by putting emphasis on their incapacity to produce viable solutions to humankind's education. She condemned totalitarianism in all its forms; still, her disillusionment with the work of democratic national governments and, more generally, the international organizations developed in the interwar period, led her to express increasingly harsh criticism toward the politics she saw as complicit in the escalation of violence occurring throughout Europe.

Montessori continued to speak about peace while sending a letter of encouragement to the War Resisters' International (WRI) congress, held in Paris in August 1937. An international association of autonomous national, regional, and local radical pacifist organizations, WRI comprised intellectuals and organizers prepared for direct collective action to prevent war and all related preparations. The 1937 congress convened antimilitarists, conscientious objectors, anti-imperialists, and nonaggressionists, and it called for the refusal of moral and practical service to war, such as refusal of military service and the use of all available means to promote antimilitarist propaganda and create resistance groups. Montessori, who sent a letter to de Ligt a few days before the conference, ironically addressed the attendees by praising them for having chosen an "easy" objective: to avoid the danger of future wars, they had decided to preach for the "resistance to the commands of the State." Although she praised the pursuit of this goal, Montessori believed this effort required "tremendous strength" from each individual, the capacity to oppose "ideals that [were] universally accepted, to resist public opinion, to renounce your country, to give up your possessions, and, eventually, even your life." What the organizers requested, according to Montessori, was a "spontaneous heroism," which seemed to her hard to achieve all at once. Such heroism would come naturally only to a few. It could, however, be achieved through "long moral training." After that, she asserted, "there would be no need of encouragement to Disarmament and Resistance to War," insofar as this new human being would not be able to endure the state of moral degradation brought about by war.[87] Though education was a necessary condition to reorganize society, the organization's goals were praiseworthy and compatible with her own peace agenda.

This continuous tension between practical and theoretical work within pacifism characterized the remainder of her speeches on the topic. According to the educator, an authentic unity among people within countries and across borders must take place to create a harmonious society. As she argued in the 1917 lectures, humankind was united from economic and intellectual standpoints. At the time, nations were so interconnected that, during wars, victorious countries had to take on the burdens of vanquished nations. The responses to this new interdependence were various, and some nations—such as Italy and Germany, which were not mentioned in the text—chose isolationism and nationalism. The only viable solution was the establishment of what Montessori calls "a single nation," or a true cooperation among governments with the common goal of respecting the rights of their most important citizens: children. This notion, which Montessori dwelled on in her 1917 lectures, is reiterated in this 1937 speech, and its importance is highlighted in relation to a new concept, that of the child as a possessor of rights.

A supranational organization was to be formed to protect the rights of "the forgotten citizen," the child.[88] On the eve of World War II, the educator issued what she termed "a sharp call to the public conscience" and advocated for the creation of the Social Party of the Child and Youth, a political party she founded while in Copenhagen.[89] She also promoted the opening of a research center and a Center for the Study of the Child in the city of Laren in the Netherlands—these two organizations had the goal of advocating on behalf of children. Until the outbreak of World War II in 1939, Montessori attempted in multiple venues to reform humanity through education and to put a halt to the contemporary belligerent political climate.

The political conversation on children's rights at the time differed deeply from Montessori's conception. As the *Times* of London put it, Montessori's "aim was to consider the child from a new standpoint," a completely new way of looking at his needs and his place in society.[90] Children's advocates instead were arguing for tutelage and protection, without recognizing children's political status and their capacity to exercise political power. Children's needs were identified and administered by adults, denying children a full membership in society and reinforcing an adultcentric notion of citizenship. The very same 1924 Declaration of the Rights of the Child that had so intensified the conversation on children's rights and influenced Montessori made no reference to their actual rights. The document fit within the realm of child welfare and reflected the undisputed assumption that children had to rely on adult protection to exercise their rights. Children remained the object, not the subject, of international law.

Maria Montessori in London, 1939. Courtesy of Association Montessori Internationale Archive, Amsterdam.

Put simply, the discourse still revolved around adults' obligations to children. From a political standpoint, children were neither seen nor heard. They were treated as a subset of something else, not, as described by historian Maggie Black, "as a category of humankind who deserves consideration in their own right."[91]

Montessori spoke of the child as the "forgotten citizen," entitled to both rights of his own and representation by specific organs such as the so-called Ministry of the Child and the Social Party of the Child.[92] In her description of the Social Party of the Child, she announced the need for a second French Revolution aimed at promoting the rights of children.[93] Though the French Revolution led to the Declaration of the Rights of Man, which included the right to receive an education, it considered education to be a burden entirely confined to childhood. On the contrary, Montessori felt education should be revolutionized and that it should be an ongoing and lifelong process. Education as people knew it did not take into account the needs of children, who had to be the subject of new legislation aimed at protecting their rights. Charitable institutions and educational societies dedicated to them were not sufficient. Only a single panhuman nation could prompt a radical change.[94]

Montessori's vision for the new child as a possessor of rights was articulated in depth and comprised several points, all of which were delineated in a pamphlet that she probably compiled when she started gathering people to form the Social Party of the Child. First, she believed that the child should have specific representatives in the legislative bodies of his country and that every government ought to include a Ministry of the Child. Childhood was to be considered a crucial period for the growth of the individual, one that needed to be respected and to receive the appropriate resources. The government had to supervise the tutelage of childhood; the child was to be considered a citizen of the state, independent from the adult.[95]

First, children had to be respected as "builders of humanity," which should be considered their occupation, and as such children should be protected by ad hoc laws, designed by committees on which children themselves should be present. Second, within the new single worldwide nation, pedagogues would form special programs to train educators and teachers on the "vital and natural needs of developing children and youth."[96] The study of child development would be mandatory for educators and specialized personnel. Third, all those who wished to marry would also be required to undergo mandatory special instruction in the physical and psychic care of the next generation, anticipating the care for children before conception. Future parents would also have to formally acknowledge their "duties toward children" before having their union legitimized by the state. Additionally, Montessori asked for governments to be deemed the "scrupulous guardian of children and assume, if found insufficient, the care taken by the family and intervene with legal power when care of the children is inadequate."[97] The child was to be considered an independent citizen of a state, not an appendix to his own parents; every national parliament must have members elected solely to represent children, she insisted. In closing her lecture, Montessori added a brief commentary on the creation of a utopian "Nation of Childhood," a nation without territorial rights and made up of children, all united under the banner to preserve two sacred interests, those of life and existence. The Nation of Childhood, just as any other nation, should also be legally represented at the League of Nations, insofar as its population is the most numerous and important. Therefore, the authority of this nation should outweigh that of all others.

With the help of Mohamed Riad Bey, a lawyer specialized in transnational affairs, Montessori went as far as drafting the statutes of the Social Party of the Child, envisioning the Le Parti Sociale de l'Enfance as an association made up of international members but, most important, of patrons who would not necessarily appreciate being called the members of a party and who would be able to give conspicuous *cotisations*, or donations, to the organization.[98] These patrons, similar to those Montessori sought for the White Cross during World War I, would attend a yearly day in support of the organization together with groups such as the Bureau International du Travail (International Labor Organization), and the Association Internationale pour la Protection de l'Enfance (International Association for the Protection of the Child).

Taken together, Montessori attempted to reverse the prevailing paradigm by suggesting that, far from needing to be sheltered from the ills of the adult world, children should in fact take an active role in political and civic debates. In this, she anticipated a conversation that would occur in the 1990s and would see actual sociological experiments involving the political participation of children, such as the *pibes unidos* (children united) in Argentina, the *meninos da rua* (street children) in Brazil, and the children's parliament experiment in Slovenia.[99] These projects, together with many others that bear the imprint of Montessori's suggestions, have been implemented to promote minors' rights, a central point in current studies on monitoring legislation for and on children.[100] The question of how to develop a participatory, comprehensive, and coherent youth policy is becoming more pressing every day, even now. A growing awareness of the specific needs of this social category has brought politicians across the globe to consider their involvement in all fields, to the extent that many governments are creating departments specifically targeting the needs of young people. These institutional changes owe much to Montessori and her followers.

Nevertheless, at the time, Montessori's pleas remained unheard. Her efforts to seek support for a party to protect children's rights and to constitute a nation that would include all children ended with the outbreak of World War II and her subsequent departure to India. The Social Party of the Child was dismantled, and its members dispersed. The war surely contributed to the failure of the initiative, though another factor was likely Montessori's envisioned structure for the organization, which resembled typical turn-of-the-century philanthropy more than modern transnational organizations based on a scientific management of humanitarianism, such as the Save the Children Fund.[101]

Montessori continued putting forward radical suggestions in favor of the Social Party of the Child from India, where she wrote "A Step Towards the Future" for the *Theosophist*, advocating in favor of the institution of the Ministry of the Child, "the powerful and essential builder of man." In addition, she pointed to the necessity of politicizing the struggle to promote children's rights: to those who think that a political party could bring an "ugly note of strife to mar the sweetness and purity of childhood," she responded that it was paramount to include the most important members of society, children, in any struggle for the betterment of that society. The concerns of the party would not be superficial or factious; they concerned humanity in its deepest form, "for in these depths the common interest [among political parties] can be found; the one universal interest which concerns the very life of humanity upon which all of us depend."[102]

Montessori would find new inspirations while in India. The impossibility of leaving the country, due to the war, and her resultant confinement in the rural village of Kodaikanal motivated Montessori's withdrawal from active political engagement in favor of expanding her methodology and rethinking the relationship between mankind and the environment, promoting an ecocritical conception of human beings and their global significance.

CHAPTER 6

The Child as Agent of Radical Change

The Years in India

I quite agree that there is a great advantage to a small child bred in the slums, having the gutter for playground, and living amid continued coarseness of gesture and word, in being placed daily in a bright, clean schoolroom hung with pictures, and often gay with flowers. There [the child] is taught to be clean, gentle, orderly; there it learns to sing and play; has toys that awaken its intelligence; learns to use its fingers deftly; is spoken to with a smile instead of a frown; is gently rebuked or coaxed instead of cursed. All this humanizes the children, arouses their brains, and renders them susceptible to intellectual and moral influences.

—Helena Petrovna Blavatsky, *The Key to Theosophy*

Among the numerous paranormal phenomena attributed to Helena Petrovna Blavatsky, the founder of the Theosophical Society, were the ability to exchange "psychic airmail" with "the Mahatmas" in Tibet and to make cigarette papers disappear into thin air.[1] But none of that can have impressed Montessorians as much as Blavatsky's vision in 1899, as described in *The Key to Theosophy*, of a school sharing a number of similarities with what would eventually become the first Casa dei Bambini in San Lorenzo.

Despite Maria Montessori's long-standing interest in the Theosophical Society, dating back to 1899, she only collaborated closely with the organization in the second half of the 1930s, when she decided to run training courses and to oversee the opening of Montessori schools while a guest at the headquarters of the organization in Madras (now Chennai), India. At the invitation of its president, George Sidney Arundale, and his wife, Rukmini Devi, a dancer and choreographer of the Indian classical dance form Bharatanatyam, Montessori and her son, Mario, spent almost a decade in

India, from 1939 to 1946 and from 1947 to 1949. During this time, Montessori was isolated from Europe because of World War II, but she remained intellectually active, stimulated by her close contact with both Theosophists and ardent Indian nationalists. The interlude furnished plenty of time to rework her pedagogical methodology. As a result, she distanced herself from her political activism of the previous decade and focused on exploring the place of the child in a larger scheme of global, ecological, and social world development. Indeed, her experiences with India convinced Montessori that by educating children, she could make a positive impact on a universal scale. Such instruction was absolutely critical to the future of humanity and the planet itself.

Within this framework, she elaborated on the concept of *cosmic education*. The specific circumstances in which she found herself—amid India's philosophical, political, and religious currents—provided fertile ground for her work. Prior to Montessori's arrival, the education of Indian youth had become a disputed subject in the country, a battleground for nationalists who wished to reclaim the right to educate Indians about local cultures, languages, and traditions, in order to break free of any intellectual subjugation by the British colonial government. All of the educator's contacts in the country were deeply engaged in this debate, and some of them had already contributed to Montessori's views on pacifism prior to her stay.

This chapter first examines the role of the Montessori approach within this debate prior to 1939, and the manner in which prominent intellectuals such as Rabindranath Tagore and Mohandas K. Gandhi helped Montessori position herself in the larger conversation on the child and the environment. Although intellectual exchanges and conversation inspired the educator to draft the idea of cosmic education in broad strokes as early as 1935, it was only her stay at the Theosophical Society in Madras that led her to develop this notion in all its strength and to fully devise a curriculum for children ages six to twelve that would implement her cosmic vision of peace.[2]

Then the rest of the chapter analyzes how Montessori was brought back to the origins of her pedagogical approach by collaborating with dancer and educator Rukmini Devi. Devi's educational philosophy emphasized muscular education and the beauty of the environment. The latter concept, one borrowed from the Theosophical tradition that figured prominently in Devi's teaching at Kalakshetra, illustrated Unity of Life. It was by way of this element, One Life, that Montessori zeroed in on the connection between human beings and their environment. This perspective allowed her to elaborate on the concept of cosmic education, by which children could find their place within the cosmos and therefore grow up with a full understanding of their global mission of peace.

Montessori's First Contacts with Eastern Mysticism, Theosophy, and Indian Nationalism

Montessori's sojourn in India is an understudied chapter of the educator's life, and it is also largely unknown to the general audience of Western Montessori teachers.[3] The reasons for her undertaking such a journey at this particular moment in her life are numerous and complex. She had received financial support from the Fascist regime of Italy until 1934. While struggling to gain financial independence in the second half of the 1930s, she had lectured throughout Europe on themes related to her larger project of societal renewal. Recent historiography has highlighted the state of turmoil in which the Montessori family lived during those years, first in Spain, where Mario probably joined a militia for the Popular Front in Huesca, under the leadership of antifascist Carlo Rosselli (who was at the head of an Italian volunteer group, Giustizia e Libertà [Justice and Freedom]) against the nationalists led by General Francisco Franco.[4] The diligent surveillance of the Montessori family by the fascist secret police OVRA spies sheds light on a series of travels and moves throughout Europe, mostly financed and given logistical support by Montessori disciples. It is thus possible that when Montessori was invited by acquaintances to India, a country for which she had long had an affinity, she went simply because she wanted a period of quiet in which to rethink her work, to write, and to train teachers in her new methods. She probably also saw the possibility of expanding her approach in South Asia.

Her relationship with India began even before her arrival in 1939. She had been a member of the Theosophical Society since May 23, 1899.[5] The Theosophical Society advocated a syncretic religion that appealed to her primarily for two reasons: it attempted to reconcile scientific naturalism and spirituality, and it was organized, not unlike the entire spiritualism movement, in a fundamentally womancentric manner.[6] When she joined, Montessori was a recent graduate from medical school, actively participating in politics and deeply involved in what Annarita Buttafuoco termed *femminismo pratico* (practical feminism)—an approach to women's rights that adopted a commitment to social charity instead of a direct political fight for political enfranchisement (discussed earlier in chapter 1).[7] Fin de siècle Rome was a city that was attempting to overcome its imperial and papal past, and it had just become a cosmopolitan hub, with a strong presence of Freemasons and other new spiritual movements.[8] Occultism, spiritualism, and Theosophical ideas had a profound impact on the Roman intellectual, social, and political elite, including professors, aristocrats, politicians, and high-ranking soldiers. In other words, the lay high bourgeoise, generally hostile to the Roman Catholic Church, were interested in the regeneration and change promised by these movements.[9] Together with her medical background and her work as an anthropologist at La Sapienza University, these surroundings had a lasting effect on the young Montessori and her pedagogical approach.[10] She had studied under the supervision of physical anthropologists Cesare Lombroso and Giuseppe Sergi, and psychiatrist Sante De Sanctis, in a school of medicine that had recently been revamped after hiring Italy's most prominent thinkers, most of whom were close to the *sinistra storica* (historical left). There, Montessori learned to rely on scientific observation, applying it to the study of children's learning behavior and viewing hygiene and medicine as having a social and progressive function in society. But her search for the spiritual growth of the child was a deep concern of her early works, which contained numerous biblical references and relied heavily on parables and stories of the lives of saints. This resulted in a hodgepodge, in which her attitudes about moral growth and spirituality often mixed with her knowledge of medical anthropology, creating what Suzanne Stewart-Steinberg calls "a modernized Christian terminology."[11]

This dualism in Montessori's work was shared by the Theosophical Society, in the form of a tension resulting from the attempt to reconcile materialism and spiritualism. In the first half of the nineteenth century, the ascent of materialism throughout Continental Europe caused a crisis of faith. While organized religions struggled to verify their truths, scientific materialism offered objective and quantifiable results that undermined the spiritual foundations of believers of various denominations. As a result, the European mind became secularized and individuals sought out new and different forms of spirituality.[12] Theosophy, like many other syncretic religions born out of this shift, endeavored to base its claims on material proofs and to give a "scientific spirituality" without demanding faith, "instead offer[ing] actual demonstration and thus objective 'proof' of its claims."[13] In *Isis Unveiled*, Blavatsky argued that "by combining science with religion, the existence of God and the immortality of man's spirit may be demonstrated like a problem by Euclid."[14] Young Montessori, a physiologist and psychiatrist, evaded what Michel Foucault has characterized as Enlightenment blackmail—the choice to embrace reason, or not—and could probably relate to this "hybrid credo" more than to the dogmatism of Catholicism.[15]

Like many other syncretic religions, Theosophy perceived spiritual development to occur through an evolutionary process, offering an intellectual framework that spoke to the Italian educator.[16] Among the main tenets of the organization, as elaborated by Blavatsky and Colonel Henry Steel Olcott, were, first, *reincarnation*, a process of returning to earth again and again—living in different physical bodies each time in order to continue the soul's journey of inner evolution, advancement, development, and unfolding—and, second, *karma*, the idea that human beings would self-actualize and reach ultimate wisdom.[17]

Both beliefs, shared with Hinduism, allowed believers to pursue spiritual development or self-actualization through a process that recalled Montessori's notion of the liberation of the child's spirit. The profound importance that Montessori attributed to the role of the environment as the cause in the evolution of all organic forms, matched with her subtle analysis of evolutionary biology in her *Antropologia Pedagogica*, demonstrates why she may have been attracted to the Theosophical movement's particular synthesis of these ideas.[18] The other foundational principles of Theosophy, that of One Life (i.e., the union between humankind and the universe) and the Universal Brotherhood of humanity (i.e., the effort to form a community of believers without distinctions of race, creed, sex, caste, or color), did not appeal to the educator as much at the turn of the century as they would in the late 1930s, when she moved to India; hence, these notions will be examined later in this chapter.

Finally, Theosophy was not immune to the feminizing trend affecting various religious frameworks, including Italian Catholicism and British occultism, in the second half of the nineteenth century—a trend that must have appealed to the Italian educator, given her significant engagement with feminism.[19] Within the Theosophical Society, this phenomenon coincided with the ascent of Annie Besant (who would, in 1907, become its second president) and resulted in an increasing number of women adepts, as well as a "new emphasis on emotion and devotion rather than study, on personal relationship rather than abstract principles, and on hierarchy and loyalty rather than individual autonomy."[20] At the same time, the society had also opened up to new ceremonial organizations such as the Universal Order of Co-Freemasonry, the first Masonic society that accepted female as well as male adepts.[21] As a result, the Theosophical Society gained a larger following among women and began to address women's issues more directly. The Universal Order of Co-Freemasonry was, in fact, among the associations that led the Theosophists to bring religious thought into the realm of feminist politics, insofar as the Co-Masons considered marches for women's suffrage to be sacramental acts.[22] Unsurprisingly, it was in this new climate, one of collaboration with women's movements, that Montessori joined the Theosophical Society.[23]

The year 1899, when Montessori allegedly became a member, coincided with a big restructuring of the organization. Isabella Cooper-Oakley, a prominent member of the organization and the personal assistant to Olcott, was sent to help the Roman branch expand its outreach. According to the periodical *Teosofia*, "It was now time for the Lodge of Rome to come out of its infantile state, and elevate it to the height of its mission," so as to make Rome "a *beacon* for the Occult in the West."[24]

Sketching a history of how the Montessori movement and Theosophy intersect is bound to be a fraught and fragmentary endeavor. That the archives of both Besant and Montessori are so scattered makes the task even more difficult. For the Italian educator, this is a history of small hints left by Montessori teachers, of digging deep into the origins of international organizations, trying to ascertain the validity of prelates' accusations. In 1900, both Montessori and Besant participated in the International Feminist Congress in London.[25] A few years later, Montessori attended a lecture by Besant on her own pedagogical experiments. Montessori's success with her first Casa dei Bambini in 1907 had impressed Besant, who identified her work as a model for reforming youth and education worldwide.[26] In the following years, Montessori schools were being inaugurated with the support of Theosophist organizations. Bolstered by the Theosophical Ligue d'éducation morale de la jeunesse (Theosophical League for Moral Youth Education), a few Montessori schools had been opened in France by two Theosophists identified as "Mesdames Pujol et Waddington," who had attended a Montessori training course in Rome.[27] According to Madame Pujol, by speaking with Montessori and her collaborators, and by reading the educator's work, one can easily infer that "the entire educational approach is based on the Theosophical conception that had also inspired us, that is to say the entire internal development of the child is the basis for any other development."[28] After World War I, Besant selected the Montessori method for one class at Guindy school, a school she inaugurated near the headquarters of the Theosophical Society in Madras.[29]

According to a 1919 report by Monsignor Umberto Benigni, a staunch opponent of Montessori, the educational movement and Theosophy were much more intertwined than sharing a few schools in Europe and in India. He argued that the influence of the Theosophical Society had been extended significantly thanks to the field of education, and thanks in particular to Montessori schools, which allowed the organization to proselytize across

Europe.[30] The prelate related that Besant, in a 1917 conference on peace in Calcutta, had argued that the child "must first of all be considered as a permanent Spiritual intelligence, covered with layers of matter; [the child] must therefore be studied with attention to be able to help him and not impose on him a method unsuitable for his development. . . . *This has actually been done in Europe and the Montessori system is proof of it.*"[31] In Benigni's view, Montessori's approach was responsible for the dissemination of the Theosophical Society's principles; in fact, it was an instrument in the hands of the organization. But there is no proof of this systematic use of the Montessori approach. As Besant herself describes it, the convergence of Theosophical ideas and Montessori's philosophy of education would come naturally, with no need to "impose Theosophical labels to have the right to educational ideas; ideas are free to all; it is only necessary to spread them in the mental atmosphere so that they are grasped by all the receptive brains."[32] And so it happened in the following decades.

The relationship with the organization continued to develop through Montessori's collaboration in the 1920s and 1930s with the New Education Fellowship (NEF), a transnational organization that, having grown out of the Theosophical Fraternity in Education, promoted debate on children's rights and education.[33] The Theosophical Society's branches in Europe, and the promotional tours by its main representatives, kept the organization's presence alive on the Continent, even though its headquarters had moved to the district of Adyar in the city of Madras, in South India.

Apart from the mutual sympathy between the society and Montessori, several Indian thinkers not associated with Theosophy had demonstrated an interest in the Italian educator's educational approach. In the decades prior to Montessori's arrival, the role of education had become a hotly contested subject in India.[34] Nationalist intellectuals vehemently protested the Westernized educational system, considering it a tool to project and cement British imperial power. Since the late 1830s, the colonial government had implemented centralized and state-sanctioned curricula, instituting a substantial break with the previous indigenous scholastic system. These curricula, as conceived at the beginning of the eighteenth century by the General Committee of Public Instruction, were designed to ensure British domination through the establishment of a "cultural dependency among education and ruling classes so that revolutionary overthrow would never be a likely alternative."[35] Students who had previously been able to study such subjects as South Asia's social and religious history, Vedic lore and astrology, and Koranic rationalism were now exposed exclusively to the works of Western thinkers, thereby fostering an alienation from indigenous cultures and traditions.[36] This was all by design. The system had been implemented with the express aim of creating a class of lower-tier bureaucrats who could act as intermediaries between the metropole and its overseas territory. The establishment and strengthening of a Western educational system came to be seen by the leaders and members of nationalist groups "as one of the most important and valuable instruments through which the British were transforming [the country]."[37]

Tagore and Gandhi

Many nationalist intellectuals—notably two of Montessori's main interlocutors in India, the first non-European Nobel laureate Tagore and the activist Gandhi—sought to reform the educational system. Their intention was to empower the Indian people and to instill a sense of pride and belonging among the indigenous populations.[38] To this end, they had two main strategies. One was to maintain the educational infrastructure implemented by the British government while reforming curricula to include the subjects of Indian cultures, religions, and traditions. Vernacular languages would be the vehicles of choice to impart this knowledge. The second strategy was a series of ethnic revivals, propelling a renaissance of indigenous Indian traditions and thus rekindling a sense of pride in the diverse populations of India.

Maria Montessori was widely supported by Indian intellectuals interested in advancing the cause of independence and was considered a valuable force for education reform. She was viewed as someone who could advance the conversation about the country's overwhelming youth-illiteracy problem.[39] Moved by a burgeoning interest in educating Indians, as well as by Montessori's fame, Tagore and Gandhi began a correspondence with her and, in turn, became valuable supporters of and participants in her work.

Montessori's support among nationalist intellectuals raises an important question: why wasn't she opposed to the degree that other Western educators were? As has been noted by education historian Carolie Elizabeth Wilson, Montessori's favorable reception came at a time when activists throughout India "were struggling to divest the country of increasing dependence on Western education and its concomitant colonial domination," which constitutes a paradox. Prior to her arrival, this tension would be resolved in part by the emergence of an "Indianized Montessori movement" connected to the Gandhian social reform movements, in which educators remained committed to the principles of the Montessori method while adapting it to the current living conditions and specific needs of the Indian people.[40]

Tagore's reading of Montessori is a notable illustration of this process. By the end of the 1920s, he had established several schools in India, and many other institutions combining his approach with Montessori's had sprung up throughout the country.[41] Tagore had met Montessori in 1925, and he had expressed admiration for her methodology.[42] In 1929, he attended the Montessori International Congress in Elsinore and spoke about his own pedagogy.[43] A member of the NEF and a forerunner of the National Education movement in India, he carried out an explicit critique of the existing educational system, which he characterized as mechanical and stifling of creativity.[44] His own pedagogical experiments opposed a school where children were "inert, like dead specimens of some museums, whilst lessons were pelted at us from high, like hailstones on flowers."[45] Tagore, much like Montessori, considered education necessary not merely for "success" or "progress" but for "illumination of heart"—that is, to foster in the child a spirit of empathy, an impulse toward service and self-sacrifice, and an ability to rise above egocentrism and ethnocentrism to a state of global consciousness.[46]

An internationalist "who wanted India . . . to rediscover its ties with Southeast and East Asia and to seek inspiration from parts of the world other than Europe," Tagore founded a school in 1901 named Shantiniketan, literally "abode" (*niketan*) of "peace" (*shanti*). He modeled it on ancient forest communities, emphasizing self-discipline, simplicity, and communion between the child and the nature.[47] Against a content-oriented approach, Tagore argued that "the highest education is that which does not merely give us information but makes our life in harmony with all existence."[48] At Shantiniketan, a teacher/guru would prompt the holistic growth of the child, promoting her intellectual and physical development in freedom and in an open-air environment.[49] Similar to Montessori, Tagore acknowledged the crucial role of early childhood education in developing empathy and the ability to emotionally connect with one's surroundings. He called specifically for a "cultivation of feelings" (*bodher tapasya/sadhana*), in which sympathy would expand to encompass the child's immediate kinship to form a deeper intuition of feeling, spearheading a connection between the child's spirit and the universe.[50] The child would acquire what literary critic Ranjan Ghosh calls "earth wisdom," the result of getting in touch with his own "ecological self," a wisdom that "transcend[ed] both individualism and holism"; he would learn amid nature, whereby his consciousness would turn into an extension of the environment itself.[51] This transformation would be accomplished through the teaching of the arts (an echo of Montessori's early writings), which would allow the child to see the interdependence between humankind and nature, between humanity and the universe, establishing a "harmonious relationship with all things with which he has dealings."[52] In both structure and content, Tagore's schools were geared toward the development of an Indian consciousness. In fact, through this ecopedagogy, students would form a profound relationship with their own cultural environment.

Although Tagore's educational innovations mostly remained within the confines of the institutions he created, his work had a deep impact on Montessori, as testified by the experiments of the two methods combined, which came about spontaneously and were not promoted or sponsored by either Montessori or Tagore. As a result of these affinities, Tagore felt somewhat grateful for Montessori's presence in India at a time when such heated debate on education was taking place. He wrote to her that he was "confident that education of the young, which must underlie all work of national reconstruction, will find a new and lasting inspiration in your presence." With Montessori's "guidance in creative self-expression," India would have new inputs for its emancipation and reconstruction.[53]

Gandhi also applied several Montessori principles to his 1937 proposal "National Scheme of Basic Education," which constituted "the coping stone of [his] socio-political edifice."[54] Inspired by his young son's education, he had been concerned with pedagogical issues since 1891.[55] He also wrote extensively about schooling throughout his life.[56] The spiritual leader's reflection on teaching and schooling, crucial as it was to his overall militancy, must be read as part of a larger project of social and political emancipation. Indeed, he was not a trained teacher and did not seek to devise an exhaustive educational approach. Instead, he studied and experimented in education to bring about social and political change. Education was to provide the tools for the Indian subcontinent to free itself from British rule.

Gandhi's pedagogical thought evolved over the course of thirty years, synthesizing Hindu texts, Western educational philosophies, and his own political activism. Aware of Montessori's work since 1915, when the first Montessori school opened in India, he would over time draw inspiration from the Italian educator or comment on her work and its application to Indian children.[57] The two met in London at the beginning of October 1931, thanks to the intercession of the founder of the Socialist Quaker Society, J. Theodore Harris.[58] Later invited by "sister Montessori," Gandhi spoke at the seventeenth Montessori International Training Course in 1931.[59] His speech at the training course shows an affinity between the two, almost an intimacy, as if they shared a higher knowledge, something unknown to others, and were called upon to spread it—demonstrated by Gandhi's kindness and profound admiration for Montessori's work. Years later, Gandhi would refer to this encounter to demonstrate his knowledge and expertise

in educational issues, arguing that "I [Gandhi] have not taken a single lesson from her and yet she has publicly awarded a certificate to me saying
that I fully understand her system and have been practicing it. This certificate was not by way of false flattery."[60]

He began his talk at the training course by stating his support for one
of the Montessori's foundational principles: the idea that we "would
learn not from grown-up learned men, but from the so-called ignorant
children," which she expressed as *il bambino è padre dell'uomo*, "the child is
the father of the man."[61] The spiritual leader argued that "the law of Love
could be best understood and learned through little children," who would
be "perfectly innocent" were it not for their parents.[62] An "inexpressible
joy" also pervaded him when he saw children in Montessori schools who
understood "the virtue of silence" and meditation, as well as their capacity
to move gracefully in "pin-drop silence," with "those beautiful rhythmic
movements."[63] In a letter to boys and girls at an ashram, he would later
describe Montessori's lesson of silence and the way it taught children to
concentrate as "the thing he liked the most in their [Montessori's] method,"
but he also admired the teaching of music to children, and the training of
"all the senses and organs of the child, that is, its hands, feet, nose, ears,
tongue, skin and the mind, and they have very carefully planned a teaching
programme with that aim in view."[64] This admiration, however, was always
tempered by a certain anxiety or tension, seen in his letters and speeches;
for instance: "I hope that it will be possible not only for the children of the
wealthy and the well-to-do, but for the children of paupers to receive training of this nature."[65]

Overall, Montessori's and Gandhi's philosophies are characterized by
many similarities and common inspirations. Both were deeply shaped by
Theosophical ideas, especially the works of Besant and Blavatsky, as well as
by the humanitarian ideals and educational principles of Leo Tolstoy.[66]
Building on the teaching of those sacred Hindu treatises, the Upanishads,
Gandhi interpreted the goal of education to be for the Self within (*Ātman*)
to connect with the essence of the universe.[67] Students would be taught to
know their inner and true Self, the first principle, and therefore to understand God, and Truth (*Satya*). Through education, a child's inner being
would be "released from the empirical bonds of darkness and ignorance,"
or, returning to a source of inspiration so dear to Montessori, the British
poet William Wordsworth, the child would be freed from "the shade of
the prison-house."[68] This cultivation of character, the development of the
child's spirit and body into self-realization, was of paramount importance
and would come before teaching any formal competencies. Gandhi also

believed in the essential principle of "unity of life," the "oneness of human-ity," whereby all beings partake of the nature of God, and therefore all citi-zens could take part in the process of self-realization through education.[69]

According to the Mahatma, schooling was to be beneficial to all beings, both male and female, including those who belonged to lower castes, fol-lowing the principle of *sarvodaya*, or uplift for all. This concern for the well-being of every member of society and for the rights of the disenfranchised governed Gandhi's scheme of education, which included compulsory mass primary education for a country that, at the time, had a high rate of illiteracy and deep-seated marginalization of certain ethnic and religious groups.[70]

Self-realization through a holistic approach that involved the training of both mind and body was also at the center of Gandhi's plan, though he did not provide a didactic apparatus and instead pointed to activities that would further this goal. Among these was manual work (or vocational training for higher grades, and adult education), which centered on the notion of self-sufficiency and the need for the student to acquire skills necessary to pro-vide for oneself and the community.[71] Similar to Montessori's activities of practical life, Gandhi's pedagogical experiments advocated for children's engagement in daily household chores. In this respect, the Indian national-ist urged educators to introduce teaching crafts such as hand spinning, which stood to represent the dignity of labor in all forms and which sym-bolized the importance of self-reliance as connected to self-rule and the emancipation of the Indian subcontinent; furthermore, it helped connect students of all classes to the plights of the poorest members of society.[72] Children's work would also be geared toward learning handcrafts. This, according to Gandhi, would lead to the creation of art objects that could be sold, enabling the school to be economically self-supporting; the aim here was an alternative to state-funded education. Advocating for compulsory vocational training, for which he would later be accused of social immobil-ism, he argued for the value of teaching students an occupation that would allow them eventually to pay for the education they had received.[73]

While Gandhi's admiration for "the learned Madam Montessori" was mainly based on her educational accomplishments, he was aware as well of the educator's ambition to teach children to value harmony, respect, and peace.[74] In a 1931 speech, he said to her:

> You have very truly remarked that if we are to reach real peace in this world
> and if we are to carry on a real war against war, we shall have to begin with
> children and if they will grow up in their natural innocence, we won't have
> the struggle, we won't have to pass fruitless idle resolutions, but we shall go

from love to love and peace to peace, until at last all the corners of the world
are covered with that peace and love for which, consciously or unconsciously,
the whole world is hungering.[75]

One could also say that Montessori had, over time, embraced Gandhian
nonviolence, as her work endorsed the notion that "if violence is scrupu-
lously avoided in education, nonviolence could and would become a means
of development and lay a sure and lasting foundation for its application to
adult social relationships."[76] Montessori had also engaged in numerous
appeals, in and out of the classroom, to rethink ways of ending violence and
conflict via an education that would lead adults to oppose war altogether.
But overall, Gandhi's writings present, as philosopher Douglas Allen points
out, a precise and subtle analysis of the "multidimensional nature of violence and the structural violence of the status quo," which Montessori
never approached systematically. Throughout the spiritual leader's vast literary corpus, violence within the classroom is not only seen as the imposition of the authoritarian teacher on the student but also as one classmate
asserting himself over another. Violence is analyzed as directly linked to
other forms of systemic violence (religious, linguistic, economic, etc.), which
are all at the center of what he conceives to be the work of peace education.
Therefore, Gandhi's contribution to peace education involved rethinking
the regnant multidimensional configurations of the aforementioned violence of the status quo.[77] This seminal contribution has led to the creation
of entire fields of study on peace and has opened up of new ways of thinking
and understanding education to peace and nonviolence, inspiring social
movements toward equity and justice.[78]

Admiration for the pedagogical approach guided Gandhi's words, and
his mission to forward the cause of Indian independence never ceased to
be at the forefront of his intellectual quest. To this end, in a 1931 interview
with Montessori, he expressed an interest in adapting her methodology to
the "children of India's hovels": "If you have children, I have children too.
Friends in India ask me to imitate you. I say to them, no, I should not imitate you but should assimilate you and the fundamental truth underlying
your method." To which Montessori responded: "As I am asking my own
children to assimilate the heart of Gandhi. I know that feeling for me in
your part of the world is deeper than here."[79] As Montessori confirmed in
the interview, Indian thinkers were in fact more and more interested in her
approach. Over the years, Gandhi himself continued referencing her work
passionately to those who requested advice on how to educate India's children.
In rethinking his own ashram, he advised Parasram Mehrotra, the general

secretary of the ashram and a Hindi teacher, to transform the entire community into a teaching experience for the children, to "make the whole atmosphere of the ashram like that of a school, and that all the grown-up men and women should regard themselves as the children's guardians and make themselves fit to be so," just as he had seen in Montessori's schools.[80] But he also staunchly continued to argue that Montessori's ideas could not be "propagated in their Western garb in Indian villages, [where] they are more likely to prove useless and might even prove harmful," as they were too expansive and would not reflect the needs and desire of the local population.[81] As he would later say about Montessori to one of his collaborators, "Imbibe whatever you find useful, and discard the rest."[82]

Montessori probably sensed the attempt by Indian educators to use the principles of her approach without having to be subordinate to her organizations. In a letter to her grandson Mario Jr. written while in Madras, she acknowledged that Gandhi was "inevitably a rival" because of his engagement in reforming India's educational system. She argued that her training course had been so successful that "it has pervaded all of India and has caused a conflict—or rather a counter movement which wants to suppress it."[83] From this private account, one can surmise Montessori's hope to see her approach spreading throughout the continent.

Rukmini Devi and George Arundale

Although it did not come from a thinker native to India, the Montessori approach, based on the notion of freedom within the classroom and favoring independent thought and self-realization, appealed to those who wanted to promote the emancipation of the Indian people from foreign domination. Among those nationalists was the president of the Theosophical Society.

The nationalist movement created an environment conducive to educational reform and thus prepared the ground for the Montessori method to take root. Within this climate, George Arundale and Rukmini Devi, the main organizers of Montessori's trip to India and both fervent Indian nationalists in their own right, favored the dissemination of her approach, while adapting it to the country's indigenous cultures and traditions. In the words of Arundale, "Dr. Montessori's visit will have a profound effect upon the new life that is beginning to animate Indian education, . . . [and] the Theosophical Society was chosen as the instrument through which her genius will fructify this great field of the Indian Nation's life."[84] Once in India, Montessori saw her methodology applied to the children of the Besant Memorial School, an institution opened in 1934 and connected to the Kalakshetra Center for the Arts. There, Devi had amplified and reworked certain foundational aspects of Montessori's approach, contextualizing them within the political framework of the Hindu ethnic revival and the basic tenets of Theosophy.

Devi's pedagogical work focused on two aforementioned foundational elements of Montessori's approach—muscular education and beauty of the environment. Yet she also borrowed heavily from the Theosophical notions of unity of the cosmos and the individual (One Life) and of Universal Brotherhood. By looking at the applications of her principles to the Besant Memorial School, and by being exposed to the notions of One Life and Universal Brotherhood, Montessori formalized her own vision of cosmic education, the connection between humankind and the world at large.

Devi and Arundale were deeply involved in the nationalist movement. George Arundale was a British man, a Theosophist living in India who worked as a principal at the Central Hindu College in Benares, later becoming chancellor of the University of Madras. He was one of the most prominent educational reformers in the interwar period. A protégé of Annie Besant, he had moved to Adyar at the beginning of the twentieth century and joined the home rule movement.[85] He was a fierce advocate for the implementation of compulsory free education for all Indian children, a reform that the British colonial government had promised but never implemented.

Following the discourse on vernacular education as a catalyst for the country's emancipation, Arundale militated for India to relinquish its cultural and ideological dependency on British domination. Indian children were to be educated by native teachers, people who could resurrect Indian languages, values, and history.

Arundale's wife, Rukmini Devi, was also very much involved in this dialogue. She approached it, however, by advancing the ethnic revival of Hindu traditions. Devi trained with Cleo Nervi, a member of the celebrated Russian ballerina Anna Pavlova's dance troupe, and was urged by Pavlova herself "to find and resuscitate India's dance."[86] Devi focused on the temple art of Bharatanatyam, an ancient southern Indian dance and music tradition with religious roots. Her goal was to resurrect this form and to encourage young people to pursue it and thus reconnect with their ethnic identity.

Current historiography has been polarized over Rukmini Devi's decision to "revive" this dance form.[87] Dance historian Matthew Harp Allen argues that she appropriated a dance tradition, the Sadir, practiced by *devadasis*, lower-caste women who sang and danced during Hindu religious-artistic services.[88] The devadasis were trained by male dance practitioners and were married to one of the gods of the Hindu temple. Devi, by contrast, was a Brahmin, a member of the highest Hindu caste, considered purer than other segments of the population, such as the devadasis. Her choice to engage with this South Indian dance tradition came after it was suppressed by the colonial government. By the early twentieth century, the antinautch movement targeted all Hindu temple dancing (more broadly known as *nautch*). In 1911, a governmental dispatch was issued "desiring nationwide action against these performances."[89] In 1930, the Legislative Council of the city of Madras, where Devi herself resided, introduced a bill banning girls from being initiated as devadasis.[90] Though formal legislation against temple dedication was not enacted until 1947, the virulent propaganda of the antinautch campaign led to a suppression of Sadir and its performances much earlier.

As a result, at the time Devi started training, Sadir was relegated to the margins of society, and the devadasis and their dances were tainted by their lower caste. According to dance scholar Uttara Asha Coorlawala, "Orientalist discourse and Christian dualist concepts of separating sensuality and spirituality generated a perception of exploited womanhood" that was often applied to devadasis.[91] Debate over the dance ensued, and one suggestion was that the practice might be renewed and "saved" by training higher-caste women with supposedly higher moral principles.[92] Influenced by this debate, Devi worked to make Sadir, which took the name of Bharatanatyam, "respectable" by eliminating its erotic components and stressing its spiritual content, contributing to the marginalization of devadasi performers.[93]

In 1936, Devi created the Kalakshetra Center for the Arts, housed at the time inside the Theosophical Society headquarters. This organization "set out the objective of achieving an international cultural renaissance, aimed at reviving throughout India the true spirit of the arts, while at the same time, and as a means to the same end, enriching education already given in the school by the addition of Art Academy."[94] Kalakshetra took its name from *kala*, or "art," and *kshetra*, "holy place," in this case referring to a venue where students could be trained in traditional dance-drama, music, painting, folk arts and crafts, and literature. Its overarching goal was to recover and revive ancient Hindu culture and to make it available to people of all castes.[95] Its students' performances were open to the public—now onstage instead of at the temple—so as to encourage participation in these ancient art forms. The institution made this revitalist ideology its foundation, "for without a spirit of dedication and a power to enter into the Spirit of ancient India, Kalakshetra would serve no useful purpose either to our motherland, India, or the world."[96] Furthermore, it fostered the growth of nationalist sentiment, by giving children a renewed and revitalized sense of cultural identity—which had previously been attenuated by Western curricula.

As argued by Tapati Guha-Thakurta, "the new nationalist ideology of Indian art, its aesthetic of self-definitions and its research for a 'tradition' had strong roots in Orientalist writing and debate."[97] Devi started working at rehabilitating this dance tradition while in dialogue with the Indian nationalist movement, "which was deeply influenced by European Orientalist thought and Victorian morality."[98] While Victorian morality did play a role in Devi's decision to purge Sadir of eroticism and the adoption of "social mores of an appropriately superior class of dancer," the marginalization of lower-caste women was not a defining element of her school program.[99] Her school was open to children of all castes. Nevertheless, the importance of systemic divisions within India society and within the ideological foundations of the Theosophical Society must be addressed. Over time, members of the organization endorsed caste divisions—in particular, the distinction between Brahmin and non-Brahmin in South India—promoting discourses and initiatives with deep racial and social ramifications.[100] This was not an issue that had started with Devi joining the ranks of the Theosophical Society, or one that occupied any space within Devi's or Arundale's writings, but it had contributed to the initial structuring of the organization.

Religious syncretism as construed by the Theosophical Society was based on a stark dichotomy between modern and ancient India, one rooted in British academia.[101] Throughout the second half of the nineteenth century, philologist Friedrich Max Müller had contributed to the shaping of the image of "celestial India," an idealized country, the cradle of the most ancient spiritual traditions. This depiction was not based on factual evidence and had little to do with the actual geopolitical entity of the Indian subcontinent in the nineteenth and early twentieth centuries.[102] Broadly, Müller argued that ancient India was the source of Western civilization, the birthplace and repository of the oldest and purest surviving knowledge. His body of work aimed at reconstructing a Hindu golden age, wherein the Aryan elite engaged in a quest for truth and enlightenment. According to this reading, the Brahmin caste and their Hindu ideology preserved the tradition of the past Aryan elite and their knowledge, which had been transmitted throughout the ages.[103] Müller argued that the so-called Aryans' lineage was connected to the high-caste Brahmins, creating a sharp divide with the non-Brahmins, or inhabitants of South India, speaking Dravidian languages.

Devi did not express support for these positions. Despite the fact that her work was part of the turn-of-the-century conversations on decorum and respectability inspired by Victorian morality (a morality which was being thrust on the Indian people of lower castes), her pedagogy did not address class distinction and did include a number of radical elements.[104] For example, she nurtured the transformation of cultural transmission by depriving male teachers of their authority to control access to the repertory. Dancers could approach the texts directly, challenging the male guru's place as a gatekeeper of the tradition.[105] As argued by dance education scholar Avanthi Meduri, Devi operated within the transnational hub of patronage offered by the Theosophical Society, and she was not a "true Brahmin," due to her marriage to Arundale, who was British and a bishop of the Liberal Catholic Church. Devi's adaptation of Sadir into Bharatanatyam must therefore not be read from a "global modernity perspective of colonialism but from within the ideological framework of Indian nationalism and 'local' modernities perspective."[106] Her work at Kalakshetra transcended nationalism because it was embedded within the Theosophical Society, a transnational organization with a global worldview that welcomed many (often dissonant) voices. Montessori, who had a cursory knowledge of Müller's thought, and who did not report, renew, or talk about being part of the Theosophical Society while she was a part of it and yet was celebrated by Theosophists, was one of the voices that constituted this cultural plurality.[107]

Montessori in India

Within a global-history approach to the study of Montessori, her move to India calls for a postcolonial reading of her influences in and from this country. In accordance with a central tenet of Edward Said's *Orientalism*, this approach proceeds from the assumption that colonialism has forced "Western" knowledge upon colonized cultures and subjects.[108] The Montessori method was not imposed upon Indians in this sense. It did come, however, from an educator deeply involved in Western (albeit reformist) educational thought at a time when Indian nationalists were striving to free themselves from it entirely. Though the educator influenced both Tagore and Gandhi, both of them adopted the basic principles of her approach but adapted them to the cultural and intellectual milieu of their country. Devi's work to recontextualize Montessori within the Bharatanatyam revival, and the inspiration drawn by Montessori from this hybridization of her own method, furnish evidence that Montessori's reflection was the product of multidirectional discourses and entangled relationships on a global scale.

Indian nationalists may have established possible ways for adapting Montessori's approach to their own national independence prior to her arrival, but it was only at Kalakshetra that her educational project took on a concrete form—while steeped in the culture of the Theosophical Society. In 1934, Devi had established five Montessori classes at the Besant Memorial

School. The aim of this initiative was to instill in children a sense of freedom and independence as they learned, in accordance with the Theosophical principles. The schools served as the basic curriculum for those attending Kalakshetra. There, Meduri observes, Devi "developed an innovative multidisciplinary pedagogy for the arts, including the learning of Sanskrit, English, and Tamil languages."[109]

Upon her arrival, the Italian educator had the chance to gauge the efficacy of her approach on the children of Kalakshetra. There, Maria and her son, Mario, resided in the headquarters of the Theosophical Society in the district of Adyar, which overlooked luxuriant gardens and temples of many faiths. She quickly organized her first instructor training course, which was held there in 1939 under palm-leafed huts built for the event, for which "as many as 315 students joined the course, comprised within 3 crowded months, men and women, young and old from all parts of India."[110]

Those who attended it described it as an enlightening experience, where an enthralling Montessori lectured in Italian for hours while her son translated her message into English. As Mario Montessori put it, since their arrival in India, "Dr. Montessori was deemed to be a seer—some Hindus

Maria Montessori delivering a lecture in India, flanked by George Arundale, *left*, and Rukmini Devi, *right*, ca. 1939. Courtesy of Surendra Narayan Archives, Theosophical Society, Adyar, Chennai.

and Theosophists considered her to be the reincarnation of some great religious teacher of the past. . . . She was considered a sort of divinely inspired teacher who had come to reveal the mental and spiritual potentialities of childhood and through them to show the way of a redeemed humanity."[111] Montessori felt at ease in this climate. Instead of the black dresses she had worn since her mother's death, she began to wear long, loose white ones, and often adorned herself with the traditional garland of lotus and jasmine flowers offered to her by her students at the beginning of each class. As Montessori's biographer Rita Kramer recounts, "Coming to this far-away place, in a way she had come home."[112] She had finally found a place where people eagerly awaited her message and asked only to help her implement her ideas.

Montessori's letters to her grandchildren confirm the educator's feelings for her stay in India, calling it "a mysterious country, which is conquering me." They also show how the educator was quite in line with her time when it came to the rhetoric used to describe Indians, whom she often saw as primitive in relation to the "world of white people [living in the city of Madras] who preserve the costumes of the civilized world over here!" She fell prey to problematic tropes such as portraying herself as "a missionary among natives!"[113] These racist comments are interspersed in an otherwise lengthy correspondence and accompanied by numerous signs of appreciation for the diversity of the people she met, yet they must be acknowledged, not dismissed as a mere reflection of her naivete.[114]

At Montessori's request, as a sign of their deep collaboration, Devi conducted art courses for the trainees—both to incorporate the arts into the curriculum and to impart a lesson in the importance of beauty in education.[115] Within her own school, Devi interpreted art to be the expression of the Theosophical concept of Universal Life, the spiritual uplifting of a human consciousness to a state of unity and harmony. In her teaching of Bharatanatyam, she emphasized the importance both of the child's muscular education and of beauty within the educational environment. Both principles served the child, teaching him to achieve harmony with his surroundings and peace in his interpersonal relationships.

In referring to these two principles, Devi borrowed from Montessori. Since the beginning of Montessori's experiments in San Lorenzo, she had argued that if the child's muscles were trained in the proper way, and if his school was inspiring and beautiful, the child would be in harmony with his own environment. Devi followed the same principles and created a school where children were in just such harmony—which, combined with the right activities, would bring them into harmony with the larger world.

Portrait of Maria Montessori in India. Courtesy of Surendra Narayan Archives, Theosophical Society, Adyar, Chennai.

Maria and Mario Montessori with Rukmini Devi in Madras, India. Courtesy of
Association Montessori Internationale Archive, Amsterdam.

In traditional school settings, learning was (and, in fact, continues to be)
achieved via activities centered on listening, reading, and writing. In the
Montessori classroom, at all levels, children learned through movement.
As scholar of psychology Angeline Lillard put it, "Montessori saw the sta-
tionary child as problematic" and believed that the development of movement and thought were strongly correlated. Movement was therefore an
integral part of school curricula.[116] For the preschool years, Montessori
advocated for muscular education to assist children in the development of
cognitive growth and physiological movement. This was achieved by the
repetitive performance of certain exercises. As a result, children would further develop their abilities to walk, breathe, and speak. They practiced muscular education via specific practical life activities. They refined their motor
skills by tying shoelaces and fastening buttons until they mastered such
activities, and by following specifically designed teaching materials. The
goal of these activities was to develop a form of bodily know-how, muscle
memory, and the improvement of fine and gross motor skills, up to age six.
This muscular education would eventually lead them to achieve *la grazia*

dei movimenti (grace in movement), or a perfect balance between themselves and their world.

A similar quest for equilibrium between muscular control and grace was at the core of Devi's dance instruction. Bharatanatyam shared Montessori's highly technical approach to muscular training. The dance was based on the narration of myths, legends, and prayers from the major Hindu texts, choreographing them by interpreting and translating them into movement. The results often reflected the syncopated meter of the writing itself, which was poetic to begin with; its verses were rendered "with arrested points in movement frozen in sculptural representation."[117] From a technical standpoint, Bharatanatyam was achieved through extended training and by reaching proficiency with certain crucial steps: for example, dancers were often called to maintain a fixed torso while either bending their legs or flexing out their knees. This positioning was accompanied by sophisticated hand- and footwork and an elaborate array of eye and facial expressions. At the Besant Memorial school, Montessori's activities to promote the refinement of motor skills served as preparation for achieving muscular control sufficient to Bharatanatyam's performances.

Devi also tapped into Montessori's work on integrating beauty into the educational experience, combining aesthetics and pedagogy. In all her schools, Montessori replaced old desks with furniture sized appropriately to children, to serve the autonomy and freedom of the children's movements. As described by Arundale, Montessori's "world contain[ed] brilliantly colored and bountiful articles of furniture, easily moved about."[118] According to Montessori, beauty would attract the children "like the colored petals attract insects," and they would approach their activities eagerly and cheerfully.[119] The beauty to which Montessori referred is not to be confused with luxury but rather the beautiful simplicity of the classroom and its furniture.[120] Commenting on Montessori, Arundale argued that this was a "beauty that calls the child to service" to engage with his surroundings in a positive fashion.[121]

In contrast with the typical schools of her time, Montessori's classroom was inspired by serenity, a feeling that would foster the child's tranquility and well-being, crucial for the development of the child's cognitive faculties. Living in a beautiful environment would stimulate in the children a sense of belonging that led them to take care of the environment at all times. This would train them, in the process, to avoid bumping into each other and being disruptive.[122]

Devi also argued that "responding to beauty is a way to uplift the human consciousness as a means of reforming human society."[123] She observed

Maria Montessori with children in a classroom in India, 1940s. Courtesy of
Association Montessori Internationale Archive, Amsterdam.

that children all over the world responded favorably to anything that they
considered beautiful, including not only color but also music and rhythm.
They needed, therefore, to have art as a component of their curriculum from
the earliest age possible. Within this beautifully designed environment,
children would grow freely, not stifled by a constrictive education but alert
to beauty in the environment and given opportunities to respond actively to
it. Devi asserted:

> Many children want to dance, and the grown-ups say, "Oh! The *tala* (rhythm)
> is not correct." Other things may also have been wrong. The child does not
> care. He dances to enjoy himself. If he can learn to express himself
> gracefully, if grace and rhythm are born in his own nature, then very quickly
> technique will follow. If the child is denied his desire to self-expression, he
> grows up feeling that something is wrong, he cannot express himself well or
> quickly because there is something he has not learned in life.[124]

Devi argued, like Montessori, that children needed to live gracefully, to
"express this exquisite culture [in which we live] in beautiful manners, in
gracious speech."[125] According to Arundale's *Indian Education for India*, the
Indian child already possessed "a spirit of deference, of graciousness . . .

respect and eager service, dignity and even reflection of India's eternal majesty."[126] With a curriculum pervaded by art, they would be able to refine this trait. Students who learned in a free environment like Kalakshetra, and were introduced to the arts in a creative way, would be able to overcome the greatest problem of their time. As Devi argued,

> It will be my greatest happiness to know that in its own humble way
> Kalakshetra is helping to make more beautiful, more artistic, the lives of
> all—that in the education of the young, creative reference for that spirit of
> the beautiful which knows no distinction of race, nation or fate as a pre-
> eminent place, that ugliness is beginning to depart from daily life, whether
> in the home or in the earning of the livelihood, that leisure finds decreasing
> satisfaction in the crude and the vulgar and that the whole world is slowly
> turning away from those barbarisms of war, of greed and of cruelty which
> still challenge its right to be called civilized.[127]

Rukmini Devi created an environment that closely resembled what Montessori described as a place where the individual was in harmony with his surroundings. But Devi brought this idea one step further, connecting a child at peace with his local environment to the entire world around him. Montessori, in turn, spent the rest of her stay in India expanding this notion. She would include a new connection between the child and the cosmos, to shape a human being who is aware of being part of an ecological and human universe, one who respects nature and worldwide ecology. It is precisely in this context that Montessori fully elaborated the notion of the cosmic education.

Witnessing Devi's Kalakshetra—and collaborating with her—prompted Montessori to delve further into the notion of the unity of humankind and the environment. The Indian revivalist had borrowed this concept herself, from the Theosophical principle of One Life, adapting it to the educational curricula of her school. One Life had been a principle of Theosophy since its inception. It had its roots in the Hermetic strain of Renaissance philosophy, particularly in Marsilio Ficino's De Vita (The Book of Life). The Theosophical term One Life was based on the idea that "as below, so it is above."[128] Put another way, both the celestial and the terrestrial worlds are constituted by the same elements. One Life, also referred to as the Absolute Deity, "formless and uncreated, procee[ed] [sic] the Universe of Lives," permeated every individual's existence.[129] It was therefore equivalent to the immanent principle, a divinity that was not a transcendent Being, but an immanent subject in an evolving world. As Blavatsky wrote in The Key to Theosophy, "we believe in the Universal Divine Principle, the root of ALL, from which all proceeds, and within which all shall be absorbed at the end of the great cycle of Being."[130] This "universal occult tradition" is best known as the *Secret Doctrine*, Blavatsky wrote.[131] As Maria Carlson observes, this doctrine "unites religion, science and philosophy into one grand synthesis that explains everything: God, the Universe, Man, Being, and Creation."[132] On a spiritual level, people did not exist as monads, as discrete parts of a universe, but as one single organism—often compared by Theosophists to "scientifically proven" natural phenomena such as electricity and magnetism.[133] As a result, the distinctions between secular and sacred, material and spiritual, and public and private dissolved. Such distinctions were superseded by the notion that division was an illusion and that only One Life existed. Besant, "the great pedagogue and theosophist," argued in *The Ancient Wisdom* that man is a God, incarnated in flesh but fallen from his so-called astral body, the spiritual world, and throughout his existence he strives to ascend to his origin.[134] His development unfolds according to an inner project, one that follows the laws of Nature—that is to say, the laws that regulate the physical realm, as well as the mental and moral.[135]

On a practical level, this reading of immanentism took the form of philanthropic work, in pursuit of the Theosophical ideal of Universal Brotherhood, a union among people without reference to race, creed, sex, caste, or color. As interpreted originally by Blavatsky, this brotherhood was inspired by the mission of secret societies such as the Freemasons and the Rosicrucians: the study of wisdom with the lofty purpose of doing good while keeping their ultimate goals, even their very existence, a secret.[136] During Besant's tenure (1907–1933), the society took concrete steps to formalize its strategies for achieving a Universal Brotherhood. Proselytes were encouraged not to retreat from the world while searching for religious truths, but rather to engage in expansive political measures "intended to bring the material realities of the 'physical plane' into harmony with the Cosmic Plan."[137] As a result, adepts who took part in these initiatives merged the idea of transforming and improving the self and subjectivity with the goal of changing the material world through activism. The notion of Universal Brotherhood had been integral to Montessori's elaboration of pacifism since 1917 (as discussed in chapter 3) and constituted the foundation for her work on cosmic education.

Before proceeding, it is important to understand the political significance that Theosophists attributed over time to the notion of immanentism and how this relates to Montessori's plan. As historian Joy Dixon has argued, the dissolution of social and bodily boundaries occurring within the Theo-

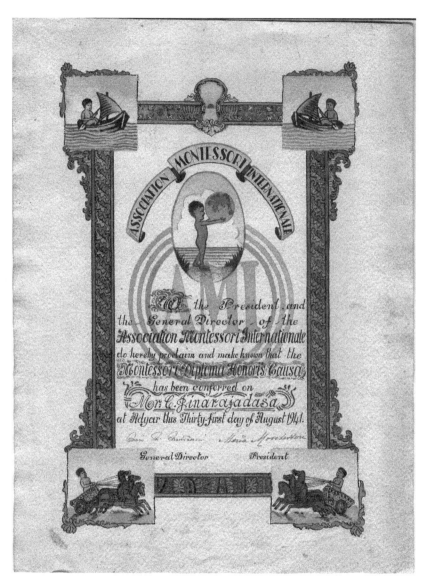

Montessori Diploma Honoris Causa to Curuppumullage Jinarajadasa, fourth
president of the Theosophical Society, 1941. Courtesy of Surendra Narayan Archives,
Theosophical Society, Adyar, Chennai.

sophical reading of immanentism provided a novel understanding of the human body and the relationship between the individual and the community.[138] Although in contemporary society, a person's actions were characterized by total independence and by the modern liberal notion of "possessive individualism," Theosophy replaced this concept with a fluid and permeable interpretation of human relationships, in which all bodies were connected to one another, on astral, mental, and spiritual levels.[139] This vision created an "occult body politics," which often granted access to "new forms of knowledge that were otherwise devalued: the bodily, the spiritual, the feminine and the eastern." Different political values could be attributed to the teaching of One Life and to the resulting occult body politics: "it could sustain both a corporatist and a collectivist vision," and over time it adapted to the changing political context, renegotiating political affiliations on both the left and the right.[140]

A political shift within the very same organization, depending on who interpreted its core writings, had characterized the Theosophical Society since its formation. It is a worthy question, whether Montessori was aware of the disparate political readings and the Theosophical Society's at times profound critique of liberal individualism through the notion of One Life. The educator has not left any direct commentary on this topic. Montessori did not ponder the political implications of One Life, which she used, figuratively, in rethinking her pedagogical approach, through a discussion of the notion of cosmic education.

Building on her previous work, she elaborated a plan to connect the child to humanity and the global environment, inserting him into a panhuman system and making him aware of his important role within it. According to Montessori, a global approach to early childhood education was necessary, in that it would connect the child with nature in order to raise an adult in harmony with the environment. Through what she termed "cosmic education," children would become active members of society; they would feel that they were citizens of a nation, an integral part of the human species, and members of a planetary ecology. Humanity would acquire a cosmic task, a more meaningful purpose than mere consumption and procreation.

To devise this overarching plan, Montessori reinterpreted the Theosophical notion of One Life. She adapted it to a structured pedagogical curriculum that sought to trace a unifying plan within the cosmos, one that would connect the birth and the development of distinct beings to the evolution of the earth itself, and ultimately to the evolution of human civilization. The Italian educator claimed that ontogenesis, the development of a single organism, did not recapitulate phylogenesis, the evolution of species and lineages: "the purpose of life is not to achieve perfection along an unlimited line of progress" but to locate oneself within the vaster evolution of the earth, to find one's purpose within cosmogenesis, the evolution of the universe, and "to achieve a definite aim within the environment."[141] While this process happened unconsciously for plants and animals—for example, microorganisms purified water in the ocean without being given specific instructions—the child must be guided by education to find his own path, Montessori argued.[142]

Montessori reported students asking, "What am I? What is the duty of mankind in this wonderful universe? Do you live here only for yourselves or do you have a more elevated task? Why do we fight and struggle? What is good and evil? Where will everything end up?"[143] Educators, according to Montessori, must help children find their place and purpose within the world by teaching an interdisciplinary curriculum that leads them to see the correlations between disciplines and fields of study, as well as the connections between different beings, their roles in society, and their relation to the environment. According to a teacher who followed Montessori to Kodaikanal and helped her and Mario develop the didactic materials for cosmic education, children ages six to twelve were ready to discern between good and evil. Furthermore, by stretching their imaginations through education, they could be prepared to acquire a "whole vision of the universe."[144] The purpose of this cosmic theory was therefore to acknowledge and cast light upon the intricacies, threads, and connections among all the various elements of the universe. Once the child saw the "complex task" of all the parts, the irreplaceable role that all elements have in the making of life on earth, he would be able to find his place among the "agents of creation":[145]

> Look at every expression of creation; hidden in the core of selfish expression of life, you will find the generous giving of unceasing work to the upkeep of the general welfare, to the procuring of the happiness of the whole and to a Cosmic Equilibrium which is kept in un-answering harmony by the ceaseless activity of everything that has been created, mountain and sea, wind and rock, desert and swamp, animal and plant, ice and fire. All have their merits and should be appreciated by the human mind, the most powerful and the most perfect of the Cosmic Agents.[146]

According to Montessori, ecology was to be the point of departure for studying these correlations. From then on, a curriculum, a "universal syllabus" for the elementary years with an ample breadth of disciplines, must be followed to provide the child with a cosmic perspective.[147]

The notion of finding one's place within the cosmos and society must not be mistaken for a suggestion on Montessori's part that social mobility be inhibited. Nor, of course, did she intend to promote a system of castes similar to what she had observed in India. Montessori did not argue that children should be educated only for a specific profession or to play only one, unchanging role in society. Instead, she explicitly argued in favor of a well-rounded education that included a multilateral development of all the child's faculties, in which manual activities are carried out in concert with intellectual ones.[148] Cosmic education would allow for the development of the children's propensities and abilities, leading them to find their natural place according to their predispositions.

This cosmic task would give every individual a place within the universe, a reason to exist within it. Mankind must find its place within this "theory of creation," that he might live not merely as a parasite, but rather participate in the care and development of the planet, Montessori asserted. She argued that people are not prepared to "dominate the environment which is composed of a 'supra-nature' created upon the earth by himself."[149] A new form of education was necessary for them to develop their latent energies, one that takes into account what Montessori defined as the new unity of humankind—an educational plan that connected the entire world under the banner of a renewed interest in the consciousness of the individual. Education would then advance "the idea of brotherhood, brotherhood so extended that it enfolds not only man, but also animals, plants, flowers, for instance."[150]

Montessori claimed that within this curriculum "all the items of culture [astronomy, geography, geology, biology, etc.] must be concerned as different aspects of the knowledge of the world and the cosmos." The connections of these aspects to one another spurred an interest "from a center towards its ramifications," igniting a rippling effect in the child's curiosity and desire to learn.[151] As Mario Montessori put it, through such curriculum "the child can experience in nature that there is something eternal, present everywhere and always, which has organized the whole universe in such a way that everything in it, merely by existing, is of service to the whole."[152] Educator David Kahn maintains that "the interdependency of life and the network of ecology [was] hardly a new insight."[153] But connecting all elements of life through the elementary school curriculum and creating a cohesive course of study with the goal of improving humanity indeed constituted a departure from other approaches.

What the educator termed *cosmic education* had the objective of promoting universal cooperation, something that would tend toward the affirmation of democracy and ultimately produce a renewed world. This last theorization is foundational for the field of *ecopedagogy*, or education for sustainability, a discipline that comprises all educational practices promoting an appreciation for the collective potential of humankind and aiming at devising culturally relevant forms of knowledge and ethical principles grounded in notions such as respect for the life of all living beings. Through the works of critical educators such as Paulo Freire, ecopedagogy has expanded to encompass related notions of planetary consciousness and students' engagement in the social, political, and racial ramifications of global problems.[154] In this twenty-first-century era of ecological decline and a renewed social responsibility to the environment expressed by a global youth movement, Montessori's educational project and political agenda loom large.

Montessori's plan was fully elaborated in her *Education for a New World* and *To Educate the Human Potential*, both dedicated to George Arundale and first published by the Kalakshetra publishing house.[155] Under the plan, a new school would be able to develop a "new man," as well as "a persuasion that mutual help among men is the most direct form of universal defense. The need or the inferiority of a people are a real danger for the whole of humanity and it is in the interest of all to find the means to satisfy those needs and to uplift man from their state of inferiority."[156]

Montessori drew extensively on another core tenet of Theosophy, the imminent advent of a new era, and she did so in her political writings on pacifism. According to Blavastky, the nineteenth century marked the end of the Kali Yuga cycle, as inspired by Hinduism, the end of the so-called dark age. In its place, a new age was about to begin: "Whether right or wrong with regard to the latter prophecy, the *blessings* of Kali Yuga are well described, and fit in admirably even with that which one sees and hears in Europe and other civilized and Christian lands in full XIXth, and at the dawn of the XXth century of our great era of ENLIGHTENMENT."[157] Montessori used this notion often, in multiple ways—as a point of departure, as a way of stressing the importance of charting a new course for humanity via education, or as an indication of the changes brought about by scientific discoveries. People risked being subjugated by what Montessori termed *supranature*, in reference to those creations and technological inventions of humankind that supersede nature and vastly modify the environment. The emergence of a new era, one in which the child would be given a cosmic education, would have allowed people to dominate the supranature—to be in harmony with nature, not dominated by it. All in all, returning to this Theosophical trope added force to her writing and urgency to her pleas.

Montessori's writing assumed a more somber tone when she discussed cosmic education, making extensive use of the notion of a dark age to reflect the distress and dire conditions endured by families during the course of the Second World War.[158] In June 1940, when Italy entered the war on the side of Germany, the British government interned Mario Montessori in a camp for civilians in Amednagar, together with the Italians residing in India, and labeled him an enemy alien. There, he struggled with military discipline and he "got into trouble on several occasions" for insubordination, "offering violence to [a] British officer," and for "having made [himself] a nuisance."[159] Some restrictions were also applied on his mother's movement. With all activities paused, Mario tried from the camp to motivate his mother to continue her "noble mission. We are two, only two, but your voice will one day be more powerful than all the guns of this crazy humanity."[160]

Although Mario was released in relatively short order thanks to the intercession of British authorities, the family was forced to wait out the end of the war in India. The climate of Adyar was not ideal for Maria Montessori, so they moved to the isolated hill city of Kodaikanal. Once there, immersed in the lush natural environment of South India, and inspired by Devi's work, Montessori focused on expanding her philosophy of peace.

A pamphlet found at the Surendra Narayan Archives at the Theosophical Society headquarters in Adyar shows Montessori's closest assistants and collaborators' lectures on cosmic education, all delivered as openings to various training courses throughout the 1940s.[161] Published in 1946, not long after the end of World War II, the pamphlet pays tribute to the fertile sources that these educators had, citing the most disparate authors and works, such as William Drumming's "Lessons from Nature" and Rudyard Kipling's "A Dedication."[162] Despite the text's hopeful tone—inspired by the impact Montessori children would eventually have in the world—the pamphlet concludes with "alarming concerns" about the political situation of the time and about experimentation with the atomic bomb. The future of humanity seemed uncertain to the authors, given that "nations were still in the grips of political aggrandizement; such dangerous experiments will send echoes of Hiroshima and Nagasaki throughout the length and breadth of the world."[163] Cosmic education was the beginning of a lofty and ambitious project that would, if adopted on a large scale, eventually yield impressive results. But that would require all the strength of a woman who was—despite her stamina and force of will (and the crucial help of her son, Mario)—in her mid-seventies. Upon her return to Europe, the Continent's physical and moral reconstruction as well as its "lost children" awaited her.[164]

Conclusion

The so-called Indian period in Maria Montessori's life had a profound impact on her; during the decade she spent in the country, she had the chance to rethink and expand her plan to promote peace and harmony from the classroom into a larger project of social renewal that would change the whole world.[165] Although her "cosmic education" is certainly a product of its own time, all its elements were present since the very beginning of Montessori's work in one form or another. They constitute a subtle thread that runs through the educator's writings, touching on issues of social justice, inequality, ecology, and sustainability. In a compelling plea to teach sexual education delivered at the 1908 Women's National Congress, Montessori argued that women had to carry on a radical change in education by speaking honestly about sexuality and procreation:

> The superb splendor, the grandiose, the marvelous harmony of the universe, is the goal [of education]. . . . In the early years, instead of *fairy tales*, children could be taught the fantastic wonders of nature, specifically plants' reproduction, or love for flowers. Pollen, the impalpable powder that rains like divine gold on the pistil of flowers, *creates* [life]. It is all the same, but it contains within itself marvelous life: the grains of pollen, so fine, are the ones that generate woods, roses, the little grass in meadows, the grain that nourishes man.[166]

Within this unity of all living beings, a harmony must be established, one that starts within a classroom and radiates throughout the cosmos, she asserted. Present throughout her writings, this notion was systematized once in India.

India's influence, an often overlooked aspect of Montessori's life, extended well beyond her actual stay in the country; it can be seen in her early interest in the possible coexistence of faith and science, as explored in Theosophical writings; her exchanges with Indian intellectuals such as Tagore and Gandhi; and later her collaboration with Devi and Arundale. Devi, though perhaps a lesser-known figure, became one of Montessori's most important interlocutors. Both women were concerned with the integration of theoretical and practical abilities and skills, with experiencing culture from its roots, with the meaning of artistic creation, and with promoting an atmosphere of quiet meditation for living and learning.[167] They were also both convinced that spreading peace was a duty of early childhood education. The Theosophical notions of One Life and the Brotherhood of Humanity gave Montessori the intellectual framework to fully elaborate on cosmic education, rethinking the curriculum for the elementary years in a comprehensive and exhaustive way. Upon her return to Europe, the great Italian educator continued to be influenced by this experience. The next and final chapter of her life would revolve around the study of newborns that she conducted in India, leading her to elaborate on the infant's capacity to absorb information and sensation from the surrounding world.

Conclusions

The Legacy of Montessori's Pacifism

In a 1944 letter to the psychoanalysts Anna Freud (Sigmund Freud's daughter) and Dorothy Burlingham, a young British mother reported that her two-year-old son, Bobby, was not doing very well now that he had moved out of the Hampstead War Nurseries:

> [Bobby] has eaten nothing since Sunday. He also has terrible nightmares, and seems to go almost mad for a bit, and screams and throws himself about. He is also afraid and screams if somebody knocks at the door or rattles anything. When he was standing outside the other day and the workmen threw some rubble on the pile, I thought he would go into a fit almost, he was so frightened. The doctor at the Welfare said she thought he probably has some sort of memory of the bombing, as it is the same house, and this flat is exactly as the top floor where we were.[1]

Separated from his mother, who had been hospitalized to give birth to a second child, and from his father, who had been deployed to India, Bobby had spent a few months at the institute founded by the psychoanalysts. Sponsored by the American Foster Parents' Plan for War Children, Freud and Burlingham ran three residential homes for evacuated children from 1941 to 1945.[2] At all three, they worked not only to repair the psychological damage caused by World War II and to prevent further harm but also to conduct "research on the essential psychological needs of children; to study their reactions to bombing, destruction, and early separation from their families; to collect facts about the harmful consequences whenever their essential needs remain unsatisfied."[3]

The Montessori approach was chosen for the nurseries "so as to afford the child the maximum increase in self-esteem and gratification by means of task completion and independent problem solving," as explained by Freud.[4] Those working at the psychoanalytic nursery attended seminars on the fundamentals of psychoanalysis, gymnastics for babies, anatomy, first aid and treatment of childhood diseases, and an introductory class to the Montessori method taught by Hedy Schwartz, who had directed a Montessori school in Vienna.[5] Among the teachers, many were young Austrian women who had fled their homes and lost their relatives to concentration camps.[6]

Anna Freud's project bore some resemblance to the White Cross, the organization for war-afflicted children that Montessori had attempted to create over the course of World War I and that constituted a crucial phase of development in Montessori's theory of pacifism, as discussed in chapter 2. As a letter by Sigmund Freud attests, Anna "consider[ed] herself a disciple of Montessori," and Sigmund himself knew about Montessori's "humanitarian understanding and endeavors"; it is likely that both Freuds were familiar with Montessori's ideas for the White Cross.[7] Just like Montessori, Anna Freud's aim was not to simply provide material assistance for the children but also to offer psychological support and rehabilitate them from the effects of war. The extensive training Freud provided to her staff, a regimen that included hygiene and gymnastics, was similar to what Montessori had envisioned for the White Cross teacher-nurses. Despite notable differences in their thought—foremost, for Montessori, the absence of infantile sexual drive—Freud's humanitarian endeavors had the same basic premises as the Italian educator's. Furthermore, Freud relied on Montessori's pedagogical approach and recognized its benefits among her own subjects: children who had experienced profound loss, displacement, and destruction during the bombing of London.[8]

Focusing on war's psychological consequences for children was uncommon when Montessori first conceived of the White Cross; this was one reason she never succeeded in securing financial support to create the organization. But the theory behind it would eventually become a standard aspect of relief work in postwar Europe, also thanks to Freud's accomplishments at the Hempstead nurseries.[9] Times had changed, and nurseries like Freud's could now make strides in influencing the international conversation on children in conflict areas, becoming "a universal lesson in human development."[10] This represented an opening for Montessori's work on peace to finally be recognized—if only in part.

Whereas interwar intergovernmental and private humanitarianism centered primarily on supporting children's material needs, in the aftermath of World War II, educators, policy makers, and social workers focused on the psychological rehabilitation of youth. Deportation, emigration, and "ethnic cleansing" had left an unprecedented number of children separated from their families and unattended, requiring a different approach to rehabilitation. With the Nazi empire's unconditional surrender, those who had lost their loved ones started to try to reunite, posting ads in newspapers, contacting international agencies, and attempting to return to their previous homes. But reuniting with family members was often impossible. National Red Cross agencies received thousands of requests to find missing children. These "unaccompanied children" became the center of a bitter political battle among international associations, governmental agencies, and social workers. New international humanitarian organizations, such as the United Nations Relief and Rehabilitation Administration (1943–1947), emphasized the importance of reinstituting prewar social norms and personal well-being, issuing reports on the psychological conditions of refugee children, and "anoint[ing] themselves agents of psychological reconstruction."[11] In the wake of a horrific global war—a conflict that left millions dead and tested the very nature of humanity—children's mental and psychological welfare seemed to be the keystone of European political and social stability.

European states also began to demonstrate a gradually declining confidence in war as an instrument of policy. Rooted in the long peace of the late nineteenth and early twentieth centuries, the slow but steady constitution of what historian James J. Sheehan calls "civilian states" transformed the post-European order. Economic prosperity, social modernization, and technological progress superseded confidence in national security and militarization, inaugurating a "non-war community" where occasional and limited conflicts arose but not ones that could jeopardize the new, civilian nature of Western Europe.[12]

Within this context, social workers, intellectuals, and politicians rethought Montessori's philosophy of education in its diverse inspirations and complex facets, finally engaging with some of her previous work on pacifism. They did so largely for two reasons. First, without opposition from nationalistic governments, Montessori's own public engagement on peace throughout the 1930s could now be appreciated and promoted across Europe. Second, in the aftermath of war, the importance of a new education—one that took a holistic view of the child and could address psychological trauma in particular—was now indisputable. Peace had to be restored, and children had to heal. Montessori could address both issues.

This intellectual climate was ideal for promoting Montessori's pedagogical research as essential to the quest for universal peace. Her work of advancing social justice in the desolate marshes of Italy's *agro romano*, her observations on refugees and displaced children of World War I, and her study of education and disarmament, among other subjects, all served now as compelling evidence to a wider audience of Montessori's tireless promotion of peace through education. But this would turn out to be yet another missed opportunity: politicians, educators, feminists, and humanitarians touted Montessori's work on peace but focused mainly on a narrow set of her speeches rather than on the deep-rooted pacifist nature of her pedagogical inquiry. This choice of focus led to a partial reassessment that did not emphasize Montessori's arguments on education as a tool to achieve peace. As a result, the campaign for explicit widespread recognition—namely, through the Nobel Peace Prize—failed. Furthermore, Montessori's death in 1952 halted further possibilities for reframing her pacifist output as central to her pedagogical inquiry. Although newly constituted international agencies such as the United Nations Educational, Scientific and Cultural Organization (UNESCO) initially engaged Montessori as an interlocutor, her death, compounded by the lack of a strong movement supporting her pacifist work, diminished the momentum of that legacy. Only decades later would they incorporate Montessori's revolutionary message on children's rights into their efforts.

The postwar climate nonetheless gave Montessori an opportunity. Destruction became an occasion for her to elucidate her vision of childhood's role in governance and democracy building. The daunting work of reconstruction in post–World War II Europe found the Italian educator full of enthusiasm, propelled by the belief that the child's hidden capacities would rebuild humanity and that politicians would finally understand the need to invest in education as the cornerstone of a new society. Montessori was particularly taken by the fact that her native Italy was among the nations that asked for her help in rethinking the future of its youngest citizens, and she felt she could not miss "the call of her own country that awaits her, that needs her."[13] While in Kodaikanal, Montessori wrote to Luigia Tincani, founder of the Unione Santa Caterina da Siena delle Missionarie della Scuola, sharing her enthusiasm for this impending reconstruction:

> Italy! Help Italy with all my strength. I did not invent my method of education—the children of San Lorenzo, forty years ago, planted the seed of this pedagogical endeavor. Roman children!! I follow them as closely as I would follow an indelible and perpetual vision—they have transformed my heart. I have tirelessly dedicated myself to them. I travelled the world like a pilgrim—a missionary—who spoke to the wind. . . . Still consolidating my work: putting roots in Italy.[14]

Montessori probably sensed that her life had come full circle and that she could at last go back to educating Italian children.

Invited by the minister of public instruction Guido Gonella to deliver a series of lectures, she arrived in Rome from India on May 1, 1947. Tincani picked her up at the airport, together with politician and pedagogue Maria De Unterrichter Jervolino, whose advocacy proved to be instrumental in Montessori's Italian trips and events.[15]

From the moment Montessori returned to Europe, Jervolino played a crucial role in the diffusion of Montessori's theory of pacifism. Jervolino attributed to Montessori her view that vanquished populations were "a danger, a burden, an obstacle to all winning nations," in that the victors became responsible for the recovery process, as would soon be demonstrated by the United States' European Recovery Program.[16] What Montessori had predicted was now the harsh reality. In Jervolino's vision, the spread of Montessori's philosophy of education would prompt a drastic societal change; it would offer the means to achieving peace and building a democratic society. Jervolino thus arranged for Montessori's trip to Italy on the basis of her global fame in early childhood education but also her engagement with pacifism, a side of her work that had been mostly ignored until then.

The political and cultural debate on education awaiting Montessori upon her return to Italy was hospitable, but it was not entirely free from tension. Italian liberal intellectuals worked to dismantle the notion of youth as elaborated by Fascism. This was a vitalistic mythology of competent and knowledgeable young men, willing not only to obey and fight but also to lead and govern; it had been adopted as a metaphor for the regime itself.[17] Twenty years of dictatorship, a second global war, new tools of mass destruction, and the schism caused by the Cold War all had a deep impact on the national conversation on education. At the time, Italy, a nation at the margins of Europe with profound aspirations to peace, was considered to be at the crossroads of opposing ideologies: home to the biggest Communist Party in the West, it still remained within the sphere of influence of the United States.

These conflicting ideologies manifested in three pedagogical camps: the lay progressives, such as Lamberto Borghi and Ernesto Codignola; the Marxists, including scholars such as Lucio Lombardo Radice and Dina Bertoni Jovine; and Catholic intellectuals such as Luigi Stefanini and Giuseppe Agazzi. Despite their differences, all three schools of thought came to identify the child as a catalyst of civic, economic, and societal growth in postwar Italy.[18] At least on a rhetorical level, they all imbued youth with the task of rebuilding the country, in order to avert the failures of the previous generation. Accordingly, the study of progressive preschool and elementary school curricula (conducted between 1943 and 1945 by Carleton Washburne of the

Education Subcommission of the Allied Control Commission, and liberal ministers of public instruction Adolfo Omodeo and Guido de Ruggero), envisioned a school that was "no longer authoritarian and competitive, but based on the notions of community and self-government, on individual and collective responsibility; [a school that aimed] at arousing a broad sense of human fraternity, instead of racist and selfish nationalism."[19] In an attempt to distance themselves from the legacy of Fascism—more specifically, from the totalitarian project of imbuing the child with Fascist principles—postwar intellectuals aimed at rethinking the role of the school, a school that did not have the objective of educating children to certain ideals but simply of providing instruction.[20] This shift was so marked that the Ministry of Education was renamed the Ministry of Instruction. Despite this change, the newly drafted national constitution would soon come to take the place of a "civic religion"—this time, however, it was no longer an imposing or dogmatic religion as compared to the Fascist years, according to philosopher Michael Walzer.[21] On a practical level, the subsequently proposed restructuring of the educational system in 1951—especially nursery schools, pre-kindergarten, and kindergarten—disavowed the principles that sanctioned this transition, but the discourse around childhood and reconstruction remained unaltered.[22]

Montessori's pedagogical work entered the quest for global peace. Her approach, as Jervolino put it, reconciled the development of each child's capacities with his social duties, eventually leading to the organic growth of the individual. This tension between individual freedom and collective responsibility, ultimately incompatible with a Fascist view of the child, represented the aspirations of the new democracy, specifically the Christian Democrats, to whom Jervolino belonged. Montessori was thus invited to take part in their ambitious project, to "help in the work of reconstruction of our youth, and our school system."[23]

Montessori's pacifism was also a perfect fit for the Italian women's movement, in all its political denominations. By advocating for the notion that children are a vehicle for peace, women's organizations could obtain legitimacy for themselves in the political arena.[24] Building on a presupposed privileged relationship among women and the fields of pacifism and early childhood education, these organizations often entered the political debate over reconstruction by advocating for practical actions in these fields.[25] Although women had acquired the right to vote fairly recently, in 1946, this achievement did not correspond to a full acceptance of their political roles. As a result, several women's associations—such as Unione Donne Italiane, open to liberal women of all stripes but run by Communists and Socialists, and the Centro Italiano Femminile, made up of Catholic women including Jervolino—focused their work on specific areas where they felt they could be effective; namely, education and pacifism. A similar phenomenon happened at the international level, as organizations such as the Women's International Democratic Federation, established in Paris in 1945, identified antifascism, world peace, child welfare, and women's emancipation as its principal areas of interest and of political action.

Jervolino's presentation of Montessori's work in front of the Constituent Assembly included similar premises. In response to those skeptical of the role of women in rebuilding the country, Jervolino countered by pointing at Montessori's scientific work and the global recognition it had received, urging the audience to regard her as "a genius guide in our new political duties," and to recognize the validity of the contributions women could make to the political life of the country.[26] All in all, therefore, Montessori could count on major political elements to back her work, and specifically to support its significance as a synthesis of education and pacifism.

The overall attempts to reframe Montessori's work in light of her inquiry into peace culminated with her three consecutive Nobel Peace Prize candidacies in 1949, 1950, and 1951. Jervolino, George Lambert, Martinus J. Langeveld, and Helena W. F. Stellwag assembled the Nobel applications on her behalf.[27] Despite their efforts, none of these applications was successful, nor did she ever make the committee's short list.[28]

Nevertheless, an analysis of the campaign behind these three applications offers insight into how Montessori's work on pacifism was reconsidered and presented to a general audience. The materials were compiled by Jervolino, president of the Opera Nazionale Montessori, and were formally endorsed by the minister of international affairs and president of the Università per Stranieri in Perugia, Carlo Sforza; the minister of public instruction Gonella; the mayor of Rome, Salvatore Rebecchini; and Count Paolo Farina.[29] Overall, the three applications were similar, in that they were all an overview of Montessori's life and accomplishments. Jervolino patched together quotations from renowned intellectuals who supported the relevance of the educator's work on peace. Among the more powerful testimonies, Adolphe Ferrière, founder of the Ligue Internationale pour l'Éducation Nouvelle, argued that "spreading globally [her educational method] would spark off a spirit of mutual tolerance and understanding and consequently a spirit of peace."[30] Aside from a few compelling points, the report reads like a biographical sketch that does not bring up the full extent of Montessori's work on global peace. Although Jervolino recognized its intrinsic pacifism, she did not analyze the method's systematic quest for harmony with the immediate environment, nor did she point out the new directions in ecopedagogy put forward by Montessori's plan on cosmic education. The only evidence cited to support her candidacy (all three times) consists of the 1930s peace lectures, collected, published, and translated into several languages. Her efforts before and after that period are only briefly mentioned, amounting to a partial reassessment of the role of pacifism in Montessori's work.

Only two other documents indicate that pacifism was not a decadelong phase for Montessori but instead a thread that ran through her entire life. The first one is a handwritten letter by disciple Anna Maria Maccheroni to the Nobel Committee. In an almost intimate missive that recalls the beginning of their friendship in 1906, Maccheroni maintained that "at the time there were no rumors of war, yet [Montessori's] teaching, her feeling, her views did strike [Maccheroni] as the most sincere faith in 'peace.'" In Maccheroni's view, Montessori interpreted peace as "the human inner power to free oneself from evil, from deviation, to become able to live 'in peace,'" referencing the educator's early work on restorative education for disadvantaged children.[31] A Montessori education led to harmonious relationships among children who would then develop into healthy adults, naturally inclined to peace. In her letter, Maccheroni recognized Montessori's self-awareness of her role as a pacifist, in that Montessori argued that she had always been solemnly opposed to war. Maccheroni closed her letter with a tirade against those who present history as a succession of conflicts and disasters, not as a series of accomplishments for humankind.

The second document that espouses a comprehensive view of Montessori's pacifism is a letter of support from a group of adult former Montessori children. This letter provided the most heartfelt, if not altogether most compelling, piece of evidence for the educator's long-standing interest in peace. Fifty Montessori students from one of the first children's houses in via Solari at the Società Umanitaria association sent a petition to support the pedagogue's 1949 nomination for the Nobel Peace Prize. As children in 1908, they had been raised according to principles that had profoundly affected them, so much so that forty years later, they still enjoyed the benefit of an education that taught them to live a "superior" existence of collaboration and mutual support. The group's intention was "to testify that a basis of practical morality is set in the first years of life, from which results a superior form of social life, one that allows children to live 'in peace,' to enjoy victories far superior to those of violence." As children of working-class parents raised in low-income housing, their upbringing and education was similar to the San Lorenzo pupils, where the Casa dei Bambini was constructed to work in collaboration with the entire building and all its tenants, involving parents in a collective project of reform. The former pupils recounted the surprise their families felt while witnessing, for the first time, an act of "uncoerced cooperation among students, activities that did not imply any form of violence, free even of the calm, authoritarian violence of those who quietly strike children with punishment, or exalt them loudly with a prize." Montessori's work, they argued, was "the practical expression of the protection of men" against the pervasive culture of aggression and competition. Their letter of support was strikingly earnest: they took pains to emphasize that they did not want to conflate these "shared conceptions of peace with politics," and they excused themselves for even thinking that their opinion could matter. They concluded by writing that in their view, "Dr. Maria Montessori's work is essentially a work for peace."[32] Their letter, like Maccheroni's, was included in the application.

Over the course of the three nominations, more letters arrived, reflecting Montessori's lifelong wanderings and multiple interests. Indian philosopher and statesman Sarvapalli Radhakrishnan, chair of the University Education Commission and later the second president of India, wrote a letter of support for the educator.[33] E. J. R. Eaglesham, professor of education at Durham University, also sent a note.[34] Politician and Catholic priest Luigi Sturzo, "who had supported this method since its inception, when Montessori only had a little school here in Rome, and was opposed by many," also endorsed the candidacy and called the prize a "well-deserved crown" to her career.[35] Organizations such as the United States Committee on Educational Reconstruction and the Institute for the Comparative Study of History, Philosophy and the Sciences sent letters of support; others, such as the World Federation for Mental Health, declined to do so.[36]

The letters of support seemed not to have been enough. Guglielmo Rulli, the Italian ambassador in Olso who advised Jervolino in assembling the application materials, emphasized that for Montessori to win the prize, she would have to benefit from galvanizing a movement:

> To get something you need to "beat the big drum" for Mrs. Montessori, and please do not think of this as something vulgar. It is necessary that the members of the Nobel Committee have the clear impression that there is a large movement of public opinion around the candidacy.[37]

As a collection of facts on Montessori's life, a series of quotations with very little contextualization, the resulting applications did not convey one of the key features of Montessori's writing on peace, her passion, nor did it adequately express the larger relevance of her pacifist work. Ultimately, Jervolino's narrative is what came to constitute the authoritative account of that work, neglecting her thorough and multifaceted writings and activism on peace before and after the 1930s. Montessori's legacy on this issue has therefore been considered marginal until now, a series of side projects she developed in times of crisis, and not a crucial component of her pedagogical inquiry. The failure to win the Nobel Prize served to crystallize this limited narrative, halting the diffusion of her ideas on peace.

The application's flaws were not the only reason that Montessori did not come to be recognized for her work on pacifism. Historian Carlo Felice Casula argues that she was not deemed worthy of the prize by the Nobel Committee for three main reasons.[38] First, the committee wanted implicitly to support the recently created United Nations (UN) by awarding the prize to people who had contributed, directly or indirectly, to the mission of that intergovernmental organization. The winners of the 1949, 1950, and 1951 Nobel Peace Prizes were, respectively: British physiologist John Boyd Orr, who was the first director of the United Nations Food and Agriculture Organization, for his research into nutrition; American political scientist Ralph Johnson Bunche, for his mediation in Israel and peacekeeping operations with the United Nations; and Léon Jouhaux, a French trade unionist, concentration camp survivor, and pacifist, for his role in setting up the International Labor Organization, which was incorporated into the UN. Second, these decisions were influenced by the committee's desire to reward those countries that had won World War II and now represented the Western bloc in the Cold War (the United Kingdom, the United States, and France). Third, gender may also have played a significant role. Before 1949, only three women had ever won the Nobel Peace Prize, all of them prominent pacifists: the Austrian antiwar novelist Baroness Bertha von Suttner in 1905, the American social reformer Jane Addams in 1931, and the American sociologist and economist Emily Greene Balch in 1946. As an Italian and as a woman, Montessori stood little chance to win.[39]

Although Montessori's failed candidacy would come to shape the prevailing narrative of her legacy for decades, other parallel initiatives were promoting Montessori's work as belonging to the crossroads of education and pacifism. The eighth Montessori Congress in San Remo, in August 1949, celebrated her pedagogy specifically from the perspective of its internationalism and ecumenicalism. Representatives of Buddhism, Christianity, Hinduism, and Islam were invited by Montessori herself to attend the event and contribute to determining the role of children in the reconstruction of the world.[40] Altogether, those in attendance included delegates from twenty nations, a delegation from UNESCO, and pacifist intellectuals such as

Aldous Huxley. Feminist associations such as the Lega Nazionale delle Donne Italiane (National League of Italian Women) sent their best wishes.

At the congress, Montessori expanded on the topics she had worked on while in India, including the interconnectedness of all human beings, the continuity between nature and culture, and the universality of the experience of childhood. In describing the steps all governments had to take to restructure their educational systems, she drew from her experience "with children of all races, of different religions, belonging to the most divergent social states; from children of royal families to children in the most abject conditions, in slums of large cities and deserts of tropical countries." She praised the efforts of organizations such as UNESCO for "trying to establish the basis of a democratic type of education and seeking the material means to install it all over the world," but she insisted that instead of working to find different solutions to each nation's economic and social problems, politicians and educators should instead look at the commonalities among all human beings and devise a transversal system of education.[41] The child's "subconscious period of development," the first years of life, presented certain commonalities across all classes, races, and nationalities. Education had to begin its work of social reconstruction starting from these common traits, as analyzed through scientific inquiry, and then to foster—without coercion—a love within the child for one's own work. The next step would be for humankind to realize the interconnectedness of each individual's behavior, as delineated by Montessori's work on cosmic education. The basis for a universal connection among every single human being already existed; people only had to come to interiorize "the real and profound existence of these bonds of interdependence and social solidarity among all the peoples of the earth."[42] The great task of education, Montessori concluded, is to make the child aware of the real depth of this union.[43]

Montessori's words were echoed throughout the conference's speeches that also stressed the importance of peace and rehabilitation to her educational work. Gustavo Colonnetti, director of the Consiglio Nazionale delle Ricerche (Italian National Council for Research), argued that children had to be educated from the most tender age to develop "a sense of personal and social responsibility" toward their environment, their peers, and their family, in order to avert new conflicts and wars.[44] The deputy lead of the UNESCO Department of Education, Cheng Chi-Pao, expressed his admiration for Montessori's work and argued that "war begins in the mind of men"; humankind must therefore understand the urgency of rethinking education so as to prevent new global conflict and mass destruction.[45] All the attendees agreed to support Montessori's first candidacy for the Nobel Prize, on the

grounds that she had demonstrated how to eliminate future war "by cultivating in the human being, starting from the earliest beginning of his life,
the conscience of the unity of all men, freed from the slavery of a useless
and oppressive education."[46]

In the years prior to her death in 1952, the world of humanitarianism
slowly started to recognize the importance of Montessori's work as a cornerstone to rebuilding a democratic society free of war and conflict. The
early postwar recognition she received from the United Nations' UNESCO
is an excellent case in point. The agency's mission shared several principles
with Montessori's vision of education, insofar as dialogue and mutual
understanding were considered foundational to building intellectual and
moral solidarity among all human beings. Providing access to high-quality
education, fighting illiteracy, fostering cultural diversity, and above all promoting a humanist vision of education were fundamentals shared deeply
by Montessori and UNESCO.

UN representatives initiated various collaborations with Montessori.
While in France to receive the Legion of Honor award in 1949, Montessori
was invited to UNESCO's International Institute of Education "to examine
together the possible implications of the application of her approach to
problems related to international understanding."[47] According to a report
in the UNESCO Courier on the 1949 Montessori Congress, Montessori had
paraphrased UNESCO's constitution in her remarks by saying that "peace
as well as war is born in the minds of men," and humankind can and must
"establish the conditions necessary in order that peace and not war may
reign among men."[48] Jaime Torres Bodet, UNESCO's director general,
introduced her at the 1950 UNESCO conference in Florence as "someone
who has become a symbol of our great expectations for education and world
peace."[49] Because of their overlapping mission, Montessori, Swiss psychologist Jean Piaget, and German-Canadian neurologist and psychiatrist Karl
Stern all attended the first meeting of the International Institute of Education in Weisbaden, West Germany, where its charter was drafted in June 1951.[50]
There, Montessori spoke imperiously, reminding all the attendees that
whereas they now addressed freedom in education, she had done it for
decades; when they mentioned the international nature of the educational
debate, she said, "Let me point out that I was active in this area at a time
when many of the people here were still children."[51] According to Montessori, all the measures suggested by this assembly had already been taken up
by internationalist enthusiasts, who later quit because of how hard it was
actually to implement these reforms. Expressing confidence in the organization, she noted that the atmosphere of this event might signal the begin-

ning of a new era for the child, if only the institute would dedicate itself to using education to support the inner life of humanity, as well as looking out for children from birth, because "they are the only people without rights."[52] Following Montessori's advice, the International Institute of Education organized a conference to be held in 1953, specifically on children during their preschool years. But Montessori would not get to attend: she died on May 6, 1952.

Montessori's death at this crucial moment in the understanding of peace and reconstruction halted the spread of her work on pacifism and thus crystallized the vision advanced in Jervolino's Nobel Peace Prize application. Her ideas, however, were carried on under the aegis of the Association Montessori Internationale and by members of the Montessori family, such as Montessori's son, Mario, and her grandchild Renilde, who worked to propel global interest in her educational and pacifist writings.

Although Montessori's ideas on children's rights were ahead of their time when formulated, they have become mainstream. The United Nations gradually adopted the key principles of Montessori education to peace and her revolutionary conception of children's rights, without attributing them; decades would have to pass before Montessori's ideas would be enshrined by transnational agencies.[53] The 1959 Declaration of the Rights of the Child, based on the structure and contents of the 1924 declaration and adopted by the United Nations General Assembly, was built on the premise that humankind owes children the best it can give. Like the 1924 version, it put implicit emphasis on the shared duties humankind has to children. But the bulk of the declaration was vague on exactly what rights children have and who is responsible for guaranteeing them. All in all, the declaration consisted of the type of nonbinding, lofty principles that seldom lead to significant, concrete political action.

The discourse on children-related concerns has progressed rapidly since 1959, eventually catching up to Montessori's strikingly modern vision. As Michael D. A. Freeman argues, the liberationist movement pushed back on the notion that the status of children would be advanced by increasing protections for them.[54] The following decades witnessed a shift from protection to independence, from providing emotional and physical nourishment and care to self-determination, from state support to justice.[55] In the 1970s, the accelerated expansion of preschool education in many countries brought nursery schools into the UNESCO Associated Schools Project, and early childhood education for peace started to receive the level of attention Montessori had demanded. UN documents such as the 1972 *Apprendre à être* by the International Institute of Education delineated how to rethink instruction in light of the students' needs and potential, and of education as a lifelong process.[56]

With the slow dissolution of colonial regimes and the emergence of violent ethnic and cultural conflicts in many parts of the world, UNESCO and all UN agencies more generally have switched from a peacekeeping approach to a peace-building one, recognizing the need to establish peace at the community level. The global integration of the world and the rise of comparative educational studies commissioned by the International Institute of Education has brought to light the commonalities among the children of the world, as Montessori preached in 1949. New programs to establish a culture of peace have finally brought recognition to Montessori's notion of using education as a tool to this end. Her work anticipated an awareness gradually developed by the aforementioned UN agencies that "action at a deeper level is called for at the earliest possible age, i.e. in the years when a child's fundamental outlook and personality are formed," as a 1985 UN report stated.[57]

In the meantime, despite a growing understanding of the value of vesting children with rights as a conflict-ending measure, it was not until the 1989 United Nations Convention on the Rights of the Child and the 1990 World Summit that watershed changes first occurred. The Declaration of the Rights of the Child recognized that children, as humans, inherently possess the same value as adults. The Convention on the Rights of the Child document furthermore stated that childhood is valuable in and of itself, not as a transitional phase that predates adulthood or simply as a training period. Vulnerable by nature, children need special support to be able to enjoy their rights in full. The so-called principle of the child's best interest, as described in Article 3 of the document, represents the most important message of the convention: that the interest of the child takes precedence over that of the parents and the state. Article 12.1, on respecting the view of the child, reflected the core of Montessori's philosophy: the idea that the child has the right to be heard and that the child's ideas must be taken seriously. Since then, the child's capacity to be an autonomous decision maker, a pillar of Montessori's philosophy of education, has slowly started to be acknowledged, at a deeper level than the largely symbolic accomplishments of previous international declarations.

This groundbreaking document also started a debate over establishing a ministry for children, something Montessori proposed almost fifty years earlier. In the wake of the Spanish Civil War, she had called for the child to become a champion of his own rights; she lamented the absence of political representation of the child, calling it a "dangerous void."[58] As she argued, children remain the largest global constituency without a political voice of their own; although they do not organize politically or lobby, they remain political subjects. Various official proposals for the sort of ministry Montessori had in mind have been put forward since the 1980s, but few countries have created any.[59] When legislation does succeed, it is done without the consultation of children themselves.

The educator's work on peace through education speaks volumes to our current times. Although the international community has at last embraced Montessori's fundamental views on peace and early childhood education, this by no means indicates that the fight for global education and children's rights is over. Thirty years after the UN Convention, the number of children with access to schools like those that Montessori herself created—a place to create and reproduce peace—remains limited. For children in many war-torn countries, a classroom as a space to grow and thrive is often not an option. Organizations such as Save the Children, Doctors Without Borders, and Human Rights Watch, for example, attend to the education and rehabilitation of children who escape wars, and who are affected by the very same symptoms and phenomena Montessori described in those who had escaped the horrors of the Great War. And yet, more than a century later, their basic needs remain unmet, their educational promise unfulfilled, their traumas untreated. Montessori's cry, more than a hundred years ago, remained unheard. Can we risk ignoring it any longer?

Notes

Archival Sources

Archivi delle Arti Applicate Italiane del XX secolo, Rome (AAI)
Archivio Antonio Gramsci, Rome
Archivio Apostolico Vaticano, Vatican City (AAV)
Archivio Casa Generalizia delle Suore Francescane Missionarie di Maria, Rome
Archivio Centrale dello Stato, Rome (ACS)
Archivio Fondazione Giovanni Gentile per gli Studi Filosofici, Rome
Archivio Ospedale Psichiatrico Santa Maria della Pietà, Rome
Archivio Storico Società Umanitaria, Milan
Association Montessori Internationale Archive, Amsterdam (AMI)
Associazione Nazionale per gli Interessi del Mezzogiorno d'Italia Archives (ANIMI)
Edwin Mortimer Standing Collection on the Montessori Method, Seattle University
Institute of Education Archive, University College London
Kalakshetra Foundation, Chennai
Opera Nazionale Montessori, Rome (ONM)
Private Archive of Francesco Randone, Rome
Surendra Narayan Archives, Theosophical Society, Adyar, Chennai
Women's International League for Peace and Freedom Records Collection, Swarthmore College Peace Collection

Introduction

1. Maude Radford Warren, *The White Flame of France* (Boston: Small & Maynard, 1918), 260.

2. Maria Montessori, *The White Cross*, in Association Montessori Internationale Archive, Amsterdam (hereafter cited as AMI). This work is a booklet of

translated excerpts of Montessori's lecture to the Woman's Board of San Diego, California, 1917.

3. The state of Montessori studies is characterized by biographies and monographs that reassert the educator's place in a line of so-called great women. Often compiled by Montessori disciples, these texts neglect the breadth of her thought and how it was informed by the debates on children and refugees' rights, war prevention, and what would later be called posttraumatic stress disorder (PTSD) rehabilitation. Furthermore, no scholarly work has so far engaged her writings with regard to human rights studies, refugee studies, and peace studies; addressing these is fundamental to recognizing the educator's contributions to these fields. The two main biographies compiled by her disciples are the following: Anna Maria Maccheroni, *A True Romance: Doctor Maria Montessori as I Knew Her* (Edinburgh: Darien Press, 1947), and E. M. Standing, *Maria Montessori: Her Life and Work* (New York: Plume, 1957). Kramer's remains the most thorough biography, though it principally relies on oral accounts from the Montessori family and seldom engages with scholarly secondary sources: Rita Kramer, *Maria Montessori: A Biography* (New York: Putnam, 1976). Renato Foschi's biography, Grazia Honegger Fresco's essays, Paola Trabalzini's analysis of the five editions of *Il Metodo*, Fulvio De Giorgi's special issue of *Annali di Storia dell'Educazione*, and the book series Montessoriana at Fefè Editore provide compelling and scholarly researched essays on Montessori's life: Renato Foschi, *Maria Montessori* (Rome: Ediesse, 2012); Paola Trabalzini, *Maria Montessori: Da "Il metodo" a "La scoperta del bambino"* (Rome: Aracne, 2003); Fulvio de Giorgi, ed., *Maria Montessori e le sue reti di relazioni* (Brescia, It.: Morcelliana, 2018); Grazia Honegger Fresco, *Maria Montessori, una storia attuale: La vita, il pensiero, le testimonianze*, ed. Marcello Grifò (Turin: Il leone verde, 2018).

4. Using the word *weapon* to symbolize education fits into Montessori's evocative and at times forceful writing style, though it also sheds light on Montessori's focus on education vis-à-vis a solid philosophical theorization on the topic. Maria Montessori, *Education and Peace*, trans. Helen Lane (Oxford: Clio Press, 1992), 28.

5. In her own writing, Montessori referred in Italian to *il bambino*, the child, in the masculine neutral form. Throughout the text, I alternate between masculine and feminine pronouns to signify a single child that could be of any gender, as Montessori did not make a distinction.

6. For further discussion of this topic, see Akira Iriye, *Cultural Internationalism and World Order* (Baltimore: Johns Hopkins University Press, 1997); Gavriel Salomon, "The Nature of Peace Education: Not All Programs Are Created Equal," in *Peace Education: The Concept, Principles, and Practices around the World*, ed. Gavriel Salomon and Baruch Nevo (Mahwah, NJ: Lawrence Erlbaum Associates, 2002).

7. Ellen Key, *Barnets århundrade* (Stockholm: A. Bonnier, 1911); Ellen Key, *The Century of the Child* (New York: G. P. Putnam's Sons, 1909). For an overview of this shift in Italy, see Franco Cambi and Simonetta Ulivieri, *Storia*

dell'infanzia nell'Italia liberale (Florence: La Nuova Italia, 1988); Patrizia Dogliani, *Storia dei giovani* (Milan: Mondadori, 2003); Carl Ipsen, *Italy in the Age of Pinocchio: Children and Danger in the Liberal Era* (New York: Palgrave Macmillan, 2006); Antonio Gibelli, *Il popolo bambino: Infanzia e nazione dalla Grande Guerra a Salò* (Turin: Einaudi, 2005). For an overview of this transnational phenomenon, see Hugh Cunningham, "Histories of Childhood," *American Historical Review* 103, no. 4 (1998): 1195–1208; Michael Grossberg, "A Protected Childhood: The Emergence of Child Protection in America," in *American Public Life and the Historical Imagination*, ed. Wendy Gamber, Michael Grossberg, and Hendrik Hartog (Notre Dame, IN: University of Notre Dame Press, 2003), 213–239. For an analysis on how the phenomenon affected single nations, see Harry Hendrick, *Children, Childhood, and English Society, 1880–1990* (Cambridge: Cambridge University Press, 1997); Colin Heywood, *Childhood in Nineteenth-Century France: Work, Health and Education among the "Classes Populaires"* (Cambridge: Cambridge University Press, 1988).

8. For an overview on this subject, see Viviana Zelizer, *Pricing the Priceless Child: The Changing Social Value of Children* (New York: Basic Books, 1985); Deborah Dwork, *War Is Good for Babies and Other Young Children: A History of the Infant and Child Welfare Movement in England 1898–1918* (London: Tavistock, 1987); Sylvia Schafer, *Children in Moral Danger and the Problem of Government in Third Republic France* (Princeton, NJ: Princeton University Press, 1997).

9. Ipsen, *Italy in the Age of Pinocchio.*

10. For an overview on this debate, see Delia Frigessi, Ferruccio Giacanelli, and Luisa Mangoni, eds., *Delitto, genio, follia* (Turin: Bollati e Boringhieri, 1995).

11. My analysis of governance and the politics of the social arise from my reading of Michel Foucault, "Governmentality," in *The Foucault Effect: Studies in Governmentality*, ed. Graham Burchell, Colin Gordon, and Peter Miller (Chicago: University of Chicago Press, 1991).

12. Nikolas Rose, *The Psychological Complex: Psychology, Politics and Society in England, 1869–1939* (London: Routledge & Kegan Paul, 1985).

13. Gibelli, *Il popolo bambino*, 3.

14. Key, *The Century of the Child.*

15. Dogliani, *Storia dei giovani.*

16. Giovanni Levi and Jean Claude Schmitt, eds., *Storia dei giovani*, vol. 2 (Turin: Laterza, 2000).

17. Peter M. Haas, "Introduction: Epistemic Communities and International Policy Coordination," *International Organization 46*, no. 1 (Winter 1992): 1–35; see also Davide Rodogno, Bernhard Struck, and Jakob Vogel, eds., *Shaping the Transnational Sphere: Experts, Networks and Issues from the 1840s to the 1930s* (New York: Berghahn Books, 2015).

18. Joëlle Droux and Rita Hofstetter, eds., *Globalisation des mondes de l'éducation: Circulations, connexions, réfractions, XIXe–XXe siècles* (Rennes, Fr.: Presses Universitaires de Rennes, 2015).

19. Émile Durkheim, *L'évolution pédagogique en france* (Paris: Presses Universitaires de France, 1990), 13.

20. For humanitarian action on disadvantaged youth, see Bruno Cabanes, *The Great War and The Origins of Humanitarianism, 1918–1924* (Cambridge: Cambridge University Press, 2014), 248–299; Dominique Marshall, "The Rise of Coordinated Action for Children in War and Peace: Experts at the League of Nations, 1924–1945," in Rodogno, Struck, and Vogel, *Shaping the Transnational Sphere*, 82–110; Dominique Marshall, "The Formation of Childhood as an Object of International Relations: The Child Welfare Committee and the Declaration of Children's Rights of the League of Nations," *International Journal of Children's Rights* 7, no. 2 (1999): 103–147; Silvia Salvatici, "Caotici anni di pace," in *Nel nome degli altri: Storia dell'umanitarismo internazionale* (Bologna: Il Mulino, 2015), 123–176.

21. The bibliography on reformist activism in Italy is vast, though only a few authors connect it to the larger conversation on human rights. For a few examples, see Stefania Bartoloni, ed., *Donne della Croce Rossa Italiana tra guerre e impegno sociale* (Venice: Marsilio, 2005); Fiorella Imprenti, *Alle origini dell'Unione Femminile: Idee, progetti e reti internazionali all'inizio del Novecento* (Milan: Biblion edizioni, 2012).

22. For further discussion on scientific philanthropy, see Edmund Fuller, *The Rights of the Child: A Chapter in Social History* (London: Victor Gollancz, 1951), 87; Caroline Moorehead, *Dunant's Dream: War, Switzerland and the History of the Red Cross* (London: Harper, 1999), 288.

23. Patricia Clavin, "Defining Transnationalism," *Contemporary European History* 14, no. 4 (2005): 422; see also C. A. Bayly et al., "AHR Conversation: On Transnational History," *American Historical Review* 111, no. 5 (2006): 1441–1464; Joëlle Droux, "L'internationalisation de la protection de l'enfance: acteurs, concurrences et projets transnationaux (1900–1925)," *Critique internationale*, no. 52 (2011): 17–33.

24. The recently constituted Global Histories of Education series, edited by Diana Vidal, Tim Allender, Eckhardt Fuchs, and Noah Sobe, engages with historical scholarship that analyzes education within a global or transnational perspective. See also Damiano Matasci, "International Congresses of Education and the Circulation of Pedagogical Knowledge in Western Europe, 1880–1914," in Rodogno, Struck, and Vogel, *Shaping the Transnational Sphere*, 218–238.

25. For an overview of Montessori public and private schools, consult the Montessori Census website, https://www.montessoricensus.org/.

26. A Casa dei Bambini for the children of the bourgeoisie opened in via Famagosta, Prati di Castello, on November 4, 1908.

27. Carolyn Sherwin Bailey, "The Freeing of 'Otello the Terrible,'" *Delineator* 83 (October 1913): 14.

28. Clavin, "Defining Transnationalism," 422; see also Bayly et al., "AHR Conversation"; Droux, "L'internationalisation de la protection de l'enfance," 17–33.

29. Matthew Pratt Guterl, "Comment: The Futures of Transnational History," *American Historical Review* 118, no. 1 (2013): 130–139.

30. Linda Mahood, *Feminism and Voluntary Action: Eglantyne Jebb and Save the Children, 1876–1928* (New York: Palgrave Macmillan, 2009); Liz Stanley, *The Auto/Biographical I: The Theory and Practice of Feminist Auto/Biography* (New York: Manchester University Press, 1992).

31. Francesca Trivellato, "Is There a Future for Italian Microhistory in the Age of Global History?" *California Italian Studies* 2, no. 1 (2011).

32. Jill Lepore, "Historians Who Love Too Much: Reflections on Microhistory and Biography," *Journal of American History* 88, no. 1 (2001): 132.

33. Lepore, "Historians Who Love Too Much," 133; see also Ronald Hoffman, introduction to *Through a Glass Darkly: Reflections on Personal Identity in Early America*, ed. Ronald Hoffman, Mechal Sobel, and Fredrika J. Teute (Chapel Hill: University of North Carolina Press, 1997), vii–viii.

34. Stanley, *Auto/Biographical I*, 8.

35. Liz Stanley, "Biography as Microscope or Kaleidoscope? The Case Of 'Power' in Hannah Cullwick's Relationship with Arthur Munby," *Women's Studies International Forum* 10, no. 1 (1987): 19–31; Barbara Caine, "Feminist Biography and Feminist History," *Women's History Review* 3, no. 2 (1994): 247–261.

36. Stanley, "Biography as Microscope or Kaleidoscope?" 22.

37. Kramer, *Maria Montessori*, 28.

38. Renato Foschi first applied this historical category of *histoire croisée* (literally, "crossed history") to the work of Maria Montessori: Renato Foschi, "*L'histoire croisée*: Contesti e soggetti nella storia della psicologia scientifica fin de siècle," *Physis* 40, no. 1 (2003): 311–323.

Chapter 1. Peace from Within

1. Maria Montessori, "Caratteri fisici delle giovani donne del Lazio (desunti dall'osservazione di 200 soggetti)," *Atti della Società Romana di Antropologia* 12, no. 1 (1906): 41. All translations are mine, unless otherwise indicated.

2. Vittorio Vidotto, *Roma contemporanea* (Turin: Laterza, 2001), 63–71.

3. David Forgacs, *Italy's Margins: Social Exclusion and Nation Formation since 1861* (Cambridge: Cambridge University Press, 2014), 28–29.

4. Montessori, "Caratteri fisici delle giovani donne del Lazio," 41.

5. Giuseppe Zucca, "La prima campana laica," *Il Marzocco*, July 14, 1912, 4.

6. The essay "Caratteri fisici delle giovani donne del Lazio" granted her the license to teach anthropology at the university level.

7. Stefano Jacini, *Atti della giunta per l'inchiesta agraria e sulle condizioni della classe agricola* (Rome: Forzani e C. Tipografi del Senato, 1881).

8. Werner Sombart, *La campagna romana* (Turin: Ermanno Loescher, 1891), 131; Sombart, *La campagna romana*, 125.

9. Sibilla Aleramo, *Andando e stando* (Milan: Feltrinelli, 1997), 7.

10. Angelo Celli, *Come vive il campagnolo nell'Agro Romano: Note e appunti* (Rome: Società Editrice Nazionale, 1900), pamphlet in Archivi delle Arti Applicate Italiane del XX secolo (hereafter cited as AAI), Duilio Cambellotti, AGRO.

11. Gaetano Salvemini, *Opere*, vol. 5 (Milan: Feltrinelli, 1966), 1042.

12. Frank Snowden, *The Conquest of Malaria: Italy, 1900–1962* (New Haven, CT: Yale University Press, 2006), 59.

13. "Croce Rossa," *La Tribuna*, July 21, 1897, in Valeria P. Babini and Luisa Lama, *Una donna nuova: Il femminismo scientifico di Maria Montessori* (Milan: Franco Angeli, 2003), 111.

14. Paolo Postempski, *La campagna antimalarica compiuta dalla Croce Rossa Italiana nell'Agro Romano nel 1900* (Rome: Tipografia cooperativa sociale, 1901).

15. Quoted in Giuseppe Tropeano, "Rivista critica della stampa," *Giornale della malaria* 1 (1907): 93–94, magazine clipping in AAI, Duilio Cambellotti, AGRO.

16. Zucca, "La prima campana laica," 4.

17. Angelo Celli, "La colonizzazione dell'Agro Romano e Pontino," *Nuova Antologia*, September 1911.

18. "Medicina sociale e malaria in Italia," *Avanti!* (Rome), July 29, 1901; Tullio Rossi-Doria, "Nuovi tempi e medici nuovi," *Avanti!* (Rome), December 6, 1900; and Giuseppe Badaloni, *La lotta contro la malaria: Relazione al Consiglio superiore di Sanità presentata nella seduta dell'11 agosto 1909* (Rome: Mantellate, 1910), 80–82. All in Archivo Centrale dello Stato, Rome (hereafter cited as ACS), MI, DGS (1900–1910), b. 117 bis, fasc. "Lotta contro la malaria."

19. Eugen Weber, *Peasants into Frenchmen: The Modernization of Rural France, 1870–1914* (Stanford, CA: Stanford University Press, 1976).

20. Weber, *Peasants into Frenchmen*, 485–496.

21. Alessandro Marcucci, *Le scuole festive nell'agro romano istituite dalla sezione romana dell'Unione Femminile Nazionale: Relazione dell'anno 1907–1908; Proposte per l'anno 1908–1909* (Rome: Tipografia dell'Unione Cooperativa, 1908), 10, in Associazione Nazionale per gli Interessi del Mezzogiorno d'Italia Archive (hereafter cited as ANIMI), Asili infantili, scuole, corsi di educazione degli adulti.

22. Sibilla Aleramo, "La vita nella Campagna romana, conferenza tenuta all'Università popolare di Milano nel 1909," *Italia Letteraria*, May 3, 1931. *Consumption* is better known today as tuberculosis.

23. Their growing presence in this field eventually pushed the government, specifically the Minister of Public Instruction Alfredo Baccelli and his successor, Orso Maria Corbino, to provide governmental support for organizations engaged in such initiatives. Marcella Bacigalupi and Piero Fossati, *Da plebe a popolo: L'educazione popolare nei libri di scuola dall'Unità d'Italia alla Repubblica* (Florence: La Nuova Italia, 1986), 3–49.

24. Alessandro Marcucci, *L'apostolato educativo di Giovanni Cena* (Rome: Le scuole per i contadini dell'agro romano e delle paludi pontine, 1928), 9, pamphlet in AAI, Duilio Cambellotti, AGRO.

25. Alessandro Marcucci, *La casa della Scuola: Dalla relazione sulle scuole per i contadini dell'agro romano e delle paludi pontine* (Rome: Le scuole per i contadini dell'agro romano e delle paludi pontine, 1925), 7, report in AAI, Duilio Cambellotti, AGRO.

26. Dino Renato Nardelli, "Le scuole per i contadini dell'agro romano," *Vita dell'Infanzia* 36, no. 6 (1987): 14–21. The expansion of Montessori schools in this and other rural areas continued to be a staple of several initiatives for rural education. T. M., "Le Scuole per i contadini dell'Agro Romano e delle Paludi Pontine," *L'idea Montessori: organo dell'Opera Nazionale Montessori* 1, no. 1 (1927): 10–11.

27. Alessandro Marcucci, *La scuola di Giovanni Cena* (Turin: Paravia, 1948), 145.

28. Giovanna Alatri, *Dal chinino all'alfabeto: Igiene, istruzione e bonifiche nella campagna romana* (Rome: Fratelli Palombi, 2000).

29. Luigi Varlez, "Appunti di un anziano," *Lavoro* [undefined], November 6, 1930, magazine clipping 19 in AAI, Duilio Cambellotti, AGRO.

30. Marcucci, *Le scuole festive nell'agro romano*, 8; Giovanni Cena, *Opere*, vol. 2, ed. Giorgio De Rienzo (Rome: Silva Editore, 1968), 306–307.

31. Enzo Catarsi, *L'asilo e la scuola dell'infanzia* (Florence: La Nuova Italia, 1994).

32. For a history of the *asilo* movement, see Enzo Catarsi and Giovanni Genovesi, *L'infanzia a scuola* (Bergamo, It.: Juvenilia, 1985).

33. The Credaro law n. 487 of June 4, 1911, instituted a school patronage with juridical power in every municipality. Among the various tasks entrusted to the patronage were the foundation of day care centers and kindergartens, the establishment of cafeterias, the granting of subsidies for clothing and footwear, and the allotment of school supplies. Tina Tomasi, *L'educazione infantile tra Chiesa e Stato* (Florence: Vallecchi, 1978), 118.

34. For further discussion of this issue, see Raffaele Romanelli, *L'Italia liberale, 1861–1900* (Bologna: Il Mulino, 1979), 349–50; see also Giovanna Farrell-Vinay, *Povertà e politica nell'Ottocento: Le opere pie nello Stato Liberale* (Turin: Scriptorium, 1997), 320–324, for a positive overview of the 1890 law. In *Italy's Social Revolution*, Maria Sophia Quine argues that the centralizing reform did not change things dramatically. Maria Sophia Quine, *Italy's Social Revolution: Charity and Welfare from Liberalism to Fascism* (New York: Palgrave, 2002). Literally translated as "pious works," *opere pie* were all those institutions of "piety, religion, and public utility" which had been founded through Christian charity and private benefaction.

35. Giovanni Genovesi, *Storia della scuola in Italia dal Settecento a oggi* (Rome: Laterza, 1998), 73–76.

36. Alessandro Marcucci, *Le scuole per i contadini dell'agro romano: Relazione del direttore delle scuole* (Rome: Tipografia poliglotta Mundus, 1913), 5. AAI, Duilio Cambellotti, AGRO, brochure.

37. Giovanna Alatri, *Gli asili d'infanzia a Roma tra Otto e Novecento* (Milan: Unicopli, 2013), 42.

38. Camillo Corradini, "Relazione presentata a S.E il ministro della Pubblica istruzione, dal direttore generale per l'istruzione primaria e popolare dott. Camillo Corradini," in *L'istruzione primaria in Italia con speciale riguardo all'anno scolastico 1907–1908*, vol. 1 (Rome: Tipografia operaia romana cooperativa, 1910), 288–334.

39. Nathan and Montessori probably knew each other through Nathan's wife, Virginia Nathan, who was also a member of the Associazione Femminile Italiana.

40. Giovanna Alatri, *Il mondo al femminile di Maria Montessori: Regine, dame e altre donne* (Rome: Fefè Editore, 2015), 142–151.

41. Pacifico Passerini, *Le scuole rurali di Roma e il bonificamento dell'Agro romano* (Rome: Tipografia Pontificia nell'Istituto Pio IX, 1908), 4.

42. "Relazione dell'assessore della Pubblica Istruzione del Comune di Roma Conti sul Bilancio Preventivo del 1909," in Giovanna Alatri, *Asili di Infanzia a Roma tra Otto e Novecento* (Milan: Unicopli, 2013), 42.42.

43. Foschi, "*L'histoire croisée*," 312.

44. Maria Montessori, "Ancora sui minorenni delinquenti: L'amore," in *La vita*, August 6, 1906, 6. *Pedagogia riparatrice* can be translated as "restorative pedagogy," but I use the terms *restorative, redemptive, rehabilitant*, and *redressing* interchangeably. Montessori saw her educational philosophy as rooted in delineating a healthy pathway of development—her techniques and approach as a practical means of providing healing for children, mending and restoring capacity and creating the space for children to return to developing naturally despite the overwhelmingly inadequate environments, unhelpful approaches, and outright obstacles adults were providing for them.

45. Montessori, "Ancora sui minorenni delinquenti," 6.

46. Henry W. Holmes, introduction to *The Montessori Method*, by Maria Montessori, trans. Anne E. George (New York: Frederick A. Stokes, 1912), ix. As quoted by Rita Kramer, Anna Maria Maccheroni describes Montessori's decision to work on the education of the child as "mystical revelation of purpose." Kramer, *Maria Montessori*, 44.

47. Maccheroni, *True Romance*, 15.

48. Renato Foschi, "Science and Culture around the Montessori's First 'Children's Houses' in Rome (1907–1915)," *Journal of the History of the Behavioral Sciences* 44, no. 3 (Summer 2008): 238–257.

49. Most of the information on Maria Montessori's personal life comes from a small circle of disciples, which has contributed to creating an aura around certain moments of the educator's life. In Valeria P. Babini, "Maria Montessori: Biografia o autobiografia?" in "Le biografie scientifiche," ed. Antonello La Vergata, special issue, *Intersezioni* 15, no. 1 (April 1995): 171–177.

50. Sante De Sanctis and Maria Montessori, *Sulle cosidette allucinazioni antagonistiche* (Rome: Società Editrice Dante Aligheri, 1897).

51. The first woman to graduate in medicine from the Istituto di Studi Superiori di Firenze was Ernestina Paper, in 1877. For a study of women in academia in fin de siècle Italy, see Vittore Ravà, *Le laureate in Italia: Notizie statistiche* (Rome: Tipografia Cecchini, 1902), 634–654.

52. Kramer, *Maria Montessori*, 41.

53. Montessori first enrolled in natural sciences at the Facoltà di scienze fisiche, matematiche e naturali in 1890. In 1892 she switched to the department of medicine.

54. Babini and Lama, *Una donna nuova*, 35–37; Giorgio Cosmacini, *Il medico materialista: Vita e pensiero di Jacob Moleschott* (Turin: Einaudi, 2005).

55. Babini and Lama, *Una donna nuova*, 37.

56. For further discussion of this issue, see Robert A. Nye, *Crime, Madness and Politics in Modern France: The Medical Concept of National Decline* (Princeton, NJ: Princeton University Press, 1984).

57. Michel Foucault, *The Birth of the Clinic: An Archeology of Medical Perception*, trans. A. M. Sheridan Smith (New York: Random House, 1975), 35–36.

58. Nye, *Crime, Madness and Politics in Modern France*, 45–48.

59. More specifically, Cesare Lombroso utilized the word *degenerato* to cover a vast array of abnormalities and therefore contributed to the diffusion of the term. Delia Frigessi, "La scienza della devianza," in Frigessi, Giacanelli, and Mangoni, *Delitto, genio, follia*, 333–373. For further discussion of this issue, see Mary Gibson, *Born to Crime: Cesare Lombroso and the Origins of Biological Criminology* (Westport, CT: Praeger, 2002).

60. Rossella Raimondo, "La 'pedagogia riparatrice' secondo Maria Montessori: Un ideale regolativo e educativo," *Rivista di storia dell'educazione* 1 (2016): 191–202.

61. Barbara Montesi, *Questo figlio a chi lo do? Minori, famiglie, istituzioni (1865–1914)* (Milan: Franco Angeli, 2007), 33.

62. Raimondo, "La 'pedagogia riparatrice' secondo Maria Montessori," 191–193; Enrico Ferri, *Sociologia criminale* (Turin: Bocca, 1900); C. F. Grosso, "Le grandi correnti del pensiero penalistico italiano tra Ottocento e Novecento," in *Storia d'Italia: Annali 12, La criminalità*, ed. Luciano Violante (Turin: Einaudi, 1997), 15.

63. Here Montessori pushes the assumption of educating mentally delayed children. Maria Montessori, *Antropologia pedagogica* (Milan: Vallardi, 1910), 7.

64. Maria Montessori, "La teoria Lombrosiana e l'educazione morale," *Rivista d'Italia* 6, no. 2 (1903): 331.

65. Montessori, "La teoria Lombrosiana," 328.

66. Maria Montessori, "Quando la scienza entrerà nella scuola," *La coltura popolare* 15 (1915): 13.

67. Foschi, "Science and Culture," 242. For a comparison between the Italian school of criminal anthropology and French intellectuals, see Nye, *Crime, Madness and Politics in Modern France*, 97–131.

68. Maria Montessori, "Influenze delle condizioni di famiglia sul livello intellettuale degli scolari," *Rivista di filosofia e scienze affini* 6, no. 2 (1904): 234–284.

69. Montessori, "Influenze delle condizioni di famiglia," 276, 282.

70. Montessori, *Antropologia pedagogica*, 25.

71. Giacomo Cives and Paola Trabalzini, *Maria Montessori tra spiritualità e azione sociale* (Rome: Anicia, 2017), 27–28.

72. For an overview of this transnational phenomenon, see Cunningham, "Histories of Childhood"; Grossberg, "Protected Childhood," 213–39. For analysis on how the phenomenon impacted single nations, see Hendrick, *Children, Childhood, and English Society*; Heywood, *Childhood in Nineteenth-Century France*; Ipsen, *Italy in the Age of Pinocchio*.

73. Key, *Century of the Child*.

74. Ipsen, *Italy in the Age of Pinocchio*, 8.

75. Michela Minesso, *Stato e infanzia nell'Italia contemporanea* (Bologna: Il Mulino, 2007).

76. Quine, *Italy Social Revolution*, 61–62.

77. On the closing of the Asdrubali maternity ward, see Maria Montessori, "Maternità, per regolamento e per pudore," *La vita*, April 2, 1907, 3. For some of her contributions on the reform of juvenile detention centers, see Maria Montessori, "Gli odierni Riformatori pei minorenni corrigendi," *La vita*, June 6, 1906, 3; "A Proposito dei Minorenni Corrigendi," *La vita*, June 3, 1906, 3; "Per i minorenni delinquenti. L'organizzazione del riformatorio di San Michele," *La vita*, July 14, 1906, 3; "Lottiamo per la Criminalità," *La vita*, September 8, 1906, 3.

78. For a comparison between Germany and Italy regarding the turn-of-the-century welfare state, see Maria Sophia Quine, "The Rise of Giolitti's 'Insurer State,'" in Quine, *Italy Social Revolution*, 67–95.

79. Maria Montessori, "Miserie Sociali e Nuovi Ritrovati della Scienza," *Roma: Rivista politica parlamentare*, July 31, 1898, 605.

80. Paola Trabalzini, "Maria Montessori: Scienza e Società," in *1907–2007 Montessori Centenary Conference Proceedings*, ed. Elena Dompè, Maria Luisa Tabasso, and Paola Trabalzini (Rome: Opera Nazionale Montessori and Associazione Montessori Internationale, 2007), 19.

81. Maria Montessori, "La questione femminile e il Congresso di Londra," in *Per la causa delle donne* (Milan: Garzanti, 2019), 7. Originally published in *L'Italia Femminile*, no. 38, October 1, 1899, 298–299; no. 39, October 8, 1899, 206–207 (italics added).

82. For a discussion of this notion, see Babini and Lama, *Una donna nuova*, 72–91; Kramer, *Maria Montessori*, 79–82.

83. Kramer, *Maria Montessori*, 86.

84. Valeria Paola Babini, "'Le donne sono antropologicamente superiori': Parola di una donna di genio," in *Se vi sono donne di genio: Appunti di un viaggio nell'antropologia dall'Unità d'Italia a oggi*, ed. Alessandro Volpone and Giovanni Destro-Bisol (Rome: Casa Editrice Università La Sapienza, 2011), 12–26.

85. Montessori, *Antropologia pedagogica*, 218.

86. Maria Montessori, "La questione femminile e il Congresso di Londra," 8, 12, 24.

87. Quoted in Giovanna Alatri, "Maria Montessori e l'educazione come rimedio ai mali sociali dell'infanzia," in *L'Infanzia Svantaggiata e Maria Montessori: Esperienze psicopedagogiche, educative e sociali dal '900 ad oggi*, ed. Leonardo De Sanctis (Rome: Fefè Editore, 2013), 39.

88. Annarita Buttafuoco, "La filantropia come politica: Esperienze dell'emancipazionismo italiano nel Novecento" in *Ragnatele di rapporti*, ed. Lucia Ferrante, Maura Palazzi, and Gianna Pomata (Turin: Rosenberg & Sellier), 166–187.

89. Buttafuoco, "La filantropia come politica," 166.

90. Maria Montessori, "La via e l'orizzonte del femminismo," *Cyrano de Bergerac* 2, no. 6 (1902): 205.

91. Annarita Buttafuoco, "Motherhood as a Political Strategy: The Role of the Italian Women's Movement in the Creation of the *Cassa Nazionale di Maternità*," in *Maternity and Gender Policies: Women and the Rise of the European Welfare States, 1880s–1950s*, ed. Gisela Bock and Pat Thane (London: Routledge, 1991), 179.

92. Buttafuoco, "Motherhood as a Political Strategy," 178–179.

93. Montessori, "La via e l'orizzonte del femminismo," 203–206.

94. On the work of two contemporaries on social maternity, see Ulla Åkerström, *La maternità sociale fra Svezia e Italia: Il carteggio Ellen Key-Ersilia Majno (1907–1917)* (Rome: Viella, 2020).

95. Caterina Botti, *Madri cattive: Una riflessione su bioetica e gravidanza* (Milan: Il Saggiatore, 2007), 39–40.

96. Catarsi and Genovesi, *L'infanzia a scuola*, 95.

97. Montessori, "La questione femminile," 8 (italics added).

98. Maria Montessori, "La donna nuova: Conferenza della dottoressa Maria Montessori," *L'Italia femminile*, February 19, 1899, 6.

99. Here with the Italian word *specie* (species), Montessori means humankind.

100. Montessori, "La questione femminile," 8; Enzo Catarsi, *La giovane Montessori* (Ferrara: Corso Editore 1995), 132 (italics added).

101. Maria Montessori, "La morale sessuale nell'educazione," *Vita: Rivista di azione per il bene* 5, no. 13–14 (July 31, 1908): 282.

102. Maria Montessori, "Intervento al Congresso di Torino," in *Atti del primo congresso pedagogico italiano-Torino 8–15 settembre 1898*, ed. G. C. Molinari and

G. C. Alesio (Turin: Stabilimento Tipografico diretto da F. Cadorna, 1899), 122–123.

103. Montessori, "Intervento al Congresso di Torino," 123.

104. Maria Montessori, "Movement and Character," *NAMTA Journal* 38, no. 2 (Spring 2013): 38.

105. Alberto Oliverio, "The Acting Mind: The Role of Motricity in Mental Representation Processes," in Dompè, Tabasso, and Trabalzini, *1907–2007 Montessori Centenary Conference Proceedings*, 27–34.

106. Maria Montessori, "La costruzione della personalità attraverso l'organizzazione dei movimenti," *Montessori: Rivista Bimestrale dell'Opera Montessori* 1, no. 6 (1932): 327–328.

107. For a history of *psychomotricité*, see Bernard Aucouturier, Ivan Darrault, and Jean Louis Empinet, *La pratique psychomotrice* (Paris: Doin, 1984); Pierre Vayer, *Educazione psicomotoria nell'età scolastica* (Rome: Armando, 1977).

108. "Legge che rende obbligatorio l'insegnamento della ginnastica educativa nelle scuole, No. 4442, July 7, 1878," *Gazzetta Ufficiale del Regno*, July 15, 1878, n. 165, quoted in Monica Ferrari and Matteo Morandi, *I programmi scolastici di "educazione fisica" in Italia. Una lettura storico-pedagogica* (Milan: Franco Angeli, 2015), 45.

109. Francesco De Sanctis, "Per l'insegnamento della ginnastica," in *Scritti e discorsi sull'educazione* (Florence: La Nuova Italia, 1967), 180, 187–188.

110. "Sull'insegnamento della ginnastica nelle scuole, relazione della Commissione sul progetto di legge presentato dal ministro della Pubblica Istruzione nella tornata del 13 maggio 1878, in AP, CD, Documenti, leg. XIII, sess. 1878, n. 48A," 2, quoted in Gaetano Bonetta, *Corpo e nazione: L'educazione ginnastica, igienica e sessuale nell'Italia liberale* (Milan: Franco Angeli, 1990), 167.

111. Bonetta, *Corpo e nazione*, 102–106.

112. Emilio Baumann, *Psico-cinesia, ovvero l'arte di formare il carattere* (printed by the author, 1900). Biblioteca comunale Augusta, Perugia.

113. Pasquale Turiello, *Saggio sull'educazione nazionale in Italia* (Naples: Luigi Pierro, 1891), 78.

114. Silvana Patriarca, *Italian Vices: Nation and Character from the Risorgimento to the Republic* (Cambridge: Cambridge University Press, 2010), 79–107.

115. Zeynep Çelik Alexander, *Kinaesthetic Knowing: Aesthetic, Epistemology, Modern Design* (Chicago: University of Chicago Press, 2017).

116. Édouard Claparède, "Opinions et Critiques," 1924, 41, quoted in Marie-Laure Bachmann, *Dalcroze Today: An Education through and into Music* (Oxford: Clarendon Press, 1991), 17.

117. Émile Jaques-Dalcroze, *Le Rythme, la Musique et l'éducation* (Paris: Librairie Fischbacher, 1920), 43.

118. Dalcroze quoted in Bachmann, *Dalcroze Today*, 19.

119. Montessori, "La costruzione della personalità," 326.

120. Bachmann, *Dalcroze Today*, 29.

121. Montessori, "La costruzione della personalità," 326.

122. Patrick Frierson, "The Moral Philosophy of Maria Montessori," *Journal of the American Philosophical Association*, forthcoming.

123. Montessori, "Per i minorenni delinquenti," 3.

124. Montessori, "Per i minorenni delinquenti," 3.

125. Montessori, "La costruzione della personalità," 327.

126. Maria Montessori, *Il metodo della pedagogia scientifica applicato all'educazione infantile* (Rome: Maglioni & Strini, 1926), 101.

127. Giovanni Pascoli, "I due fanciulli," *Primi poemetti* (Bologna: Zanichelli, 1907), 141 (italics added). Pascoli probably knew Montessori, since he signed in 1898 to support the Comitato Provvisorio della Lega Nazionale per i bambini deficienti (Provisional Committee of the National League for the Care and Education of Mentally Deficient Children).

128. Montessori, *Il metodo della pedagogia scientifica*, 117, 111.

129. Montessori, *Il metodo della pedagogia scientifica*, 111, 120.

130. Paula Polk Lillard, *Montessori: A Modern Approach* (New York: Schocken Books, 1972), 31.

131. Maria Montessori, *The Absorbent Mind* (Wheaton, IL: Theosophical Publishing House, 1964), 147.

132. Montessori, "Movement and Character," 39.

133. Montessori, *Il metodo della pedagogia scientifica*, 122.

134. "From these considerations, we criticized both Montessori and Froebel, the one that she does not provide situations for more adequate social cooperation, the other that the cooperation comes too largely from outside suggestion and from adult considerations." William Kilpatrick, *The Montessori System Examined* (Boston: Houghton Mifflin, 1914), 20.

135. Maria Montessori, *Spontaneous Activity in Education* (New York: Shocken Books, 1965), 311.

136. Carolyn Sherwin Bailey, "The Christ in Bruno: A True Montessori Christmas Story," *Delineator* 83 (December 1913): 5.

137. ANIMI was founded in 1910 under the honorary presidency of Pasquale Villari and the effective presidency of Senator Leopoldo Franchetti. Between 1911 and 1914, ANIMI opened several nursery schools that followed the Montessori method. Umberto Zanotti-Bianco, *L'Associazione nazionale per gli interessi del Mezzogiorno d'Italia, nei suoi primi cinquant'anni di vita* (Rome: Collezione Meridionale Editrice, 1960).

138. For more information on Leopoldo Franchetti's role in the promotion of the method, see Roberta Fossati, "Alice Hallgarten Franchetti e le sue iniziative alla Montesca," *Fonti e Documenti* 16–17 (1987–1988): 269–347; Paolo Pezzino and Alvaro Tacchino, *Leopoldo e Alice Franchetti e il loro tempo* (Città di Castello, It.: Petruzzi Editore, 2002).

139. Bailey, "Christ in Bruno," 5.

140. Bailey, "Christ in Bruno," 5 (italics added).

141. Bailey, "Christ in Bruno," 6.

142. Maria Montessori, "Norme per una classificazione dei deficienti in rapporto ai metodi speciali di educazione," in *Atti del Comitato Ordinatore del II Congresso Pedagogico Italiano 1899–1901* (Naples: Trani, 1902), 145.

143. This essay was a lecture that Montessori was supposed to deliver at the Congresso Pedagogico di Napoli (Pedagogical Congress of Naples), which was postponed for two years; ultimately only the precirculated papers were published.

144. Augusto Scocchera refers to this schism as "divorzio scientifico" in Augusto Scocchera, *Maria Montessori: Una storia per il nostro tempo* (Rome: Opera Nazionale Montessori, 1997), 35.

145. Maria Montessori, "La prolusione della dott.ssa Montessori," *I diritti della scuola*, January 28, 1906, 172.

146. Montessori, "Norme per una classificazione dei deficienti," 146.

147. Montessori, "Norme per una classificazione dei deficienti," 147.

148. Maria Montessori, *Pedagogical Anthropology*, trans. Frederic Taber Cooper (New York: Frederick A. Stokes, 1913), 16.

149. Maria Montessori, "L'antropologia pedagogica: Una conferenza dimenticata del 1903," *Vita dell'Infanzia* 46, no.8 (October 1997): 13 (italics added).

150. Montessori, "Ancora sui minorenni delinquenti," 6.

151. Montessori, "La teoria Lombrosiana," 331.

152. Montessori, "Norme per una classificazione dei deficienti," 3.

153. Maria Montessori, "Norme per una classificazione dei deficienti," 3.

154. Arthur Schopenhauer, *The World as Will and Representation* (Cambridge: Cambridge University Press, 2018).

155. The original quotation reads, "Ciò che si manifesta di comune nei degenerati, i quali formano una serie infinita di varietà, è una speciale deficienza del così detto 'senso morale,' cioè 'della simpatia,' la 'tendenza altruistica,' il 'sentimento di giustizia' sono diminuiti, o aboliti o pervertiti la rappresentazione del bene e del male altrui lascia insensibili: l'egoismo trionfa con le sue conseguenze." Montessori, "Norme per una classificazione dei deficienti," 19.

156. Raniero Regni, "Il romanticismo e l'infanzia tra nostalgia e promessa," in *Infanzia e società in Maria Montessori: Il bambino padre dell'uomo* (Rome: Armando Editore, 2007), 55–58.

157. "Intellettualisti e volontaristi Schopenhauer e la sua teoria sulla volontà. Indirizzo moderno che riconosce vere le idee di Schopenhauer, in quanto stabilisce essere nella volontà e nei sentimenti l'essenza intima di ciascun individuo; una rigetta il fatalismo di Seguin ritenendo la volontà e il sentimento educabile appunto perché scaturiscono, oltrechè dall'organizzazione individuale, modificabile con la igiene della generazione, anche dalle condizioni fisiologiche e dalla suggestione dell'ambiente che possono essere variabili secondo esigenze speciali. Necessità dunque di studiare metodi da cui può scaturire la potenzialità individuale, e quelli con cui la medesima si può modificare e correggere,

ecc.; in modo da risultarne un individuo perfettamente adatto all'ambiente." (Intellectualists and voluntarists, Schopenhauer and his theory of the will: A modern address that recognizes Schopenhauer's ideas as true, establishing that the intimate essence of each individual is in the will and feelings; one rejects Seguin's fatalism, deeming emotions and will as something that can be taught precisely because they arise not only from the individual, modifiable with hygiene, but also from physiological conditions and the influence of the environment, which can vary according to special needs. Therefore, it is necessary to study methods from which the potential of each individual can spring, and those with which it can be modified and corrected, etc.; in order to result in an individual perfectly suited to the environment.) Ospedale S. Maria Della Pietà Archives, Rome, Clodomiro Bonfigli 1892–1904, Lega per la protezione dei fanciulli deficienti, Transcript of first year classes, Doctor Giuseppe Montesano 1900–1901, Lesson 1, Monday December 3, 1900, 20, folder 19, envelope 4.

158. Clodomiro Bonfigli, *Dei fattori sociali della pazzia in rapporto con l'educazione infantile* (Rome: Tipografia delle Mantellate, 1894).

159. Valeria Paola Babini, *La questione dei frenastenici: Alle origini della psicologia scientifica in Italia (1870–1910)* (Milan: Franco Angeli, 1996), 67–74.

160. Montessori, "Miserie sociali," 608.

161. Montessori, "Miserie sociali," 608.

162. Babini and Lama, *Una donna nuova*, 73.

163. Fulvio De Giorgi, "Maria Montessori Modernista," *Annali di storia dell'educazione e delle istituzioni scolastiche* 16 (2009): 216.

164. Montessori, "Norme per una classificazione dei deficienti," 17.

165. Maria Montessori, *Il metodo della pedagogia scientifica applicato all'educazione infantile nelle case dei bambini. Edizione Critica* (Rome: Opera Nazionale Montessori, 2000), 327–331.

166. Giovanna Caterina De Feo, "Maria Montessori, Francesco Randone e la scuola d'arte educatrice," in *La cura dell'anima in Maria Montessori: L'educazione religiosa, spirituale e religiosa dell'infanzia*, ed. Leonardo De Sanctis (Rome: Fefè Editore, 2011), 67–77; Giovanna Caterina De Feo, "La scuola d'arte educatrice," in *Trucci, Trucci Cavallucci . . . Infanzia a Roma tra Otto e Novecento* (Rome: Palombi Editore, 2001), 70–77; Giovanna Caterina De Feo, *Francesco Randone: Il Maestro delle Mura* (Rome: Associazione Amici di Villa Strohl, 2000); Flavia Matitti, "La 'bottega mistica' di Francesco Randone (1864–1935): Arte ed esoterismo a Roma tra Otto e Novecento," *Luce e Ombra* 116, no. 1 (2016): 41–50.

167. Giuseppe Zucca, "Una scuola d'arte educatrice," *Rassegna contemporanea* 7, no. 2 (December 25, 1914): 680.

168. Maria Montessori, "Arte Educatrice," *La vita*, August 6, 1907, 7.

169. Connected to the Roman symbolist movement, to the futurist artist Giacomo Balla and author Filippo Tommaso Marinetti, Randone was also a Freemason who organized soirees with séances and gathered all those interested in arts. Many of Giovanna Caterina De Feo's articles delve into the connections

between Randone and the Theosophical Society. For more Randone and theosophy, see Rolando Bellini and Mara Folini, eds., *Fuoco ad Arte! Artisti e Fornaci: La felice stagione della ceramica a Roma e nel Lazio tra simbolismo, Teosofia e altro 1880–1930* (Locarno, Switz.: Tipografia Bassi, 2005).

170. Montessori, *Il metodo della pedagogia scientifica applicato all'educazione infantile nelle case dei bambini: Edizione Critica*, 328.

171. "Prima scuola d'Arte Educatrice, Roma, Mura del Belisario, Programma didattico n.3 per l'anno 18," in De Feo, "Maria Montessori, Francesco Randone e la scuola d'arte educatrice," 67–68.

172. Montessori, "Arte Educatrice."

173. Francesco Randone, *Per nova itinera: Insegnamento dell'arte educatrice negli asili d'infanzia, scuole elementari e secondarie; La lavagna* (Tivoli: Stabilimento Tipografico Majella di A. Chicca, 1914), 10.

174. Francesco Randone, *Scuola d'Arte Educatrice* (Rome: Edizioni Scuola d'Arte Educatrice, 1930), 20.

175. Randone, *Per nova itinera*, 3.

176. Palmira Melesi Fanti, "La Settimana della Bontà," in Randone, *Scuola d'Arte Educatrice*, 12.

177. Maria Montessori, *La casa dei bambini dell'Istituto Romano dei Beni Stabili: Conferenza tenuta il 7 aprile 1907* (Rome: Istituto Romano dei Beni Stabili, 1907), 8.

178. Giuseppe Talamo, "Dagli inizi del secolo all'avvento del fascismo," in Giuseppe Talamo and Gaetano Bonetta, *Roma nel '900: Da Giolitti alla Repubblica* (Rome: Cappelli, 1987), 98–102.

179. Mario Sanfilippo, *San Lorenzo 1870–1945: Storia e storie di un quartiere popolare romano* (Rome: Edilazio, 2003), 24.

180. G. Talamo, "Dagli inizi del secolo all'avvento del fascismo," 139.

181. "Roma: 'La Casa dei Bambini,'" *La vita*, January 7, 1907, 4.

182. Montessori specifically references the moral decay of the district: "In quarters where poverty and vice ruled, a work of moral redemption is going on." Maria Montessori, *The Montessori Method*, trans. Anne Everett George (New York: Frederick A. Stokes, 1912), 48.

183. Rose, *Psychological Complex*, 47–49 (italics in original). See also Jones Gareth Stedman, *Outcast London: A Study in the Relationship between Classes in Victorian Society* (Harmondsworth, UK: Penguin, 1976).

184. For more on the construction of the urban periphery through an analysis of San Lorenzo, see Forgacs, *Italy's Margins*, 14–66.

185. Montessori, *Il metodo della pedagogia scientifica applicato all'educazione infantile nelle case dei bambini: Edizione Critica*, 143.

186. Sibilla Aleramo, *Una donna* (Milan: Feltrinelli, 2003), 106.

187. "Roma: 'La Casa dei Bambini.'"

188. Montessori, *Il metodo della pedagogia scientifica applicato all'educazione infantile nelle case dei bambini: Edizione Critica*, 145, 142.

189. Irene De Guttry, "The Design Reform Movement in Rome at the Beginning of the Century," *Journal of Decorative and Propaganda Arts* 13 (Summer 1989): 68.

190. Emidio Agostinoni, "Duilio Cambellotti," *Il Secolo XX*, no. 3 (1908), newspaper clipping in AAI, Duilio Cambellotti, AGRO.

191. Among others: Febea [Olga Ossani Lodi], "Quel che occorre sapere: L'industria e l'igiene," *La Casa* 1, no. 3 (July 1908): 51–52; Febea [Olga Ossani Lodi], "Sul pianerottolo (novella)," *La Casa* 1, no. 9 (October 1908): 174–175.

192. L. F., "La casa e il primo congresso delle donne Italiane," *La Casa*, no. 2 (June 1908): 17–18.

193. Ivan Ricca, "Architettura razionale," *La Casa*, no. 3 (August 1908): 86.

194. Duilio Cambellotti, "Progetto di casa per famiglie di lavoratori: La casa," *La Casa* 1, no. 11 (November 1908): 207.

195. Duilio Cambellotti, "Progetto di casa per famiglie di lavoratori: L'arredamento," *La Casa* 1, no. 13 (December 1, 1908): 247. For an analysis of Cambellotti's contribution to *La Casa*, see Irene De Guttry, Maria Paola Maino, and Gloria Raimondi, *Duilio Cambellotti: Arredi e Decorazioni* (Rome: Laterza, 1999), 15–24.

196. Irene De Guttry, "Cambellotti Architetto," in *Cambellotti (1876–1960)*, ed. Giovanna Buonsegale, Anna Maria Damigella, and Bruno Mantura (Rome: Edizioni De Luca, 1999), 39–42.

197. Alma [Teresita Bonfatti Pasini], "Un buon affare e un'opera buona: La 'casa moderna,'" *La Casa* 1, no. 11 (November 16, 1908): 226–231.

198. Edoardo Talamo, *La casa moderna nell'opera dell'Istituto Romano dei Beni Stabili* (Rome: Società Beni Stabili, 1910), 10.

199. Maria Montessori, *Corso Nazionale Montessori: Lezioni della dottoressa Montessori* (Milan: Litografia Mariani, 1926), 17 (italics added).

200. E. Talamo, *La casa moderna*, 12; Montessori, *Il metodo della pedagogia scientifica applicato all'educazione infantile nelle case dei bambini. Edizione Critica*, 139.

201. Montessori, *Il metodo della pedagogia scientifica*, 146, 151.

202. Montessori, *Il metodo della pedagogia scientifica*, 155–56.

203. E. Talamo, *La casa moderna*, 15–16.

204. E. Talamo, *La casa moderna*, 15.

205. Montessori, *Antropologia pedagogica*, 120 (italics added).

206. Tiziana Pironi, "Educating to Beauty: The Aesthetical Value of Child of Infants' Educative Institutions in The Twentieth Century's Pedagogy," *Journal of Theories and Research in Education* 12, no. 1 (2017): 111–122.

207. Key, *Century of the Child*, 262.

208. William Grandi, "Orizzonti sociali, progetti riformatori e proposte educative in Robert Owen, John Ruskin e William Morris," *Ricerche di Pedagogia e Didattica* 5, no. 2 (2010): 1–25.

209. Tiziana Pironi, *Femminismo ed educazione in età giolittiana: Conflitti e sfide della modernità* (Pisa: Edizioni ETS, 2011), 113; Tiziana Pironi, "Da Ellen

Key a Maria Montessori: La progettazione di nuovi spazi educativi per l'infanzia," *Ricerche di Pedagogia e Didattica* 5, no. 1 (2010): 1–11.

210. Maria Montessori, *L'autoeducazione nelle scuole elementari* (Rome: P. Maglione and C. Strini, 1916), 107.

211. Montessori, *L'autoeducazione nelle scuole elementari*, 107.

212. Maria Montessori, *The Discovery of the Child*, trans. Mary A. Johnstone (Chennai: Kalakshetra, 1948), 182.

213. Montessori, *Discovery of the Child*, 182.

214. Montessori, *L'autoeducazione nelle scuole elementari*, 107.

215. Alessandro Marcucci, *La decorazione nella scuola: A proposito della prima scuola decorata dell'Agro Romano* (Varese, It.: Premiata Tipografia Coopertiva Varesina, 1912), 3.

216. Marcucci, *La scuola di Giovanni Cena*, 70.

217. Marcucci, *La scuola di Giovanni Cena*, 70, 72.

218. Montessori, *Antropologia pedagogica*, 120.

219. Babini and Lama, *Una donna nuova*, 155–157.

220. For Montessori's speech at the conference, see Montessori, "La morale sessuale nell'educazione." For a collection of Montessori's writings on feminist issues, see Catarsi, *La giovane Montessori*.

221. E. M. Standing, *Maria Montessori: Her Life and Work* (New York: New American Library, 1962), 61–62.

222. Kramer, *Maria Montessori*, 156.

223. Maria Montessori, *Il Metodo della pedagogia scientifica applicato all'educazione infantile nelle case dei bambini* (Rome: Loescher, 1913).

224. Montessori, *Montessori Method*.

225. Montessori, *L'autoeducazione nelle scuole elementari*, 276–277.

Chapter 2. The White Cross

1. Maria Montessori, "La scuola e la guerra: La Croce Bianca," *La Coltura Popolare* 7, no. 9 (1917): 661.

2. "The White Cross," *Times Educational Supplement* (London), September 20, 1917, 5.

3. Mary R. Cromwell, "Il metodo Montessori in Francia durante la guerra," *La Coltura Popolare* 9, no. 1 (1919): 50, 51.

4. For a history of the German invasion of Belgium, see Michael R. Marrus, *The Unwanted: European Refugees in the Twentieth Century* (New York: Oxford University Press, 1985); Susan Grayzel, *Women and the First World War* (London: Longman, 2002), 16–19; Sophie De Schaepdrijver, "Belgium," in *A Companion to World War I*, ed. John Horne (Oxford: Wiley-Blackwell, 2010), 386–402; John Horne and Alan Kramer, *German Atrocities, 1914: A History of Denial* (New Haven, CT: Yale University Press, 2001); Philippe Nivet, "Rifugiati," in *La prima guerra mondiale*, ed. Stéphane Audoin-Rouzeau and Jean-Jacques Becker (Turin: Einaudi, 2007), 229–241.

5. Pierre Purseigle, "'A Wave on to Our Shores': The Exile and Resettlement of Refugees from the Western Front," *Contemporary European History* 16, no. 4 (2007): 429.

6. Olivier Faron, *Les Enfants du deuil* (Paris: La Découverte, 2001), 74–85.

7. The Geneva Convention of 1906 was a revision of the Red Cross Convention concluded in the same city on August 22, 1864. Broadly, the conference aimed at ameliorating the condition of soldiers wounded in armies in the field, but it also reiterated that arbitration was the most effective and equitable means to adjust differences that had not been resolved through diplomatic channels. It identified the Permanent Court at The Hague as a preferable site for arbitration. See *The Geneva Convention of 1906 for the Amelioration of the Condition of the Wounded in Armies in the Field* (Washington, DC: Carnegie Endowment for International Peace, 1916). For more information on the role of the American Red Cross during World War I, see Marian Moser Jones, *The American Red Cross from Clara Barton to the New Deal* (Baltimore: Johns Hopkins University Press, 2013), esp. 157–175; Julia F. Irwin, *Making the World Safe: The American Red Cross and a Nation's Humanitarian Awakening* (New York: Oxford University Press, 2013).

8. Dorothea and Gladys, sisters of Mary, had joined the American Red Cross in France in February 1918 as canteen volunteers.

9. Firmin Roz, *L'amérique et nous* (Brussels: Éditions du globe, 1946), 264.

10. Montessori, *White Cross*, 1, AMI.

11. Montessori, *White Cross*, 1, AMI.

12. Cromwell, "Il metodo Montessori in Francia," 51.

13. Maria Montessori to Pope Benedict XV, August 27, 1918, Erigenda Croce Bianca, Archivio Apostolico Vaticano (hereafter cited as AAV), Segreteria di Stato, Guerra 1914–1918, folder 469, f. 10r.

14. Montessori to Benedict XV, August 27, 1918, 10v.

15. Montessori, "La scuola e la guerra," 662.

16. Montessori, "La scuola e la guerra," 662; For an analysis of the notion of degeneration in Morel, see Mauro Simonazzi, *Degenerazionismo: Psichiatria, eugenetica e biopolitica* (Milan: Mondadori, 2013).

17. "White Cross," *Times Educational Supplement.*

18. "Of General Interest," *School World: A Monthly Magazine of Educational Work and Progress* 19, no. 6 (October 1917): 351; see also Cromwell, "Il metodo Montessori in Francia," 50.

19. "The White Cross," *Daily News* (UK), September 18, 1916.

20. Cromwell, "Il metodo Montessori in Francia," 51.

21. To make sure Cardinal Pompilj would receive her letter, Montessori sent a copy to her disciple Anna Maria Maccheroni, who took it to a priest, Miguel de Esplugas. Anna Maccheroni to Miguel de Esplugas, Barcelona, October 23, 1917, AAV, Fondo Benigni, folder 48, f. 29r.

22. Here Montessori refers to smocks, used by children of both sexes. Montessori, *White Cross*, 3, AMI.

23. While working for the Lega per i fanciulli deficienti, Montessori had been in touch with both Morselli and Tamburini. On her relationship with them, see Babini and Lama, *Una donna nuova*, 66–74. On the debate on mental diseases, see Sophie Delaporte, "Medicina e guerra," in Audoin-Rouzeau and Becker, *La prima guerra mondiale*, 299–306.

24. Bruna Bianchi, "Psichiatria e guerra," in Audoin-Rouzeau and Becker, *La prima guerra mondiale*, 309–322.

25. Bianchi, "Psichiatria e guerra," 312–313.

26. Warren, *White Flame of France*, 253, 258, 261.

27. For further discussion of this topic, see Sergio Giuntini, *Sport, scuola e caserma dal Risorgimento al primo conflitto mondiale* (Padua, It.: Centro Grafico Editoriale, 1988); Giuseppe Conti, "L'educazione nazionale militare nell'Italia liberale: I convitti nazionali militarizzati," *Storia contemporanea* 23, no. 6 (1992): 939–999; Ester De Fort, *La scuola elementare: Dall'unità alla caduta del fascismo* (Bologna: Il Mulino, 1996).

28. For a general introduction to this debate, see Philippe Ariès, *Centuries of Childhood: A Social History of Family Life* (New York: Alfred A. Knopf, 1962); Zelizer, *Pricing the Priceless Child*. For an analysis of the impact of this debate in Italy, see Cambi and Ulivieri, *Storia dell'infanzia nell'Italia liberale*; Jean-Noël Luc, "I primi asili infantili e l'invenzione del bambino," in *Storia dell'infanzia: Dal Settecento a oggi*, ed. Egle Becchi and Dominique Julia (Rome: Laterza, 1996), 282–305; Ipsen, *Italy in the Age of Pinocchio*.

29. Bonetta, *Corpo e nazione*, 167.

30. Gaetano Bonetta, "La scuola dell'infanzia," in *La scuola italiana dall'Unità ai giorni nostri*, ed. Giacomo Cives (Florence: La Nuova Italia, 1990), 29–30.

31. Trabalzini, *Maria Montessori: Da "Il metodo,"* 83.

32. The debate addressed the care of children ages three to six.

33. The decree's full name was Royal Decree January 4, 1914, N. 27, *Istruzioni, programmi e orari per gli Asili infantili e Giardini d'Infanzia*. Catarsi, *L'Asilo e scuola d'infanzia*, 369–406.

34. Giuseppe Sergi, "Alcune idee sull'educazione," *Nuova Antologia*, March 1, 1914, 65.

35. Giuseppe Sergi, "Froebelianismo," *L'educazione Nazionale* 1, no. 39 (June 128, 890): 313, calling the process "marionettismo." See also Giuseppe Sergi, *Educazione e istruzione: Pensieri* (Milan: Trevisini, 1892), 95.

36. Sergi, "Alcune idee sull'educazione," 66.

37. Giuseppe Franzè, *Fanciulli oggi, uomini domani: Agazzi, Pizzigoni, Montessori. Itinerari didattici* (Rome: Edizioni Magi, 2006), 104–158.

38. Catarsi and Genovesi, *L'infanzia a scuola*, 96.

39. Trabalzini, *Maria Montessori: Da "Il metodo,"* 83–84.

40. Emma Boghen Conigliani, *Il giardino infantile modello di Mompiano giudicato sotto l'aspetto sociale* (Brescia, It.: Canossi, 1902), 97.

41. Dina Bertoni Jovine, *La scuola italiana dal 1870 ai giorni nostri* (Rome: Editori Riuniti, 1958), 97–101.

42. Sergi, "Alcune idee sull'educazione," 69.

43. Sergi, "Alcune idee sull'educazione," 69.

44. Bonetta, "La scuola dell'infanzia," 29.

45. Gibelli, *Il popolo bambino*. For a general overview of the topic, see Bruna Bianchi, *Crescere in tempo di guerra: Il lavoro e la protesta dei ragazzi in Italia 1915–1918* (Venice: Libreria Editrice Cafoscarina, 1995); Andrea Fava, "La guerra a scuola: Propaganda, memoria, rito," *Materiali di lavoro* 3–4 (1986): 53–126; Andrea Fava, "All'origine di nuove immagini dell'infanzia: Gli anni della Grande Guerra," in *Il bambino nella storia*, ed. Maria Cristina Giuntella and Isabella Nardi (Naples: Edizioni Scientifiche Italiane, 1993), 181–204; Fabiana Loparco, *I bambini e la guerra: Il Corriere dei Piccoli e il primo conflitto mondiale (1915–1918)* (Florence: Edizioni Nerbini, 2011).

46. Gibelli, *Il popolo bambino*, 15.

47. Alberto Caracciolo, "Caratteristiche della vita privata," in *La vita privata: Il Novecento*, ed. Philippe Ariès and Georges Duby (Rome: Laterza, 1998), 4–6. As historian Alberto Caracciolo argues, the twentieth century was inaugurated by a massive event, the Great War, the sheer scale of which violated the division between private and public, familiar and political, and forced the family to adapt to the sudden absence of fathers and often mothers.

48. Gibelli, *Il popolo bambino*, 102–103. Although the sources analyzed are different, both Fava and Gibelli affirm the centrality of children in state campaigns, in literary and sociological magazines, and in various ephemera during World War I. Antonio Gibelli carries on his analysis using a wide variety of sources: propaganda posters, postcards, and literary sources. Fava's research uses the Ministry of Education archive, the Ministry of Internal Affairs archive, and teachers unions' archives.

49. Sylvia Schafer analyzes this process for France, but her work ends before World War I. Sylvia Schafer, *Children in Moral Danger*. Historian Kristen Stromberg Childers investigates how paternity was at the heart of issues of citizenship and nationhood in early twentieth-century France. Kristen Stromberg Childers, *Fathers, Families, and the State in France 1914–1945* (Ithaca, NY: Cornell University Press, 2003).

50. Fava, "All'origine di nuove immagini dell'infanzia," 145–200.

51. Andrea Fava, "War, 'National Education,' and the Italian Primary School," in *State, Society and Mobilization in Europe during the First World War*, ed. John Horne (Cambridge: Cambridge University Press, 1997), 60; Arianna Arisi Rota, "Eroi, martiri, concittadini patrioti: I necrologi come pedagogia del ricordo," in *Patrioti si diventa: Luoghi e linguaggi di pedagogia patriottica nell'Italia unita*, ed. Arianna Arisi Rota, Monica Ferrari, and Matteo Morandi (Milan: Franco Angeli, 2009), 143–156.

52. Quoted phrase in the title of this section is taken from Maria Montessori to Cardinal Pompilj in favor of the Constitution of the White Cross, San Diego, before August 30, 1917, AAV, Fondo Benigni, folder 48, ff. 28r–31r, 31.

53. Daniele Ceschin, *Gli esuli di Caporetto: I profughi in Italia durante la Grande Guerra* (Rome: Laterza, 2006); Diego Leoni, Camillo Zadra, and Quinto Antonelli, *La città di legno: Profughi trentini in Austria 1915–1918* (Trento: Temi, 1995); Luciana Palla, *Fra realtà e mito: La grande guerra nelle valli ladine* (Milan: Angeli, 1991), 103–140; Annette Becker, *Oubliés de la Grande Guerre: Humanitaire et culture de guerre 1914–1918. Populations occupées, déportés civils, prisonniers de guerre* (Paris: Noêsis, 1998).

54. For transnational humanitarian aid for children, see Heather Jones, "International or Transnational? Humanitarian Action during the First World War," *European Review of History* 16, no.5 (2009): 697–713; Julia F. Irwin, "*Sauvons les bébés*: Child Health and U.S. Humanitarian Aid in the First World War Era," *Bulletin of the History of Medicine* 86, no.1 (2012): 37–65; Michael R. Marrus, *The Unwanted: European Refugees from the First World War through the Cold War* (Philadelphia: Temple University Press, 2002); Claudena M. Skran, *Refugees in Inter-war Europe* (Oxford: Oxford University Press, 1995).

55. Antonio Gibelli, "Nefaste meraviglie: Grande Guerra e apoteosi della modernità," in *Storia d'Italia: Annali 18, Guerra e Pace*, ed. Walter Barberis (Turin: Einaudi, 2002), 549–589.

56. On Giacomo Della Chiesa, see Alberto Monticone, "Il pontificato di Benedetto XV," in *Storia della Chiesa: La Chiesa e la società industriale (1878–1922)*, ed. Elio Guerriero and Annibale Zambarbieri (Frascati, It.: Edizioni Paoline, 1990), 155–200; Gabriele De Rosa, "Benedetto XV," in *Enciclopedia dei Papi*, vol. 3 (Rome: Istituto della Enciclopedia Italiana, 2000), 608–617; Alberto Melloni, Giovanni Cavagnini, and Giulia Grossi, eds., *Benedetto XV: Papa Giacomo Della Chiesa nel mondo dell' "inutile strage"* (Bologna: Il Mulino, 2017).

57. John Pollard, *The Unknown Pope: Benedict XV (1914–1922) and the Pursuit of Peace* (London: Geoffrey Chapman, 2000), 112.

58. On diplomacy to aid the victims, see Melloni, Cavagnini, and Grossi, *Benedetto XV*.

59. Pollard, *Unknown Pope*, 112.

60. Kramer, *Maria Montessori*, 247–251. This institute later evolved into the larger Escola Montessori, with infant and primary departments for three-to-ten-year-olds, and the Seminari Laboratori de Pedagogiá, a center for research, teaching, and training.

61. Maria Montessori, *I bambini viventi nella Chiesa* (Naples: Morano, 1922), 11.

62. Montessori, *I bambini viventi nella Chiesa*, 13.

63. These experiments also resulted in the publication of Montessori's *La Santa Messa spiegata ai bambini* (Milan: Garzanti, 1949).

64. Montessori, *I bambini viventi nella Chiesa*, 10–11.

65. Erica Moretti and Alejandro Mario Dieguez, "I progetti di Maria Montessori impigliati nella rete di mons. Umberto Benigni," *Annali di storia dell'educazione e delle istituzioni scolastiche* 25 (2018): 89–114.

66. The bulk of the letters were found at the Archivio Apostolico Vaticano (AAV) and at the Association Montessori Internationale (AMI) archive.

67. Montessori's disciple Edwin Mortimer Standing copied parts of the letter and mistakenly identified Cardinal Pompilj as Pomeili. Extract from a letter by Maria Montessori to his excellency cardinal Pomeili 1917, Edwin Mortimer Standing Collection on the Montessori Method, Special Collections, Lemieux Library and McGoldrick Learning Commons, Seattle University (hereafter cited as E. M. Standing Collection), Series IV, 110, 1917. Cf. Margie Mayfield, "Maria Montessori: Advocate for Children," *Communications* 2 (2006): 4–9.

68. AAV, Fondo Benigni, folder 48, f. 27, page 2.

69. *Captation benevolentie* is a rhetorical device used to capture the goodwill of the papacy at the beginning of the appeal. Edward Mortimer Standing, "Extract from a Letter by Maria Montessori to His Excellency Cardinal Pomeili-1917," Montessori Studies Center, E. M. Standing Collection (duplicate copy).

70. Standing, "Extract from a Letter by Maria Montessori to His Excellency Cardinal Pomeili-1917," 1.

71. Montessori to Benedict XV, August 27, 1918, f. 10r.

72. From the letter: "There is another question regarding the children: what to do with the multitude of little Germans left in France and Belgium as living consequences of the horrors of the war. These children incite hatred in the local population. Various French people here in the US have said that we will need to send Americans, or other foreigners, that could take care of them." The Italian is as follows: "C'è anche un'altra questione—ed è della moltitudine di piccoli tedeschi lasciati in Francia e in Belgio come conseguenza vivente degli orrori della guerra; questi bambini destano odio nelle popolazioni locali: e varie persone francesi hanno detto qui in America che bisognerebbe che delle americane o in genere delle straniere andassero a prendersi cura di questi bambini." Montessori to Benedict XV, August 27, 1918, f. 10r.

73. Salvatore Messina, "Le donne violentate in guerra e il diritto all'aborto," *Scuola positiva* 6, no. 4 (1915): 290.

74. Scipio Sighele, *La folla delinquente* (Turin: Fratelli Bocca, 1891).

75. Scipio Sighele, *La crisi dell'infanzia e la delinquenza dei minorenni* (Florence: La Rinascita del Libro, 1911), 20.

76. Luigi Maria Bossi, *In difesa della donna e della razza* (Genoa: Quintieri, 1917), 79–80.

77. On monsignor Umberto Benigni, see Pietro Scoppola, "Benigni, Umberto," in *Dizionario Biografico degli Italiani* (Rome: Istituto della Enciclopedia Italiana,1966): 504–508. Pius X died in August 1914 and was succeeded by Benedict XV the following month.

78. Maria Montessori to Pope Benedict XV, August 15, 1918, AAV, Segreteria Stato, 1918, rubricelle 244, fasc. X, folder 469.

79. Montessori to Benedict XV, August 27, 1918, f. 11r.

80. Montessori, *White Cross*. The image of this "voluntary heroine" recalls that of the "true missionary, a moral queen among the people" described in the "Inaugural Speech." Montessori, *Il Metodo della pedagogia scientifica applicato all'educazione infantile nelle case dei bambini*, 151.

81. Montessori to Benedict XV, August 15, 1918, f. 11r. (italics added).

82. Montessori to Benedict XV, August 15, 1918, f. 10r.

83. Montessori to Benedict XV, August 15, 1918, f. 10r.

84. The phrase "Save the Children" is from Società Umanitaria (Milan, Italy), "Una sala bambini per i figli dei profughi," in *L'Umanitaria e la sua opera* (Milan: Cooperativa Grafica degli Operai, 1922), 165.

85. Condulmari quoted in Claudio A. Colombo and Maria Beretta Dragoni, eds., *Maria Montessori e il sodalizio con l'Umanitaria* (Milan: Raccolto, 2008), 52.

86. Irene Pozzi, "La Società Umanitaria e la diffusione del metodo Montessori," *Ricerche di Pedagogia e Didattica* 10, no. 2 (2015): 106.

87. Antonella Andriani, "Il design per l'infanzia, quando il 'design' in Italia non esisteva ancora," in Colombo and Dragoni, *Maria Montessori e il sodalizio con l'Umanitaria*, 34–35.

88. Colombo and Dragoni, *Maria Montessori e il sodalizio con l'Umanitaria*, 51.

89. Società Umanitaria, "Una sala bambini per i figli dei profughi," 165. For an overview of the Società Umanitaria's major projects, see Società Umanitaria, *L'Umanitaria e la sua opera*.

90. Società Umanitaria, *L'Umanitaria e la sua opera*, 433.

91. Augusto Osimo, "Salviamo i bambini: Prime adesioni e contributi d'idee e di azione al nostro appello," *La Coltura Popolare* 8, no. 4 (1918): 235.

92. Società Umanitaria, *L'Umanitaria e la sua opera*, 267–268.

93. Società Umanitaria, *L'Umanitaria e la sua opera*, 268.

94. Maria Montessori, "La Croce Bianca," in *Il metodo del bambino e la formazione dell'uomo: Scritti e documenti inediti e rari*, ed. Augusto Scocchera (Rome: Edizioni Opera Nazionale Montessori, 2002), 250.

95. Società Umanitaria, *L'Umanitaria e la sua opera*, 268, 269.

96. Giacomo Cives, "Maria Montessori tra scienza, spiritualità e laicità," *Studi sulla formazione* 17, no. 2 (2014): 123.

97. Fulvio De Giorgi, "Rileggere Maria Montessori: Modernismo cattolico e rinnovamento educativo," in *Maria Montessori, Dio e il bambino e altri scritti inediti*, ed. Fulvio De Giorgi (Brescia, It.: La Scuola, 2013), 5–104.

98. Montessori, *Il metodo del bambino e la formazione dell'uomo*, 275.

Chapter 3. Ending Conflict with Education

1. The four lectures are stored at the AMI Archive, Amsterdam.

2. Maria Montessori, *First Lecture on Peace Delivered on 17 Feb. 1917*, San Diego Course: document 3984, AMI, 1918, 1.

3. Montessori, *First Lecture on Peace*, 1.

4. Erica Moretti, "Teaching Peace in a Time of War: Maria Montessori's 1917 Lectures," *AMI Journal* 1–2 (2013): 17–31.

5. Recent scholarship has highlighted the influence these experiences had on her thinking over the course of those two decades. Babini and Lama, *Una donna nuova*; Anna Matellicani, *La "Sapienza" di Maria Montessori: Dagli studi universitari alla docenza (1890–1919)* (Rome: Aracne, 2007).

6. For an overview, see Thomas Hippler and Miloš Vec, eds., *Paradoxes of Peace in Nineteenth-Century Europe* (Oxford: Oxford University Press, 2015); Bo Stråth, *Europe's Utopias of Peace: 1815, 1919, 1951* (London: Bloomsbury Academic, 2016); Roger Chickering, *Imperial Germany and a World without War: The Peace Movement and German Society, 1892–1914* (Princeton, NJ: Princeton University Press, 1975); Sandi E. Cooper, *Patriotic Pacifism: Waging War on War in Europe, 1815–1914* (New York: Oxford University Press, 1991); Paul Laity, *The British Peace Movement, 1870–1914* (Oxford: Clarendon Press, 2002).

7. Cooper, *Patriotic Pacifism*, 103–119.

8. David Nicholls, "Richard Cobden and the International Peace Congress Movement, 1848–1853," *Journal of British Studies* 30, no. 4 (1991): 351–376.

9. Johan Galtung and Dietrich Fischer, *Johan Galtung: Pioneer of Peace Research* (Basel, Switz.: Springer, 2013).

10. Cooper, *Patriotic Pacifism*, 9.

11. Francesca Canale Cama, *La pace dei liberi e dei forti: La rete di pace di Ernesto Teodoro Moneta* (Bologna: Bononia University Press, 2012); Claudio Ragaini, *Giù le armi! Ernesto Teodoro Moneta e il progetto di pace internazionale* (Milan: Franco Angeli, 1999); Ute Buse, *Ernesto Teodoro Moneta (1833–1918): Leben und Werk eines italienischen Pazifisten* (Frankfurt am Main: Lang, 1996); Maria Combi, *Ernesto Teodoro Moneta, premio Nobel per la pace 1907* (Milan: U. Mursia, 1968).

12. Beatrice Pisa, "Ernesto Teodoro Moneta: Storia di un pacifista 'con le armi in mano,'" *Giornale di storia contemporanea* 12, no. 2 (2009): 21–56.

13. Victor Hugo to Giuseppe Garibaldi, December 20, 1863, Istituto per la Storia del Risorgimento Italiano. Giuseppe Garibaldi Papers, B242 (CCXLII) no. 36 (1).

14. Giuseppe Mazzini and Dora Melegari, *La giovane Italia e la giovane Europa: Dal carteggio inedito di Giuseppe Mazzini a Luigi Amedeo Melegari* (Milan: Fratelli Treves, 1906).

15. Bruna Bianchi and Geraldine Ludbrook, *Living War, Thinking Peace (1914–1924): Women's Experiences, Feminist Thought, and International Relations* (Newcastle, UK: Cambridge Scholars Publishing, 2016).

16. Franca Pieroni Bortolotti, *La donna, la pace, l'Europa: L'associazione internazionale delle donne dalle origini alla Prima Guerra Mondiale* (Milan: Franco Angeli, 1985).

17. Catia Papa, *Sotto altri cieli: L'Oltremare nel movimento femminista italiano* (Rome: Viella, 2009).

18. Catia Papa, "Suffragiste d'inizio Novecento: Maria Montessori e la via italiana al voto femminile," in *Maria Montessori e la società del suo tempo*, ed. Fabio Fabbri, 194–207 (Rome: Castelvecchi, 2020).

19. Babini and Lama, *Una donna nuova*, 49.

20. Valeria Babini, "Science, Feminism and Education: The Early Work of Maria Montessori," *History Workshop Journal* 49, no. 1 (2000): 50.

21. Movimento Femminile e Notizie, "Comizio femminile e proteste contro la guerra d'Africa," *Vita femminile: Organo del movimento femminile italiano* 2, no. 4 (April 1896): 32.

22. *Alle donne italiane* (March 1, 1896) Manifesto Associazione Femminile di Roma, Museo Centrale del Risorgimento di Roma, *Alina e Felice Albani*, b. 1084, f. 1 (10), quoted in Papa, *Sotto altri cieli*, 93–94.

23. Nicola Labanca, *In marcia verso Adua* (Turin: Einaudi, 1993), 78.

24. Babini and Lama, *Una donna nuova*, 51.

25. Maria Montessori, "Movimento femminile," *L'Italia femminile*, July 30, 1899, 29.

26. *International Council of Women: Report of Transactions of the Second Quinquennial Meeting held in London, July 1899*, vol. 1 (London: T. Fisher Unwin Paternoster Square, 1900), 228–230.

27. Johan Galtung, *Peace: Research, Education, Action* (Copenhagen: Ejlers, 1975), 317–333. Originally delivered as lectures in 1971–72.

28. Milena Santerini, *Cittadini del mondo: Educazione alle relazioni interculturali* (Brescia, It.: La Scuola, 1994).

29. Tiziana Pironi, "Educazione e pacifismo nelle lettere tra Ellen Key e Romain Rolland," *Studi sulla formazione* 19, no. 1 (2016): 87–103.

30. Ellen Key, *The Younger Generation* (London: Putnam & Sons, 1914), 68–72.

31. "Such an education will remain in the mind of the adult and will grow into a voluntary self-control and sincere obedience to the demands of society, and from this state of mind of the individuals of a nation will an international self-control be developed." Ellen Key, *War, Peace, and the Future: A Consideration of Nationalism and Internationalism, and of the Relation of Women to War* (London: Putnam & Sons, 1916), 156.

32. Key, *Younger Generation*, 67–88.

33. Maria Montessori, *Il segreto dell'infanzia* (Milan: Garzanti, 1992), 268.

34. Witherspoon was also a cofounder and executive secretary of the New York Bureau of Legal Advice, which provided the first organized assistance to conscientious objectors in the country. She was affiliated with the Women's Suffrage Party and the Woman's Peace Party.

35. It is fair to assume that her distancing in 1908 is the reason she did not attend the 1915 International Congress of Women that convened at The Hague, Netherlands.

36. Frances M. Witherspoon to Maria Montessori, January 13, 1917, Women's International League for Peace and Freedom Records Collection, Swarthmore College Peace Collection, Reel 12.22: Correspondence, 1916–19, WPP/NYC.

37. Elda Guerra, *Il dilemma della pace: Femministe e pacifiste sulla scena internazionale, 1914–1939* (Rome: Viella, 2014), 19–29; "what is left of the internationalism which met in congresses, socialist, feminist, pacifist, and boasted of a coming of an era of peace and amity?" Mary Sheepshanks, "Patriotism and Internationalism," *Jus Suffragii; Monthly Organ of the International Woman's Alliance* 9, no. 2 (1914): 184.

38. Alberto Castelli, "Il pacifismo alla prova: Ernesto Moneta e il conflitto italo-turco," in *Nazione democrazia e pace: Tra Ottocento e Novecento*, ed. Giovanna Angelini (Milan: Franco Angeli, 2012), 111–142.

39. Edoardo Teodoro Moneta, "Sulla Morale," *La vita internazionale*, April 4, 1905.

40. Bruna Bianchi argues that feminist organizations continued fighting for peace throughout the conflict. Bruna Bianchi, "Towards a New Internationalism: Pacifist Journals Edited by Women," in *Gender and the First World War*, ed. Christa Hämmerle, Oswald Überegger, and Birgitta Bader-Zaar (Basingstoke, UK: Palgrave MacMillan, 2014), 176–194.

41. Gaetano Salvemini, "La guerra e la pace," *L'Unità*, August 28, 1914.

42. The United States would formally enter World War I on April 6, 2017, less than two weeks after Montessori completed her series of lectures there. Spain remained neutral throughout the war.

43. Maria Montessori, *Maria Montessori Sails to America: A Private Diary, 1913*, trans. Carolina Montessori (Amsterdam: Pierson Publishing, 2013); Maria Montessori, *Maria Montessori Writes to her Father: Letters from California, 1915*, trans. Carolina Montessori (Amsterdam: Pierson Publishing, 2015); Maria Montessori, *The California Lectures of Maria Montessori, 1915: Collected Speeches and Writings*, ed. Robert G. Buckenmeyer (Oxford: Clio, 1997).

44. Gerald L. Gutek and Patricia Gutek, *Bringing Montessori to America: S. S. Mcclure, Maria Montessori, and the Campaign to Publicize Montessori Education* (Tuscaloosa: University of Alabama Press, 2016).

45. William Kilpatrick, "What America Thinks of Montessori's Educational Crusade," *Current Opinion* 56 (February 12, 1914): 127–129; Kramer, *Maria Montessori*, 212–216; Montessori, *California Lectures*.

46. The scholarship on the movement is prolific but scattered. For a recent debate on this topic, see Charles Magnin and Rita Hofstetter, eds., "New Education: Genesis and Metamorphosis," special issue, *Paedagogica Historica* 42, no. 1–2 (2006). In particular, see the article in that issue by Alberto Felice Arújo on Montessori's role in the movement: Alberto Felice Arújo, "Le thème de l'enfant nouveau chez Montessori: Vers une mythanalyse en éducation," 143–159.

47. William Boyd and Wyatt Rawson, *The Story of the New Education* (London: Heinemann, 1965).

48. Montessori, *First Lecture on Peace*, 1.

49. Montessori, *Antropologia pedagogica*.

50. Kramer, *Maria Montessori*, 356–357.

51. These transcriptions are all that survive of the lectures and have been preserved and catalogued as typewritten manuscripts by the archivists of the Association Montessori Internationale in Amsterdam. No professional translator or editor has ever reviewed them until now.

52. Kramer, *Maria Montessori*, 376.

53. Montessori, *First Lecture on Peace*, 1.

54. Montessori, *First Lecture on Peace*, 10–11.

55. Montessori, *First Lecture on Peace*, 1.

56. Montessori, *First Lecture on Peace*, 2.

57. For a general overview of irredentism, see Markus Kornprobst, *Irredentism in European Politics: Argumentation, Compromise and Norms* (Cambridge: Cambridge University Press, 2008); Thomas Ambrosio, *Irredentism: Ethnic Conflict and International Politics* (Westport, CT: Praeger, 2001); Fabio Todero, ed., *L'Irredentismo armato: Gli irredentismi europei davanti alla guerra* [. . .] (Trieste: Istituto regionale per la storia del movimento di liberazione nel Friuli-Venezia Giulia, 2015); Marina Cattaruzza, *L'Italia e il confine orientale* (Bologna: Il mulino, 2007).

58. Woodrow Wilson, "Address to the Senate of the United States: 'A World League for Peace,'" ed. Gerhard Peters and John T. Woolley, American Presidency Project, https://www.presidency.ucsb.edu/node/206603.

59. Wilson, "Address to the Senate."

60. Montessori, *First Lecture on Peace*, 12.

61. Maria Montessori, *Second Lecture on Peace Delivered on 11 March 1917*, San Diego Course: document 3985, AMI, 1918.

62. Montessori, *Second Lecture on Peace*, 2.

63. Montessori, *Montessori Method*, 346.

64. Montessori, *Second Lecture on Peace*, 4.

65. Montessori does not mention what those principles are, but here it seems clear that she is referencing the principles of Roman Catholicism.

66. Montessori, *Second Lecture on Peace*, 9.

67. Montessori, *Montessori Method*, 377.

68. Jane Roland Martin, "Romanticism Domesticated: Maria Montessori and the Casa dei Bambini," in *The Educational Legacy of Romanticism*, ed. John Willinsky (Waterloo, ON: Wilfrid Laurier University Press, 1990), 159–174.

69. Montessori, *Il Metodo della pedagogia scientifica applicato all'educazione infantile nelle Case dei Bambini: Edizione Critica*, 683.

70. Fabio Pruneri, "L'Umanitaria e la massoneria," *Annali di storia dell'educazione e delle istituzioni scolastiche* 11 (2004): 133–151.

71. Maria Montessori, *Third Lecture on Peace Delivered on 18 March 1917*, San Diego Course: document 3986, AMI, 1918.

72. Maria Montessori, *The Absorbent Mind* (Wheaton, IL: Theosophical Publishing House, 1964), 148.

73. Montessori, *Montessori Method*, 105.

74. Montessori, *Montessori Method*, 106.

75. Montessori, *Montessori Method*, 62.

76. Montessori, *Montessori Method*, 359.

77. Montessori, *Third Lecture on Peace*, 7.

78. Montessori, *Third Lecture on Peace*, 9, 10.

79. Montessori, *Third Lecture on Peace*, 11. See also Montessori, *Montessori Method*, 98.

80. Maria Montessori, *Fourth Lecture on Peace Delivered on 25 March 1917*, San Diego Course: document 3987, AMI, 1918.

81. Montessori, *Fourth Lecture on Peace*. Montessori argued that the child experiences four specific phases, or planes, of development: from birth to age six, from age six to twelve, from twelve to eighteen, and from eighteen to twenty-four. Each period corresponds to a particular set of characteristics, learning modes, and developmental necessities. Each plane therefore necessitates a specific educational approach. Montessori further developed this theory in *Education for a New World*, *The Absorbent Mind*, and *The Child, Society and the World*. See Maria Montessori, *Education for a New World* (Madras: Kalakshetra Press, 1946); Montessori, *Absorbent Mind*; Maria Montessori, *The Child, Society and the World* (Amsterdam: Montessori-Pierson, 2008).

82. Montessori, *Fourth Lecture on Peace*, 3.

83. Montessori, *Fourth Lecture on Peace*, 8, 10.

84. Here Montessori is probably referring to Carmen Sylva, the literary name of Pauline Elisabeth Ottilie Luise zu Wied, wife of King Carol I of Romania. For more information on the writer, see Gabriel Badea-Päun, *Carmen Sylva: Uimitoarea Regină Elisabeta a României, 1843–1916* (Bucharest: Humanitas, 2008).

85. Montessori, *Fourth Lecture on Peace*, 10.

86. "He that loveth father or mother more than Me, is not worthy of Me: and he that loveth son or daughter more than Me, is not worthy of Me." Matt. 10:37 (authorized version).

87. Montessori, *Fourth Lecture on Peace*, 11.

88. Montessori, *Education and Peace*, 14.

Chapter 4. Montessori in Fascist Italy

1. Maria Montessori to Benito Mussolini, Milan, April 4, 1927, ACS, Segreteria Particolare del Duce, Corrispondenza Ordinaria 1922–1943, B. 288, f. 15279/2.

2. Maria Montessori to Benito Mussolini, May 26, 1928, ACS, Segreteria Particolare del Duce, Corrispondenza Ordinaria 1922–1943, B. 288, f. 15279/2.

3. Several secondary sources mention a lecture on peace Montessori delivered at the International Bureau of Education (IBE) in 1926, which has never

been found. The lecture does not exist in the Jean Jacques Institute Archives, where all the IBE papers are kept, and there is no mention of Montessori being invited in the IBE director Pierre Bovet's correspondence. Scholars have probably confused this with her 1932 lecture.

4. Maria Montessori to Emilio Bodrero, May 16, 1931, ACS, Presidenza Del Consiglio Dei Ministri 1934–36 f. 5, n. 2069.

5. Angelo Ventura, *Intellettuali: Cultura e Politica tra fascismo e antifascismo* (Rome: Donzelli, 2017), 171.

6. Clara Tornar, "Maria Montessori durante il fascismo," *Giornale italiano di pedagogia sperimentale* 13, no. 2 (2005): 6; Augusto Scocchera, *Introduzione a Mario Montessori* (Rome: Edizioni Opera Nazionale Montessori, 1999), 46; Augusto Scocchera, *Maria Montessori: Quasi un ritratto inedito* (Florence: La Nuova Italia, 1990); Paola Trabalzini, *Maria Montessori: Da "Il Metodo,"* 95–99.

7. Montessori, *L'autoeducazione nelle scuole elementary*, 212.

8. Foschi, *Maria Montessori*, 94–95. G. Cives, *Giuseppe Lombardo Radice: Didattica e pedagogia della collaborazione* (Florence: La Nuova Italia, 1970).

9. For an overview of the relationship between intellectuals and Fascism, see Ventura, *Intellettuali*; Gabriele Turi, *Il fascismo e il consenso degli intellettuali* (Bologna: Il Mulino, 1980); Giovanni Sedita, *Gli intellettuali di Mussolini: La cultura finanziata dal fascismo* (Florence: Le Lettere, 2010). On this topic, scholarly attention has also been given to other pedagogues who took part in the drafting of the Gentile reform and benefited from or collaborated with the Fascist regime and, over the course of the 1920s, eventually distanced themselves. Among them, see Gabriele Turi, *Lo Stato educatore: Politica e Intellettuali* (Laterza: Rome-Bari, 2002) 168–186; Giacomo Cives, *Attivismo e antifascismo in Giuseppe Lombardo Radice: "Critica didattica" o "didattica critica"?* (Florence: La Nuova Italia, 1983); Lamberto Borghi, *Educazione e autorità nell'Italia Moderna* (Florence: La Nuova Italia, 1951); Franco Cambi, *Antifascismo e pedagogia 1930–1945* (Florence: Vallecchi Editore, 1980); Tina Tomasi, *Idealismo e fascismo nella scuola italiana* (Florence: La Nuova Italia, 1969).

10. Almost all the contributions on Montessori and Fascism are in Italian. See Scocchera, *Maria Montessori: Quasi un ritratto inedito*, 57–59; Hélène Leenders, "Con viva fede nel lavoro a venire: Intorno alla pubblicazione della terza edizione italiana del Metodo della pedagogia scientifica, 1926," *I problemi della pedagogia* 42, no. 4–6 (July–December 1996): 349–357; Marjan Schwegman, *Maria Montessori* (Bologna: Il Mulino, 1999), 97–110; Hélène Leenders, *Montessori en fascistisch Italië: Een receptiegeschiedenis* (Baarn, Neth.: Intro, 1999); Giuliana Marazzi, "Montessori e Mussolini: La Collaborazione e la Rottura," *Dimensioni e problemi della ricerca storica*, 13, no. 1 (2000): 177–195; Luisa Lama, "Maria Montessori nell'Italia Fascista: Un Compresso Fallito," *Il Risorgimento* 54, no. 2 (2000): 309–341; Suzanne Stewart-Steinberg, *The Pinocchio Effect: On Making Italians, 1860–1920* (Chicago: University of Chicago Press, 2007), 289–326;

Fabio Fabbri, "Maria Montessori di fronte al fascismo," in *Maria Montessori e la società del suo tempo*, ed. Fabio Fabbri, 208–229 (Rome: Castelvecchi, 2020).

11. Montessori, *Il metodo della pedagogia scientifica*.

12. Cabanes, *Great War and Origins of Humanitarianism*.

13. Iriye, *Cultural Internationalism and World Order*, 91–105.

14. Mona Siegel, *The Moral Disarmament of France: Education, Pacifism, and Patriotism, 1914–1940* (Cambridge: Cambridge University Press, 2004).

15. Kramer, *Maria Montessori*, 280. Giovanni Gentile, *La riforma della scuola in Italia*, vol. 3, ed. H. A. Cavallera (Florence: Le Lettere, 2003); Gabriele Turi, *Giovanni Gentile: Una biografia* (Turin: Utet, 2006); Jean-Yves Fretigne, *Les conceptions educatives de Giovanni Gentile: Entre elitisme et fascisme* (Paris: L'Harmattan, 2006).

16. Daniela Coli, ed., *Giovanni Gentile filosofo e pedagogista* (Florence: Le Lettere, 2004).

17. Kramer, *Maria Montessori*, 280–281.

18. Kramer cites the AMI Archives, but I have not been able to verify the existence or content of this specific letter. In Kramer, *Maria Montessori*, 281.

19. Kramer, *Maria Montessori*, 278–293.

20. Montessori, *Il metodo della pedagogia scientifica*, 554.

21. Montessori to Mussolini, April 4, 1927.

22. In Leenders, "Con viva fede nel lavoro a venire," 353.

23. "Circolare ai prefetti delle città sedi universitarie del 6 dicembre 1923," in Edoardo and Duilio Susmel, eds., *Opera omnia di Benito Mussolini*, vol. 20, *Dal viaggio negli Abruzzi al delitto Matteotti (23 agosto 1923–13 giugno 1924)* (Florence: La Fenice, 1956), 366.

24. Tomasi, *Idealismo e fascismo nella scuola italiana*, 40–41. Gentile himself brings back to the study of a Royal Committee in 1905 his elaboration of the main principles of the reform. In Giovanni Gentile, *Scritti pedagogici*, vol. 3, *La riforma della scuola in Italia* (Milan: Sandron, 1932), 312.

25. Alessandra Tarquini, *Il Gentile dei fascisti: Gentiliani e antigentiliani nel regime fascista* (Bologna: Il Mulino, 2009).

26. Tomasi, *Idealismo e fascismo nella scuola italiana*; Giacomo Cives, *La Scuola italiana dall'Unità ai nostri giorni.* (Florence: La Nuova Italia, 2000); Giovanni Gentile, Giuseppe Lombardo Radice, and Ernesto Codignola, *Il pensiero pedagogico dell'idealismo*, ed. Armando Carlini (Brescia, It.: La scuola, 1968); Giuseppe Ricuperati, *La scuola italiana e il fascismo* (Bologna: Consorzio provinciale pubblica lettura, 1977); Michel Ostenc, *La scuola italiana durante il fascismo* (Rome: Laterza, 1981).

27. Ernesto Codignola, *Il problema dell'educazione nazionale in Italia* (Florence: Vallecchi Editore, 1925), 149.

28. Dante L. Germino, *The Italian Fascist Party in Power: A Study in Totalitarian Rule* (Minneapolis: University of Minnesota Press, 1959), 62.

29. For more on this part of his philosophy, see, for example, Giovanni Gentile, *Fascismo e cultura*, vol. 1 (Milan: Fratelli Treves, 1928).

30. Giovanni Gentile, *Il fascismo al governo della scuola* (Florence: Remo Sandron, 1924), 129.

31. Elena D'ambrosio, *A scuola col duce: L'istruzione primaria nel ventennio fascista* (Como, It.: Istituto di Storia Contemporanea Pier Amato Perretta, 2001), 12.

32. More specifically, the government circulars of September 29, 1870, and of July 12, 1871, modified the 1859 Casati Law. According to the Casati Law, the teaching of religion was included among the mandatory subjects at the elementary level. Parents who wanted their children to abstain from this subject could request to withdraw their children. For more on religion education in Italy, see Luigi Ambrosoli, *Libertà e religione nella riforma Gentile* (Florence: Vallecchi, 1980); Alberto Aquarone, *Lo Stato catechista* (Florence: Parenti, 1961); Carmen Betti, *La religione a scuola fra obbligo e facoltatività (1859–1923)* (Florence: Manzuoli, 1989); Emilio Butturini, *La religione a scuola dall'Unità a oggi* (Brescia, It.: Queriniana, 1987), 28–59; Luciano Pazzaglia, "Lo Stato laico e l'insegnamento religioso in alcuni dibattiti del primo Novecento," *Pedagogia e Vita* 39, no. 4 (April–May 1981): 379–416; Luciano Pazzaglia, *Scuola e religione in età giolittiana* (Milan: ISU Università Cattolica Editore, 2000); Gaetano Bonetta, "L'istruzione religiosa nell'Italia liberale, Studi e ricerche sull'Italia liberale," *Italia Contemporanea*, no. 162 (March 1986): 27–54.

33. Borghi, *Educazione e autorità nell'Italia moderna*, 243–244. After 1926 and during his progressive detachment from Fascism, Lombardo Radice criticized Montessori's pedagogy. See Giuseppe Lombardo Radice, *Il problema dell'educazione infantile* (Florence: La Nuova Italia, 1948), 26; Giuseppe Lombardo Radice, *Athena fanciulla: Scienza e poesia della scuola serena* (Florence: R. Bemporad, 1925), 16–24.

34. Borghi, *Educazione e autorità nell'Italia moderna*, 243–244.

35. Giovanni Gentile, "Il metodo Montessori," in *L'educazione nazionale* 4, no. 7 (July 1922): 27, quoted in Salvatore Valituttti, "Giovanni Gentile e il metodo Montessori," *Vita dell'infanzia* 17, no. 6–7 (June–July 1968): 10–16.

36. Giuseppe Lombardo Radice, "A proposito del metodo Montessori," *L'educazione nazionale* 8, no. 7 (July 1926): 21.

37. The 1926 edition presented many changes, including six new chapters. Giacomo Cives, "Carattere e senso delle varianti di Il Metodo," in Montessori, *Il Metodo della pedagogia scientifica applicato all'educazione infantile nelle case dei bambini: Edizione critica*, xvii.

38. Trabalzini, *Maria Montessori: Da "Il Metodo,"* 185–186. Maria Montessori, *Il Metodo della pedagogia scientifica applicato all'educazione infantile nelle case dei bambini: Edizione critica*, 75n61.

39. Tomasi, *Idealismo e fascismo nella scuola italiana*, 16.

40. Trabalzini, *Maria Montessori: Da "Il metodo,"* 187.

41. See De Giorgi, *Maria Montessori e le sue reti di relazioni*; Foschi, *"L'histoire croisée."*

42. Fulvio De Giorgi, "Montessori tra modernisti, antimodernisti e gesuiti," *Annali di storia dell'educazione* 25 (2018): 27–73; Moretti and Dieguez, "I progetti di Maria Montessori impigliati nella rete di mons. Umberto Benigni," 89–114.

43. Royal Decree, October 1, 1923, n. 1285, article 3.

44. Tracy H. Koon, *Believe, Obey, Fight* (Chapel Hill: University of North Carolina Press, 1985), 60.

45. "The papal benediction . . . is a pledge of those graces and celestial favors with which we wish to render *Il Metodo della Pedagogia Scientifica applicato all'educazione infantile nelle case dei bambini* fertile with goodness." Benedictus S.S. XV, November 21, 1918. Maria Montessori, *Il Metodo della pedagogia scientifica*, 64.

46. "Le 'Case dei bambini' della Montessori e l' 'autoeducazione,'" *La Civiltà Cattolica*, 70 (1919), II, 37–49.

47. Maria Montessori and Fulvio De Giorgi, *I bambini viventi nella chiesa*; Maria Montessori, *Il peccato originale* (Brescia, It.: Scholé, 2019); Maria Montessori, *La vita in Cristo* (Rome: Stabilimento Tipografico Ferri, 1931); Maria Montessori, *Mass Explained to Children* (London: Sheed & Ward, 1932). *Mass Explained to Children* summarizes two previous versions in Italian. It was published in English to reach a wider audience.

48. Leenders, "Con viva fede nel lavoro a venire," 349–356. Trabalzini also supports this thesis. Trabalzini, *Maria Montessori: Da "Il metodo,"* 202–210.

49. Moretti and Dieguez, "I progetti di Maria Montessori impigliati nella rete di mons. Umberto Benigni."

50. Erminio Lora and Rita Simionati, eds. *Enchiridion delle encicliche*, vol. 5, *Pio XI (1922–1939)* (Bologna: Edizioni Dehoniane, 1995), n. 370.

51. Carl Ipsen, *Dictating Demography: The Problem of Population in Fascist Italy* (Cambridge: Cambridge University Press, 1996); Elizabeth Dixon Whitaker, *Measuring Mamma's Milk: Fascism and the Medicalization of Maternity in Italy* (Ann Arbor: University of Michigan Press, 2000).

52. The foundation was created though a royal decree issued by King Vittorio Emanuele III under the patronage of Queen Margherita. Queen Margherita had supported Maria Montessori's initiatives from the very beginning. She had, in fact, sponsored the second training course held by Montessori at the Suore Francescane Missionarie di Maria in via Giusti.

53. Pietro Fedele to Benito Mussolini, August 7, 1926, ACS, Presidenza del Consiglio dei Ministri, 1934–1936, folder 5, no. 2069.

54. "Inaugurazione del Corso magistrale Montessori svoltosi a Milano presso la Società Umanitaria da febbraio ad agosto 1926," *Note sul Metodo Montessori*, ed. Comitato di Milano dell'Opera Nazionale Montessori (Rome: Bestetti e Tumminelli, 1926), 42.

55. In Scocchera, *Maria Montessori: Quasi un ritratto inedito*, 57.

56. Schwegman, *Maria Montessori*, 97–110; Lama, "Maria Montessori nell'Italia fascista."

57. Pietro Fedele to Benito Mussolini, June 30, 1926, "Appunti relativi al metodo Montessori circa la NOTA di S.E. il Governatore di Roma, 30 giugno 1926," ACS, Presidenza del Consiglio dei Ministri, 1934–36, folders 1–3, no. 2069, Carteggio "Roma Opera Montessori."

58. Settimio Carassali, "Giardino di Froebel o Casa dei Bambini?," *La Stampa* (Turin), July 12, 1926, 4.

59. Maria Montessori to Mussolini, February 9, 1928, ACS, Segreteria Particolare del Duce, Corrispondenza Ordinaria 1922–1943, B. 288, f. 15279/2.

60. Adrian Lyttelton, *The Seizure of Power: Fascism in Italy (1919–1929)* (London: Routledge, 2004), 406.

61. Marc Raboy, *Marconi: The Man Who Networked the World* (New York: Oxford University Press, 2016), 552.

62. Turi, *Lo Stato educatore*, 61–75.

63. Sedita, *Gli intelllettuali di Mussolini*, 39.

64. Ventura, *Intellettuali*; Ruth Ben-Ghiat, *Fascist Modernities: Italy, 1922–1945* (Berkeley: University of California Press, 2009); Turi, *Il fascismo e il consenso degli intellettuali*; Albertina Vittoria, "Totalitarismo e intellettuali: L'Istituto nazionale fascista di cultura dal 1925 al 1937," *Studi Storici* 23, no. 4 (October–December 1982): 897–918; Gisella Longo, "L'istituto Nazionale Fascista di Cultura durante la Presidenza di Giovanni Gentile," *Storia Contemporanea* 23, no. 2 (1992): 181–282.

65. Vincenzo Cardarelli to unknown recipient, October 21, 1932, in ACS, Minculpop, Cabinet, deposit 11, b. 3., fasc. Cardarelli Vincenzo, as quoted in Ventura, *Intellettuali*, 37.

66. Instat, *Annuario statistico italiano*, 1926, as cited in Hélène Leenders, "A Special Meaning of 'Health': Towards a Theory-Immanent Explanation for the Use of Montessori Pedagogy in Fascist Italy (1926–1934)," *Annali di storia dell'educazione* 25 (2018): 202.

67. Speech delivered by Mario M. Montessori at *Zeist*, September 1, 1962, 1–3, document in Surendra Narayan Archives, Theosophical Society, Adyar, Chennai.

68. Lama, "Maria Montessori nell'Italia fascista," 325.

69. Kramer, *Maria Montessori*, 300.

70. Giuseppe Lombardo Radice, "Accanto ai maestri," *L'educazione nazionale* 8, no. 9 (August–September 1924): 2.

71. Bacigalupi and Fossati, *Da plebe a popolo*, 191–212.

72. Montessori to Mussolini, April 4, 1927.

73. Scocchera, *Maria Montessori: Quasi un ritratto inedito*, 59.

74. Montessori to Bodrero.

75. Anonymous note, October 10, 1932, Rome, ACS, Ministero dell'Interno, Polizia politica.

76. This episode certainly had repercussions on Mussolini's behavior during interactions with Montessori. See Lama, *Maria Montessori nell'Italia fascista*, 334–335.

77. Peter Cahalan, *Belgian Refugee Relief in England during the Great War* (New York: Garland, 1982); Peter Gatrell, *A Whole Empire Walking: Refugees in Russia during World War I* (Bloomington: Indiana University Press, 1999); Marrus, *Unwanted*; Philippe Nivet, *Les réfugiés français de la Grande Guerre, 1914/1920: Les "Boches du Nord"* (Paris: Economica, 2004).

78. Dominique Marshall, "Humanitarian Sympathy for Children in Times of War and the History of Children's Rights, 1919–1959," in *Children and War: A Historical Anthology*, ed. James Marten (New York: New York University Press, 2002), 184–200.

79. Paul Weindling, "Introduction: Constructing International Health Between the Wars," in *International Health Organizations and Movements 1918–1939*, ed. Paul Weindling (Cambridge University Press, 1995), 2.

80. Carol Miller, "The Social Section and Advisory Committee on Social Questions of the League of Nations," in Weindling, *International Health Organizations and Movements*, 154–175.

81. Salvatici, *Nel nome degli altri*, 136–137.

82. Marshall, "Rise of Coordinated Action for Children."

83. Ellen Boucher, "Cultivating Internationalism: Save the Children Fund, Public Opinion and the Meaning of Child Relief, 1919–24," in *Brave New World: Imperial and Democratic Nation-Building in Britain between the Wars*, ed. Laura Beers and Geraint Thomas (London: University of London, 2011), 182.

84. Marshall, "Formation of Childhood as Object of International Relations."

85. Historian Bruno Cabanes defines the transition from war to peace, or *sortie de guerre*, as a unique moment wherein all citizens and organizations experienced a profound reorganization to adapt to peacetime requirements. Bruno Cabanes, *La Victoire endeuillée: La sortie de guerre des soldats français (1918–1920)* (Paris: Seuil, 2004); Patrick O. Cohrs, *The Unfinished Peace after World War I: America, Britain and the Stabilisation of Europe, 1919–1932* (Cambridge: Cambridge University Press, 2006).

86. Boucher, "Cultivating Internationalism," 178–180.

87. Clare Mulley, *The Woman Who Saved the Children* (London: Oneworld, 2019), 301. Linda Mahood, *Feminism and Voluntary Action*, 194–200.

88. Mahood, *Feminism and Voluntary Action*, 197–199.

89. Murray Last, "Putting Children First," *Disaster* 8, no. 3 (September 1994): 192–202.

90. Cabanes, *Great War and Origins of Humanitarianism*, 293.

91. "Declaration of the Rights of the Child 1924," in *International Documents on Children*, ed. Geraldine Van Bueren (Boston: Martinus Nijhoff, 1993), 3.

92. Susan Pedersen, "Back to the League of Nations," *American Historical Review* 112, no. 4 (October 2007): 1111.

93. Van Bueren, *International Documents on Children*, xv.

94. Mark Mazower, "The Strange Triumph of Human Rights, 1933–1950," *Historical Journal* 47, no. 2 (2004): 382.

95. See chapter 10, "The Contribution of the League of Nations to the Evolution of International Law," in J. G. Starke, *Studies in International Law* (London: Butterworth, 1965). See also A. H. Robertson, *Human Rights in the World* (Manchester: University of Manchester Press, 1972).

96. Philip E. Veerman, *The Rights of the Child and the Changing Image of Childhood* (Dodrecht, Neth.: Martinius Nijhoff, 1992), 325–328.

97. Maria Montessori, "La morale sessuale nell'educazione," in *Atti del I Congresso Nazionale delle donne italiane, Rome 24–30 April 1908* (Rome: Stabilimento Tipografico della Società Editrice Laziale, 1912), 272–281. In her talk, the educator had emphasized the relationship between sexual education and individual responsibility in the betterment of the human species, with the goal of preventing congenital defects. According to Montessori, sexual education had to be taught in school by trained personnel; it was part of a larger plan for female emancipation, one that emphasized women's role as mothers and bearers of the human race, freeing them from "the tacit prohibition for the woman, even as a mother, to intrude in any way in matters of sexuality," a ban that confined women to a never-ending childhood in that they "ignored the basic facts of life and its struggles, dwarfed in their thought and in their conscience" (274–275).

98. Daniel Hameline, *L'éducation dans le miroir du temps* (Lausanne, Switz.: Édition des sentiers, 2002), 181.

99. Pierre Bovet, *La paix par l'école: Travaux de la Conférence internationale tenue à Prague du 16 au 20 avril 1927* (Geneva: Bureau International d'Éducation, 1927).

100. Regina Helena De Freitas Campos, "Les psychologues et le mouvement de l'Éducation pour la paix à Genève (1920–1940)," in *Les psycologues et les guerres*, ed. Élisabeth Chapuis, Jean Pierre Pétard, and Régine Plas (Paris: L'Harmattan, 2010), 96.

101. Davide Rodogno, Bernhard Struck, and Jakob Vogel, introduction to Rodogno, Struck, and Vogel, *Shaping the Transnational Sphere*, 1–22.

102. John Howlett, "The Formation, Development and Contribution of the New Ideals in Education Conferences, 1914–1937," *History of Education* 46, no. 4 (2017): 459–479.

103. Kevin J. Brehony, "A New Education for a New Era: Contribution of the Conferences of the New Education Fellowship to the Disciplinary Field of Education 1921–1938," *Paedagogica Historica* 40, nos. 5/6 (October 2004): 733–755; Maxwell Donald Lawson, "The New Education Fellowship: The Formative Years," *Journal of Educational Administration and History* 13, no. 2 (1981): 24–28.

104. Ensor and Rotten were deeply involved to the vast array of networks devoted to aid for children affected by famine and poverty in the postwar period. Ensor worked for the organization Famine Area Children's Hospitality, bringing Austrian and Hungarian children to England, where they were relocated with host families. Rotten, a pacifist and member of the Women's International League for Peace and Freedom, had done humanitarian work through the Emergency and War Victims Relief Committee of the English Society of Friends together with Frédéric Ferrière (father of Adolphe Ferrière), the Swiss doctor and delegate of the International Committee of the Red Cross who was responsible for the first accounts of children starving in German and Austrian cities.

105. The New Education Fellowship, First International Report, London, 1932, Institute of Education Archive, University of London, Records of the World Education Fellowship, 43b.

106. New Education Fellowship, First International Report.

107. Editorial, *Pour l'ère nouvelle* 7, no. 35 (1928): 25.

108. Editorial, *Pour l'ère nouvelle* 6, no. 29 (1927): 110.

109. Beatrice Ensor, "Le congrès de Calais," *Pour l'ère nouvelle* 1, no. 1 (January 1922): 5.

110. Jean-François Condette and Antone Savoye, "Une éducation pour une ère nouvelle: Le congrès international d'éducation de calais (1921)," *Les études sociales*, 1, no. 163 (2016): 43–77.

111. "Chronique de l'enseignement primaire en France: Le congrès international de Calais," *Revue pédagogique* 79, no. 1 (July–December 1921): 294.

112. Ensor, "Le congrès de Calais," 6; Condette and Savoye, "Une éducation pour une ère nouvelle," 63.

113. Giulio Cesare Ferrari, "L'education de l'activité spontanée chez les enfants," *Pour l'ère nouvelle* 1 (January 1922): 19–20; Roger Cousinet, "La Nouvelle Èducation" *Pour l'ère nouvelle* 1, no. 1 (January 1922): 10.

114. Béatrice Haenggeli-Jenni, "Le rôle de la Ligue Internationale pour l'Éducation nouvelle dans la circulation des savoirs pédagogiques (1920–1940)" in Droux and Hofstetter, *Globalisation des mondes de l'éducation*, 75–95. See, e.g., Maria Valli, "L'esprit de la méthode Montessori," *Pour l'ère nouvelle* 1, no. 2 (1922): 37–39; Louise Briod, "La méthode Montessori dans les écoles primaires du Tessin," *Pour l'ère nouvelle* 3, no. 12 (1924): 65–67; Maria Montessori, "La discipline et la liberté," *Pour l'ère nouvelle* 6, no. 29 (June 1927): 111–113.

115. R. Gerber and V. Czak, *Vie et œuvre d'Adolphe Ferrière (1879–1960): Chronologie de son existence (1879–1936)* (Geneva: Université de Genève, Faculté de psychologie et des sciences de l'éducation, 1989–2018), 38, https://www.unige.ch/archives/aijjr/files/1215/3676/4096/R_Gerber_corrige_1.pdf.

116. Adolphe Ferrière, "Une visite aux pionniers de l'école active en Italie," *Pour l'ère nouvelle* 5, no. 23 (November 1926): 151.

117. Montessori quoted in William Boyd, *Report on the Fifth World Conference of the NEF* (London: University of London Institute of Education, 1930), 106.

Chapter 5. Montessori's First Public Lectures on Peace, 1932–1939

1. Montessori's lectures on peace came at a time when this issue was vigorously debated. In 1939, Albert Einstein and Sigmund Freud had notoriously debated the question, "Is there any way of delivering mankind from the menace of war?" Requested by the League of Nations, the publication of this debate had a large circulation. Freud's response to this query claimed a direct link between aggression as the behavior of individuals and the phenomenon of war. They were both caused by the same drive system. According to the psychoanalyst, war is "just another of life's odious importunities, [. . .] biologically sound, practically unavoidable" as it responds to the human death instinct. This instinct becomes an impulse of destruction when it is directed toward external objects. By explaining the occurrence of war at the level of the individual, Freud explained the phenomenon as an externalization of the death instinct. For her part, Montessori did not address the notion of war as posited by Freud. Albert Einstein and Sigmund Freud, *Why War? A Correspondence between Albert Einstein and Sigmund Freud*, trans. Stuart Gilbert (London: Peace Pledge Union, 1939).

2. Montessori, *Education and Peace*, 13–14.

3. Maria Montessori, "Social Status of Children," *Times* (London), January 9, 1932.

4. The International Bureau of Education is identified by the translator, Helen Lane, as the International Office of Education. The International Bureau of Education published the lecture, but it is not clear whether this was a lecture Montessori delivered at the second International Montessori Congress in Nice in July 1932 or a lecture she delivered in Geneva in March of the same year. According to a 1949 article in *Opera Montessori*, the lecture was first delivered at the second International Montessori Congress in Nice. A typescript of the lecture in Italian, preserved at the AMI Archive, is dated March 1932. Montessori probably delivered the same lecture twice. Maria Montessori, "Montessori e la pace," in Maria Montessori, *La pace e l'educazione* (Rome: Opera Montessori, 1959), 3–6; Maria Montessori, *Peace and Education* (Geneva, Switz.: Publications of the International Bureau of Education, 1932); Maria Montessori, "Peace," in Montessori, *Education and Peace*, 5–23.

5. Quoted in Rita Hofstetter, "Building an 'International Code for Public Education': Behind the Scenes at the International Bureau of Education (1925–1946)," *Prospects* 45, no. 1 (2015): 36.

6. On "la nouvelle génération," see Rita Hofstetter et al., "Genève dans le contexte international," in *Passion, Fusion, Tension: New Education and Educational Sciences*, ed. Rita Hofstetter and Bernard Schneuwly (Berne: Peter Lang, 2006), 131. See also Silvia Parrat-Dayan, "Les activités de Piaget Durant les deux guerres mondiales," in Chapuis, Pétard, and Plas, *Les psychologues et la guerre*, 201–215; Gerry P. T. Finn, "Piaget, Vygotsky and the Social Dimension," in *Piaget, Vygotsky and Beyond: Future Issues for Developmental Psychology and Edu-*

cation, ed. Leslie Smith, Julie Dockrell, and Peter Tomlinson (London: Routledge, 1997), 93–94.

7. Jean Piaget, "La biologie et la guerre," *Feuille centrale de la Société suisse de Zofingue* 58, no. 5 (1918): 380.

8. Charles Magnin and Astrid Thomann. "Jean Piaget, diplomate de l'éducation," in *L'éducation dans tous ses états,* ed. A Philippart, L. Vandevelde (Brussels: CEDEF, 2001), 279–289.

9. Jean Piaget, "Is an Education for Peace Possible?" trans. Hans G. Furth, in "Piaget Peace and War," ed. Hans G. Furth, special issue, *Genetic Epistemologist* 17, no. 3 (1989): 5.

10. Montessori, "Peace," 21.

11. An antimilitarist and activist against conscription, Albert Einstein campaigned in favor of peace and international understanding. For a study on Einstein's work on peace in the interwar period, see Albert Einstein, "Internationalism and European Security 1922–1932," in *Einstein on Politics: His Private Thoughts and Public Stands on Nationalism, Zionism, War, Peace, and the Bomb,* ed. David E. Rowe and Robert Schulmann, 189–222 (Princeton, NJ: Princeton University Press, 2007).

12. Montessori, "Peace," 23, 14.

13. Montessori, "Peace," 16, 17.

14. Montessori, "Peace," 19.

15. Montessori, "Peace," 19.

16. Montessori, "Peace," 19.

17. Celia Jenkins, "New Education and its Emancipatory Interests (1920–1950)," *History of Education* 29, no. 2 (2000): 139–151.

18. Beatrice Ensor, "Outlook Tower," *New Era,* 10, no. 37 (1929): 133.

19. Giuliana Sorge to Benito Mussolini, April 10, 1932, ACS, Presidenza del Consiglio dei Ministri, 1876–1943, f. 14.3, n. 5006. The text of the speech is attached to the letter.

20. Bodrero was a Fascist deputy elected to parliament in 1924. He served as assistant to the minister of public instruction Pietro Fedele from 1925 to 1928. He became senator in 1934 and deputy to the League of Nations. He served as the director of the Opera Nazionale Montessori for three years, vexing Montessori for the entire time he was in office.

21. Emilio Bodrero to Benito Mussolini, August 7, 1932, ACS, Segreteria particolare Duce, Co, b. 288, f. 15279.

22. The comment is added by pen to the margins of a copy of the letter originally sent to Montessori. Emilio Bodrero to Maria Montessori, August 26, 1932, ACS, Ministero dell'Interno, Divisione Polizia Politica: Cartella personale Montessori, n. inventario 13–157–5, package 859, folder 52, Montessori, n. 22.

23. Foschi, *Maria Montessori,* 88–91; Carlo M. Fiorentino, *All'ombra di Pietro: La Chiesa cattolica e lo spionaggio fascista in Vaticano, 1929–1939* (Florence: Le Lettere, 1999), 20–29.

24. Moretti and Dieguez, "I progetti di Maria Montessori impigliati nella rete di mons. Umberto Benigni"; Erica Moretti and Alejandro Dieguez, "Il difficile equilibrio tra cattolicesimo e teosofia," in *Il destino di Maria Montessori: Promozioni, rielaborazioni, censure, opposizioni al metodo*, ed. Renato Foschi, Erica Moretti, and Paola Trabalzini (Rome: Fefè Editore, 2018), 95–112.

25. Monsignor Umberto Benigni's report on Maria Montessori, Rome, October 29, 1932, ACS, Ministero dell'Interno, Divisione Polizia Politica: Cartella personale Montessori. On Benigni and Fascism, see Nina Valbousquet, *Les réseaux transnationaux de l'antisémitisme catholique: France, Italie, 1914–1934* (Paris: CNRS Éditions, 2020), 300–308.

26. Montessori, *Education and Peace*, 21.

27. Renzo De Felice, *Mussolini il duce: Gli anni del consenso, 1929–1936* (Turin: Einaudi, 1974), 35–36.

28. Maria Montessori, "Disarmament in Education," *New Era* 13 (September 1932): 257–59; quotations at 257.

29. Thomas R. Davies, *Possibilities of Transnational Activism: The Campaign for Disarmament between the Two World Wars* (Leiden, Neth.: Brill, 2006), 87.

30. Otto Nathan and Heinz Norden, eds., *Einstein on Peace* (New York: Schocken Books, 1960), 105. The manifesto appeared in a German version in *Die Menscherechte* 5, no. 5/6 (July 20, 1930).

31. Quoted in Nathan and Norden, *Einstein on Peace* (New York: Schocken Books, 1960), 168–169.

32. For an analysis of the debate, see Elly Hermon, "The International Peace Education Movement 1919–1939," in *Peace Movements and Political Cultures*, ed. Charles Chatfield and Peter Ven Den Dungen (Knoxville: University Tennessee Press, 1988), 127–142; Elly Hermon, "Le désarmement moral, facteur dans les relations internationales pendant l'entre-deux-guerres," *Guerres mondiales et conflits contemporains* 156 (October 1989): 23–36.

33. Caroline E. Playne, "Le desarmement moral," *Le mouvement pacifiste*, July 1923, 81, as translated and quoted by Elly Hermon in Hermon, "International Peace Education Movement," 130.

34. Théodore Ruyssen, "Le desarmement moral," *La paix par le droit*, September 1924, 326–333.

35. Siegel, *Moral Disarmament of France*, 191–220.

36. League of Nations, *Conference on the Reduction and Limitation of Armaments: Moral Disarmament*, no. Conf. D. 98, Geneva, February 24, 1932, https://libraryresources.unog.ch/ld.php?content_id=31320509.

37. Elisabetta Tollardo, *Fascist Italy and the League of Nations 1922–1935* (London: Palgrave, 2016), 21–64.

38. Benito Mussolini, "Discorso di Firenze," in *Opera Omnia di Benito Mussolini*, ed. Edoardo Susmel and Duilio Susmel, vol. 24 (Florence: La Fenice, 1951), 113.

39. Carolyn Kitching, *Britain and the Geneva Disarmament Conference: A Study in International History* (Houndmills, UK: Palgrave Macmillan, 2003), 66–88.

40. Maria Montessori, *Educazione alla guerra o educazione alla pace? La pace e l'educazione* (Milan: Società Anonima Editrice Dante Alighieri, 1933). Excerpt from Maria Montessori, "Educazione alla guerra o educazione alla pace? La pace e l'educazione," *Rivista pedagogica*, no. 3 (November–December 1933), 786–801. This lecture was then edited and published in Maria Montessori, *Educazione e Pace* (Milan: Garzanti, 1970).

41. Montessori, "Disarmament in Education," 258–259.

42. Marazzi, "Montessori e Mussolini," 186–188.

43. "Progetto di una organizzazione assistenziale per le persone civili divenute invalide o ammalate in seguito alla guerra di Spagna," May 15, 1937, ACS, Ministero dell'Interno, Divisione Polizia Politica: Cartella personale Montessori.

44. "La labor del Ministerio de Instrucción Pública: Una visita a la Delegación Central de Colonias," *El Magisterio Español*, no. 6696 (1937): 302, cited in Sjaak Braster and María del Mar del Pozo Andrés, "Education and the Children's Colonies in the Spanish Civil War (1936–1939): The Images of the Community Ideal," *Paedagogica Historica* 51, no. 4 (August 2015): 462. For literature on the evacuation of children during the Spanish Civil War, see Dorothy Lagarreta, *The Guernica Generation: Basque Refugee Children of the Spanish Civil War* (Reno: University of Nevada Press, 1984); Eduard Pons Prades, *Los niños republicanos: El exilio* (Madrid: Oberón, 2005); Eduard Pons Prades, *Las guerras de los niños republicanos, 1936–1995* (Madrid: Compañía Literaria, 1997).

45. Foschi, *Maria Montessori*, 95–96.

46. Francis Paul Walters, *A History of the League of Nations* (London: Oxford University Press, 1952), 706.

47. Rachel Mazuy, "Le Rassemblement Universel pour la Paix (1931–1939): Une organisation de masse?," *Matériaux pour l'histoire de notre temps* no. 30 (1993): 40–44.

48. Tollardo, *Fascist Italy*; Robert Mallett, *Mussolini in Ethiopia, 1919–1935: The Origins of Fascist Italy's African War* (New York: Cambridge University Press, 2015); Susan Pedersen, *The Guardians: The League of Nations and the Crisis of Empire* (Oxford: Oxford University Press, 2015).

49. "Manifeste du congrès de Rassemblement Universel pour la Paix," *L'Esprit international,* September 5, 1936, 568–569.

50. Elly Hermon, "Une ultime tentative du sauvetage de la Société des Nations: La campagne du Rassemblement Universel pour la Paix," in *Le pacifisme en Europe des années 1920s aux années 1950,* ed. Maurice Vaïsse (Brussels: Etablissements Emile Bruylant, 1993), 193–220; Hermon, "International Peace Education Movement," 127–142.

51. Montessori, *Education and Peace*, 25–26.

52. Montessori, *Education and Peace*, 24.

53. "Resoconto di Santorre Vezzari su Maria e Mario Montessori, Bruxelles, September 1st, 1936," ACS, Polizia Politica: Cartella personale Montessori.

54. "Resoconto di Santorre Vezzari su Maria e Mario Montessori," August 11, 1936, ACS, Ministero dell'Interno, Divisione Polizia Politica; Foschi, *Maria Montessori*, 93–96.

55. "Resoconto di Santorre Vezzari sulle frequentazioni della famiglia Montessori in Spagna," Barcelona, February 27, 1933, ACS, Ministero dell'Interno, Divisione Polizia Politica; Foschi, *Maria Montessori*, 91–92.

56. Mazuy, "Le Rassemblement Universel."

57. "Circa la professoressa Montessori," Lugano, September 8, 1936, ACS, Ministero dell'Interno, Polizia Politica: Cartella personale Montessori, document 27232.

58. Unsigned letter to the police, August 11, 1936, ACS, Ministero dell'Interno, Polizia Politica: Cartella personale Montessori.

59. In the original: "Questa miserabile donna fu salvata anni or sono per l'intercessione del Ministro dell'Educazione Nazionale."

60. "Varie," October 10, 1932, ACS, Ministero dell'Interno, Polizia Politica: Cartella personale Montessori.

61. In her *Maria Montessori: A Biography*, Rita Kramer mentions that Montessori was a member of the Fascist Party. However, there is no record of her affiliation, neither among her papers nor in the administration of the party.

62. Herman Noordegraaf, "The Anarchopacifism of Bart de Ligt," in *Challenge to Mars: Essays on Pacifism from 1918 to 1945*, ed. Peter Brock and Thomas P. Socknat (Toronto: University of Toronto Press, 1999), 98.

63. Bart de Ligt, *Introduction to the Science of Peace: The Initial Lecture of the First Summer School of the Peace Academy Held in Jouy-en-Josas France in August 1938* (London: Peace Pledge Union, 1939), 31. Quoted in Herman Noordegraaf, "Anarchopacifism of Bart de Ligt," 89–100.

64. C. L. de Ligt-Van Rossem, "Un témoignage Hollandais en faveur de la Méthode Montessori," *Pour l'ère nouvelle* 6, no. 29 (June 1927): 113–115.

65. De Ligt borrows extensively from the work of Mary Patricia Willcocks, *Towards New Horizons* (London: John Lane, 1919), 201–202. Bart de Ligt, *The Conquest of Violence: An Essay on War and Revolution* (London: George Routledge & Sons, 1937), 126–127.

66. De Ligt, *Introduction to the Science of Peace*, 127, 20.

67. Maria Montessori, "Cittadinanza adulta, cittadinanza bambina," in *Il metodo del bambino e la formazione dell'uomo: Scritti e documenti inediti e rari*, by Maria Montessori and Augusto Scocchera (Rome: Opera Nazionale Montessori, 2002), 101.

68. Kramer, *Maria Montessori*, 337.

69. Montessori, *Education and Peace*, 45, 48.

70. Montessori only hints at the role of the environment in the child. She will delve into this subject later. In chapter 6, the role of the environment will be further discussed through an analysis of the series of lectures titled The Formation of Man and of the lecture text "Cosmic Education."

71. Reference to "spiritual embryo" in Montessori, *Education and Peace*, 37. In her lecture, Montessori mentions the concept of "spiritual gestation" and references her 1936 book *The Secret of Childhood*. See Maria Montessori, *The Secret of Childhood* (New York: Random House, 1966), 29–36.

72. Emel Ultanir, "An Epistemological Glance at the Constructivist Approach: Constructivist Learning in Dewey, Piaget, and Montessori," *International Journal of Instruction* 5, no. 2 (2012): 195–212.

73. Montessori, *Secret of Childhood*, 29, 28.

74. Montessori, *Education and Peace*, 53, 50.

75. One of the speeches, the most explicitly political one, was not included in the collection *Education and Peace* and only published in 1986 in *Communications*, the Association Montessori Internationale journal. Here, the lecture is cited from a reprinted version, Montessori and Montessori, "Peace through Education."

76. Montessori and Montessori, "Peace through Education," 51.

77. Here, Montessori does not refer to the contemporaneous definition of unitarian states, according to which a unitary state is a state governed as a single power wherein the central government is supreme and all the administrative divisions exercise only powers that the central governments delegates. She refers to regimes that centralized their powers during the 1930s. Montessori and Montessori, "Peace through Education," 52.

78. Montessori and Montessori, "Peace through Education," 52.

79. "Resoconto di Pietro Gerbore sulla professoressa Maria Montessori," August 2, 1937, ACS, Ministero dell'Interno, Polizia Politica: Cartella personale Montessori, document 441/03829.

80. Montessori and Montessori, "Peace through Education," 52.

81. Montessori and Montessori, "Peace through Education," 52.

82. Montessori and Montessori, "Peace through Education," 53.

83. Eckhardt Fuchs, "Contextualizing School Textbooks Revision," in *Journal of Educational Media, Memory and Society* 2, no.2 (2010): 1–12.

84. Montessori and Montessori, "Peace through Education," 54.

85. Montessori and Montessori, "Peace through Education," 54.

86. Montessori, *Education and Peace*, 63–64.

87. Maria Montessori, "Message to the International Congress against War and Militarism at Paris 1–5 August 1937,"in Bart de Ligt, *The Conquest of Violence: An Essay on War and Revolution* (London: George Routledge & Sons, 1937), 286.

88. Montessori, *Education and Peace*, 38.

89. Maria Montessori, *The Permanent Relevance of Montessori's Plea* (Amsterdam: AMI, 2004), 17.

90. "The Child's Place in Society," *Times* (London), March 13, 1939, clipping, AMI.

91. Maggie Black, *Children First: The Story of UNICEF, Past and Present* (Oxford: Oxford University Press, 2006), 3.

92. Montessori, *Education and Peace*, 74–75.

93. Maria Montessori, "The Aims of the Social Party of the Child," *Communications* 1–2 (2013): 56–57. Originally published as Maria Montessori, "A Step Towards the Future: The Social Party of the Child," *Theosophist* 62 (May 1941): 105.

94. Montessori, *Education and Peace*, 73–74.

95. Montessori, "Child's Place in Society."

96. Ginni Sackett, *A Sharp Call to the Public Conscience: Maria Montessori and the Social Party of the Child* (Rochester, NY: Association Montessori Internationale USA, 2010), 3.

97. Montessori, *Permanent Relevance of Montessori's Plea*, 7–9.

98. *Explanatory Note on the Annexed Draft of the Statues*, October 12, 1937, AMI.

99. Francesca Bosisio, "Il Percorso dell'Infanzia nel Mondo dei Diritti," in *Viaggio Attraverso i Diritti dell'Infanzia e dell'Adolescenza*, ed. Francesca Mazzucchelli (Milan: Franco Angeli, 2006), 34; Zoran Pavlovic, "Children's Parliament in Slovenia," in *Monitoring Children's Rights*, ed. Eugeen Verhellen (The Hague: Martinus Nijhoff, 1996), 327–346.

100. Paula S. Fass, "A Historical Context for the United Nations Convention on the Rights of the Child," *The Annals of the American Academy of Political and Social Science* 633 (January 2011): 17–29.

101. Rebecca Gil, "'The Rational Administration of Compassion': The Origins of British Relief in War," *Le Movement Social* 227 (April–June 2009): 9–26, cited in Droux, "L'internationalisation de la protection de l'enfance," 24.

102. Montessori, "Step Towards the Future," 106, 111.

Chapter 6. The Child as Agent of Radical Change

1. J. Jeffrey Franklin, *The Lotus and the Lion: Buddhism and the British Empire* (Ithaca, NY: Cornell University Press, 2008), 65. This phenomenon is reported in Joy Dixon, *Divine Feminine: Theosophy and Feminism in England* (Baltimore: Johns Hopkins University Press, 2001), 26; Dixon, in turn, cites Alfred Percy Sinnett, *The Occult World* (London: Truber, 1883), 56. The opening epigraph is from Helena Petrovna Blavatsky, *The Key to Theosophy* (Los Angeles: United Lodge of Theosophists, 1920), 209.

2. Maria Montessori, "Man's Place in Creation: VI/1. Lecture in a Convent, London 1935," in Montessori, *The Child, Society and the World*, 95–99.

3. The literature on this topic is scarce and often not academic. Carolie Elizabeth Wilson, "Montessori Was a Theosophist," *History of Education Society Bulletin* 36 (1985): 52–54; Carolie Elizabeth Wilson, "A Study of the Application of Her Method in a Developing Country" (PhD diss., University of Sydney, 1987); Paola Giovetti, *Maria Montessori: Una biografia* (Rome: Edizioni Mediterranee, 2009); Maxwell Donald Lawson, "Montessori: The Indian Years," *Forum of Education* 33, no. 1 (1974): 36–49; Prasanna Srinavasan et al., *Montessori in India: 70 Years* (Chennai: Indian Montessori Foundation, 2007); Tiziana Leucci,

"Maria Montessori en Inde: Adoption et adaptation d'une méthode pédagogique," in *L'Inde et l'Italie: Rencontres intellectuelles, politiques et artistiques*, ed. Marie Fourcade, Claude Markovits, and Tiziana Leucci (Paris: Éditions de l'École des hautes études, 2018), 245–285; Letterio Todaro, *L'alba di una nuova era: teosofia ed educazione in Italia agli inizi del Novecento* (Santarcangelo di Romagna, Italy: Maggioli Editore, 2020).

4. Foschi, *Maria Montessori*, 88–91.

5. Wilson, "Montessori Was a Theosophist," 52–54.

6. Alex Owen, *The Darkened Room: Women, Power, and Spiritualism in Late Victorian England* (Philadelphia: University of Pennsylvania Press, 1990); Janet Oppenheim, *The Other World: Spiritualism and Psychical Research in England, 1850–1914* (Cambridge: Cambridge University Press, 1985); Marlene Tromp, *Altered States: Sex, Nation, Drugs, and Self-Transformation in Victorian Spiritualism* (Albany: State University of New York Press, 2006), 47; Franklin, *Lotus and Lion*, 56.

7. Buttafuoco, "La filantropia come politica," 166–87.

8. Vittorio Vidotto, *Roma contemporanea* (Rome: Laterza, 2001), 72–141; Marco Pasi, "Teosofia e antroposofia nell'Italia del primo Novecento," in *Storia d'Italia: Annali 25, Esoterismo*, ed. Gian Mario Cazzaniga (Turin: Einaudi, 2010), 569–798.

9. Lucetta Scaraffia, "Emancipazione e rigenerazione spirituale," in *Donne Ottimiste: Femminismo e associazioni borghesi nell'Otto e Novecento*, by Lucetta Scaraffia and Anna Maria Asastia (Bologna: Il Mulino, 2002), 19–126.

10. Babini and Lama, *Una donna nuova*, 148–164.

11. Stewart-Steinberg, *Pinocchio Effect*, 311.

12. Owen Chadwick, *The Secularization of the European Mind in the Nineteenth Century* (Cambridge: Cambridge University Press, 1975).

13. Owen, *The Darkened Room*, 245.

14. Helena Petrovna Blavatsky, *Isis Unveiled: A Master-Key to the Mysteries of Ancient and Modern Science and Theosophy*, vol. 2, *Theology* (Pasadena, CA: Theosophical University Press, 1877), xlv.

15. Michel Foucault, "What Is Enlightenment?" in *The Foucault Reader*, ed. Paul Rabinow (New York: Pantheon Books, 1984), 43. For the definition of "hybrid credo," see Franklin, *Lotus and Lion*.

16. Franklin, *Lotus and Lion*, 71.

17. Henri Steel Olcott, "The Genesis of Theosophy," *National Review* (London), October 14, 1889, 208–217.

18. Montessori, *Antropologia pedagogica*.

19. For the phenomenon in Catholic Italy, see Emma Fattorini, *Il culto mariano fra Ottocento e Novecento: Simboli e devozione* (Milan: Franco Angeli, 1999); Emma Fattorini, "A Voyage to the Madonna," in *Women and Faith: Catholic Religious Life in Italy from Late Antiquity to the Present*, ed. Lucetta Scaraffia and Gabriella Zarri (Cambridge, MA: Harvard University Press, 1999), 281–295.

For the feminization of spiritualism and Theosophy, see Owen, *Darkened Room*; Oppenheim, *Other World*; Marlene Tromp, "Spirited Sexuality: Sex, Marriage, and Victorian Spiritualism," *Victorian Literature and Culture* 31, no. 1 (2003): 67–81; Dixon, *Divine Feminine*, 67–93.

20. Dixon, *Divine Feminine*, 68.

21. Through this organization, prominent women such as Francesca Arundale, adoptive mother of George Sidney Arundale, came to collaborate with the Theosophical Society. She soon became a friend and collaborator of both Blavatsy and Besant, and she adopted her great-nephew George Arundale, who would in turn become the president of the organization in the 1930s. Among her most prominent works is Francesca Arundale, *Education in the Light of Theosophy* (Madras: Vasantā Press, 1913).

22. Elizabeth Severs, "The Co-Masons and the Women's Suffrage Procession," *Co-Mason* 3 (July 1911): 129.

23. Diana Burfield, "Theosophy and Feminism: Some Explorations in Nineteenth Century Biography," in *Women's Religious Experience: Cross-Cultural Perspectives*, ed. Pat Holden (London: Croom Helm, 1983), 28–45.

24. *Teosofia*, periodico mensile della Sez. Teosofica di roma, October 1899, AAV, Fondo Benigni, folder 49, f. 468v. Italics in the original.

25. Lawson, "Montessori: The Indian Years," 36–49.

26. Transcript of talk by Sankara Menon titled "Dr. Maria Montessori," on radio program *All India*, August 31, 1970, quoted in Lawson, "Montessori: The Indian Years," 36.

27. Fabienne Serina-Karsky, "L'éducation nouvelle incarnée dans les classes: Marie Aimée Niox-Chateau, une Montessorienne a l'école nouvelle," research paper, CIRCEFT-HEDUC, University of Paris, August 18, 2019, hal-02267122, https://hal.archives-ouvertes.fr/hal-02267122/document.

28. *Travaux et projets de la Ligue d'éducation morale de la jeunesse*, Rapport de Madame Pujol, 11, Archivio Casa Generalizia delle Suore Francescane Missionarie di Maria, Rome, series 18, n. 491.

29. Giovetti, *Maria Montessori: Una biografia*, 99.

30. "Il movimento Teosofico," 460–468, AAV, Fondo Benigni, folder 49.

31. "Che per educare bene il fanciullo, egli deve essere anzitutto considerato come una intelligenza Spirituale permanente, rivestita di involucri di materia e quindi bene studiato affine di poterlo aiutare e non imporgli invece un metodo inadatto al suo sviluppo. Il grande Istruttore ci à consigliato di far penetrare le idee Teosofiche nell'Educazione. *Questo effettivamente è stato fatto in Europa ed il sistema Montessori ne è una prova.*" "Il movimento Teosofico," 460, italics in the original.

32. "Il movimento Teosofico," 467.

33. C. W. Dijkgraff, ed., *Transactions of the Eighth Congress of the Federation of European National Society Held in Vienna July 21st to 26th 1923* (Amsterdam: Council of the Federation, 1923); Brehony, "New Education for a New Era."

34. For a general overview of the subject of nationalism and education in imperial India, see Aparna Basu, *The Growth of Education and Political Development in India, 1898–1920* (Delhi: Oxford University Press, 1974); Manu Bhagavan, *Sovereign Sphere: Princes, Education and Empire in Colonial India* (New Delhi: Oxford University Press, 2003); Bhattacharya Sabyasachi, ed., *The Contested Terrain: Perspective on Education in India* (New Delhi: Orient Longman, 1998).

35. Martin Carnoy, *Education as Cultural Imperialism* (New York: Longman, 1974), 100.

36. Hayden J. A. Bellenoit, *Missionary Education and Empire in Late Colonial India 1860–1920* (London: Pickering & Chatto, 2007), 2; Nita Kumar, *Lessons from Schools: The History of Education in Banaras* (New Delhi: Sage, 2000).

37. Sanjay Seth, *Subject Lessons: The Western Education of Colonial India* (Durham, NC: Duke University Press, 2007), 159.

38. Glyn Richards, *Gandhi's Philosophy of Education* (New Delhi: Oxford University Press, 2001); Rabindranath Tagore, *The Oxford India Tagore: Selected Writings on Education and Nationalism*, ed. Uma Dasgupta (Delhi: Oxford University Press, 2010); William Cenkner, *The Hindu Personality in Education: Tagore, Gandhi, Aurobindo* (New Delhi: Manohar, 1994).

39. Maria Montessori, *The Formation of Man*, trans. A. M. Joosten (Amsterdam: Montessori Pierson Publishing, 2007), 75–76.

40. Wilson, "Study of the Application," 4, 70.

41. Kramer, *Maria Montessori*, 306–307.

42. "La dedica di Tagore a Montessori," *Il quaderno Montessori* (Summer 1993): 4–5.

43. Kramer, *Maria Montessori*, 306–307.

44. The journal *Pour l'ère nouvelle* reviewed the approach in a 1928 piece. Moriz Winternitz, "L'école de Rabindranath Tagore à Santiniketan," *Pour l'ère nouvelle* 7, no. 38 (1928): 99–100.

45. Rabindranath Tagore, "To Teachers," in *A Tagore Reader*, ed. Amiya Chakravarty (New York: Macmillan, 1961), 214.

46. Mohammad A. Quayum, "Education for Tomorrow: The Vision of Rabindranath Tagore," *Asian Studies Review* 40, no. 1 (2016): 1–16.

47. Ratna Ghosh, M. Ayaz Naseem, and Ashok Vijh, "Tagore and Education: Gazing Beyond the Colonial Cage," in *Decolonizing Philosophies of Education*, ed. Ali A. Abdi (Rotterdam: Sense Publishers, 2012), 63.

48. Rabindranath Tagore, *Personality* (New York: Macmillan, 1917), 142.

49. The figure of the teacher/guru differs drastically from Montessori's conception of the teacher. For a definition of this figure in Tagore, see Ranjan Ghosh, "Caught in the Cross Traffic: Rabindranath Tagore and the Trials of Child Education," *Comparative Education Society* 59, no. 3 (2015): 409–410.

50. Tagore quoted in Swati Lal, "Rabindranath Tagore's Ideals of Aesthetic Education," *Journal of Aesthetic Education* 18, no. 2 (1984): 31–39.

51. Ranjan Ghosh, "A Poet's School: Rabindranath Tagore and the Politics of Aesthetic Education," *South Asia: Journal of South Asian Studies* 35, no. 1 (2012): 18.

52. Rabindranath Tagore, "The Artist," in *The Religion of Man* (London: George Allen & Unwin, 1961), 83–84.

53. *Maria Montessori: A Centenary Anthology 1870–1970* (Amsterdam: Association Montessori International, 1970), 49.

54. J. B. Kripalani, *The Latest Fad: Basic Education* (Bombay: Vora, 1946), 107.

55. M. K. Gandhi, *An Autobiography: The Story of My Experiments with Truth*, trans. Mahadev Desai (London: Jonathan Cape, 1966), 77.

56. Richard L. Johnson, ed., *Gandhi's Experiments with Truth: Essential Writings by and about Mahatma Gandhi* (Lanham, MD: Lexington Books, 2006).

57. The first Montessori school was established in the Gujarati-speaking state of Baroda, in the city of Vaso. Social workers Matibhai Amin and Darbar Gopaldas, who had read several articles on Montessori in *The Times of India*, opened it. Wilson, "Study of the Application," 127–128. Gandhi said he had been aware of Montessori since 1915, when he visited a small school in Amreli. Mohandas Gandhi, "Speech at Montessori Training College, London, October 28, 1931," *Young India*, November 19, 1931, quoted in Mohandas K. Gandhi, *The Collected Works of Mahatma Gandhi*, vol. 54, *October 13, 1931–February 8, 1932* (New Delhi: Publications Division Government of India, 1999), 238–240.

58. Mohandas K. Gandhi to J. Theodore Harris, September 29, 1931, in Gandhi, *Collected Works*, vol. 53, *July 2, 1931–October 12, 1931*, 435–436.

59. Gandhi calls her "sister Montessori" in a 1945 letter to Saraladevi Sarabhai, who asked him if he knew the Montessori method. Mohandas K. Gandhi to Saraladevi Sarabhai, January 21, 1945, in Gandhi, *Collected Works*, vol. 79, *July 16, 1940–December 27, 1940*, 53.

60. Mohandas K. Gandhi, "Speech at Inauguration of Bal Mandir, Nadiad, May 3, 1935," in Gandhi, *Collected Works*, vol. 68, *September 23, 1935–May 15, 1936*, 391.

61. Montessori, *Education and Peace*, 33.

62. Gandhi, "Speech at Montessori Training College," 54:238.

63. Gandhi, "Speech at Montessori Training College," 54:239.

64. The Sabarmati Ashram was Gandhi's hermitage, spiritual home, and political headquarters. It served as an institution where the spiritual leader conducted his search for Truth, as well as a place where disparate political groups interested in nonviolence would gather to discuss. Mohandas K. Gandhi to Ashram Boys and Girls, January 30, 1932, in Gandhi, *Collected Works*, vol. 54, *October 13, 1931–February 8, 1932*, 429.

65. Gandhi, "Speech at Montessori Training College," 54:240.

66. Mark Bevir, "Theosophy and the Origins of the Indian National Congress," *International Journal of Hindu Studies* 7, no. 1–3 (2003): 99–115; Michael Bergunder, "Experiments with Theosophical Truth: Gandhi, Esotericism, and

Global Religious History," *Journal of the Modern Academy of Religion* 82, no. 2 (2014): 398–426.

67. Richards, *Gandhi's Philosophy of Education*, 2–3.

68. William Wordsworth, "Intimations of Immortality from Recollections of Early Childhood," in *The Poetical Works of Wordsworth*, ed. Thomas Hutchinson (Oxford: Oxford University Press, 1973), 78.

69. Richards, *Gandhi's Philosophy of Education*, 16.

70. Gandhi advocated for a comprehensive restructuring of the education system that included also adult education as a tool for self-reliance and peace. Dev Parkash Nayyar, *Building for Peace, or Gandhi's Ideas on Social (Adult) Education* (Delhi: Ama Ram & Sons, 1952).

71. Mohandas K. Gandhi, *Selections from Gandhi*, ed. N. K. Bose (Ahmedabad, India: Navajivan Trust, 1968), 52.

72. Mohandas K. Gandhi, *The Moral and Political Writings of Mahatma Gandhi*, vol. 3, ed. Raghavan Iyer (Oxford: Clarendon Press, 1987), 382.

73. Several other points of Gandhi's educational plan have been under attack. One is, for example, considering the teaching of the arts "sheer waste" which would result in the unemployment of students upon the completion of their degrees. Richards, *Gandhi's Philosophy of Education*, 36.

74. Gandhi, "Speech at Inauguration of Bal Mandir," 68:121.

75. Gandhi, "Speech at Montessori Training College," 54:240.

76. Albert Joosten, "Gandhi and Maria Montessori," *Communications* 1–2 (2013): 67.

77. Douglas Allen, "Mahatma Gandhi on Violence and Peace Education," *Philosophy East & West* 57, no. 3 (2007): 294, 297.

78. Monisha Bajaj, "Conjectures on Peace Education and Gandhian Studies: Method, Institutional Development and Globalization," *Journal of Peace Education* 7, no. 1 (2010): 47–63.

79. Mohandas K. Gandhi, "Interview with Maria Montessori, October 9, 1931," in Gandhi, *Collected Works*, vol. 53, *July 2, 1931–October 12, 1931*, 475.

80. Mohandas K. Gandhi to Parasram Mehrotra, April 18, 1932, in Gandhi, *Collected Works*, vol. 55, *February 10, 1932–June 15, 1932*, 10.

81. Mohandas K. Gandhi to Saraladevi Sarabhai, April 12, 1945, in Gandhi, *Collected Works*, vol. 86, *March 4, 1945–May 28, 1945*, 169.

82. Mohandas K. Gandhi to Tarabehn Modak, October 16, 1945, in Gandhi, *Collected Works*, vol. 88, *August 30, 1945–December 6, 1945*, 163.

83. Maria Montessori, *Maria Montessori Writes to Her Grandchildren: Letters from India (1939–1946)*, trans. Carolina Montessori (Amsterdam: Montessori Pierson Publishing, 2020), 64–65.

84. *The Theosophical Society Yearbook*, 1941, 76, in Surendra Narayan Archives, Theosophical Society, Adyar, Chennai.

85. Mark Bevir, "In Opposition to the Raj: Annie Besant and the Dialectic of Empire," *History of Political Thought* 19, no. 1 (1998): 61–77; Mark Bevir, "The

Formation of the All-India Home Rule League," *Indian Journal of Political Science* 52, no. 3 (1991): 341–356; Joanne Stafford Mortimer, "Annie Besant and India 1913–1917," *Journal of Contemporary History* 18, no. 1 (1983): 61–78.

86. Matthew Harp Allen, "Rewriting the Script for South Indian Dance," *TDR (1988–)* 41, no. 3 (1997): 93.

87. Harp Allen and Meduri confront each directly on this controversy; see Harp Allen, "Rewriting the Script"; Avanthi Meduri, "Bharatanatyam as Global Dance: Some Issues in Research, Teaching and Practice," *Dance Research Journal* 36, no. 2 (2004): 11–29.

88. Harp Allen, "Rewriting the Script."

89. Amrit Srinivasan, "Reform and Revival: The Devadasi and Her Dance," *Economic and Political Weekly* 20, no. 44 (1985): 1873.

90. Leela Venkataraman and Avinash Pasricha, *Indian Classical Dance: Tradition in Transition* (New Delhi: Lustre Press, 2002), 21.

91. Uttara Asha Coorlawala, "The Sanskritized Body," *Dance Research Journal* 36, no. 2 (2004): 51–52.

92. Venkataraman and Pasricha, *Indian Classical Dance*, 28.

93. Rukmini Devi Arundale, "The Spiritual Background of Bharata Natyam," in *Classical and Folk Dances of India* (Bombay: Marg Publications, 1963); Avanthi Meduri, ed., *Rukmini Devi Arundale (1904–1986): A Visionary Architect of Indian Culture and Performing Arts* (Delhi: Motilal Banarsidass Publishers, 2005).

94. *The Besant Cultural Center Adyar Madras-20*, Surendra Narayan Archives, document 76.13.1, 2.

95. *Besant Cultural Center Adyar Madras-20*, 32.

96. Rukmini Devi to students who intended to join Kalakshetra, 1944, quoted in Leela Samson, "Imbibing Culture at Kalakshetra," *India International Centre Quarterly* 29, no. 3–4 (2002–2003): 39.

97. Tapati Guha-Thakurta, *The Making of a New "Indian" Art: Artists, Aesthetics and Nationalism in Bengal, c. 1850–1920* (Cambridge: Cambridge University Press, 1992), 146.

98. Harp Allen, "Rewriting the Script," 94.

99. Here Srinivasan refers to "a vegetarian diet, early rising and prayers, *puja* on the stage." Srinivasan, "Reform and Revival," 1875.

100. Already in 1893, when Besant first sailed to India, she manifested her identification with the India and the birthplace of the Aryans. According to this vision, the Brahmins were the inheritor of the Aryans. Isaac Lubelsky, *Celestial India: Madame Blavatsky and the Birth of Indian Nationalism* (Oakville, CT: Equinox, 2012), 255–256.

101. Mark Bevir, "The West Turns Eastward: Madame Blavatsky and the Transformation of the Occult Tradition," *Journal of the American Academy of Religion* 62, no. 3 (1994): 747–767.

102. Lubelsky, *Celestial India*, 39–76.

103. Friedrich Max Müller, *India: What Can It Teach Us?* (Escondido, CA: Book Tree, 1999), 232; Friedrich Max Müller, *Life and Religion: An Aftermath from the Writings of the Right Honorable Professor F. Max Müller*, ed. Georgina Max Müller (London: Constable, 1915), 100.

104. Tim Allender, "'Better Mothers': Feminine and Feminist Educators and Thresholds of Indian Female Interaction, 1870–1932," in *Learning Femininity in Colonial India, 1820–1932* (Manchester: Manchester University Press, 2016), 233–266.

105. Coorlawala, "Sanskritized Body," 54.

106. Meduri, "Bharatanatyam as Global Dance," 19, 12. The Liberal Catholic Church was independent from the Roman Catholic Church but followed many Catholic practices. The Liberal Christian Church existed all over the world and was characterized by an interest in esoteric beliefs.

107. Maria Montessori, "Cosmic Education: VI/4 Lecture, India 1946," in *The Child, Society and The World*, 108–109.

108. Edward W. Said, *Orientalism* (New York: Vintage Books, 1979).

109. Meduri, *Rukmini Devi Arundale*, 15; see also Ramani Shakuntala, *Shraddahanjali: Brief Pen Portraits of Great People Who Laid the Foundation of Kalakshetra* (Chennai: Kalakshetra Foundation, 2003).

110. *Celebrations: 13 Oct.–15 Oct. '89*, Kalakshetra, Madras, Montessori in India 1939–1989, 3, pamphlet, Surendra Narayan Archives.

111. Mario M. Montessori, "The Impact of India," *NAMTA Journal* 23, no. 2 (1998): 29.

112. Kramer, *Maria Montessori*, 343.

113. Montessori, *Maria Montessori Writes to Her Grandchildren*, 51, 45–47.

114. Britt Hawthorne, "Dr. Montessori's Racism," *AMI/USA Journal* (Spring 2019): 61.

115. Sarada Hoffman, "Rukmini Devi: The Educator," in Meduri, *Rukmini Devi Arundale*, 87.

116. Angeline Stoll Lillard, *Montessori: The Science Behind the Genius* (New York: Oxford University Press, 2005), 39.

117. Venkataraman and Pasricha, *Indian Classical Dance*, 12.

118. George S. Arundale, *Education: Lectures and Supporting Statistics of George S. Arundale*, n.d., 204, Surendra Narayan Archives, George Sidney Arundale Notebooks, document 392bb.

119. Maria Montessori, *La scoperta del bambino* (Milan: Garzanti, 2011), 114.

120. Montessori, *Il metodo della pedagogia scientifica applicato all'educazione infantile nelle case dei bambini*, 185.

121. Arundale, *Education*, 204.

122. Montessori, *Il metodo della pedagogia scientifica applicato all'educazione infantile nelle case dei bambini*, 130.

123. Radha Burnier, "Rukmini Devi as a Theosophist," in Meduri, *Rukmini Devi Arundale*, 63.

124. Rukmini Devi Arundale, *Art and Education* (Madras: Theosophical Publishing House, n.d.), 3.

125. Devi Arundale, *Art and Education*, 11.

126. George S. Arundale, "Indian Education in India," in G. S. Arundale, *Education*, 66.

127. *Kalakshetra Foundation Prospectus*, Rukmini Devi College of Fine Arts, 8–9, Surendra Narayan Archives.

128. Marsilio Ficino, *The Book of Life*, trans. Charles Boer (Irving, TX: Spring Publications, 1980).

129. Helena Petrovna Blavatsky, *The Secret Doctrine*, vol. 1, *Cosmogenesis*, ed. Boris de Zirkoff (Madras: Quest Books, 1993), 250.

130. Blavatsky, *Key to Theosophy*, 63.

131. Blavatsky, *Secret Doctrine*, vol. 1, *Cosmogenesis*, 118.

132. Maria Carlson, *No Religion Higher Than Truth: A History of The Theosophical Movement in Russia, 1875–1922* (Princeton, NJ: Princeton University Press, 1993), 114.

133. Dixon, *Divine Feminine*, 123.

134. Annie Besant, *The Ancient Wisdom: An Outline of Theosophical Teachings* (Madras: Theosophical Publishing House, 1897), 245–246.

135. Winfried Böhm, "Educazione e grazia: Agostino, Rousseau, Montessori," *Pedagogia e vita* 58, no. 4 (2000): 27–41.

136. Lubelsky, *Celestial India*, 155–159.

137. Dixon, *Divine Feminine*, 121.

138. Dixon, *Divine Feminine*, 121–151.

139. C. B. Macpherson, *The Political Theory of Possessive Individualism: Hobbes to Locke* (Oxford: Clarendon Press, 1992).

140. Dixon, *Divine Feminine*, 124, 150.

141. Montessori, "Cosmic Education," 106. Biologist Ernst Haeckel elaborated the theory according to which ontogenesis is a brief recapitulation of phylogenesis. For an introduction to Heackel's thought on this subject, see Robert J. Richards, *The Tragic Sense of Life: Ernst Haeckel and the Struggle over Evolutionary Thought* (Chicago: University of Chicago Press, 2009).

142. Maria Montessori, *Come educare il potenziale umano* (Milan: Garzanti, 1992), 57–64.

143. Montessori, *Come educare il potenziale umano*, 21.

144. Ms. Vaidhesswaren, "How We Came to the Advanced Montessori Course at Kodaikanal," *NAMTA Journal* (June 1982): 31–34.

145. Montessori, "Cosmic Education," 107.

146. Maria Montessori, "Foreword," December 11, 1943, quoted in M. Subrahmanyam, *The Cosmic Plan of Creation* (Madras: n.p., 1946), 2–3, pamphlet in Surendra Narayan Archives, document 32965.

147. Montessori, "Cosmic Education," 110.

148. Montessori, *Come educare il potenziale umano*, 26–27.

149. Montessori, "Cosmic Education," 110.

150. Maria Montessori, *Dr. Maria Montessori's 1946 Lectures, Karachi, India*, ed. Lakshmi Kripalani (Houston: Houston Montessori Center, 2002), 7.

151. Montessori, "Cosmic Education," 111–112.

152. Mario Montessori quoted in David Kahn, "The Kodaikanal Experience: Kahn-Montessori Interview," *NAMTA Quarterly* 5, no. 1 (1979): 59.

153. Kahn, "Kodaikanal Experience," 58.

154. Paulo Freire, *Pedagogia da indignação: Cartas pedagógicas e outros escritos* (São Paulo: UNESP, 2000).

155. Montessori, *Education for a New World*; Maria Montessori, *To Educate the Human Potential* (Madras: Kalakshetra Publications, 1948); single lectures were also published in Montessori, *The Child, Society and the World*, 93–113.

156. Montessori, "Cosmic Education," 113.

157. Blavatsky, *Secret Doctrine*, vol. 1, *Cosmogenesis*, 378.

158. Montessori, *Formation of Man*, 12.

159. Montessori, *Maria Montessori Writes to Her Grandchildren*, 131.

160. Mario Montessori to Maria Montessori, June 13, 1940, in *Maria Montessori Writes to Her Grandchildren*, 119.

161. Subrahmanyam, *Cosmic Plan of Creation*.

162. William Drummond and William C. Ward, *The Poems of William Drummond of Hawthornden* (London: G. Routledge & Sons, 1920); Rudyard Kipling, *The Years Between* (New York: Barnes & Noble Digital Library, 2011), https://www.overdrive.com/media/848285/the-years-between.

163. Subrahmanyam, *Cosmic Plan of Creation*, 64.

164. Tara Zahra, *The Lost Children: Reconstructing Europe's Families after World War II* (Cambridge, MA: Harvard University Press, 2011).

165. Giacomo Cives, "Il periodo indiano di Maria Montessori," *Studi sulla formazione* 13, no. 1 (2010): 95–98.

166. Montessori, "La morale sessuale nell'educazione," 284.

167. Eckert, "Concretizing Cosmic Education in India."

Conclusions

1. Anna Freud and Dorothy Burlingham, *The Writings of Anna Freud*, vol. 3, *1939–1945, Infants without Families: Report on the Hampstead Nurseries* (New York: International Universities Press, 1973), 403.

2. This was not Anna Freud's first experience with children affected by war. In 1918, she had worked with a group of Austro-Hungarian displaced children who had been evacuated from Vienna to the Hungarian countryside during World War I.

3. Anna Freud and Dorothy Burlingham, *Young Children in War-Time: A Year's Work in a Residential War Nursery* (London: George Allen & Unwin, 1942), 12.

4. The complete quotation reads, "In this nursery school method [Montessori's] the play material is selected so as to afford the child the maximum

increase in self-esteem and gratification by means of task completion and independent problem solving, and children can be observed to respond positively to such opportunities almost from the toddler stage onward." Anna Freud, *Normality and Pathology in Childhood: Assessments of Development* (London: Routledge, 1989), 81.

5. Nick Midgley, "Anna Freud: The Hampstead War Nurseries and the Role of the Direct Observation of Children for Psychoanalysis," *International Journal of Psychoanalysis* 88, no. 4 (2007): 943.

6. Christiane Ludwig-Körner, "Anna Freud and her Collaborators in the Early Post-War Period," in *The Anna Freud Tradition: Lines of Development; Evolution of Theory and Practice Over the Decades*, ed. Norka T. Malberg and Joan Raphael-Leff (London: Routledge, 2012), 17.

7. Sigmund Freud to Maria Montessori, [December 20, 1917], Sigmund Freud Collection, General Correspondence, 1871–1996, Library of Congress. The letter is wrongly cataloged under 1927 instead of 1917.

8. The Italian pedagogue had early in her career distanced herself from psychoanalysis. She underlined the absence of infantile sexuality, a phenomenon that, when present at all, only corresponded to the influence of a corrupt environment. Montessori's official distance from this discipline relies on her idea that the child is empty, free from original sin and from sexual and violent drives. Scholar Edith Kurzweil argues that Montessori was influenced more by psychologist Wilhelm Wundt and the philosopher Johann Friederich Herbart than by Freud. Kurzweil maintains that Montessori's idea of the natural inclinations of the child can be linked to Freud's viable discipline. The Austrian pupil of Montessori Lili Roubiczek worked on the relationship between psychoanalysis and education and led a series of biweekly seminars with Anna Freud. Edith Kurzweil, *The Freudians: A Comparative Perspective* (New Brunswick, NJ: Transaction Publishers, 1998), 132. See also Kramer, *Maria Montessori*, 320.

9. For an analysis of the relationship between Anna Freud and Montessori and their respective works, see Edgar Mortimer Standing, "Sviluppo storico del movimento Montessori," in *Maria Montessori: Cittadina del mondo*, ed. Marziolina Pignattari (Rome: Comitato Italiano dell OMEP, 1967); Kramer, *Maria Montessori*, 319–321; Grazia Honegger Fresco, "Anna Freud e l'esperienza Montessori," *Il quaderno Montessori* 20, no. 76 (2002–2003) 47–64; Paola Trabalzini, "Maria Montessori e i rapporti con Sigmund Freud," *Annali di storia dell'educazione e delle istituzioni scolastiche* 25 (2018): 146–162.

10. Zahra, *Lost Children*, 64.

11. Zahra, *Lost Children*, 89.

12. James J. Sheehan, *Where Have All the Soldiers Gone? The Transformation of Modern Europe* (Boston: Mariner Books, 2009), 223.

13. "Maria Jervolino's Radio Interview to Maria Montessori," manuscript, handwritten by Luigia Tincani, [May 1947], Archivio Storico delle Missionarie

della Scuola c.21, quoted in Roberto P. Violi, *Maria de Unterrichter Jervolino (1902–1975): Donne, educazione e democrazia nell'Italia del Novecento* (Rome: Studium, 2014), 196.

14. Montessori to Luigia Tincani, in Montessori, *Il metodo del bambino e la formazione dell'uomo*, 274.

15. In addition to being a teacher and politician, Jervolino was also a prominent member of the Christian Democracy Party (DC), a member of the constituent assembly and the first three legislatures of Republican Italy, a delegate of the Women's Movement of the DC, the undersecretary of state for public education, the president (from 1947 to 1975) of Opera Nazionale Montessori (ONM), and vice president of the Association Montessori Internationale (AMI).

16. *Atti dell'Assemblea Costituente, seduta pomeridiana*, May 3, 1947, 3501–3502, quoted in Violi, *Maria de Unterrichter Jervolino*, 194–195.

17. Luisa Passerini, "La giovinezza metafora del cambiamento sociale: Due dibattiti sui giovani nell'Italia fascista e negli Stati Uniti degli anni Cinquanta," in Levi and Schmitt, *Storia dei giovani*, 2:383–459.

18. Luciano Pazzaglia, "Ideologie e scuola fra ricostruzione e sviluppo," in *Scuola e società nell'Italia unita*, ed. Luciano Pazzaglia and Roberto Sani (Florence: La Scuola, 2001), 463–471; Catarsi, *L'asilo e la scuola dell'infanzia*, 207–234; Giorgio Vecchio, "Il conflitto tra cattolici e comunisti: Caratteri ed effetti (1945–1958)," in *Chiesa e progetto educativo nell'Italia del secondo dopoguerra: (1945–1958)* (Brescia, It.: La Scuola, 1988), 443–475.

19. Tina Tomasi, *La scuola italiana dalla dittatura alla Repubblica (1943–48)* (Rome: Editori Riuniti, 1976), 25. For an analysis of John Dewey's philosophy in Italy, see Steven F. White, "Carleton Washburne: L'influenza deweyana nella scuola italiana," *Scuola e città* 40, no. 2 (1989): 49–57.

20. Lorenzo Benadusi, "Il fascismo e la formazione dell'uomo nuovo: Dalla scuola laica all'educazione politica," in *Fare il cittadino: La formazione di un nuovo soggetto sociale nell'Europa tra il XIX e il XXI secolo*, ed. Inge Botteri, Elena Riva, and Adolfo Scotto di Luzio (Catanzaro, It.: Rubettino, 2012), 147–160.

21. Michael Walzer, *On Toleration* (New Haven, CT: Yale University Press, 1997), 76–79.

22. In reality, the law proposal on *scuola materna* (nursery school) put forward by Minister Gonella left parents in charge of deciding whether to send their children to nursery schools and provided little funding (though double what was allocated before) for supporting the opening of nursery schools. Genovesi, *Storia della scuola in Italia*, 177; Bonetta, "La scuola dell'infanzia," 36–39.

23. Violi, *Maria de Unterrichter Jervolino*, 133–137, 194.

24. Anna Scarantino, "Associazioni di donne per la pace nell'Italia di De Gasperi," in *Guerra e pace nell'Italia del Novecento: Politica estera, cultura politica e correnti dell'opinione pubblica*, ed. Luigi Goglia, Renato Moro, and Leopoldo Nuti (Bologna: Il Mulino, 2006), 319–355.

25. Berenice A. Carroll, "Feminism and Pacifism: Historical and Theoretical Connections," in *Women and Peace: Theoretical, Historical, and Practical Perspectives*, ed. Ruth Roach Pierson (London: Croom Helm, 1987), 2–28.

26. *Atti dell'Assemblea Costituente*, quoted in Violi, *Maria de Unterrichter Jervolino*, 196.

27. The viscount George Lambert was a member of the British Liberal Party. Martinus J. Langeveld and Helena W. F. Stellwag were professors at the Universities of Utrecht and Amsterdam, respectively.

28. Because Maria Montessori never made the Nobel Prize committee's short list, there are no reports written on her candidacy at the Norwegian Nobel Committee Archives.

29. Montessori's second candidacy was not supported by Carlo Sforza, who instead wrote in favor of the North American journalist Clarence Streit. Carlo Felice Casula, "Maria Montessori: la candidatura al Premio Nobel per la pace e la proposta della nomina a senatore a vita e di un assegno vitalizio," in *Maria Montessori e la società del suo tempo*, ed. Fabio Fabbri, 243–280 (Rome: Castelvecchi, 2020).

30. Premio Nobel per la pace a Maria Montessori, 1950, Proposta dell'Onorevole Maria Jervolino: Promemoria, 2, Fascicolo Premio Nobel per la Pace, Opera Nazionale Montessori (hereafter cited as ONM) Archive, Rome.

31. Anna Maria Maccheroni to the Nobel Prize Committee, February 23, 1949, 1–2, AMI.

32. Document 748, in Messaggi e Adesioni Italiane e Straniere alla Proposta dell'opera Montessori per il Premio Nobel della Pace a Maria Montessori (hereafter cited as Montessori Support Documents), ONM.

33. Sarvepalli Radhakrishnan to Nobel Prize Committee, New Delhi, March 27, 1949, Nobel Peace Support Papers, AMI.

34. E. J. R. Eaglesham to Nobel Prize Committee [by May 18], 1949, Nobel Peace Support Papers, AMI.

35. Don Luigi Sturzo to Maria Jervolino, June 16, 1949, document 748, Montessori Support Documents, ONM.

36. "Premio Nobel della Pace: Elenco delle adesioni," 1949, in Montessori Support Documents, ONM; Nobel Peace Candidacy, AMI.

37. Legazione d'Italia Olso, 1/VI/49, Protocollo N. 910, 1949, document 711, Montessori Support Documents, ONM.

38. Casula, *Maria Montessori: Il mancato Premio Nobel per la pace*.

39. *A Century of Nobel Prize Laureates, 1901–2005: From Peace Movements to the United Nations* (Geneva: United Nations, 2006).

40. Statement by Maria Montessori announcing the Eighth International Montessori Conference in San Remo, 1, Nobel Peace Support Papers, AMI.

41. Statement by Maria Montessori, 1–2.

42. Maria Montessori, "La solidarietà umana nel tempo e nello spazio: Seconda conferenza della dottoressa Montessori," in *La formazione dell'uomo nella ricostruzione mondiale* (Rome: Ente Opera Montessori, 1950), 200.

43. Maria Montessori, "Il grande compito dell'educazione è quello di rendere conscio il bambino della profondità reale di questa unione," in *La formazione dell'uomo nella ricostruzione mondiale*, 203.

44. Gustavo Colonnetti, "Un senso di responsabilità personale e sociale," in Montessori, *La formazione dell'uomo nella ricostruzione mondiale*, 89.

45. Cheng Chi-Pao, "Address Before the VIII International Montessori Congress," in Montessori, *La formazione dell'uomo nella ricostruzione mondiale*, 269.

46. Maria Jervolino to August Schon, General Secretary of Det Norske Stortings Nobelkomite, September 9, 1949, document 948, Comitato italiano per l'assegnazione del Premio Nobel per la Pace a Maria Montessori 1949, ONM.

47. "The Doctor Who Opened a New Door to Education," *UNESCO Courier* 2, no. 12 (1950): 4.

48. "Case dei Bambini Became Model for the World," *UNESCO Courier* 2, no. 10 (1949): 17.

49. "The 1950 UNESCO Conference in Florence," *UNESCO Courier* 2, no. 11 (1949): 9.

50. Victoria Barres, "Maria Montessori and UNESCO," Centenary of the Montessori Movement 2007, http://www.montessoricentenary.org/srunesco article.htm.

51. "Laissez-moi remarquer que j'étais active dans ce domaine à une époque où un grand nombre des personnes ici présentes étaient encore des enfants." Quoted in *Apprendre sans limites: 50 ans Institut de l'UNESCO pour l'Éducation* (Hamburg: Drückerei in St. Pauli, 2002), 32.

52. *Apprendre sans limites*, 33.

53. Barres, "Maria Montessori and UNESCO."

54. Michael Freeman, "Introduction: Rights, Ideologies, and Children," in *The Ideologies of Children's Rights*, ed. Michael Freeman and Philip Veerman (Dordrecht, Neth.: Martinus Nijhoff, 1992), 3–7.

55. Carl M. Rogers, "Attitudes Toward Children's Rights: Nurturance or Self-Determination?" *Journal of Social Issues* 34, no. 2 (1978): 59–68.

56. Edgar Faure, *Apprendre à être* (Paris: UNESCO, 1972).

57. United Nations Educational, Scientific and Cultural Organization (UNESO), *Seeds for Peace: The Role of Pre-School Education in International Understanding and Education for Peace* (Paris: UNESCO, 1985), 1.

58. Maria Montessori, "Radio-Associaciò de Catalunya, 1936, 3°, 4°, 5° lectures," quoted in Montessori, *Il metodo del bambino e la formazione dell'uomo*.

59. Joan Lestor, "A Minister for Children," in *The Handbook of Children's Rights: Comparative Policy and Practice*, ed. Bob Franklin (London: Routledge, 1995), 100–106.

Bibliography

Agostinoni, Emidio. "Duilio Cambellotti." *Il Secolo XX* 8, no. 3 (1908): 229–231.

Åkerström, Ulla. *La maternità sociale fra Svezia e Italia: Il carteggio Ellen Key-Ersilia Majno (1907–1917).* Rome: Viella, 2020.

Alatri, Giovanna. *Dal chinino all'alfabeto: Igiene, istruzione e bonifiche nella campagna romana.* Rome: Fratelli Palombi, 2000.

Alatri, Giovanna. *Gli asili d'infanzia a Roma tra Otto e Novecento.* Milan: Unicopli, 2013.

Alatri, Giovanna. *Il mondo al femminile di Maria Montessori: Regine, dame e altre donne.* Rome: Fefè Editore, 2015.

Alatri, Giovanna. "Maria Montessori e l'educazione come rimedio ai mali sociali dell'infanzia." In *L'Infanzia Svantaggiata e Maria Montessori: Esperienze psicopedagogiche, educative e sociali dal '900 ad oggi,* edited by Leonardo De Sanctis, 21–45. Rome: Fefè Editore, 2013.

Aleramo, Sibilla. *Andando e stando.* Milan: Feltrinelli, 1997.

Aleramo, Sibilla. "La vita nella Campagna romana, conferenza tenuta all'Università popolare di Milano nel 1909." *Italia Letteraria,* May 3, 1931.

Aleramo, Sibilla. *Una donna.* Milan: Feltrinelli, 2003.

Allen, Douglas. "Mahatma Gandhi on Violence and Peace Education." *Philosophy East & West* 57, no. 3 (2007): 290–310.

Allender, Tim. "'Better Mothers': Feminine and Feminist Educators and Thresholds of Indian Female Interaction, 1870–1932." In *Learning Femininity in Colonial India, 1820–1932,* 233–66. Manchester: Manchester University Press, 2016.

Alma [Teresita Bonfatti Pasini]. "Un buon affare e un'opera buona: La 'casa moderna.'" *La Casa* 1, no. 11 (November 16, 1908): 226–231.

Ambrosio, Thomas. *Irredentism: Ethnic Conflict and International Politics.* Westport, CT: Praeger, 2001.

Ambrosoli, Luigi. *Libertà e religione nella riforma Gentile.* Florence: Vallecchi, 1980.

Andriani, Antonella. "Il design per l'infanzia, quando il 'design' in Italia non esisteva ancora." In Colombo and Dragoni, *Maria Montessori e il sodalizio con l'Umanitaria*, 34–35.

Apprendre sans limites: 50 ans Institut de l'UNESCO pour l'Éducation. Hamburg: Drückerei in St. Pauli, 2002.

Aquarone, Alberto. *Lo Stato catechista.* Florence: Parenti, 1961.

Ariès, Philippe. *Centuries of Childhood: A Social History of Family Life.* New York: Alfred A. Knopf, 1962.

Arisi Rota, Alberto. "Eroi, martiri, concittadini patrioti: I necrologi come pedagogia del ricordo." In *Patrioti si diventa: Luoghi e linguaggi di pedagogia patriottica nell'Italia unita*, edited by Arianna Arisi Rota, Monica Ferrari, and Matteo Morandi, 143–156. Milan: Franco Angeli, 2009.

Arújo, Alberto Felice. "Le thème de l'enfant nouveau chez Montessori: Vers une mythanalyse en éducation." In Magnin and Hofstetter, "New Education," 143–159.

Arundale, Francesca. *Education in the Light of Theosophy.* Madras: Vasantā Press, 1913.

Aucouturier, Bernard, Ivan Darrault, and Jean Louis Empinet. *La pratique psychomotrice.* Paris: Doin, 1984.

Audoin-Rouzeau, Stéphane, and Jean-Jacques Becker, eds. *La prima guerra mondiale.* Turin: Einaudi, 2007.

Babini, Valeria Paola. *La questione dei frenastenici: Alle origini della psicologia scientifica in Italia (1870–1910).* Milan: Franco Angeli, 1996.

Babini, Valeria Paola. "'Le donne sono antropologicamente superiori': Parola di una donna di genio." In *Se vi sono donne di genio: Appunti di un viaggio nell'antropologia dall'Unità d'Italia a oggi*, edited by Alessandro Volpone and Giovanni Destro-Bisol, 12–26. Rome: Casa Editrice Università La Sapienza, 2011.

Babini, Valeria Paola. "Maria Montessori: Biografia o autobiografia?" In "Le biografie scientifiche," edited by Antonello La Vergata, special issue, *Intersezioni* 15, no. 1 (1995): 171–177.

Babini, Valeria Paola. "Science, Feminism and Education: The Early Work of Maria Montessori." *History Workshop Journal* 49, no. 1 (2000): 44–67.

Babini, Valeria Paola, and Luisa Lama. *Una donna nuova: Il femminismo scientifico di Maria Montessori.* Milan: Franco Angeli, 2003.

Bachmann, Marie-Laure. *Dalcroze Today: An Education through and into Music.* Oxford: Clarendon Press, 1991.

Bacigalupi, Marcella, and Piero Fossati. *Da plebe a popolo: L'educazione popolare nei libri di scuola dall'Unità d'Italia alla Repubblica.* Florence: La Nuova Italia, 1986.

Badaloni, Giuseppe. *La lotta contro la malaria: Relazione al Consiglio superiore di Sanità presentata nella seduta dell'11 agosto 1909.* Rome: Mantellate, 1910.

Badea-Päun, Gabriel. *Carmen Sylva: Uimitoarea Regină Elisabeta a României, 1843–1916*. Bucharest: Humanitas, 2008.

Bailey, Carolyn Sherwin. "The Christ in Bruno: A True Montessori Christmas Story." *Delineator* 83 (December 1913): 5–6.

Bailey, Carolyn Sherwin. "The Freeing of 'Otello the Terrible.'" *Delineator* 83 (October 1913): 16.

Bajaj, Monisha. "Conjectures on Peace Education and Gandhian Studies: Method, Institutional Development and Globalization." *Journal of Peace Education* 7, no. 1 (2010): 47–63.

Barres, Victoria. "Maria Montessori and UNESCO." Centenary of the Montessori Movement 2007. http://www.montessoricentenary.org/srunescoarticle.htm.

Bartoloni, Stefania. *Donne della Croce Rossa italiana tra guerre e impegno sociale*. Venice: Marsilio, 2005.

Basu, Aparna. *The Growth of Education and Political Development in India, 1898–1920*. Delhi: Oxford University Press, 1974.

Baumann, Emilio. *Psico-cinesia, ovvero l'arte di formare il carattere*. Printed by the author, 1900. Biblioteca comunale Augusta, Perugia.

Bayly, C. A., Sven Beckert, Matthew Connelly, Isabel Hofmeyr, Wendy Kozol, and Patricia Seed. "AHR Conversation: On Transnational History." *American Historical Review* 111, no. 5 (2006): 1441–1464.

Becker, Annette. *Oubliés de la Grande Guerre: Humanitaire et culture de guerre 1914–1918. Populations occupées, déportés civils, prisonniers de guerre*. Paris: Noêsis, 1998.

Bellenoit, Hayden J. A. *Missionary Education and Empire in Late Colonial India 1860–1920*. London: Pickering & Chatto, 2007.

Bellini, Rolando, and Mara Folini, eds. *Fuoco ad Arte! Artisti e Fornaci: La felice stagione della ceramica a Roma e nel Lazio tra simbolismo, Teosofia e altro 1880–1930*. Locarno, Switz.: Tipografia Bassi, 2005.

Benadusi, Lorenzo. "Il fascismo e la formazione dell'uomo nuovo: Dalla scuola laica all'educazione politica." In *Fare il cittadino: La formazione di un nuovo soggetto sociale nell'Europa tra il XIX e il XXI secolo*, edited by Inge Botteri, Elena Riva, and Adolfo Scotto di Luzio, 147–160. Catanzaro, It.: Rubettino, 2012.

Ben-Ghiat, Ruth. *Fascist Modernities: Italy, 1922–1945*. Berkeley: University of California Press, 2009.

Bergunder, Michael. "Experiments with Theosophical Truth: Gandhi, Esotericism, and Global Religious History." *Journal of the Modern Academy of Religion* 82, no. 2 (2014): 398–426.

Bertoni Jovine, Dina. *La scuola italiana dal 1870 ai giorni nostri*. Rome: Editori Riuniti, 1958.

Besant, Annie. *The Ancient Wisdom: An Outline of Theosophical Teachings*. Madras: Theosophical Publishing House, 1897.

Betti, Carmen. *La religione a scuola fra obbligo e facoltatività (1859–1923)*. Florence: Manzuoli, 1989.

Bevir, Mark. "The Formation of the All-India Home Rule League." *Indian Journal of Political Science* 52, no. 3 (1991): 341–356.

Bevir, Mark. "In Opposition to the Raj: Annie Besant and the Dialectic of Empire." *History of Political Thought* 19, no. 1 (1998): 61–77.

Bevir, Mark. "Theosophy and the Origins of the Indian National Congress." *International Journal of Hindu Studies* 7, no. 1–3 (2003): 99–115.

Bevir, Mark. "The West Turns Eastward: Madame Blavatsky and the Transformation of the Occult Tradition." *Journal of the American Academy of Religion* 62, no. 3 (1994): 747–767.

Bhagavan, Manu. *Sovereign Sphere: Princes, Education and Empire in Colonial India*. New Delhi: Oxford University Press, 2003.

Bianchi, Bruna. *Crescere in tempo di guerra: Il lavoro e la protesta dei ragazzi in Italia 1915–1918*. Venice: Libreria Editrice Cafoscarina, 1995.

Bianchi, Bruna. "Psichiatria e guerra." In Audoin-Rouzeau and Becker, *La prima guerra mondiale*, 309–322.

Bianchi, Bruna. "Towards a New Internationalism: Pacifist Journals Edited by Women." In *Gender and the First World War*, edited by Christa Hämmerle, Oswald Überegger, and Birgitta Bader-Zaar, 176–194. Basingstoke, UK: Palgrave MacMillan, 2014.

Bianchi, Bruna, and Geraldine Ludbrook. *Living War, Thinking Peace (1914–1924): Women's Experiences, Feminist Thought, and International Relations*. Newcastle, UK: Cambridge Scholars Publishing, 2016.

Black, Maggie. *Children First: The Story of UNICEF, Past and Present*. Oxford: Oxford University Press, 2006.

Blavatsky, Helena Petrovna. *Isis Unveiled: A Master-Key to the Mysteries of Ancient and Modern Science and Theosophy*. Vol. 2, *Theology*. Pasadena, CA: Theosophical University Press, 1877.

Blavatsky, Helena Petrovna. *The Key to Theosophy*. Los Angeles: United Lodge of Theosophists, 1920.

Blavatsky, Helena Petrovna. *The Secret Doctrine*. Vol. 1, *Cosmogenesis*, edited by Boris de Zirkoff. Madras: Quest Books, 1993.

Boghen Conigliani, Emma. *Il giardino infantile modello di Mompiano giudicato sotto l'aspetto sociale*. Brescia, It.: Canossi, 1902.

Böhm, Winfried. "Educazione e grazia: Agostino, Rousseau, Montessori." *Pedagogia e vita* 58, no. 4 (2000): 27–41.

Bonetta, Gaetano. *Corpo e nazione: L'educazione ginnastica, igienica e sessuale nell'Italia liberale*. Milan: Franco Angeli, 1990.

Bonetta, Gaetano. "La scuola dell'infanzia." In *La scuola italiana dall'Unità ai giorni nostri*, edited by Giacomo Cives, 22–39. Florence: La Nuova Italia, 1990.

Bonetta, Gaetano. "L'istruzione religiosa nell'Italia liberale." *Italia contemporanea*, no. 162 (1986): 27–54.

Bonfigli, Clodomiro. *Dei fattori sociali della pazzia in rapporto con l'educazione infantile*. Rome: Tipografia delle Mantellate, 1894.

Borghi, Lamberto. *Educazione e autorità nell'Italia Moderna*. Florence: La Nuova Italia, 1951.

Bosisio, Francesca. "Il percorso dell'infanzia nel mondo dei diritti." In *Viaggio attraverso i diritti dell'infanzia e dell'adolescenza*, edited by Francesca Mazzucchelli, 25–48. Milan: Franco Angeli, 2006.

Bossi, Luigi Maria. *In difesa della donna e della razza*. Genoa: Quintieri, 1917.

Botti, Caterina. *Madri cattive: Una riflessione su bioetica e gravidanza*. Milan: Il Saggiatore, 2007.

Boucher, Ellen. "Cultivating Internationalism: Save the Children Fund, Public Opinion and the Meaning of Child Relief, 1919–24." In *Brave New World: Imperial and Democratic Nation-Building in Britain between the Wars*, edited by Laura Beers and Geraint Thomas, 169–188. London: University of London Press, 2011.

Bovet, Pierre. *La paix par l'école: Travaux de la conférence internationale tenue à Prague du 16 au 20 avril 1927*. Geneva: Bureau International d'Éducation, 1927.

Boyd, William. *Report on the Fifth World Conference of the NEF*. London: University of London Institute of Education, 1930.

Boyd, William, and Wyatt Rawson. *The Story of the New Education*. London: Heinemann, 1965.

Braster, Sjaak, and María del Mar del Pozo Andrés. "Education and the Children's Colonies in the Spanish Civil War (1936–1939): The Images of the Community Ideal." *Paedagogica Historica* 51, no. 4 (2015): 455–477.

Brehony, Kevin J. "A New Education for a New Era: Contribution of the Conferences of the New Education Fellowship to the Disciplinary Field of Education 1921–1938." *Paedagogica Historica* 40, nos. 5/6 (October 2004): 733–755.

Briod, Louise. "La méthode Montessori dans les écoles primaires du Tessin." *Pour l'ère nouvelle* 3, no. 12 (1924): 65–67.

Burfield, Diana. "Theosophy and Feminism: Some Explorations in Nineteenth Century Biography." In *Women's Religious Experience: Cross-Cultural Perspectives*, edited by Pat Holden, 28–45. London: Croom Helm, 1983.

Burnier, Radha. "Rukmini Devi as a Theosophist." In Meduri, *Rukmini Devi Arundale*, 61–66.

Buse, Ute. *Ernesto Teodoro Moneta (1833–1918): Leben und Werk eines italienischen Pazifisten*. Frankfurt am Main: Lang, 1996.

Buttafuoco, Annarita. "La filantropia come politica: Esperienze dell'emancipazionismo italiano nel Novecento." In *Ragnatele di rapporti*, edited by Lucia Ferrante, Maura Palazzi, and Gianna Pomata, 166–187. Turin: Rosenberg & Sellier.

Buttafuoco, Annarita. "Motherhood as a Political Strategy: The Role of the Italian Women's Movement in the Creation of the *Cassa Nazionale di Maternità*."

In *Maternity and Gender Policies: Women and the Rise of the European Welfare States, 1880s–1950s*, edited by Gisela Bock and Pat Thane, 178–195. London: Routledge, 1991.

Butturini, Emilio. *La religione a scuola dall'Unità a oggi.* Brescia, It.: Queriniana, 1987.

Cabanes, Bruno. *The Great War and the Origins of Humanitarianism, 1918–1924.* Cambridge: Cambridge University Press, 2014.

Cabanes, Bruno. *La victoire endeuillée: La sortie de guerre des soldats français (1918–1920).* Paris: Seuil, 2004.

Cahalan, Peter. *Belgian Refugee Relief in England during the Great War.* New York: Garland, 1982.

Caine, Barbara. "Feminist Biography and Feminist History." *Women's History Review* 3, no. 2 (1994): 247–261.

Cambellotti, Duilio. "Progetto di casa per famiglie di lavoratori: L'arredamento." *La Casa* 1, no. 13 (December 1, 1908): 246–248.

Cambellotti, Duilio. "Progetto di casa per famiglie di lavoratori: La casa." *La Casa* 1, no. 11 (November 16, 1908): 206–208.

Cambi, Franco. *Antifascismo e pedagogia 1930–1945.* Florence: Vallecchi Editore, 1980.

Cambi, Franco, and Simonetta Ulivieri. *Storia dell'infanzia nell'Italia liberale.* Florence: La Nuova Italia, 1988.

Canale Cama, Francesca. *La pace dei liberi e dei forti: La rete di pace di Ernesto Teodoro Moneta.* Bologna: Bononia University Press, 2012.

Caracciolo, Alberto. "Caratteristiche della vita privata." In *La vita privata: Il Novecento*, edited by Philippe Ariès and Georges Duby, 4–18. Rome: Laterza, 1998.

Carassali, Settimio. "Giardino di Froebel o Casa dei Bambini?" *La Stampa* (Turin), July 12, 1926.

Carlson, Maria. *No Religion Higher Than Truth: A History of The Theosophical Movement in Russia, 1875–1922.* Princeton, NJ: Princeton University Press, 1993.

Carnoy, Martin. *Education as Cultural Imperialism.* New York: Longman, 1974.

Carroll, Berenice A. "Feminism and Pacifism: Historical and Theoretical Connections." In *Women and Peace: Theoretical, Historical, and Practical Perspectives*, edited by Ruth Roach Pierson, 2–28. London: Croom Helm, 1987.

Castelli, Alberto. "Il pacifismo alla prova: Ernesto Moneta e il conflitto italo-turco." In *Nazione democrazia e pace: Tra Ottocento e Novecento*, edited by Giovanna Angelini, 111–142. Milan: Franco Angeli, 2012.

Casula, Carlo Felice. "Maria Montessori: la candidatura al Premio Nobel per la pace e la proposta della nomina a senatore a vita e di un assegno vitalizio." In *Maria Montessori e la società del suo tempo*, edited by Fabio Fabbri, 243–280. Rome: Castelvecchi, 2020.

Catarsi, Enzo. *La giovane Montessori.* Ferrara, It.: Corso Editore 1995.

Catarsi, Enzo. *L'asilo e la scuola dell'infanzia.* Florence: La Nuova Italia, 1994.

Catarsi, Enzo, and Giovanni Genovesi. *L'infanzia a scuola: L'educazione infantile in Italia dalle sale di custodia alla materna statale.* Bergamo, It.: Juvenilia, 1985.

Cattaruzza, Marina. *L'Italia e il confine orientale.* Bologna: Il Mulino, 2007.

Çelik Alexander, Zeynep. *Kinaesthetic Knowing: Aesthetic, Epistemology, Modern Design.* Chicago: University of Chicago Press, 2017.

Celli, Angelo. *Come vive il campagnolo nell'agro romano: Note e appunti.* Rome: Società Editrice Nazionale, 1900.

Celli, Angelo. "La colonizzazione dell'agro romano e Pontino." *Nuova Antologia,* September 1, 1911.

Cena, Giovanni. *Opere.* Vol. 2, edited by Giorgio De Rienzo. Rome: Silva Editore, 1968.

Cenkner, William. *The Hindu Personality in Education: Tagore, Gandhi, Aurobindo.* New Delhi: Manohar, 1994.

Centin, Alfio. "Un giudizio di Giovanni Gentile su Maria Montessori." *Vita dell'infanzia* 41, no. 9 (1992): 3–4.

Ceschin, Daniele. *Gli esuli di Caporetto: i profughi in Italia durante la Grande Guerra.* Rome: Laterza, 2006.

A Century of Nobel Prize Laureates, 1901–2005: From Peace Movements to the United Nations. Geneva: United Nations, 2006.

Chadwick, Owen. *The Secularization of the European Mind in the Nineteenth Century.* Cambridge: Cambridge University Press, 1975.

Chapuis, Élisabeth, Jean Pierre Pétard, and Régine Plas, eds. *Les psychologues et les guerres.* Paris: L'Harmattan, 2010.

Chickering, Roger. *Imperial Germany and a World without War: The Peace Movement and German Society, 1892–1914.* Princeton, NJ: Princeton University Press, 1975.

Childers, Kristen Stromberg. *Fathers, Families, and the State in France 1914–1945.* Ithaca, NY: Cornell University Press, 2003.

"Chronique de l'Enseignement primaire en France." *Revue pédagogique* 79, no. 10 (July–December 1921): 292–308.

Cives, Giacomo. *Attivismo e antifascismo in Giuseppe Lombardo Radice: "Critica didattica" o "didattica critica"?* Florence: La Nuova Italia, 1983.

Cives, Giacomo. "Carattere e senso delle varianti di Il Metodo." In Montessori, *Il Metodo della pedagogia scientifica applicato all'educazione infantile nelle case dei bambini: Edizione critica,* xv–xxvii.

Cives, Giacomo. *Giuseppe Lombardo Radice: Didattica e pedagogia della collaborazione.* Florence: La Nuova Italia, 1970.

Cives, Giacomo. "Il periodo indiano di Maria Montessori." *Studi sulla formazione* 13, no. 1 (2010): 95–98.

Cives, Giacomo. *La Scuola italiana dall'Unità ai nostri giorni.* Florence: La Nuova Italia, 2000.

Cives, Giacomo. *Maria Montessori: Pedagogista complessa.* Pisa: Edizioni ETS, 2001.

Cives, Giacomo. "Maria Montessori tra scienza, spiritualità e laicità." *Studi sulla formazione* 2, no. 2 (2014): 123.

Cives, Giacomo, and Paola Trabalzini. *Maria Montessori tra spiritualità e azione sociale*. Rome: Anicia, 2017.

Clavin, Patricia. "Defining Transnationalism." *Contemporary European History* 14, no. 4 (2005): 422.

Codignola, Ernesto. *Il problema dell'educazione nazionale in Italia*. Florence: Vallecchi, 1925.

Cohrs, Patrick O. *The Unfinished Peace after World War I: America, Britain and the Stabilisation of Europe, 1919–1932*. Cambridge: Cambridge University Press, 2006.

Coli, Daniela, ed. *Giovanni Gentile filosofo e pedagogista*. Florence: Le Lettere, 2004.

Colombo, Claudio A., and Maria Beretta Dragoni, eds. *Maria Montessori e il sodalizio con l'Umanitaria*. Milan: Raccolto, 2008.

Combi, Maria. *Ernesto Teodoro Moneta, premio Nobel per la pace 1907*. Milan: U. Mursia, 1968.

Comitato di Milano dell'Opera Nazionale Montessori, ed. *Note sul Metodo Montessori*. Rome: Bestetti e Tumminelli, 1926.

Condette, Jean-François, and Antoine Savoye. "Une éducation pour une ère nouvelle: Le congrès international d'éducation de Calais (1921)." *Les Études Sociales* 163, no. 1 (2016): 43–77.

Conti, Giuseppe. "L'educazione nazionale militare nell'Italia liberale: I convitti nazionali militarizzati." *Storia contemporanea* 23, no. 6 (1992): 939–999.

Cooper, Sandi E. *Patriotic Pacifism: Waging War on War in Europe, 1815–1914*. New York: Oxford University Press, 1991.

Coorlawala, Uttara Asha. "The Sanskritized Body." *Dance Research Journal* 36, no. 2 (2004): 50–63.

Corradini, Camillo. *L'istruzione primaria in Italia con speciale riguardo all'anno scolastico 1907–1908*. Vol. 1. Rome: Tipografia operaia romana cooperativa, 1910.

Cosmacini, Giorgio. *Il medico materialista: Vita e pensiero di Jacob Moleschott*. Turin: Einaudi, 2005.

Cousinet, Roger. "La Nouvelle Éducation." *Pour l'ère nouvelle* 1, no. 1 (1922): 10–12.

Cromwell, Mary Rebecca. "Il metodo Montessori in Francia durante la guerra." *La Coltura Popolare* 9, no. 1 (1919): 50–53.

Cunningham, Hugh. "Histories of Childhood." *American Historical Review* 103, no. 4 (1998): 1195–1208.

Dalcroze, Émile Jaques-. *Le Rythme, la Musique et l'éducation*. Paris: Librairie Fischbacher, 1920.

D'Ambrosio, Elena. *A scuola col Duce: L'istruzione primaria nel ventennio fascista*. Como, It.: Istituto di Storia Contemporanea Pier Amato Perretta, 2001.

Davies, Thomas R. *The Possibilities of Transnational Activism: The Campaign for Disarmament between the Two World Wars.* Leiden, Neth.: Brill, 2006.

"Declaration of the Rights of the Child 1924." In *International Documents on Children,* edited by Geraldine Van Bueren, 3–6. Boston: Martinus Nijhoff, 1993.

De Felice, Renzo. *Mussolini il duce: Gli anni del consenso, 1929–1936.* Turin: Einaudi, 1974.

De Feo, Giovanna Caterina. *Francesco Randone: Il Maestro delle Mura.* Rome: Associazione Amici di Villa Strohl, 2000.

De Feo, Giovanna Caterina. "La scuola d'arte educatrice." In *Trucci, Trucci Cavallucci . . . Infanzia a Roma tra Otto e Novecento.* Rome: Palombi Editore, 2001.

De Feo, Giovanna Caterina. "Maria Montessori, Francesco Randone e la scuola d'arte educatrice." In L. De Sanctis, *La cura dell'anima in Maria Montessori,* 67–77.

De Fort, Ester. *La scuola elementare: Dall'unità alla caduta del fascismo.* Bologna: Il Mulino, 1996.

De Freitas Campos, Regina Helena. "Les psychologues et le mouvement de l'Éducation pour la paix à Genève (1920–1940)." In Chapuis, Pétard, and Plas, *Les psychologues et les guerres,* 95–10.

De Giorgi, Fulvio, ed. *Maria Montessori e le sue reti di relazioni.* Brescia, It.: Morcelliana, 2018.

De Giorgi, Fulvio. "Maria Montessori Modernista." *Annali di storia dell'educazione e delle istituzioni scolastiche* 16 (2009): 199–216.

De Giorgi, Fulvio. "Montessori tra modernisti, antimodernisti e gesuiti." *Annali di storia dell'educazione e delle istituzioni scolastiche* 25 (2018): 27–73.

De Giorgi, Fulvio. "Rileggere Maria Montessori: Modernismo cattolico e rinnovamento educativo." In *Maria Montessori, Dio e il bambino e altri scritti inediti,* edited by Fulvio De Giorgi, 5–114. Brescia, It.: La Scuola, 2013.

De Guttry, Irene. "Cambellotti Architetto." In *Cambellotti (1876–1960),* edited by Giovanna Buonsegale, Anna Maria Damigella and Bruno Mantura, 39–42. Rome: Edizioni De Luca, 1999.

De Guttry, Irene. "The Design Reform Movement in Rome at the Beginning of the Century." *Journal of Decorative and Propaganda Arts* 13 (Summer 1989): 52–75.

De Guttry, Irene, Maria Paola Maino, and Gloria Raimondi. *Duilio Cambellotti: Arredi e Decorazioni.* Rome: Laterza, 1999.

Delaporte, Sophie. "Medicina e guerra." In Audoin-Rouzeau and Becker, *La prima guerra mondiale,* 299–306.

de Ligt, Bart. *The Conquest of Violence: An Essay on War and Revolution.* London: George Routledge & Sons, 1937.

de Ligt, Bart. *Introduction to the Science of Peace: The Initial Lecture of the First Summer School of the Peace Academy Held in Jouy-en-Josas France in August 1938.* London: Peace Pledge Union, 1939.

de Ligt-van Rossem, C. L. "Un témoignage Hollandais en faveur de la Méthode Montessori." *Pour l'ère nouvelle* 6, no. 29 (1927): 113–115.

De Rosa, Gabriele. "Benedetto XV." In *Enciclopedia dei Papi*, vol. 3, 608–617. Rome: Istituto della Enciclopedia Italiana, 2000.

De Sanctis, Francesco. *Scritti e discorsi sull'educazione*. Florence: La Nuova Italia, 1967.

De Sanctis, Leonardo, ed. *La cura dell'anima in Maria Montessori: L'educazione religiosa, spirituale e religiosa dell'infanzia*. Rome: Fefè Editore, 2011.

De Sanctis, Sante, and Montessori, Maria. *Sulle cosidette allucinazioni antagonistiche*. Rome: Società Editrice Dante Aligheri, 1897.

De Schaepdrijver, Sophie. "Belgium." In *A Companion to World War I*, edited by John Horne, 386–402. Oxford: Wiley-Blackwell, 2010.

Devi Arundale, Rukmini. *Art and Education*. Madras: Theosophical Publishing House, n.d.

Devi Arundale, Rukmini. "The Spiritual Background of Bharata Natyam." In *Classical and Folk Dances of India*. Bombay: Marg Publications, 1963.

Dijkgraff, C. W., ed. *Transactions of the Eighth Congress of the Federation of European National Society Held in Vienna July 21st to 26th 1923*. Amsterdam: Council of the Federation, 1923.

Dixon, Joy. *Divine Feminine: Theosophy and Feminism in England*. Baltimore: Johns Hopkins University Press, 2001.

Dogliani, Patrizia. *Storia dei giovani*. Milan: Mondadori, 2003.

Dompè, Elena, Maria Luisa Tabasso, and Paola Trabalzini, eds. *1907–2007 Montessori Centenary Conference Proceedings*. Rome: Opera Nazionale Montessori and Association Montessori Internationale, 2007.

Droux, Joëlle. "L'internationalisation de la protection de l'enfance: Acteurs, concurrences et projets transnationaux (1900–1925)." *Critique internationale*, no. 52 (2011): 17–33.

Droux, Joëlle, and Rita Hofstetter, eds. *Globalisation des mondes de l'éducation: Circulations, connexions, réfractions, XIXe–XXe siècles*. Rennes, Fr.: Presses Universitaires de Rennes, 2015.

Drummond, William, and William C. Ward. *The Poems of William Drummond of Hawthornden*. London: G. Routledge & Sons, 1920.

Durkheim, Émile. *L'évolution pédagogique en France*. Paris: Presses Universitaires de France, 1990.

Dwork, Deborah. *War Is Good for Babies and Other Young Children: A History of the Infant and Child Welfare Movement in England 1898–1918*. London: Tavistock, 1987.

Eckert, Ela. "Concretizing Cosmic Education in India: A Montessori Historical Account." *NAMTA Journal* 30, no. 2 (2005): 195–225.

Einstein, Albert. "Internationalism and European Security 1922–1932." In *Einstein on Politics: His Private Thoughts and Public Stands on Nationalism, Zion-*

ism, War, Peace, and the Bomb, edited by David E. Rowe and Robert Schulmann, 189–222. Princeton, NJ: Princeton University Press, 2007.

Einstein, Albert, and Sigmund Freud. *Why War? A Correspondence between Albert Einstein and Sigmund Freud*. Translated by Stuart Gilbert. London: Peace Pledge Union, 1939.

Ensor, Beatrice. "Le congrès de Calais." *Pour l'ère nouvelle* 1, no. 1 (January 1922): 5–7.

Ensor, Beatrice. "Outlook Tower." *New Era* 10, no. 37 (1929): 133.

Fabbri, Fabio. "Maria Montessori di fronte al fascismo." In *Maria Montessori e la società del suo tempo*, edited by Fabio Fabbri, 208–229. Rome: Castelvecchi, 2020.

Fanti, Palmira Melesi. "La Settimana della Bontà." In Randone, *Scuola d'Arte Educatrice*, 12.

Faron, Olivier. *Les Enfants du deuil*. Paris: La Découverte, 2001.

Farrell-Vinay, Giovanna. *Povertà e politica nell'Ottocento: Le opere pie nello Stato Liberale*. Turin: Scriptorium, 1997.

Fass, Paula S. "A Historical Context for the United Nations Convention on the Rights of the Child." *The Annals of the American Academy of Political and Social Science* 633 (January 2011): 17–29.

Fattorini, Emma. *Il culto mariano fra Ottocento e Novecento: Simboli e devozione*. Milan: Franco Angeli, 1999.

Fattorini, Emma. "A Voyage to the Madonna." In *Women and Faith: Catholic Religious Life in Italy from Late Antiquity to the Present*, edited by Lucetta Scaraffia and Gabriella Zarri, 281–295. Cambridge, MA: Harvard University Press, 1999.

Faure, Edgar. *Apprendre à être*. Paris: UNESCO, 1972.

Fava, Andrea. "All'origine di nuove immagini dell'infanzia: Gli anni della Grande Guerra." In *Il bambino nella storia*, edited by Maria Cristina Giuntella and Isabella Nardi, 181–204. Naples: Edizioni Scientifiche Italiane, 1993.

Fava, Andrea. "La guerra a scuola: Propaganda, memoria, rito." *Materiali di lavoro* 3–4 (1986): 53–126.

Fava, Andrea. "War, 'National Education,' and the Italian Primary School." In *State, Society and Mobilization in Europe during the First World War*, edited by John Horne, 53–70. Cambridge: Cambridge University Press, 1997.

Febea [Olga Ossani Lodi]. "Quel che occorre sapere: L'industria e l'igiene." *La Casa* 1, no. 3 (July 1908): 51–52.

Febea [Olga Ossani Lodi]. "Sul pianerottolo (novella)." *La Casa* 1, no. 9 (October 1908): 174–175.

Ferrari, Giulio Cesare. "L'education de l'activité spontanée chez les enfants." *Pour l'ère nouvelle* 1, no. 1 (January 1922): 19–20.

Ferrari, Monica, and Matteo Morandi. *I programmi scolastici di "educazione fisica" in Italia. Una lettura storico-pedagogica*. Milan: Franco Angeli, 2015.

Ferri, Enrico. *Sociologia criminale*. Turin: Bocca, 1900.

Ferrière, Adolphe. "Une visite aux pionniers de l'école active en Italie." *Pour l'ère nouvelle* 5, no. 23 (November 1926): 150–156.

Ficino, Marsilio. *The Book of Life*. Translated by Charles Boer. Irving, TX: Spring Publications, 1980.

Finn, Gerry P. T. "Piaget, Vygotsky and the Social Dimension." In *Piaget, Vygotsky and Beyond: Future Issues for Developmental Psychology and Education*, edited by Leslie Smith, Julie Dockrell, and Peter Tomlinson, 92–99. London: Routledge, 1997.

Fiorentino, Carlo M. *All'ombra di Pietro: La Chiesa cattolica e lo spionaggio fascista in Vaticano, 1929–1939*. Florence: Le Lettere, 1999.

Forgacs, David. *Italy's Margins: Social Exclusion and Nation Formation since 1861*. Cambridge: Cambridge University Press, 2014.

Foschi, Renato. "*L'histoire croisée*: Contesti e soggetti nella storia della psicologia scientifica fin de siècle." *Physis* 40, no. 1 (2003): 311–323.

Foschi, Renato. *Maria Montessori*. Rome: Ediesse, 2012.

Foschi, Renato. "Né scomuniche, né annessioni: La complessa sociabilità di Maria Montessori." *Erasmo notizie* 15, no. 1–2 (2014): 10–11.

Foschi, Renato. "Science and Culture around the Montessori's First 'Children's Houses' in Rome (1907–1915)." *Journal of the History of the Behavioral Sciences* 44, no. 3 (Summer 2008): 238–257.

Fossati, Roberta. "Alice Hallgarten Franchetti e le sue iniziative alla Montesca." *Fonti e Documenti* 16–17 (1987–1988): 269–347.

Foucault, Michel. *The Birth of the Clinic: An Archeology of Medical Perception*. Translated by A. M. Sheridan Smith. New York: Random House, 1975.

Foucault, Michel. *The Foucault Effect: Studies in Governmentality*. Edited by Graham Burchell, Colin Gordon, and Peter Miller. Chicago: University of Chicago Press, 1991.

Foucault, Michel. "What Is Enlightenment?" In *The Foucault Reader*, edited by Paul Rabinow, 32–50. New York: Pantheon Books, 1984.

Franklin, J. Jeffrey. *The Lotus and the Lion: Buddhism and the British Empire*. Ithaca, NY: Cornell University Press, 2008.

Franzè, Giuseppe. *Fanciulli oggi, uomini domani: Agazzi, Pizzigoni, Montessori; Itinerari didattici*. Rome: Edizioni Magi, 2006.

Freeman, Michael. "Introduction: Rights, Ideologies, and Children." In *The Ideologies of Children's Rights*, edited by Michael Freeman and Philip Veerman, 3–7. Dordrecht, Neth.: Martinus Nijhoff, 1992.

Freire, Paulo. *Pedagogia da indignação: Cartas pedagógicas e outros escritos*. São Paulo: UNESP, 2000.

Fretigne, Jean-Yves. *Les conceptions éducatives de Giovanni Gentile: Entre élitisme et fascisme*. Paris: L'Harmattan, 2006.

Freud, Anna. *Normality and Pathology in Childhood: Assessments of Development*. London: Routledge, 1989.

Freud, Anna, and Dorothy Burlingham. *The Writings of Anna Freud*. Volume 3, *1939–1945, Infants without Families: Report on the Hampstead Nurseries*. New York: International Universities Press, 1973.

Freud, Anna, and Dorothy Burlingham. *Young Children in War-Time: A Year's Work in a Residential War Nursery*. London: George Allen & Unwin, 1942.

Frierson, Patrick. "The Moral Philosophy of Maria Montessori." *Journal of the American Philosophical Association*. Forthcoming.

Frigessi, Delia. "La scienza della devianza." In Frigessi, Giacanelli, and Mangoni, *Delitto, genio, follia*, 333–373.

Frigessi, Delia, Ferruccio Giacanelli, and Luisa Mangoni, eds. *Delitto, genio, follia*. Turin: Bollati e Boringhieri, 1995.

Fuchs, Eckhardt. "Contextualizing School Textbooks Revision." *Journal of Educational Media, Memory, and Society* 2, no. 2 (2010): 1–12.

Fuller, Edmund. *The Rights of the Child: A Chapter in Social History*. London: Victor Gollancz, 1951.

Galtung, Johan. *Peace: Research, Education, Action*. Copenhagen: Ejlers, 1975.

Galtung, Johan, and Dietrich Fischer. *Johan Galtung: Pioneer of Peace Research*. Basel, Switz.: Springer, 2013.

Gandhi, Mohandas K. *An Autobiography: The Story of My Experiments with Truth*. Translated by Mahadev Desai. London: Jonathan Cape, 1966.

Gandhi, Mohandas K. *The Collected Works of Mahatma Gandhi*. 98 vols. New Delhi: Publications Division Government of India, 1999. https://www.gandhiashramsevagram.org/gandhi-literature/collected-works-of-mahatma-gandhi-volume-1-to-98.php.

Gandhi, Mohandas K. *The Moral and Political Writings of Mahatma Gandhi*. Vol. 3, edited by Raghavan Iyer. Oxford: Clarendon Press, 1987.

Gandhi, Mohandas K. *Selections from Gandhi*. Edited by N. K. Bose. Ahmedabad, India: Navajivan Trust, 1968.

Gatrell, Peter. *A Whole Empire Walking: Refugees in Russia during World War I*. Bloomington: Indiana University Press, 1999.

The Geneva Convention of 1906 for the Amelioration of the Condition of the Wounded in Armies in the Field. Washington, DC: Carnegie Endowment for International Peace, 1916.

Genovesi, Giovanni. *Storia della scuola in Italia dal Settecento a oggi*. Rome: Laterza, 1998.

Gentile, Giovanni. *Fascismo e cultura*. Milan: Fratelli Treves, 1928.

Gentile, Giovanni. *Il fascismo al governo della scuola*. Florence: Remo Sandron, 1924.

Gentile, Giovanni. "Il metodo Montessori." *L'educazione nazionale* 4, no. 7 (1922): 25–27.

Gentile, Giovanni. *La riforma della scuola in Italia*. Edited by H. A. Cavallera. Florence: Le Lettere, 2003.

Gentile, Giovanni. *Scritti pedagogici*. Vol. 3, *La riforma della scuola in Italia*. Milan: Sandron, 1932.

Gentile, Giovanni, Giuseppe Lombardo Radice, and Ernesto Codignola. *Il pensiero pedagogico dell'idealismo*. Edited by Armando Carlini. Brescia, It.: La Scuola, 1968.

Gerber, R., and V. Czak. *Vie et œuvre d'Adolphe Ferrière (1879–1960): Chronologie de son existence (1879–1936)*. Geneva: Université de Genève, Faculté de psychologie et des sciences de l'éducation, 1989–2018. https://www.unige.ch/archives/aijjr/files/1215/3676/4096/R_Gerber_corrige_1.pdf.

Germino, Dante L. *The Italian Fascist Party in Power: A Study in Totalitarian Rule*. Minneapolis: University of Minnesota Press, 1959.

Ghosh, Ranjan. "Caught in the Cross Traffic: Rabindranath Tagore and the Trials of Child Education." *Comparative Education Society* 59, no. 3 (2015): 409–410.

Ghosh, Ranjan. "A Poet's School: Rabindranath Tagore and the Politics of Aesthetic Education." *South Asia: Journal of South Asian Studies* 35, no. 1 (2012): 13–32.

Ghosh, Ratna, M. Ayaz Naseem, and Ashok Vijh. "Tagore and Education: Gazing beyond the Colonial Cage." In *Decolonizing Philosophies of Education*, edited by Ali A. Abdi, 59–71. Rotterdam: Sense Publishers, 2012.

Gibelli, Antonio. *Il popolo bambino: Infanzia e nazione dalla Grande Guerra a Salò*. Turin: Einaudi, 2005.

Gibelli, Antonio. "Nefaste meraviglie: Grande Guerra e apoteosi della modernità." In *Storia d'Italia: Annali 18, Guerra e Pace*, edited by Walter Barberis, 549–589. Turin: Einaudi, 2002.

Gibson, Mary. *Born to Crime: Cesare Lombroso and the Origins of Biological Criminology*. Westport, CT: Praeger, 2002.

Gil, Rebecca. "The Rational Administration of Compassion: The Origins of British Relief in War." *Le Movement Social*, no. 227 (April–June 2009): 9–26.

Giovetti, Paola. *Maria Montessori: Una biografia*. Rome: Edizioni Mediterranee, 2009.

Giuntini, Sergio. *Sport, scuola e caserma dal Risorgimento al primo conflitto mondiale*. Padua, It.: Centro Grafico Editoriale, 1988.

Grandi, William. "Orizzonti sociali, progetti riformatori e proposte educative in Robert Owen, John Ruskin e William Morris." *Ricerche di Pedagogia e Didattica* 5, no. 2 (2010): 1–25.

Grayzel, Susan. *Women and the First World War*. London: Longman, 2002.

Grossberg, Michael. "A Protected Childhood: The Emergence of Child Protection in America." In *American Public Life and the Historical Imagination*, edited by Wendy Gamber, Michael Grossberg, and Hendrik Hartog, 213–239. Notre Dame, IN: University of Notre Dame Press, 2003.

Grosso, C. F. "Le grandi correnti del pensiero penalistico italiano tra Ottocento e Novecento." In *Storia d'Italia: Annali 12, La criminalità*, edited by Luciano Violante, 5–34, Turin: Einaudi, 1997.

Guerra, Elda. *Il dilemma della pace: Femministe e pacifiste sulla scena internazionale, 1914–1939*. Rome: Viella, 2014.

Guha-Thakurta, Tapati. *The Making of a New "Indian" Art: Artists, Aesthetics and Nationalism in Bengal, c. 1850–1920*. Cambridge: Cambridge University Press, 1992.

Gutek, Gerald L., and Patricia Gutek. *Bringing Montessori to America: S. S. McClure, Maria Montessori, and the Campaign to Publicize Montessori Education*. Tuscaloosa: University of Alabama Press, 2016.

Guterl, Matthew Pratt. "Comment: The Futures of Transnational History." *American Historical Review* 118, no. 1 (2013): 130–139.

Haas, Peter M. "Introduction: Epistemic Communities and International Policy Coordination." *International Organization* 46, no. 1 (Winter 1992): 1–35.

Haenggeli-Jenni, Béatrice. "Le rôle des femmes de la Ligue Internationale pour l'éducation nouvelle dans la circulation des savoirs pédagogiques (1920–1940)." In Droux and Hofstetter, *Globalisation des mondes de l'éducation*, 75–95.

Hameline, Daniel. *L'éducation dans le miroir du temps*. Lausanne, Switz.: Édition des sentiers, 2002.

Harp Allen, Matthew. "Rewriting the Script for South Indian Dance." *TDR (1988–)* 41, no. 3 (1997): 63–100.

Hawthorne, Britt. "Dr. Montessori's Racism." *AMI/USA Journal* (Spring 2019): 61.

Hendrick, Harry. *Children, Childhood, and English Society, 1880–1990*. Cambridge: Cambridge University Press, 1997.

Hermon, Elly. "The International Peace Education Movement, 1919–1939." In *Peace Movements and Political Cultures*, edited by Charles Chatfield and Peter Ven Den Dungen, 127–142. Knoxville: University of Tennessee Press, 1988.

Hermon, Elly. "Le désarmement moral, facteur dans les relations internationales pendant l'entre-deux-guerres." *Guerres mondiales et conflits contemporains* 156 (October 1989): 23–36.

Hermon, Elly. "Une ultime tentative du sauvetage de la Société des Nations: La campagne du Rassemblement Universel pour la Paix." In *Le pacifisme en Europe des années 1920s aux années 1950*, edited by Maurice Vaïsse, 193–220. Brussels: Bruylant, 1993.

Heywood, Colin. *Childhood in Nineteenth-Century France: Work, Health and Education among the "Classes Populaires."* Cambridge: Cambridge University Press, 1988.

Hippler, Thomas, and Miloš Vec, eds. *Paradoxes of Peace in Nineteenth-Century Europe*. Oxford: Oxford University Press, 2015.

Hoffman, Ronald. Introduction to *Through a Glass Darkly: Reflections on Personal Identity in Early America*, edited by Ronald Hoffman, Mechal Sobel, and Fredrika J. Teute, vii–viii. Chapel Hill: University of North Carolina Press, 1997.

Hoffman, Sarada. "Rukmini Devi: The Educator." In Meduri, *Rukmini Devi Arundale*, 85–89.

Hofstetter, Rita. "Building an 'International Code for Public Education': Behind the Scenes at the International Bureau of Education (1925–1946)." *Prospects* 45, no. 1 (2015): 31–48.

Hofstetter, Rita, Bernard Schneuwly, Valérie Lussi, and Béatrice Haenggeli-Jenni. "L'engagement scientifique et réformiste en faveur de la 'nouvelle pédagogie': Genève dans le contexte international; Premières décades du 20e siècle." In *Passion, Fusion, Tension: New Education and Educational Sciences*, edited by Rita Hofstetter and Bernard Schneuwly, 107–141. Bern: Peter Lang, 2006.

Holmes, Henry W. Introduction to *The Montessori Method*, by Maria Montessori, xvii–xlii. Translated by Anne E. George. New York: Frederick A. Stokes Company, 1912.

Honegger Fresco, Grazia. "Anna Freud e l'esperienza Montessori." *Il quaderno Montessori* 20, no. 76 (2002–2003): 47–64.

Honegger Fresco, Grazia. *Maria Montessori, una storia attuale: La vita, il pensiero, le testimonianze.* Edited by Marcello Grifò. Turin: Il leone verde, 2018.

Horne, John, and Alan Kramer. *German Atrocities, 1914: A History of Denial.* New Haven, CT: Yale University Press, 2001.

Howlett, John. "The Formation, Development and Contribution of the New Ideals in Education Conferences, 1914–1937." *Journal of the History of Education Society* 46, no. 4 (2017): 459–479.

Imprenti, Fiorella. *Alle origini dell'Unione Femminile: Idee, progetti e reti internazionali all'inizio del Novecento.* Milan: Biblion edizioni, 2012.

International Council of Women: Report of Transactions of the Second Quinquennial Meeting Held in London, July 1899. Vol. 1. London: T. Fisher Unwin Paternoster Square, 1900.

Ipsen, Carl. *Dictating Demography: The Problem of Population in Fascist Italy.* Cambridge: Cambridge University Press, 1996.

Ipsen, Carl. *Italy in the Age of Pinocchio: Children and Danger in the Liberal Era.* New York: Palgrave Macmillan, 2006.

Iriye, Akira. *Cultural Internationalism and World Order.* Baltimore: Johns Hopkins University Press, 1997.

Irwin, Julia F. *Making the World Safe: The American Red Cross and a Nation's Humanitarian Awakening.* New York: Oxford University Press, 2013.

Irwin, Julia F. "*Sauvons les bébés*: Child Health and U.S. Humanitarian Aid in the First World War Era." *Bulletin of the History of Medicine* 86, no.1 (2012): 37–65.

Jacini, Stefano. *Atti della giunta per l'inchiesta agraria e sulle condizioni della classe agricola.* Rome: Forzani e C. Tipografi del Senato, 1881.

Jenkins, Celia. "New Education and Its Emancipatory Interests (1920–1950)." *History of Education* 29, no. 2 (2000): 139–151.

Johnson, Richard L., ed. *Gandhi's Experiments with Truth: Essential Writings by and about Mahatma Gandhi.* Lanham, MD: Lexington Books, 2006.

Jones, Heather. "International or Transnational? Humanitarian Action during the First World War." *European Review of History* 16, no. 5 (2009): 697–713.

Jones, Marian Moser. *The American Red Cross from Clara Barton to the New Deal.* Baltimore: Johns Hopkins University Press, 2013.

Joosten, Albert. "Gandhi and Maria Montessori." *Communications* 1–2 (2013): 66–68.

Kahn, David. "The Kodaikanal Experience: Kahn-Montessori Interview." *NAMTA Quarterly* 5, no. 1 (1979): 56–59.

Key, Ellen. *Barnets århundrade.* Stockholm: A. Bonnier, 1911.

Key, Ellen. *The Century of the Child.* New York: G. P. Putnam's Sons, 1909.

Key, Ellen. *War, Peace, and the Future: A Consideration of Nationalism and Internationalism, and of the Relation of Women to War.* London: Putnam & Sons, 1916.

Key, Ellen. *The Younger Generation.* London: Putnam & Sons, 1914.

Kilpatrick, William. *The Montessori System Examined.* Boston: Houghton Mifflin, 1914.

Kilpatrick, William. "What America Thinks of Montessori's Educational Crusade." *Current Opinion* 56 (February 1914): 127–129.

Kipling, Rudyard. *The Years Between.* New York: Barnes & Noble Digital Library, 2011. https://www.overdrive.com/media/848285/the-years-between.

Kitching, Carolyn. *Britain and the Geneva Disarmament Conference: A Study in International History.* Houndmills, UK: Palgrave Macmillan, 2003.

Koon, Tracy H. *Believe, Obey, Fight: Political Socialization of Youth in Fascist Italy, 1922–1943.* Chapel Hill: University of North Carolina Press, 1985.

Kornprobst, Markus. *Irredentism in European Politics: Argumentation, Compromise and Norms.* Cambridge: Cambridge University Press, 2008.

Kramer, Rita. *Maria Montessori: A Biography.* New York: Putnam, 1976.

Kripalani, J. B. *The Latest Fad: Basic Education.* Bombay: Vora, 1946.

Kumar, Nita. *Lessons from Schools: The History of Education in Banaras.* New Delhi: Sage, 2000.

Kurzweil, Edith. *The Freudians: A Comparative Perspective.* New Brunswick, NJ: Transaction Publishers, 1998.

Labanca, Nicola. *In marcia verso Adua.* Turin: Einaudi, 1993.

Lagarreta, Dorothy. *The Guernica Generation: Basque Refugee Children of the Spanish Civil War.* Reno: University of Nevada Press, 1984.

Laity, Paul. *The British Peace Movement, 1870–1914.* Oxford: Clarendon Press, 2002.

Lal, Swati. "Rabindranath Tagore's Ideals of Aesthetic Education." *Journal of Aesthetic Education* 18, no. 2 (1984): 31–39.

Lama, Luisa. "Maria Montessori nell'Italia fascista: Un compromesso fallito." *Il Risorgimento: Rivista di storia del Risorgimento e di storia contemporanea* 54, no. 2 (2000): 309–341.

Last, Murray. "Putting Children First." *Disaster* 8, no. 3 (September 1994): 192–202.

Lawson, Maxwell Donald. "Montessori: The Indian Years." *Forum of Education* 33, no. 1 (1974): 36–49.

Lawson, Maxwell Donald. "The New Education Fellowship: The Formative Years." *Journal of Educational Administration and History* 13, no. 2 (1981): 24–28.

League of Nations. *Conference on the Reduction and Limitation of Armaments: Moral Disarmament; Documentary Material Forwarded by the International Organisation on International Cooperation.* No. Conf. D. 98. Geneva, February 24, 1932. https://libraryresources.unog.ch/ld.php?content_id=31320509.

Leenders, Hélène. "Con viva fede nel lavoro a venire: Intorno alla pubblicazione della terza edizione italiana del *Metodo della pedagogia scientifica* di Montessori, Maria, 1926." *I problemi della pedagogia* 42, no. 4–6 (July–December 1996): 349–357.

Leenders, Hélène. *Montessori en fascistisch Italië: Een receptiegeschiedenis.* Baarn, Neth.: Intro, 1999.

Leenders, Hélène. "A Special Meaning of 'Health': Towards a Theory-Immanent Explanation for the Use of Montessori Pedagogy in Fascist Italy (1926–1934)." *Annali di storia dell'educazione e delle istituzioni scolastiche* 25 (2018): 196–208.

Leoni, Diego, Camillo Zadra, and Quinto Antonelli, eds. *La città di legno: Profughi trentini in Austria 1915–1918.* Trento: Temi, 1995.

Lepore, Jill. "Historians Who Love Too Much: Reflections on Microhistory and Biography." *Journal of American History* 88, no. 1 (2001): 129–144.

Lestor, Joan. "A Minister for Children." In *The Handbook of Children's Rights: Comparative Policy and Practice,* edited by Bob Franklin, 100–106. London: Routledge, 1995.

Leucci, Tiziana. "Maria Montessori en Inde: Adoption et adaptation d'une méthode pédagogique." In *L'Inde et l'Italie: Rencontres intellectuelles, politiques et artistiques,* edited by Marie Fourcade, Claude Markovits, and Tiziana Leucci, 245–285. Paris: Éditions de l'École des hautes études, 2018.

Levi, Giovanni, and Jean Claude Schmitt, eds. *Storia dei giovani.* Vol. 2. Turin: Laterza, 2000.

L. F. "La casa e il primo congresso delle donne Italiane." *La Casa* 1, no. 1 (June 1908): 17–18.

Lillard, Paula Polk. *Montessori: A Modern Approach.* New York: Schocken Books, 1972.

Lombardo Radice, Giuseppe. "Accanto ai maestri." *L'educazione nazionale* 8, no. 9 (August–September 1924): 2.

Lombardo Radice, Giuseppe. "A proposito del metodo Montessori." *L'educazione nazionale* 8, no. 7 (July 1926): 21.

Lombardo Radice, Giuseppe. *Athena fanciulla: Scienza e poesia della scuola serena.* Florence: R. Bemporad, 1925.

Lombardo Radice, Giuseppe. *Il problema dell'educazione infantile.* Florence: La Nuova Italia, 1948.

Longo, Gisella. "L'istituto Nazionale Fascista di Cultura durante la Presidenza di Giovanni Gentile." *Storia Contemporanea* 23, no. 2 (1992): 181–282.

Loparco, Fabiana. *I bambini e la guerra: Il Corriere dei Piccoli e il primo conflitto mondiale (1915–1918)*. Florence: Edizioni Nerbini, 2011.

Lora, Erminio, and Rita Simionati, eds. *Enchiridion delle encicliche*. Vol. 5, *Pio XI (1922–1939)*. Bologna: EDB, 1995.

Lubelsky, Isaac. *Celestial India: Madame Blavatsky and the Birth of Indian Nationalism*. Oakville, CT: Equinox, 2012.

Luc, Jean-Noël. "I primi asili infantili e l'invenzione del bambino." In *Storia dell'infanzia: Dal Settecento a oggi*, edited by Egle Becchi and Dominique Julia, 282–305. Rome: Laterza, 1996.

Ludwig-Körner, Christiane. "Anna Freud and Her Collaborators in the Early Post-War Period." In *The Anna Freud Tradition: Lines of Development; Evolution of Theory and Practice Over the Decades*, edited by Norka T. Malberg and Joan Raphael-Leff, 17–29. London: Routledge, 2012.

Lyttelton, Adrian. *The Seizure of Power: Fascism in Italy (1919–1929)*. London: Routledge, 2004.

M., T., "Le Scuole per i contadini dell'Agro Romano e delle Paludi Pontine." *L'idea Montessori: organo dell'Opera Nazionale Montessori* 1, no. 1 (1927): 10–11.

Maccheroni, Anna Maria. *A True Romance: Doctor Maria Montessori as I Knew Her*. Edinburgh: Darien Press, 1947.

Macpherson, C. B. *The Political Theory of Possessive Individualism: Hobbes to Locke*. Oxford: Clarendon Press, 1992.

Magnin, Charles, and Rita Hofstetter, eds. "New Education: Genesis and Metamorphosis." Special issue, *Paedagogica Historica* 42, no. 1–2 (2006).

Magnin, Charles, and Astrid Thomann. "Jean Piaget, diplomate de l'éducation: Essai historique sur sa façon de concevoir l'influence du Bureau international d'éducation (BIE) dans le domaine éducatif entre 1929 et 1950." In *L'éducation dans tous ses états: Influences européennes et internationales sur les politiques nationales d'éducation et de formation; Actes du colloque international organisé en commun à Bruxelles du 9 au 12 mai 2001*, edited by André Philippart and Louis Vandevelde, 279–289. Brussels: CEDEF, 2001.

Mahood, Linda. *Feminism and Voluntary Action: Eglantyne Jebb and Save the Children, 1876–1928*. New York: Palgrave Macmillan, 2009.

Mallett, Robert. *Mussolini in Ethiopia, 1919–1935: The Origins of Fascist Italy's African War*. New York: Cambridge University Press, 2015.

"Manifeste du congrès de Rassemblement Universel pour la Paix." *L'Esprit international*, September 5, 1936, 568–569.

Marazzi, Giuliana. "Montessori e Mussolini: La collaborazione e la rottura." *Dimensioni e problemi della ricerca storica* 13, no. 1 (2000): 177–195.

Marcucci, Alessandro. *La casa della scuola: Dalla relazione sulle scuole per i contadini dell'agro romano e delle paludi pontine*. Rome: Le scuole per i contadini dell'agro romano e delle paludi pontine, 1925.

Marcucci, Alessandro. *La decorazione nella scuola: A proposito della prima scuola decorata dell'agro romano; Estratto da coltura popolare.* Varese, It.: Premiata Tipografia Coopertiva Varesina, 1912.

Marcucci, Alessandro. *L'apostolato educativo di Giovanni Cena.* Rome: Le scuole per i contadini dell'agro romano e delle paludi pontine, 1928.

Marcucci, Alessandro. *La scuola di Giovanni Cena.* Turin: Paravia, 1948.

Marcucci, Alessandro. *Le scuole festive nell'agro romano istituite dalla sezione romana dell'Unione Femminile Nazionale: Relazione dell'anno 1907–1908, Proposte per l'anno 1908–1909.* Rome: Tipografia dell'Unione Cooperativa, 1908.

Marcucci, Alessandro. *Le scuole per i contadini dell'agro romano: Relazione del direttore delle scuole.* Rome: Tipografia poliglotta Mundus, 1913.

Maria Montessori: A Centenary Anthology 1870–1970. Amsterdam: Association Montessori International, 1970.

Marrus, Michael R. *The Unwanted: European Refugees from the First World War through the Cold War.* Philadelphia: Temple University Press, 2002.

Marrus, Michael R. *The Unwanted: European Refugees in the Twentieth Century.* New York: Oxford University Press, 1985.

Marshall, Dominique. "The Formation of Childhood as an Object of International Relations: The Child Welfare Committee and the Declaration of Children's Rights of the League of Nations." *International Journal of Children's Rights* 7, no. 2 (1999): 103–147.

Marshall, Dominique. "Humanitarian Sympathy for Children in Times of War and the History of Children's Rights, 1919–1959." In *Children and War: A Historical Anthology,* edited by James Marten, 184–200. New York: New York University Press, 2002.

Marshall, Dominique. "The Rise of Coordinated Action for Children in War and Peace: Experts at the League of Nations, 1924–1945." In Rodogno, Struck, and Vogel, *Shaping the Transnational Sphere,* 82–110.

Martin, Jane Roland. "Romanticism Domesticated: Maria Montessori and the Casa dei Bambini." In *The Educational Legacy of Romanticism,* edited by John Willinsky, 159–174. Waterloo, ON: Wilfrid Laurier University Press, 1990.

Matasci, Damiano. "International Congresses of Education and the Circulation of Pedagogical Knowledge in Western Europe, 1880–1914." In Rodogno, Struck, and Vogel, *Shaping the Transnational Sphere,* 218–238.

Matellicani, Anna. *La "Sapienza" di Maria Montessori: Dagli studi universitari alla docenza (1890–1919).* Rome: Aracne, 2007.

Matitti, Flavia. "La 'bottega mistica' di Francesco Randone (1864–1935): Arte ed esoterismo a Roma tra Otto e Novecento." *Luce e Ombra* 116, no. 1 (2016): 41–50.

Mayfield, Margie. "Maria Montessori: Advocate for Children." *Communications* 2 (2006): 4–9.

Mazower, Mark. "The Strange Triumph of Human Rights, 1933–1950." *Historical Journal* 47, no. 2 (2004): 379–398.

Mazuy, Rachel. "Le Rassemblement Universel pour la Paix (1931–1939): Une organisation de masse?" *Matériaux pour l'histoire de notre temps*, no. 30 (1993): 40–44.

Mazzini, Giuseppe, and Dora Melegari. *La giovane Italia e la giovane Europa: Dal carteggio inedito di Giuseppe Mazzini a Luigi Amedeo Melegari.* Milan: Fratelli Treves, 1906.

"Medicina sociale e malaria in Italia." *Avanti!* (Rome), July 29, 1901.

Meduri, Avanthi. "Bharatanatyam as Global Dance: Some Issues in Research, Teaching and Practice." *Dance Research Journal* 36, no. 2 (2004): 11–29.

Meduri, Avanthi, ed. *Rukmini Devi Arundale (1904–1986): A Visionary Architect of Indian Culture and Performing Arts.* Delhi: Motilal Banarsidass, 2005.

Melloni, Alberto, Giovanni Cavagnini, and Giulia Grossi, eds. *Benedetto XV: Papa Giacomo Della Chiesa nel mondo dell'"inutile strage."* Bologna: Il Mulino, 2017.

Messina, Salvatore. "Le donne violentate in guerra e il diritto all'aborto." *Scuola positiva* 6, no. 4 (1915): 289–294.

Midgley, Nick. "Anna Freud: The Hampstead War Nurseries and the Role of the Direct Observation of Children for Psychoanalysis." *International Journal of Psychoanalysis* 88, no. 4 (2007): 939–959.

Miller, Carol. "The Social Section and Advisory Committee on Social Questions of the League of Nations." In Weindling, *International Health Organizations and Movements*, 154–175.

Minesso, Michela. *Stato e infanzia nell'Italia contemporanea.* Bologna: Il Mulino, 2007.

Moneta, Edoardo Teodoro. "Sulla Morale." *La vita internazionale*, April 4, 1905.

Montesi, Barbara. *Questo figlio a chi lo do? Minori, famiglie, istituzioni (1865–1914).* Milan: Franco Angeli, 2007.

Montessori, Maria. *The Absorbent Mind.* Wheaton, IL: Theosophical Publishing House, 1964.

Montessori, Maria. "The Aims of the Social Party of the Child." *Communications* 1–2 (2013): 56–57.

Montessori, Maria. "Ancora sui minorenni delinquenti: L'amore." *La vita*, August 6, 1906.

Montessori, Maria. *Antropologia pedagogica.* Milan: Vallardi, 1910.

Montessori, Maria. "A Proposito dei Minorenni Corrigendi." *La vita*, June 3, 1906.

Montessori, Maria. "Arte Educatrice." *La vita*, August 6, 1907.

Montessori, Maria. *The California Lectures of Maria Montessori, 1915: Collected Speeches and Writings.* Edited by Robert G. Buckenmeyer. Oxford: Clio, 1997.

Montessori, Maria. "Caratteri fisici delle giovani donne del Lazio (desunti dall'osservazione di 200 soggetti)." *Atti della Società Romana di Antropologia* 12, no. 1 (1906): 37–120.

Montessori, Maria. *The Child, Society and the World.* Amsterdam: Montessori-Pierson Publishing, 2008.

Montessori, Maria. "Cittadinanza adulta, cittadinanza bambina." In *Il metodo del bambino e la formazione dell'uomo: Scritti e documenti inediti e rari*, by Maria Montessori and Augusto Scocchera, 99–110. Rome: Opera nazionale Montessori, 2002.

Montessori, Maria. *Come educare il potenziale umano*. Milan: Garzanti, 1992.

Montessori, Maria. *Corso Nazionale Montessori: Lezioni della dottoressa Montessori*. Milan: Litografia Mariani, 1926.

Montessori, Maria. *La Santa Messa spiegata ai bambini*. Milan: Garzanti, 1949.

Montessori, Maria. "Cosmic Education: VI/4 Lecture, India 1946." In Montessori, *The Child, Society and the World*, 108–109.

Montessori, Maria. "Disarmament in Education." *New Era* 13 (1932): 257–259.

Montessori, Maria. *The Discovery of the Child*. Translated by Mary A. Johnstone. Madras: Kalakshetra, 1948.

Montessori, Maria. *Dr. Maria Montessori's 1946 Lectures, Karachi, India*. Edited by Lakshmi Kripalani. Houston: Houston Montessori Center, 2002.

Montessori, Maria. *Education and Peace*. Translated by Helen Lane. Oxford: Clio Press, 1992.

Montessori, Maria. *Education for a New World*. Madras: Kalakshetra Press, 1946.

Montessori, Maria. *Educazione alla guerra o educazione alla pace? La pace e l'educazione*. Milan: Società Anonima Editrice Dante Alighieri, 1933.

Montessori, Maria. "Educazione alla guerra o educazione alla pace? La pace e l'educazione." *Rivista pedagogica*, no. 3 (1933): 786–801.

Montessori, Maria. *Educazione e pace*. Milan: Garzanti, 1970.

Montessori, Maria. *The Formation of Man*. Translated by A. M. Joosten. Amsterdam: Montessori Pierson Publishing, 2007.

Montessori, Maria. "Gli odierni Riformatori pei minorenni corrigendi." *La vita*, June 6, 1906.

Montessori, Maria. *I bambini viventi nella Chiesa*. Naples: Morano, 1922.

Montessori, Maria. *Il metodo del bambino e la formazione dell'uomo: Scritti e documenti inediti e rari*. Edited by Augusto Scocchera. Rome: Edizioni Opera Nazionale Montessori, 2002.

Montessori, Maria. *Il metodo della pedagogia scientifica applicato all'educazione infantile*. Rome: Maglioni & Strini, 1926.

Montessori, Maria. *Il metodo della pedagogia scientifica applicato all'educazione infantile nelle case dei bambini*. Rome: Loescher, 1913.

Montessori, Maria. *Il metodo della pedagogia scientifica applicato all'educazione infantile nelle case dei bambini: Edizione Critica*. Rome: Opera Nazionale Montessori, 2000.

Montessori, Maria. *Il segreto dell'infanzia*. Milan: Garzanti, 1992.

Montessori, Maria. "Influenze delle condizioni di famiglia sul livello intellettuale degli scolari." *Rivista di filosofia e scienze affini* 6, no. 2 (1904): 234–284.

Montessori, Maria. "Intervento al Congresso di Torino." In *Atti del primo congresso pedagogico italiano-Torino 8–15 settembre 1898*, edited by G. C. Molinari and

G. C. Alesio, 122–123. Turin: Stabilimento Tipografico diretto da F. Cadorna, 1899.

Montessori, Maria. *La casa dei bambini dell'Istituto Romano dei Beni Stabili: Conferenza tenuta il 7 aprile 1907.* Rome: Istituto Romano dei Beni Stabili, 1907.

Montessori, Maria. "La costruzione della personalità attraverso l'organizzazione dei movimenti." *Montessori: Rivista Bimestrale dell'Opera Montessori* 1, no. 6 (1932): 323–329.

Montessori, Maria. "La Croce Bianca." In Montessori, *Il metodo del bambino e la formazione dell'uomo,* 250.

Montessori, Maria. "La discipline et la liberté." *Pour l'ère nouvelle* 6, no. 29 (June 1927): 111–113.

Montessori, Maria. "La donna nuova: Conferenza della dottoressa Maria Montessori." *L'Italia femminile,* February 19, 1899.

Montessori, Maria. *La formazione dell'uomo nella ricostruzione mondiale.* Rome: Ente Opera Montessori, 1950.

Montessori, Maria. "La morale sessuale nell'educazione." In *Atti del I congresso nazionale delle donne italiane: Roma 24–30 aprile 1908,* 272–283. Rome: Stabilimento Tipografico Società Editrice Laziale, 1912.

Montessori, Maria. "La morale sessuale nell'educazione." *Vita: Rivista di azione per il bene* 5, no. 13–14 (July 31, 1908): 282–290.

Montessori, Maria. "L'antropologia pedagogica: Una conferenza dimenticata del 1903." *Vita dell'Infanzia* 46, no. 8 (1997): 8–15.

Montessori, Maria. *La pace e l'educazione.* Rome: Opera Montessori, 1959.

Montessori, Maria. "La prolusione della dott.ssa Montessori." *I diritti della scuola,* January 28, 1906, 172.

Montessori, Maria. "La questione femminile e il Congresso di Londra." In Montessori, *Per la causa delle donne,* 7. Originally published in *L'Italia Femminile,* no. 38, October 1, 1899, 298–299; no. 39, October 8, 1899, 206–207.

Montessori, Maria. *La scoperta del bambino.* Milan: Garzanti, 2011.

Montessori, Maria. "La scuola e la guerra: La Croce Bianca." *La Coltura Popolare* 7, no. 9 (1917): 661–663.

Montessori, Maria. "La teoria Lombrosiana e l'educazione morale." *Rivista d'Italia* 6, no. 2 (1903): 326–331.

Montessori, Maria. *L'autoeducazione nelle scuole elementari.* Rome: P. Maglione and C. Strini, 1916.

Montessori, Maria. "La via e l'orizzonte del femminismo." *Cyrano de Bergerac* 2, no. 6 (1902): 204.

Montessori, Maria. *La vita in Cristo.* Rome: Stabilimento Tipografico Ferri, 1931.

Montessori, Maria. "Lottiamo per la Criminalità." *La vita,* September 8, 1906.

Montessori, Maria. *Maria Montessori Sails to America: A Private Diary, 1913.* Translated by Carolina Montessori. Amsterdam: Pierson Publishing, 2013.

Montessori, Maria. *Maria Montessori Writes to Her Father: Letters from California, 1915.* Translated by Carolina Montessori. Amsterdam: Pierson Publishing, 2015.

Montessori, Maria. *Maria Montessori Writes to Her Grandchildren: Letters from India (1939–1946).* Translated by Carolina Montessori. Amsterdam: Montessori Pierson Publishing, 2020.

Montessori, Maria. *Mass Explained to Children.* London: Sheed & Ward, 1932.

Montessori, Maria. "Maternità, per regolamento e per pudore." *La vita,* April 2, 1907.

Montessori, Maria. "Message to the International Congress against War and Militarism at Paris 1–5 August 1937." In de Ligt, *Conquest of Violence,* 286.

Montessori, Maria. "Miserie sociali e nuovi ritrovati della scienza." *Roma: Rivista politica parlamentare,* July 31, 1898, 604–608.

Montessori, Maria. *The Montessori Method.* Translated by Anne Everett George. New York: Frederick A. Stokes, 1912.

Montessori, Maria. "Movement and Character." *NAMTA Journal* 38, no. 2 (Spring 2013): 37–44.

Montessori, Maria. "Movimento femminile." *L'Italia femminile,* July 30, 1899.

Montessori, Maria. "Norme per una classificazione dei deficienti in rapporto ai metodi speciali di educazione." In *Atti del Comitato Ordinatore del II Congresso Pedagogico Italiano 1899–1901,* 144–167. Naples: Trani, 1902.

Montessori, Maria. *Pedagogical Anthropology.* Translated by Frederic Taber Cooper. New York: Frederick A. Stokes, 1913.

Montessori, Maria. "Per i minorenni delinquenti: L'organizzazione del riformatorio di San Michele." *La vita,* July 14, 1906.

Montessori, Maria. *Per la causa delle donne.* Milan: Garzanti, 2019.

Montessori, Maria. *The Permanent Relevance of Montessori's Plea.* Amsterdam: AMI, 2004.

Montessori, Maria. "Quando la scienza entrerà nella scuola." *La coltura popolare* 15 (1915): 12–14.

Montessori, Maria. *The Secret of Childhood.* New York: Random House, 1966.

Montessori, Maria. "Social Status of Children." *Times* (London), January 9, 1932.

Montessori, Maria. *Spontaneous Activity in Education.* New York: Shocken Books, 1965.

Montessori, Maria. "A Step Towards the Future: The Social Party of the Child." *Theosophist* 62 (May 1941): 105–107.

Montessori, Maria. *To Educate the Human Potential.* Madras: Kalakshetra Publications, 1948.

Montessori, Maria. *The White Cross.* AMI.

Montessori, Maria, and Fulvio De Giorgi. *Il peccato originale.* Brescia, It.: Scholé, 2019.

Montessori, Maria, and Mario M. Montessori. "Peace through Education." *Communications* 1–2 (2013): 51–55.

Montessori, Mario M. "The Impact of India." *NAMTA Journal* 23, no. 2 (1998): 26–32.

Monticone, Alberto. "Il pontificato di Benedetto XV." In *Storia della Chiesa: La Chiesa e la società industriale (1878–1922)*, edited by Elio Guerriero and Annibale Zambarbieri, 155–200. Frascati, It.: Edizioni Paoline, 1990.

Moorehead, Caroline. *Dunant's Dream: War, Switzerland and the History of the Red Cross.* London: Harper, 1999.

Moretti, Erica. "Teaching Peace in a Time of War: Maria Montessori's 1917 Lectures." *Communications AMI Journal* 1–2 (2013): 17–31.

Moretti, Erica, and Alejandro Dieguez. "Il difficile equilibrio tra cattolicesimo e teosofia." In *Il destino di Maria Montessori: Promozioni, rielaborazioni, censure, opposizioni al metodo*, edited by Renato Foschi, Erica Moretti, and Paola Trabalzini, 95–112. Rome: Fefè Editore, 2018.

Moretti, Erica, and Alejandro Mario Dieguez. "I progetti di Maria Montessori impigliati nella rete di mons. Umberto Benigni." *Annali di storia dell'educazione e delle istituzioni scolastiche* 25 (2018): 89–114.

Mortimer, Joanne Stafford. "Annie Besant and India 1913–1917." *Journal of Contemporary History* 18, no. 1 (1983): 61–78.

Müller, Friedrich Max. *India: What Can It Teach Us?* Escondido, CA: Book Tree, 1999. First published 1883.

Müller, Friedrich Max. *Life and Religion: An Aftermath from the Writings of the Right Honorable Professor F. Max Müller.* Edited by Georgina Max Müller. London: Constable, 1915.

Mulley, Clare. *The Woman Who Saved the Children: A Biography of Eglantyne Jebb, Founder of Save the Children.* London: Oneworld, 2019.

Mussolini, Benito. "Discorso di Firenze." In *Opera omnia di Benito Mussolini*, edited by Edoardo Susmel and Duilio Susmel, vol. 24, 113–117. Florence: La Fenice, 1951.

Nardelli, Dino Renato. "Le scuole per i contadini dell'agro romano." *Vita dell'Infanzia* 36, no. 6 (1987): 14–21.

Nathan, Otto, and Heinz Norden, eds. *Einstein on Peace.* New York: Schocken Books, 1960.

Nayyar, Dev Parkash. *Building for Peace, or Gandhi's Ideas on Social (Adult) Education.* Delhi: Ama Ram & Sons, 1952.

Nicholls, David. "Richard Cobden and the International Peace Congress Movement, 1848–1853." *Journal of British Studies* 30, no. 4 (1991): 351–376.

Nivet, Philippe. *Les réfugiés français de la Grande Guerre, 1914–1920: Les "Boches du Nord."* Paris: Economica, 2004.

Nivet, Philippe. "Rifugiati." In Audoin-Rouzeau and Becker, *La prima guerra mondiale*, 229–241.

Noordegraaf, Herman. "The Anarchopacifism of Bart de Ligt." In *Challenge to Mars: Essays on Pacifism from 1918 to 1945*, edited by Peter Brock and Thomas P. Socknat, 89–100. Toronto: University of Toronto Press, 1999.

Nye, Robert A. *Crime, Madness and Politics in Modern France: The Medical Concept of National Decline.* Princeton, NJ: Princeton University Press, 1984.

"Of General Interest." *School World: A Monthly Magazine of Educational Work and Progress* 19 (October 1917): 351.

Olcott, Henri Steel. "The Genesis of Theosophy." *National Review* (London), October 14, 1889, 208–217.

Oliverio, Alberto. "The Acting Mind: The Role of Motricity in Mental Representation Processes." In Dompè, Tabasso, and Trabalzini, *1907–2007 Montessori Centenary Conference Proceedings,* 27–34.

Oppenheim, Janet. *The Other World: Spiritualism and Psychical Research in England, 1850–1914.* Cambridge: Cambridge University Press, 1985.

Osimo, Augusto. "Salviamo i bambini: Prime adesioni e contributi d'idee e di azione al nostro appello." *La Coltura Popolare* 8, no. 4 (1918): 235.

Ostenc, Michel. *La scuola italiana durante il fascismo.* Rome: Laterza, 1981.

Owen, Alex. *The Darkened Room: Women, Power, and Spiritualism in Late Victorian England.* Philadelphia: University of Pennsylvania Press, 1990.

Palla, Luciana. *Fra realtà e mito: La grande guerra nelle valli ladine.* Milan: Franco Angeli, 1991.

Papa, Catia. *Sotto altri cieli: L'Oltremare nel movimento femminista italiano.* Rome: Viella, 2009.

Papa, Catia. "Suffragiste d'inizio Novecento: Maria Montessori e la via italiana al voto femminile." In *Maria Montessori e la società del suo tempo,* edited by Fabio Fabbri, 194–207. Rome: Castelvecchi, 2020.

Parrat-Dayan, Silvia. "Les activités de Piaget Durant les deux guerres mondiales." In Chapuis, Pétard, and Plas, *Les psychologues et les guerres,* 201–215.

Pascoli, Giovanni. "I due fanciulli." In *Primi poemetti,* 141–143. Bologna: Zanichelli, 1907.

Pasi, Marco. "Teosofia e antroposofia nell'Italia del primo Novecento." In *Storia d'Italia: Annali 25, Esoterismo,* edited by Gian Mario Cazzaniga, 569–798. Turin: Einaudi, 2010.

Passerini, Luisa. "La giovinezza metafora del cambiamento sociale: Due dibattiti sui giovani nell'Italia fascista e negli Stati Uniti degli anni Cinquanta." In *Storia dei giovani,* vol. 2, edited by Giovanni Levi and Jean-Claude Schmitt, 383–459. Rome: Laterza, 2000.

Passerini, Pacifico. *Le scuole rurali di Roma e il bonificamento dell'agro romano.* Rome: Tipografia Pontificia nell'Istituto Pio IX, 1908.

Patriarca, Silvana. *Italian Vices: Nation and Character from the Risorgimento to the Republic.* Cambridge: Cambridge University Press, 2010.

Pavlovic, Zoran. "Children's Parliament in Slovenia." In *Monitoring Children's Rights,* edited by Eugeen Verhellen, 327–346. The Hague: Martinus Nijhoff, 1996.

Pazzaglia, Luciano. "Ideologie e scuola fra ricostruzione e sviluppo." In *Scuola e società nell'Italia unita,* edited by Luciano Pazzaglia and Roberto Sani, 463–471. Florence: La Scuola, 2001.

Pazzaglia, Luciano. "Lo Stato laico e l'insegnamento religioso in alcuni dibattiti del primo Novecento." *Pedagogia e vita* 39, no. 4 (April–May 1981): 379–416.

Pazzaglia, Luciano. *Scuola e religione in età giolittiana.* Milan: ISU Università Cattolica Editore, 2000.

Pedersen, Susan. "Back to the League of Nations." *American Historical Review* 112, no. 4 (October 2007): 1091–1117.

Pedersen, Susan. *The Guardians: The League of Nations and the Crisis of Empire.* Oxford: Oxford University Press, 2015.

Pezzino, Paolo, and Alvaro Tacchino. *Leopoldo e Alice Franchetti e il loro tempo.* Città di Castello, It.: Petruzzi Editore, 2002.

Piaget, Jean. "Is an Education for Peace Possible?" Translated by Hans G. Furth. In "Piaget Peace and War," edited by Hans G. Furth. Special issue, *Genetic Epistemologist* 17, no. 3 (1989): 5–9.

Piaget, Jean. "La biologie et la guerre." *Feuille centrale de la Société suisse de Zofingue* 58, no. 5 (1918): 374–380.

Pieroni Bortolotti, Franca. *La donna, la pace, l'Europa: L'associazione internazionale delle donne dalle origini alla Prima Guerra Mondiale.* Milan: Franco Angeli, 1985.

Pironi, Tiziana. "Da Ellen Key a Maria Montessori: La progettazione di nuovi spazi educativi per l'infanzia." *Ricerche di Pedagogia e Didattica* 5, no. 1 (2010): 1–11.

Pironi, Tiziana. "Educating to Beauty: The Aesthetical Value of Child of Infants' Educative Institutions in the Twentieth Century's Pedagogy." *Journal of Theories and Research in Education* 12, no. 1 (2017): 111–122.

Pironi, Tiziana. "Educazione e pacifismo nelle lettere tra Ellen Key e Romain Rolland." *Studi sulla formazione* 19, no. 1 (2016): 87–103.

Pironi, Tiziana. *Femminismo ed educazione in età giolittiana: Conflitti e sfide della modernità.* Pisa: Edizioni ETS, 2011.

Pisa, Beatrice. "Ernesto Teodoro Moneta: Storia di un pacifista 'con le armi in mano.'" *Giornale di storia contemporanea* 12, no. 2 (2009): 21–56.

Pollard, John. *The Unknown Pope: Benedict XV (1914–1922) and the Pursuit of Peace.* London: Geoffrey Chapman, 2000.

Pons Prades, Eduard. *Las guerras de los niños republicanos, 1936–1995.* Madrid: Compañía Literaria, 1997.

Pons Prades, Eduard. *Los niños republicanos: El exilio.* Madrid: Oberón, 2005.

Postempski, Paolo. *La campagna antimalarica compiuta dalla Croce Rossa Italiana nell'agro romano nel 1900.* Rome: Tipografia cooperativa sociale, 1901.

Pozzi, Irene. "La Società Umanitaria e la diffusione del metodo Montessori." *Ricerche di pedagogia e didattica* 10, no. 2 (2015): 103–114.

Pruneri, Fabio. "L'Umanitaria e la massoneria." *Annali di storia dell'educazione e delle istituzioni scolastiche* 11 (2004): 133–151.

Purseigle, Pierre. "'A Wave on to Our Shores': The Exile and Resettlement of Refugees from the Western Front." *Contemporary European History* 16, no. 4 (2007): 427–444.

Quayum, Mohammad A. "Education for Tomorrow: The Vision of Rabindranath Tagore." *Asian Studies Review* 40, no. 1 (2016): 1–16.

Quine, Maria Sophia. *Italy Social Revolution: Charity and Welfare from Liberalism to Fascism.* New York: Palgrave Macmillan, 2002.

Raboy, Marc. *Marconi: The Man Who Networked the World.* New York: Oxford University Press, 2016.

Ragaini, Claudio, and Ernesto Teodoro Moneta. *Giù le armi! Ernesto Teodoro Moneta e il progetto di pace internazionale.* Milan: Franco Angeli, 1999.

Raimondo, Rossella. "La 'pedagogia riparatrice' secondo Maria Montessori: Un ideale regolativo e educativo." *Rivista di storia dell'educazione* 1 (2016): 191–202.

Randone, Francesco. *Per nova itinera: Insegnamento dell'arte educatrice negli asili d'infanzia, scuole elementari e secondarie; La lavagna.* Tivoli, It.: Stabilimento Tipografico Majella di A. Chicca, 1914.

Randone, Francesco. *Scuola d'Arte Educatrice.* Rome: Edizioni Scuola d'Arte Educatrice, 1930.

Ravà, Vittore. *Le laureate in Italia: Notizie statistiche.* Rome: Tipografia Cecchini, 1902.

Regni, Raniero. *Infanzia e società in Maria Montessori: Il bambino padre dell'uomo.* Rome: Armando Editore, 2007.

Ricca, Ivan. "Architettura razionale." *La Casa,* no. 3 (August 1908): 86–88.

Richards, Glyn. *Gandhi's Philosophy of Education.* New Delhi: Oxford University Press, 2001.

Richards, Robert J. *The Tragic Sense of Life: Ernst Haeckel and the Struggle over Evolutionary Thought.* Chicago: University of Chicago Press, 2009.

Ricuperati, Giuseppe. *La scuola italiana e il fascismo.* Bologna: Consorzio provinciale di pubblica lettura, 1977.

Robertson, Arthur Henry. *Human Rights in the World.* Manchester: University of Manchester Press, 1972.

Rodogno, Davide, Bernhard Struck, and Jakob Vogel, eds. *Shaping the Transnational Sphere: Experts, Networks and Issues from the 1840s to the 1930s.* New York: Berghahn Books, 2015.

Rogers, Carl M. "Attitudes Toward Children's Rights: Nurturance or Self-Determination?" *Journal of Social Issues* 34, no. 2 (1978): 59–68.

"Roma: 'La Casa dei Bambini.'" *La vita,* no. 5 (January 7, 1907): 4.

Romanelli, Raffaele. *L'Italia liberale, 1861–1900.* Bologna: Il Mulino, 1979.

Rose, Nikolas. *The Psychological Complex: Psychology, Politics and Society in England, 1869–1939.* London: Routledge & Kegan Paul, 1985.

Rossi-Doria, Tullio. "Nuovi tempi e medici nuovi." *Avanti!* (Rome), December 6, 1900.

Roz, Firmin. *L'amérique et nous*. Brussels: Éditions du globe, 1946.

Ruyssen, Théodore. "Le desarmement moral." *La paix par le droit*, September 14, 1924, 326–333.

Sabyasachi, Bhattacharya, ed. *The Contested Terrain: Perspective on Education in India*. New Delhi: Orient Longman, 1998.

Sackett, Ginni. *A Sharp Call to the Public Conscience: Maria Montessori and the Social Party of the Child*. Rochester, NY: Association Montessori Internationale USA, 2010.

Said, Edward W. *Orientalism*. New York: Vintage Books, 1979.

Salomon, Gavriel. "The Nature of Peace Education: Not All Programs Are Created Equal." In *Peace Education: The Concept, Principles, and Practices around the World*, edited by Gavriel Salomon and Baruch Nevo, 3–14. Mahwah, NJ: Lawrence Erlbaum Association, 2002.

Salvatici, Silvia. *Nel nome degli altri: Storia dell'umanitarismo internazionale*. Bologna: Il Mulino, 2015.

Salvemini, Gaetano. "La guerra e la pace." *L'Unità*, August 28, 1914.

Salvemini, Gaetano. *Opere*. Vol. 5. Milan: Feltrinelli, 1966.

Samson, Leela. "Imbibing Culture at Kalakshetra." *India International Centre Quarterly* 29, no. 3–4 (2002–2003): 39–46.

Sanfilippo, Mario. *San Lorenzo 1870–1945: Storia e storie di un quartiere popolare romano*. Rome: Edilazio, 2003.

Santerini, Milena. *Cittadini del mondo: Educazione alle relazioni interculturali*. Brescia, It.: La Scuola, 1994.

Scaraffia, Lucetta. "Emancipazione e rigenerazione spirituale." In *Donne Ottimiste: Femminismo e associazioni borghesi nell'Otto e Novecento*, by Lucetta Scaraffia and Anna Maria Asastia, 19–126. Bologna: Il Mulino, 2002.

Scarantino, Anna. "Associazioni di donne per la pace nell'Italia di De Gasperi." In *Guerra e pace nell'Italia del Novecento: Politica estera, cultura politica e correnti dell'opinione pubblica*, edited by Luigi Goglia, Renato Moro, and Leopoldo Nuti, 319–355. Bologna: Il Mulino, 2006.

Schafer, Sylvia. *Children in Moral Danger and the Problem of Government in Third Republic France*. Princeton, NJ: Princeton University Press, 1997.

Schopenhauer, Arthur. *The World as Will and Representation*. Cambridge: Cambridge University Press, 2018.

Schwegman, Marjan. *Maria Montessori*. Bologna: Il Mulino, 1999.

Scocchera, Augusto. *Introduzione a Mario M. Montessori*. Rome: Edizioni Opera Nazionale Montessori, 1999.

Scocchera, Augusto. *Maria Montessori: Quasi un ritratto inedito*. Florence: La Nuova Italia, 1990.

Scocchera, Augusto. *Maria Montessori: Una storia per il nostro tempo*. Rome: Opera Nazionale Montessori, 1997.

Scoppola, Pietro. "Benigni, Umberto." In *Dizionario Biografico degli Italiani*, 504–508. Rome: Istituto della Enciclopedia Italiana,1966.

Sedita, Giovanni. *Gli intellettuali di Mussolini: La cultura finanziata dal fascismo.* Florence: Le Lettere, 2010.

Sergi, Giuseppe. "Alcune idee sull'educazione." *Nuova Antologia,* March 1, 1914, 65–69.

Sergi, Giuseppe. *Educazione e istruzione: Pensieri.* Milan: Trevisini, 1892.

Sergi, Giuseppe. "Froebelianismo." *L'educazione Nazionale* 1, no. 39 (June 28, 1890): 313–316.

Serina-Karsky, Fabienne. "L'éducation nouvelle incarnée dans les classes: Marie Aimée Niox-Chateau, une Montessorienne a l'école nouvelle." Research paper, CIRCEFT-HEDUC, University of Paris, August 18, 2019. https://hal.archives-ouvertes.fr/hal-02267122/document.

Seth, Sanjay. *Subject Lessons: The Western Education of Colonial India.* Durham, NC: Duke University Press, 2007.

Severs, Elizabeth. "The Co-Masons and the Women's Suffrage Procession." *Co-Mason* 3 (July 1911): 124–132.

Shakuntala, Ramani. *Shraddahanjali: Brief Pen Portraits of Great People Who Laid the Foundation of Kalakshetra.* Chennai: Kalakshetra Foundation, 2003.

Sheehan, James J. *Where Have All the Soldiers Gone? The Transformation of Modern Europe.* Boston: Mariner Books, 2009.

Sheepshanks, Mary. "Patriotism and Internationalism." *Jus Suffragii; Monthly Organ of the International Woman's Alliance* 9, no. 2 (1914): 184–185.

Siegel, Mona L. *The Moral Disarmament of France: Education, Pacifism, and Patriotism, 1914–1940.* Cambridge: Cambridge University Press, 2004.

Sighele, Scipio. *La crisi dell'infanzia e la delinquenza dei minorenni.* Florence: La Rinascita del Libro, 1911.

Sighele, Scipio. *La folla delinquente.* Turin: Fratelli Bocca, 1891.

Simonazzi, Mauro. *Degenerazionismo: Psichiatria, eugenetica e biopolitica.* Milan: Mondadori, 2013.

Sinnett, Alfred Percy. *The Occult World.* London: Truber, 1883.

Skran, Claudena M. *Refugees in Inter-war Europe: The Emergence of a Regime.* Oxford: Oxford University Press, 1995.

Snowden, Frank. *The Conquest of Malaria: Italy, 1900–1962.* New Haven, CT: Yale University Press, 2006.

Società Umanitaria. *L'Umanitaria e la sua opera.* Milan: Cooperativa Grafica degli Operai, 1922.

Sombart, Werner. *La campagna romana.* Turin: Ermanno Loescher, 1891.

Srinavasan, Prasanna, et al. *Montessori in India: 70 Years.* Chennai: Indian Montessori Foundation, 2007.

Srinivasan, Amrit. "Reform and Revival: The Devadasi and Her Dance." *Economic and Political Weekly* 20, no. 44 (1985): 1869–1876.

Standing, E. M. *Maria Montessori: Her Life and Work.* New York: New American Library, 1962.

Standing, E. M. *Maria Montessori: Her Life and Work*. New York: Plume, 1957.

Standing, E. M. "Sviluppo storico del movimento Montessori." In *Maria Montessori: Cittadina del mondo*, edited by Marziolina Pignattari, 67–82. Rome: Comitato Italiano dell'OMEP, 1967.

Stanley, Liz. *The Auto/Biographical I: The Theory and Practice of Feminist Auto/Biography*. New York: Manchester University Press, 1992.

Stanley, Liz. "Biography as Microscope or Kaleidoscope? The Case of 'Power' in Hannah Cullwick's Relationship with Arthur Munby." *Women's Studies International Forum* 10, no. 1 (1987): 19–31.

Starke, J. G. *Studies in International Law*. London: Butterworth, 1965.

Stedman, Jones Gareth. *Outcast London: A Study in the Relationship between Classes in Victorian Society*. Harmondsworth, UK: Penguin, 1976.

Stewart-Steinberg, Suzanne. *The Pinocchio Effect: On Making Italians, 1860–1920*. Chicago: University of Chicago Press, 2007.

Stoll Lillard, Angeline. *Montessori: The Science behind the Genius*. New York: Oxford University Press, 2005.

Stråth, Bo. *Europe's Utopias of Peace: 1815, 1919, 1951*. London: Bloomsbury Academic, 2016.

Susmel, Edoardo, and Duilio Susmel, eds. *Opera omnia di Benito Mussolini*. Vol. 20, *Dal viaggio negli Abruzzi al delitto Matteotti (23 agosto 1923–13 giugno 1924)*. Florence: La Fenice, 1956.

Tagore, Rabindranath. "The Artist." In *The Religion of Man*, 83–84. London: George Allen & Unwin, 1961.

Tagore, Rabindranath. *The Oxford India Tagore: Selected Writings on Education and Nationalism*, edited by Uma Dasgupta. Delhi: Oxford University Press, 2010.

Tagore, Rabindranath. *Personality*. New York: Macmillan, 1917.

Tagore, Rabindranath. "To Teachers." In *A Tagore Reader*, ed. Amiya Chakravarty, 214. New York: Macmillan, 1961.

Talamo, Edoardo. *La casa moderna nell'opera dell'Istituto Romano dei Beni Stabili*. Rome: Società Beni Stabili, 1910.

Talamo, Giuseppe. "Dagli inizi del secolo all'avvento del fascismo." In Talamo and Bonetta, *Roma nel '900*, 98–102.

Talamo, Giuseppe, and Gaetano Bonetta. *Roma nel '900: Da Giolitti alla Repubblica*. Rome: Cappelli, 1987.

Tarquini, Alessandra. *Il Gentile dei fascisti: Gentiliani e antigentiliani nel regime fascista*. Bologna: Il Mulino, 2009.

Todaro, Letterio. *L'alba di una nuova era: teosofia ed educazione in Italia agli inizi del Novecento*. Santarcangelo di Romagna, Italy: Maggioli Editore, 2020.

Todero, Fabio, ed. *L'Irredentismo armato: Gli irredentismi europei davanti alla guerra: Atti del Convegno di studi, Gorizia, 25 maggio, Trieste 26–27 maggio 2014*. Trieste: Istituto regionale per la storia del movimento di liberazione nel Friuli-Venezia Giulia, 2015.

Tollardo, Elisabetta. *Fascist Italy and the League of Nations 1922–1935*. London: Palgrave, 2016.

Tomasi, Tina. *Idealismo e fascismo nella scuola italiana*. Florence: La Nuova Italia, 1969.

Tomasi, Tina. *La scuola italiana dalla dittatura alla Repubblica (1943–48)*. Rome: Editori Riuniti, 1976.

Tomasi, Tina. *L'educazione infantile tra Chiesa e Stato*. Florence, Vallecchi, 1978.

Tornar, Clara. "Maria Montessori durante il fascismo." *Giornale italiano di pedagogia sperimentale* 13, no. 2 (2005): 7–22.

Trabalzini, Paola. *Maria Montessori: Da "Il metodo" a "La scoperta del bambino."* Rome: Aracne, 2003.

Trabalzini, Paola. "Maria Montessori e i rapporti con Sigmund Freud." *Annali di storia dell'educazione e delle istituzioni scolastiche* 25 (2018): 146–162.

Trabalzini, Paola. "Maria Montessori: Scienza e Società." In Dompè, Tabasso, and Trabalzini, *1907–2007 Montessori Centenary Conference Proceedings*, 18–22.

Trivellato, Francesca. "Is There a Future for Italian Microhistory in the Age of Global History?" *California Italian Studies* 2, no. 1 (2011). https://escholarship.org/uc/item/0z94n9hq.

Tromp, Marlene. *Altered States: Sex, Nation, Drugs, and Self-Transformation in Victorian Spiritualism*. Albany: State University of New York Press, 2006.

Tromp, Marlene. "Spirited Sexuality: Sex, Marriage, and Victorian Spiritualism." *Victorian Literature and Culture* 31, no. 1 (2003): 67–81.

Tropeano, Giuseppe. "Rivista critica della stampa." *Giornale della malaria* 1 (1907): 93–94.

Turi, Gabriele. *Giovanni Gentile: Una biografia*. Turin: Utet, 2006.

Turi, Gabriele. *Il fascismo e il consenso degli intellettuali*. Bologna: Il Mulino, 1980.

Turi, Gabriele. *Lo Stato educatore: Politica e intellettuali*. Rome: Laterza, 2002.

Turiello, Pasquale. *Saggio sull'educazione nazionale in Italia*. Naples: Luigi Pierro, 1891.

Ultanir, Emel. "An Epistemological Glance at the Constructivist Approach: Constructivist Learning in Dewey, Piaget, and Montessori." *International Journal of Instruction* 5, no. 2 (2012): 195–212.

United Nations Educational, Scientific and Cultural Organization (UNESCO). *Seeds for Peace: The Role of Pre-School Education in International Understanding and Education for Peace*. Paris: UNESCO, 1985.

Vaidhesswaren, Ms. "How We Came to the Advanced Montessori Course at Kodaikanal." *NAMTA Journal* (June 1982): 31–34.

Valbousquet, Nina. *Les réseaux transnationaux de l'antisémitisme catholique: France, Italie, 1914–1934*. Paris: CNRS Éditions, 2020.

Valitutti, Salvatore, ed. "Giovanni Gentile e il metodo Montessori." *Vita dell'infanzia* 17, no. 6–7 (June–July 1968): 10–16.

Valli, Maria. "L'esprit de la méthode Montessori." *Pour l'ère nouvelle* 1, no. 2 (1922): 37–39.

Van Bueren, Geraldine, ed. *International Documents on Children*. Boston: Martinus Nijhoff, 1993.

Vayer, Pierr. *Educazione psicomotoria nell'età scolastica*. Rome: Armando, 1977.

Vecchio, Giorgio. *Chiesa e progetto educativo nell'Italia del secondo dopoguerra (1945–1958)*. Brescia, It.: La Scuola, 1988.

Veerman, Philip E. *The Rights of the Child and the Changing Image of Childhood*. Dordrecht, Neth.: Martinus Nijhoff, 1992.

Venkataraman, Leela, and Avinash Pasricha. *Indian Classical Dance: Tradition in Transition*. New Delhi: Lustre Press, 2002.

Ventura, Angelo. *Intellettuali: Cultura e politica tra fascismo e antifascismo*. Rome: Donzelli, 2017.

Vidotto, Vittorio. *Roma contemporanea*. Rome: Laterza, 2001.

Violi, Roberto P. *Maria de Unterrichter Jervolino (1902–1975): Donne, educazione e democrazia nell'Italia del Novecento*. Rome: Studium, 2014.

Vittoria, Albertina. "Totalitarismo e intellettuali: L'Istituto nazionale fascista di cultura dal 1925 al 1937." *Studi Storici* 23, no. 4 (October–December 1982): 897–918.

Walters, Francis Paul. *A History of the League of Nations*. London: Oxford University Press, 1952.

Walzer, Michael. *On Toleration*. New Haven, CT: Yale University Press, 1997.

Warren, Maude Radford. *The White Flame of France*. Boston: Small & Maynard, 1918.

Weber, Eugen. *Peasants into Frenchmen: The Modernization of Rural France, 1870–1914*. Stanford, CA: Stanford University Press, 1976.

Weindling, Paul, ed. *International Health Organizations and Movements, 1918–1939*. Cambridge: Cambridge University Press, 1995.

Weindling, Paul. "Introduction: Constructing International Health Between the Wars." In Weindling, *International Health Organizations and Movements*, 1–16.

Whitaker, Elizabeth Dixon. *Measuring Mamma's Milk: Fascism and the Medicalization of Maternity in Italy*. Ann Arbor: University of Michigan Press, 2000.

White, Steven F. "Carleton Washburne: L'influenza deweyana nella scuola italiana." *Scuola e città* 40, no. 2 (1989): 49–57.

"The White Cross." *Daily News*, September 18, 1916.

"The White Cross." *Times Educational Supplement* (London), September 20, 1917, 5.

Willcocks, Mary Patricia. *Towards New Horizons*. London: John Lane, 1919.

Wilson, Carolie Elizabeth. "Montessori Was a Theosophist." *History of Education Society Bulletin* 36 (1985): 52–54.

Wilson, Carolie Elizabeth. "A Study of the Application of Her Method in a Developing Country." PhD diss., University of Sydney, 1987.

Wilson, Woodrow. "Address to the Senate of the United States: 'A World League for Peace,'" January 22, 1917. Edited by Gerhard Peters and John T. Woolley. American Presidency Project. https://www.presidency.ucsb.edu/node/206603.

Winternitz, Moriz. "L'école de Rabindranath Tagore à Santiniketan." *Pour l'ère nouvelle* 7, no. 38 (1928): 99–100.

Wordsworth, William. "Intimations of Immortality from Recollections of Early Childhood." In *The Poetical Works of Wordsworth*, edited by Thomas Hutchinson, 112. Oxford: Oxford University Press, 1973.

Zahra, Tara. *The Lost Children: Reconstructing Europe's Families after World War II.* Cambridge, MA: Harvard University Press, 2011.

Zanotti-Bianco, Umberto. *L'Associazione nazionale per gli interessi del Mezzogiorno d'Italia, nei suoi primi cinquant'anni di vita.* Rome: Collezione Meridionale Editrice, 1960.

Zelizer, Viviana. *Pricing the Priceless Child: The Changing Social Value of Children.* New York: Basic Books, 1985.

Zucca, Giuseppe. "La prima campana laica." *Il Marzocco,* July 14, 1912, 4.

Zucca, Giuseppe. "Una scuola d'arte educatrice." *Rassegna contemporanea* 7, no. 2 (December 25, 1914): 680.

Index